DATE DUE

BRODART	Cat. No. 23-221

Cambridge Studies in Historical Geography 10

URBAN HISTORICAL GEOGRAPHY

Cambridge Studies in Historical Geography

Series editors:
ALAN R. H. BAKER   J. B. HARLEY   DAVID WARD

Cambridge Studies in Historical Geography encourages exploration of the philosophies, methodologies and techniques of historical geography and publishes the results of new research within all branches of the subject. It endeavours to secure the marriage of the traditional scholarship with innovative approaches to problems and to sources, aiming in this way to provide a focus for the discipline and to contribute towards its development. The series is an international forum for publication in historical geography which also promotes contact with workers in cognate disciplines.

URBAN HISTORICAL GEOGRAPHY

Recent Progress in Britain and Germany

Edited by

DIETRICH DENECKE

Lecturer in Geography, University of Göttingen

and

GARETH SHAW

Senior Lecturer in Geography, University of Exeter

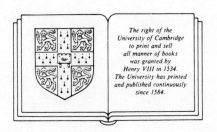

The right of the
University of Cambridge
to print and sell
all manner of books
was granted by
Henry VIII in 1534.
The University has printed
and published continuously
since 1584.

CAMBRIDGE UNIVERSITY PRESS

CAMBRIDGE

NEW YORK   NEW ROCHELLE   MELBOURNE   SYDNEY

Published by the Press Syndicate of the University of Cambridge
The Pitt Building, Trumpington Street, Cambridge CB2 1RP
32 East 57th Street, New York, NY 10022, USA
10 Stamford Road, Oakleigh, Melbourne 3166, Australia

First published 1988

Printed in Great Britain at the Bath Press, Avon

British Library cataloguing in publication data

Urban historical geography: recent progress
in Britain and Germany. – (Cambridge
studies in historical geography; 10).
1. Cities and towns – Great Britain –
History   2. Cities and towns – Germany –
History
I. Denecke, Dietrich   II. Shaw, Gareth
941'.009'732   HT133

Library of Congress cataloguing in publication data

Urban historical geography.
(Cambridge studies in historical geography; 10)
Includes index.
1. Cities and towns – Great Britain – History.
2. Cities and towns – Germany – History.   3. Cities and
towns, Medieval.   I. Denecke, Dietrich.   II. Shaw,
Gareth.   III. Series.
HT133.U685   1988   307.7'6'0941   87-25600
ISBN 0 521 34362 3

Contents

Figures

Tables

Contributors

E. Baigent *St Hugh's College, University of Oxford*

Professor H. Carter *Department of Geography, University College of Wales, Aberystwyth*

Professor M. R. G. Conzen *Department of Geography, University of Newcastle upon Tyne*

Dr D. Denecke *Geographisches Institut, Universität Göttingen*

Dr R. Dennis *Department of Geography, University College, London*

Dr C. Dyer *Department of History, University of Birmingham*

Professor C. Erdmann *Geographisches Institut, der Rheinisch-Westfälischen Technischen Hochschule, Aachen*

Dr B. Graham *School of Environmental Sciences, University of Ulster at Jordanstown*

Professor H. Heineberg *Institut für Geographie, Universität Münster*

Professor J. Lafrenz *Institut für Geographie und Wirtschaftsgeographie, Universität Hamburg*

Dr N. de Lange *Institut für Geographie, Universität Münster*

Professor R. Lawton *Department of Geography, University of Liverpool*

Dr C. G. Pooley *Department of Geography, University of Lancaster*

H. C. Prince *Department of Geography, University College, London*

L. Proudfoot *Department of Geography, Queen's University, Belfast*

Dr G. Shaw *Department of Geography, University of Exeter*

Dr T. Slater *Department of Geography, University of Birmingham*

Dr H.-G. Stephan *Seminar für Ur- und Frühgeschichte, Universität Göttingen*

Professor H. Steuer *Institut für Ur- und Frühgeschichte, Universität Freiburg*

Dr J. Whitehand *Department of Geography, University of Birmingham*

1

Introduction

DIETRICH DENECKE and GARETH SHAW

The occasion

This book represents the result of two Anglo-German seminars on urban historical geography. The initial idea to organise these joint conferences was born from a concern to find new ways of contact and cooperation, together with a desire for a more effective form of international seminars between British and German historical geographers.

The first of the seminars was held in West Germany during 1982 and involved a number of field excursions held between Lübeck and Bonn, together with a series of papers. It was the success of this meeting that stimulated the demand for a further seminar, which was held in Britain during 1983. At the outset there was never an attempt to impose any rigid themes, indeed it quickly became apparent that the small group of participants had fairly eclectic interests. Such research foci varied both in terms of approach, subject matter, as well as historical periods. However, in contrast to this background of diversity the group was bound together by an interest in urban fieldwork, as reflected in the many excursions undertaken in both meetings. The reports and reactions underline that this specific form of a 'moving conference', which was developed and applied here, was especially rewarding in many respects, giving the opportunity to develop discussions within the field and helping to knit these together with the paper sessions.[1] Besides this concept of management it was important, and a basic strategy of these seminars, that all the participants were involved in personal active research in urban historical geography.

More importantly the ideas for these seminars grew from a concern that contact between British and German historical geographers was extremely limited, especially by comparison with Anglo-French or Anglo-American initiatives. It was certainly becoming the case that a whole generation of British geographers was missing out on potentially rewarding contacts with their German counterparts.[2] This situation had prompted Geipel to

1

comment that 'relatively little information has reached the English-speaking academic community concerning developments in German geography since 1939'; which, whilst something of an overstatement, does highlight the frustration felt by many German-speaking geographers.[3] In this respect the situation within historical geography contrasts with the position among urban historians both in Britain and more especially in the United States, where contact with German colleagues is far greater.[4]

The idea of the seminars was to provide the means by which British and German historical geographers could understand each others' work. This was to be achieved at a number of different levels, starting from the basic one of introducing the historical geography of urban settlement in the two countries. The obvious difference was between the political patchwork of states that conditioned the growth of German cities until the final quarter of the nineteenth century, as opposed to the relatively early uniformity of Britain. The difficulties of making direct comparisons between British and German urban settlements was a constant theme running through much of the field work and following discussions. Greater common ground was perhaps more visible in terms of methodology and approach. In most respects the basic techniques of analysis were similar, although slight differences in emphasis emerged in many of the papers.

Though direct empirical or objective comparison usually turned up differences between Britain and Germany, there was also a strong emphasis to find general lines of a comparative urban historical geography. Indeed, this is a general methodological aim which needs much further development on an international basis. Some progress has been made; for example, in Münster there exists an 'Institute of Comparative Urban History' (Institut für vergleichende Städtegeschichte), together with a long-term research project, 'Vergleichende geschichtliche Städteforschung', whilst in Japan there has been launched a new journal in 1982 under the title: *The Comparative Urban History Review*. Indeed, this whole problem of comparative study has been recently emphasised by Clarke and Simms who conclude their two volumes on *The comparative history of urban origins in non-Roman Europe*: 'When we have learned to ask comparable questions in a comparable manner and in comparable language, we may eventually succeed in building the foundations of a comparative history of urban origins.'[5]

The whole question of internationalising historical geography has been widely discussed, especially following the success in 1957 of the first colloquium on the evolution of rural landscape in Europe. This and subsequent meetings suggested there was much to be gained by making cross-cultural comparisons of the development of field systems, settlement patterns and farming practices.[6] Within urban historical work similar moves towards the breaking down of national barriers were being made particularly through the historic towns atlas project.[7] Perhaps of greater significance was the establishment in 1976 of the I.G.U. 'Working Group on Historical Changes in Spatial Organisation', which during its eight years of operation did much to promote international cooperation.[8]

This relative increase in international contacts between historical geographers has certainly improved lines of communication, although coverage is still somewhat patchy.[9] Moreover, whilst such links provide a necessary springboard for comparative work, important problems associated with such historical studies remain to be resolved. Early discussions among historians highlighted many of the difficulties as well as stressing the significance of such an approach.[10] For example, Bloch believed that comparative history had three equally important uses. First, to test explanatory hypotheses; second, it could be used to discover the uniqueness of different societies; and finally to formulate new areas of study for historical research.[11] Whilst few would doubt the value of a comparative approach, the problems associated with this form of study have often been ignored by urban historical geographers. In contrast, Bloch drew attention to the fact that 'for each aspect of European social life, in each historical instant, the appropriate geographical framework has to be found'.[12] To some extent this is a basic starting point, yet significantly little attention has been given to the problems of 'unit delinitiation'.

This raises a further general problem of international understanding and scientific cooperation, which has to be discussed more intensively in the near future, namely the international terminology of urban history and urban historical geography. International understanding and cooperation in research also means that there has to be a common terminological framework, a 'comparable language'. The 'International Working Group for the Geographical Terminology of the Agricultural Landscape' made remarkable efforts to lay a foundation for establishing terminological frameworks. This is in the form of tables which offer criteria and terms for the understanding of existing phenomena and for the definition of established terms for different languages.[13] Unfortunately, there is nothing comparable yet for the field of urban historical geography and urban history, and such an international and interdisciplinary project is badly needed.

The aims of the book

Following on from the ideas of the two seminars this book aims to bring together a diverse collection of papers that reflect the state of present day urban historical geography in both countries. In one respect it represents the first major attempt to confront similar research projects and approaches in Britain with those in West Germany, and in this sense the joint publication may be regarded as a comparative literature. Conversely, it may also be seen as marking a starting point from which full comparative and collaborative research projects can develop.

In the British, as well as in the German, contributions directly comparative aspects will rarely be found, since the concept was to give in most of the contributions a general review of recent research within selected fields of work in each country. In some contributions a particular case study is summarised and presented as an example for a specific approach or field of research. The proposal was to cover more or less the most important approaches and questions of research that have been followed in Britain as well as in Germany. In order to gain a reasonable coverage a few contributions were obtained from non-participants in the seminars, although even in these circumstances the authors had expressed an interest in the aims of these meetings.

The book is wide ranging and starts with two chapters that provide a general overview of recent research in Britain and Germany. Whilst it is possible to see common threads between these two papers the contrasts are perhaps more revealing. For example, Richard Dennis and Hugh Prince stress changes in approach based around a variety of stimuli, whereas Dietrich Denecke gives greatest emphasis to the influence of techniques and methodology, referring to a greater number of special fields of research. More significantly, these chapters highlight some major philosophical differences towards the study of urban historical geography, although it is far from certain that such contrasts follow any nationalistic lines. In the absence of any comprehensive bibliographies these two chapters also serve to provide general comparative guides to the British and German literature.[14]

In Part Two of the book emphasis is given to settlement evolution and aspects of medieval town development. This section also highlights the links between geographers, archaeologists and historians in the two countries; with the contributions by Chris Dyer, Heiko Steuer and Hans Stephan. These three papers, together with that by Brian Graham, examine the evolution of urban settlement in a national and regional context. In contrast Terry Slater's paper concentrates on those factors influencing the internal design and layout of the medieval town.

It is evident from these chapters that medieval urban archaeologists are playing a leading role especially in researching the development phase of proto-towns, as reflected in long-term projects, in specific conferences and substantial publications of collected papers.[15] It is also clear that there are many regional and topographical aspects, as well as functional and spatial relations, involved in this research which means that geographical questions are raised. To solve them, not only finds, dates and archaeological evidence are needed, but also geographical approaches, interpretations, theories and models of explanation. Historical geographers are still far away from a noticeable input of geographical aspects or of joint research, but they try at least to follow the results of recent archaeology. Certainly in the German context one example of an introduction of a geographical concept which has already found its fruitful application has been the central place model.[16]

The remainder of the book approaches the historical geography of the town from a thematic rather than an historic or chronological perspective; starting in Part Three with a review of work on social areas, social patterns and social processes. Three major themes emerge from these papers. The first concerns the long-standing debate over the timing of change between the pre-industrial and industrialising city. The applications of such ideas are most prominent in the essays by Elizabeth Baigent and Claudia Erdmann. These two chapters not only tackle in some detail the nature of social structure prior to industrialisation, but also, as in the case of Aachen, highlight the cultural-political dimension. Furthermore the similarities between these two studies also perhaps refute some of the assertions by Lichtenberger on the uniqueness of the continental European city, and suggest that further studies are required on a wider range of the larger cities for the eighteenth and nineteenth centuries.[17]

The second main theme highlighted in this section is the contrast between the strong interest in the social structure, more precisely, the social topography and the pattern of social indices of the early modern town in Germany, as illustrated in Dietrich Denecke's paper, and the relative lack of interest among British historical geographers on this period. Such a balance of interest is significantly reversed however when one compares the work on the social geography of nineteenth-century British cities, as discussed by Colin Pooley and Richard Lawton, with in this case the more limited research emanating from Germany. The final paper, by Lindsay Proudfoot, draws attention to a more specialised influence on social patterns, as well as reminding us of another dimension to the diversity of British towns.

Part Four considers the economic and functional components of urban settlements, which as the papers illustrate is a rather fragmented research area. In Germany there has been considerable emphasis and long-term interest on urban hierarchies and the measurement of centrality. Not only did such work start earlier, through the influence of Christaller, it has also remained a more significant focus of research in more recent times than is the case in Britain. Unfortunately, there is no representative paper for such work, but interested readers are referred to Blotevogel's work and Denecke's review in Chapter 3.[18] In Britain similar goals have been pursued by Harold Carter as represented by his wide-ranging study of the urban hierarchy in England and Wales.

The remaining two papers in this section highlight the growing interest in the internal economic structure of cities. Heinz Heineberg and Norbert de Lange's chapter focusses on the locational dynamics of office functions and emphasises the changing nature of site influences in German cities. In contrast Gareth Shaw's paper considers the growth of retail functions and their impact on urban land use patterns. Both papers either directly or indirectly allude to a significant gap in the lack of any work on manufacturing industries in nineteenth-century cities.

The final section of the book covers two main themes, namely urban morphology and the conservation of historic townscapes. The first of these provides perhaps more than anything else the early bridge between British and German historical geographers. At a personal level this link owes much to the efforts of M.R.G. Conzen and his work on town plan analysis. Indeed, Conzen played an active role in both of the seminar meetings, and his paper shows the understanding of town growth that can be provided by town plan analysis. At a wider level the many contacts between English- and German-speaking geographers through the interest in urban morphology have been recently reviewed by Conzen.[19] Jeremy Whitehand's contribution represents a substantial extension to this early work, and demonstrates the importance of using detailed building records. In terms of research in Germany the approach developed by Whitehand from the morphogenetic studies of Conzen is indeed innovative, as there as yet are no comparable studies of this type. The work of Jürgen Lafrenz draws attention to a much more specialised aspect of recent work on urban morphology and town topography being undertaken within German-speaking countries, using the techniques of metrological analysis.

The paper by Terry Slater and Gareth Shaw highlights the contrasting approaches taken towards the conservation and management of historic towns. In both countries it is the pressure for commercial development that constitutes the greatest threat, but in Germany conservation planners are at an advantage over their British counterparts, because of the more enlightened general attitude and the past history of such work. Indeed, in Britain urban historical geographers have already noticed the necessity to contribute to this field of an applied research, and in Germany there is a growing interest and production of applied studies for planning and conservation purposes.[20]

PART ONE

Recent trends in urban historical geography

2

Research in British urban historical geography

RICHARD DENNIS and HUGH PRINCE

This chapter reviews current trends in British research in urban historical geography. First, it traces new developments since 1970, identifying convergent interests that have drawn together geographers, planners, architects, archaeologists and historians as well as divergent interests that have pulled apart geographers and historians. The review then examines progress from well-established fields of inquiry such as urban morphogenesis through to social area analysis, initiated during the quantitative revolution and fostered by the release of vast quantities of nineteenth-century census data. Interest is then directed towards ideological questions, introducing recent Marxist interpretations of urban patterns and processes, classical economic interpretations of urban hierarchies and systems and psycho-cultural interpretations of symbols and images in built environments. Finally, the contribution of historical geographers to conserving historic townscapes is briefly mentioned.

Progress in British urban historical geography since 1970

To judge from the volume of published work, urban historical geography is thriving in Britain. Recent texts on urban geography offer substantial accounts of historical changes and developments and urban historical geography now has an introductory text of its own.[1] Knowledge of urban historical geography of countries beyond England has begun to be brought together in book form, with new titles on Ireland, Scotland and Wales.[2] New periodicals have been founded to provide outlets for an increasing flow of articles. These include the *Urban History Yearbook* (founded in 1974), *Journal of Historical Geography* (1975), *London Journal* (1975) and the *Planning History Bulletin* (1979). Special issues of the *Transactions of the Institute of British Geographers*, in addition to regular individual contributions to major journals, major research seminars financed by the Social Science Research Council (now the Economic and Social Research

9

Table 2.1 *Types of urban history research*

	No.	%
Undated (including studies of the		
evolution of particular towns)	13	10
Medieval and earlier	13	10
Early modern	7	5
Eighteenth century	12	9
1800–1914	69	53
Post-1914 (mostly on conservation issues)	16	12

Council) and many funded research projects, all indicate an apparently flourishing specialism.[3]

Urban historical geography has been stimulated by a parallel growth in urban history which gained respectability through such influential works as Asa Briggs' *Victorian cities*, published in 1963, and partly through the evangelistic efforts of H. J. Dyos, whose own *Victorian suburb* (1961) provided a model for urban historical research, and whose cottage industry of *Urban History Newsletters* paved the way for the substantial *Urban History Yearbook*. A further stimulus was given by social historians who began to collect written and oral testimony about the history of common people living in towns and cities, working in mines and mills.[4] At the first international conference on urban history held in Britain, out of forty-three participants three (Carter, Conzen and Freeman) were geographers and others were sympathetic to geographical perspectives. Of the sixteen papers subsequently published in *The study of urban history* (1968) two were by geographers, both concerned more with morphology and built environments than with urban society.[5]

This impression of vigorous growth is less obvious in the statistics collected in two recent surveys. The *Register of research in urban history 1984* lists a total of 630 entries of which 80 are definitely associated with geography departments, but among this apparently large tally, several titles are followed by the words 'project abandoned' or 'suspended'.[6] In the *Register of research in historical geography 1984*, out of 495 projects 130 are primarily urban in focus but absolute numbers are inflated by enumerating projects rather than researchers. Several enterprising researchers list different aspects of their work as separate projects.[7] Whilst absolute numbers are on the high side, the distribution by period more truly indicates the orientation of current research, as shown in Table 2.1.

There is an overwhelming concentration on cities in and since the industrial revolution, for which few special skills (e.g. in palaeography or medieval languages) are required. More research has been undertaken by urban geographers delving into the past than by historical geographers, moving away from their traditional concern for agrarian landscapes.[8] Of the geographical research on medieval and early modern cities that has been carried out, much has been undertaken by social and economic historians rather than by geographers.[9]

Urban morphogenesis

Until the 1960s most urban geographers concerned with the internal structure of cities focused on morphology, and most urban morphology was historical, plotting the ages and types of buildings, identifying diverse historical components of town plans.[10] Little of this research attracted mainstream historical geographers, whose primary concern was the distant, preindustrial past, when urban populations were small and only a few major cities possessed an identifiable spatial structure. Even in Darby's *A new historical geography of England* (1973), towns were treated primarily as points, as markets, ports, spas or places of manufacture. Their internal social geography received less attention.[11]

The potential for *urban* historical geography, as distinct from *historical* urban geography, clearly existed. If the layout of medieval field systems was worth studying, so was the pattern of landownership and its implications for the layout of streets and buildings in urban areas. The relationship between tenant farmers and their landlords could be paralleled by that between tenant builders and ground landlords in urban areas. Enclosure and the ensuing reorganization of landownership and use generated similar legal processes and similar forms of documentation to compulsory purchase, slum clearance and the redistribution of building land in cities. Some of these connections between sources used for reconstructing the morphology of urban and of rural landscapes have been made in recent publications.[12] But in the 1960s and 1970s, *historical* urban geography was practised by researchers whose approaches were more urban than historical, more *ecological* or sociological than cultural – disciples of the quantitative revolution, whose language and technical orientation alienated them from researchers into *landscape* and, as critically, from the growing army of urban historians.[13]

Social area analysis

As urban geography became more sociological and more quantitative, so it lost favour with urban historians. Geographers were conspicuously absent from two later interdisciplinary celebrations of urban history: *The Victorian city: images and realities* (1973) and *The pursuit of urban history* (1983).[14] In their introduction to the latter, Fraser and Sutcliffe commented that 'geography has remained trapped in microscopic studies of urban land use and its minor contribution to this volume compared to that of 1968 is itself evocative of a failure to generate a general theory of urban geography which advances significantly beyond that of the Chicago School'.[15] By the early 1980s urban history had espoused Marxist social history and social anthropology. Geography, it appeared, was still in a theoretical Dark Age. Writing in 1986, we might observe that historical geography now has its fair share of Marxists, structuralists, humanists, idealists and realists. But, often *because* they adopt these perspectives, they would reject the label 'urban' or even 'historical' geographer. The most interesting investigations are being carried out on the borders between specialisms and between established disciplines.

Geographers primarily concerned with the social geography of nine-teenth-century cities drew on ecological theory from the Chicago School – reasonably enough, given that the theory of human ecology was formu-lated in the first decades of the twentieth century, and nineteenth-century British cites were certainly much closer in spirit to free-market Chicago than were many post-war cities to which the theory was also applied. Less defensibly, they also espoused social area theory, which had first been developed for urban areas in California in the late 1940s and 1950s. Multi-variate statistical methods (multiple regression, factor analysis, cluster analysis) were used to analyse social area data derived from a limited number of standard sources, especially the census enumerators' books (see Chapter 12 below). Although the range of information was narrower than that covered in modern censuses, the detailed information on individuals made possible endless cross-tabulations and index calculations that could be mapped and correlated at a variety of scales, using tailor-made areal boundaries – individuals, households, streets, blocks, enumeration districts, grid squares, wards.[16] The enumerators' books (now available for each census from 1841 to 1881) recorded nothing about housing conditions, but a great deal on family and household structure, occupation and birthplace.[17] Hence the emphasis in research shifted from the morphology of the built environment to the morphology of the social environment. Attempts to link the two were usually rather crude, because researchers had detailed quantitative information on the social environment but, unless they ven-tured into estate papers and local government building records, only crude presence/absence data on characteristics of the built environment.[18]

Social areas as an index of modernity

The objective of social area analysis was to reconstruct 'spatial structure' and compare it with a few standard types: Sjoberg's preindustrial city, Burgess' concentrically zoned city, Hoyt's sectors. Then the city in question could be located somewhere along a transition from 'preindustrial' to 'modern'.[19] Hence, David Ward's question: 'Victorian cities: how modern?'[20]

In accord with social area theory, a modern city was defined as one in which socio-economic status, family status and ethnic status were uncorrelated and displayed different spatial patterns. From factor analyses it was inferred that mid-nineteenth-century cities were already modern. But given a census that provided information only on aspects of socio-economic status, household and family structure, and birthplace, it was hardly surprising that statistical analyses produced separate dimensions that fitted with social area theory.[21] Nor was it surprising that historians found these analyses irrelevant to their own interests.[22]

Over time, the concept of modernity has become more subtle and more historical; not just defined by a modern spatial pattern, but by modern attitudes, perceptions, political philosophies and forms of class consciousness.[23] But in the 1970s studies were still principally descriptive; only the most general of processes, such as 'modernization', were invoked to account for observed changes. And processes were inferred from studies that were static and cross-sectional, tied to particular census years. Even adventurous geographers who researched earlier periods still tied their analyses to models of spatial structure and modernization. Were medieval or early modern cities closer to Sjoberg's or Vance's models of preindustrial urbanism?[24]

While these studies provided a valuable descriptive base to set alongside contemporaries' own perceptions of their cities, and a useful training in handling standard sources, they rarely gathered data in the right format to answer questions posed by subsequent generations of researchers. In the short run, social area analyses offered a useful benchmark for process-oriented studies that were still positivist in approach but tapped more diverse sources and used techniques of historic record linkage to relate names and locations in different records; studies of social interaction,[25] residential mobility [26] and journeys to work, church and pub.[27] But by the mid-1980s urban historical geography was as likely to be humanist or structuralist as positivist.[28] Even studies of residential segregation, the most statistical branch of urban historical geography, are now more concerned with the meaning and experience of segregation than with its objective measurement.[29]

Ideology and research

In this methodological environment theories can no longer be tested or verified. Instead, theories are 'meant to inform the questions posed by researchers inquiring into real situations in actual places'.[30] Data are no more than illustrative and selective. No study can be absolutely conclusive, comprehensive, objective or value-free. Historians constantly reinterpret the past in the light of the present, and the interaction of researcher and researched; likewise historical geographers reinterpret past environments in the light of their own current concerns and experience.

In the 1960s an optimistic belief in progress and freedom was reflected in urban geography in 'models of urban development' and a form of behavioural geography which emphasized individual choice. Much of this research was imitative of American urban geography, which assumed a free market in land, a purely private housing market and an unlimited potential for social mobility. None of these conditions prevailed in British cities, where government intervention in planning and the provision of public housing, historical peculiarities of land tenure and a far from classless society all distorted the operation of free-market forces. The myth that human geography was apolitical and value-free was able to flourish in an era of consensus politics, in which successive Conservative and Labour governments displayed broadly similar attitudes to the welfare state. It was easy to ignore the ideological context, when it was apparently unchanging, and especially when the advent of powerful computers, and quantitative techniques to match, allowed researchers to concentrate on technical problems of handling large data sets.

As the economic and political climate changed, so urban geographers sought alternative approaches. The assumption that private individuals were free to choose was the first to be challenged.[31] In modern urban studies, *managerialism* focused on *gatekeepers* who controlled access to different kinds of housing, education, welfare, transport, all of which were now regarded as scarce resources, for which need, if not demand, exceeded supply.[32] Urban historians had been examining the activities of creators and controllers of the built environment, especially landowners, developers and builders, ever since Dyos' pioneering study of Camberwell,[33] and their efforts culminated in several monographs acknowledging the significance of geography though not of spatial analysis: Cannadine's examination of the role of the aristocracy, especially in the context of suburban Edgbaston and seaside Eastbourne, Chalklin's study of the building process in Georgian towns, Thompson's and Olsen's research on estates in north-west London and – a model for urban historical geographers to follow – Daunton's reconstruction of landownership, development, house ownership and resultant patterns of segregation and mobility in late nineteenth-century Cardiff.[34]

The conjunction of these historical case studies with managerialist theory prompted a variety of responses by urban and historical geographers. Springett's focus on the activities in Huddersfield of the Ramsden and

Thornhill families, their agents and the local builders who developed their estates, built on earlier products of a Leeds School of urban historical geography in which the emphasis had been less on individual actors than the overall pattern.[35] In other studies the connection between urban history and managerialist theory was more explicit. Pooley progressed from a census-based study of social areas in Liverpool to an examination of local authority housing provision and management in the same city, and Dennis followed his study of community structure in mid-nineteenth-century Huddersfield, based on censuses, marriage registers and other nominal lists, with research on the practice of philanthropic housing agencies in inner London, based on tenants' registers, annual reports and minute books.[36] In each case, the new research grew out of the old, beginning with the objective of showing how decisions in the housing market affected the social ecology of the chosen city. How did Liverpool Corporation facilitate a process of working-class suburbanization? How did slum clearance and the erection of new blocks of flats contribute to processes of filtering and ecological succession? But subsequently their research became less ecological, more concerned with the internal dynamics of the housing market and the ideology of decision-makers. What were the objectives of philanthropists? Who, indirectly as well as directly, was intended to benefit from new housing? How was subsidized housing related to industrial wage levels, the stability of the labour market and the social reproduction of labour?

Among morphologists, Whitehand shifted from a classical economic model of urban development – comparing the bid-rent curves of different land uses under different economic conditions – to a concern with individual architects, builders and developers.[37] Gordon argues that morphological research now demands the study of individual *actors* operating on a *stage* which includes not only geographical characteristics, but also legislative, political and technical environments.[38]

Are towns distinctive historical-geographical entities?

These developments raise doubts about the *urban-ness* of urban historical geography. At a theoretical level, the study of urban managers and gatekeepers is no different from the study of their rural counterparts. Indeed, the theoretical coherence of *urban* studies has been questioned by a succession of Marxist and structuralist critics. In the early days of urban history, Hobsbawm warned that it would degenerate into 'a large container, with ill-defined, heterogeneous and sometimes indiscriminate contents'.[39] Dyos did not object to the methodological pluralism of his subject, but he *was* anxious that urban history should focus on 'the city as a whole', on characteristics *of* cities rather than merely *in* cities.[40] In practice, very few historians were wholeheartedly committed to urban history. Most urban history was undertaken by economic, social, political, demographic or planning historians who happened for a time to be examining urban aspects of their specialism. While this may not have produced total urban history, the results were often original and challenging. By contrast, much urban historical geography was practised by full-time urban geographers whose research tended to be accumulative and, ultimately, repetitive, but less frequently innovative, perhaps *because* they were too committed to a particular methodology.[41] More recently, urban historical geography has gone the way of urban history; it has become more diverse, methodologically and topically, more imaginative, but also less distinctively urban.

The attack on the notion that towns possess their own unique histories and geographies has been conducted on several fronts. From historical sociology, Philip Abrams argued that towns could not be regarded as social entities, changing independently of their socio-economic environment. Instead we should treat the town 'as a resource for the understanding of the structures and processes of a more inclusive reality it expressed and epitomized'. Abrams concluded that 'we need many studies of towns – because that is where the process in its many varieties occurs. But we can do without studies of the town.'[42] In *The pursuit of urban history*, Ray Pahl was cast as the mole capable of undermining the entire urban enterprise. Like Abrams, Pahl considered it valuable to study cities as concrete expressions of the socio-political systems in which they were situated, but he noted that attempts to explain urban patterns and other characteristics of towns without reference to their socio-political context were invariably trivial and naive.[43] Other criticisms, by Castells and Saunders, were directed at the integrity of urban sociology.[44]

The attack has not gone unanswered. Carter has conceded the validity of Castells' and Abrams' critiques; in his own view 'the city is a dependent variable'; and he admits that urban historical geography lacks theory. Yet he disputes the feasibility of a structuralist urban geography, in which *social* theory is brought to bear on urban situations, observing that 'to follow the lines proposed by structuralists would involve an outline (but surely better still a deep and penetrating study) of the whole of human history from which all the characteristics of the city would be derived'. Furthermore, Carter regards structuralism as eroding the differences between historical geography and socio-economic history, leading to the abandonment of 'the central geographical concern with spatial structure'. He wants to maintain a clear distinction between urban history, 'more concerned with urban life and townspeople and their formal and informal institutions', and urban geography, 'more concerned with patterning and distribution'.[45]

In practice, even structuralists acknowledge the independence of 'the urban variable' in particular situations. Sutcliffe notes that Marxist political economists are now arguing that towns not only *express* some crucial contradictions of capitalism but also *promote* processes of change in industrial society.[46] Urbanization may have been coincident with the growth of industrial capitalism, but the resultant 'urban problem' was not simply a problem of capitalist society. The *urban* characteristics of the inner city – its location, density and heterogeneity – are fundamental to today's inner-city crisis.[47] Marxists are fond of noting that Marx ignored the separation of town and country in capitalist society, yet he did recognize the validity of the distinction in feudal society; and, as the *Communist Manifesto* records, capitalist industrial society provided the context in which socialism could develop, by bringing together a class-conscious proletariat in an *urban* setting.[48] Saunders noted that there was nothing urban about the urban sociology he had been taught, yet he accepted that 'the city may constitute a valid object of analysis for the historian'.[49] So we must beware of assuming that critiques of contemporary urban sociology necessarily apply to all kinds of urban studies. Theories of spatial structure lend a unique status to urban geography.

On empirical grounds, it is evident that in the past class structure varied between rural and urban areas; social relations were different because large numbers of people were obliged to live in close proximity to one another. The physical density of urban agglomerations in the past generated problems of health and sanitation that were neither as obvious nor as urgent in rural environments. The anonymity of city life offered opportunities for crime and a social milieu in which deviant subcultures could flourish. The separation of housing capital and industrial capital, so that the relation between employer and employee differed from that between landlord and tenant, was primarily an urban phenomenon. Contemporary observers throughout history, from the author of Genesis onwards, recognized the differences between urban and rural life and values; and nineteenth-century commentators were keen to distinguish between their praise for industrialization and their fears for the consequences of urban agglomeration.[50] Consider the stereotypes of different kinds of rural and urban society in Disraeli's *Sybil* or Mrs Gaskell's *North and south*.[51]

Marxist interpretations

Despite David Harvey's pioneering efforts, and despite the influence of important historical analyses by Foster and Stedman Jones, Marxist urban historical geography has made slow progress in Britain.[52] An important collection of essays, Dear and Scott's *Urbanization and urban planning in capitalist society*, contains several papers by British urban historians and contemporary urban geographers; Doherty has contributed a provocative Marxist perspective on urbanization to a collection of essays on Scottish historical geography; and recent papers by Cambridge historical geographers adopt a broadly Marxian humanist stance, reflecting their adoption of methodologies derived from Giddens' theory of structuration, Foucault's work on discipline and power or Sartre's existentialism.[53]

In each inquiry the objective has been to show the interaction between structure, human agency and individual experience. In some studies, such as Billinge's examination of the class struggle between old and new middle classes in late eighteenth-century Manchester, the focus is far from spatial. Billinge's interpretation rests on deciphering the connections between culture, class and community.[54] Other studies concentrate on the role of institutions, whether the underlying components of the cultural formation such as rationalism or utilitarianism, particular organizations, including school boards, poor law unions and housing trusts, or the institutional buildings themselves – board schools, workhouses, asylums, model dwellings.[55] The central geographical concern for man and environment is being recovered in the ways in which people create, use and interpret their surroundings. There is a convergence of this kind of institutional historical geography with a purer form of humanistic geography, that has its roots in environmental perception, where an initial concern for the experience of landscape or townscape is now being interpreted in an ideological context.[56]

Rather more urban geographers have reacted to allegations of the irrelevance or triviality of their quantitative analyses by retaining a broadly positivist approach but focusing on welfare issues; a historical geography of social well-being. Most studies of disease, mortality and sanitation have remained in an ecological mould, but a concern for the ideology behind the statistics is now emerging.[57] The historical geography of urban crime remains uncharted territory, despite continuing interest by social historians, and some routine references to rookeries and Victorian theories of criminality in geographies of modern urban crime.[58]

Spatial variations in poverty were central to Booth's pioneering inquiries in the 1880s and 1890s.[59] Stedman Jones took up this theme in his major study of poverty and the labour process in *Outcast London*, and a recent thesis by David Green develops this connection for London in the early nineteenth century.[60] Yet for all the interest in the *social* geography of cities, there has been little work on their *economic* geography. Green examines the geography of poverty in London in the context of deskilling and the shift from bespoke West End trades to slop or sweated manufacture and outwork in the East End; but there are few other studies of manufacturing, and even fewer of commercial activities, such as warehousing and office-work, at an intra-urban scale.[61] Retailing has attracted more attention, researchers tracing the development of markets, bazaars, department stores, multiples, co-operatives and fixed-shop retailing generally, and examining the connection between poverty and street-trading.[62] But the linking of retail change to social and residential change remains more a pious hope than a coherent theory.

Inter-urban studies

In a much-cited article published at the height of the quantitative revolution, Brian Berry used the memorable phrase – 'cities as systems in systems of cities' – to link inter-urban networks, defined in terms of central place theory and the rank size rule, with intra-urban density gradients.[63] So far we have discussed only intra-urban historical geography. In fact, the study of urban systems and inter-urban relationships has been neglected lately, and its methodology has not been debated at all.

For pre-census periods, any substantial statistical analysis is limited by the doubtful accuracy of population estimates, especially where information for different towns has been gathered from diverse sources: religious or civil enumerations of male household heads, poll taxes, lay subsidies, hearth taxes – with variable multipliers to allow for women, children, the poor and anybody else who escaped enumeration.[64] For an early modern urban system John Patten has provided a solid foundation, primarily derived from his own research in East Anglia; but for earlier periods, urban historians have been more active than geographers, pursuing a vigorous inquiry into the question of urban decay in the later middle ages.[65] Geographical research has examined less controversial issues, such as the spacing of market centres and the nature of regional urban hierarchies.[66]

Once into the nineteenth century, there is unlimited scope for statistical modelling, best exemplified by Brian Robson's analysis of urban growth in England and Wales between 1801 and 1911.[67] Robson assumed that population growth responded to rates of innovation adoption. He developed a simple model in which innovations diffused down the urban hierarchy to successively smaller places, and according to a distance-decay function to ever more remote places. He also assumed that the rate at which new innovations were generated varied cyclically. The statistical results were, at best, inconclusive, but Robson's examination of particular infrastructural innovations – financial services, gas works, telephone exchanges – neatly foreshadowed current research into variations in municipal expenditure on services such as roads, parks and housing in the Edwardian and inter-war years. As with much recent historical research, this interest connects with contemporary studies of the geography of public finance, and current political debate on central government control of local authority expenditure.[68]

Images of cities

At a time when historical geographers have become aware of their own predilections for ideologically convenient pasts, so they have begun to examine ways in which past environments were themselves moulded by political, religious and aesthetic beliefs shared by designers and patrons. An extensive literature on symbolism in urban planning has been revived by Carter[69] and subtle analyses of iconography and imagery in art and landscape are currently enjoying a vogue. Contributions to Dyos and Wolff's many-sided portrait of the Victorian city set the trend towards critical appraisals of nineteenth-century image making, probing attitudes towards railways, slums, suburbs, pollution, poverty, wealth – the awful sublimity of the growing city.[70] Olsen comments on the symbolic significance of designs of hotels, restaurants, clubs and theatres[71] and Dellheim examines in detail the architecture of civic monuments including Manchester Town Hall, 'the best place to study the meanings and functions of medievalism' in the Victorian city.[72] Daniels has shown how planning and building of Yorkshire mill towns were dictated by local manufacturers, asserting their ideals of moral order. A new kind of industrial paternalism was expressed through the layout of public parks, the distancing of industrial buildings from rural landscapes, the design of different grades of housing for different grades of employee and the provision of morally uplifting services in schools, institutes, churches, libraries and allotment gardens.[73]

Cosgrove surveys a longer span of time and a wider range of countries, relating the creation of symbolic landscapes and associated scientific and technical innovations such as perspective and surveying to changes in social formation, from feudalism to mercantile and industrial capitalism.[74] His thesis ranges over art, landscape and townscape, but concentrates particularly on renaissance Italy and the city-states of Venice and Vicenza. As well as discussing the content of messages that creators or illustrators of landscape intended to convey, he is also concerned with the reinterpretation of environment by subsequent generations, for example, the meaning of Venice to nineteenth-century British visitors such as John Ruskin.[75] David Harvey has now formulated connecting theories explaining the relations between money, time and space in the structure of city forms in advanced capitalist societies. Most interestingly, he has related the interactions of capital and labour in the redevelopment of central Paris between 1850 and 1870, and has examined the mythical and monumental significance of the building of the basilica of Sacré Coeur, enshrining the class conflicts running through the history of the Third Republic.[76]

In humanistic as in structuralist research, there is no methodological difference between urban and rural studies. Indeed, many geographers have focused their attention upon the interface between town and country;

observing rustic elements such as parks, cottages with gardens and winding lanes embedded in ordered townscapes, industrial features such as mills, furnaces and railways erupting in rural landscapes, migrants from rural areas encountering and then adjusting to urban life. These studies also bridge the divide between contemporary and historical human geography. Much of the art and literature examined by humanistic geographers happens to date from the eighteenth and nineteenth centuries, because at that time painters and novelists were most acutely aware of changes in their physical and social environments and were deeply influenced by prevailing determinist theories.[77] As sources for geographical interpretation, fine art and polite literature are dangerously elitist or atypical, reflecting the views of wealthy patrons and exceptionally sensitive and articulate artists, some of whom enjoyed private incomes. But the viewpoints of writers and painters are no more selective or biased than those imposed by census enumerators who assigned individuals to households whatever their domestic state, or the definitions imposed by positivist geographers on the status, class or ethnicity of families that may have thought or acted according to quite different models of society. Humanistic geographers have succeeded to a higher degree than most positivist geographers in appraising the value and limitations of their source materials but they have been less successful than literary historians or art historians in exposing and interpreting layers of meaning to be discovered in particular texts or pictures.[78]

A promising beginning has been made in elucidating city images in popular art forms. Pop music, vaudeville, commercial art, commercial architecture, journalistic stereotypes of the inner city and suburbs have begun to attract the interest of humanistic geographers.[79] Gigantic, threatening, alienating images of a futuristic metropolis in cinema have been examined by Reyner Banham, Anthony Sutcliffe and John Gold.[80] In the search for everyday perspectives on urban life, geographers and historians have turned to working-class diaries, letters, autobiographies and oral evidence.[81] All these sources, especially the latter, imply a colonization of the early and middle years of the twentieth century, until recently a period that merited the description, 'the real Dark Ages as far as historical geographers are concerned'.[82]

Conservation of historic buildings and townscapes

Past and present are also linked through the contributions of historical geographers to debates on the conservation of historic townscapes. Lowenthal has reflected on our attitudes to the past, attempting to discover the social, psychological and aesthetic causes for attachment to relics from the past, and examining the benefits brought by that attachment and the burdens it imposes. The questions raised go far beyond ethical questions about preserving, restoring or reviving the fabric of past landscapes; they enter into the character of historical records and the kinds of history or historical geography that draw upon preserved, restored or fabricated evidence.[83]

Case studies of conservation in particular towns have been contributed by Kain and Clout, working in France, and Slater in the English Midlands.[84] Slater has shown how even in the 1980s planners betray their ignorance of the past by producing plans 'directly at odds with the historical development of the town plan and its natural divisions'; in Stratford-on-Avon, efforts to maintain or enhance aesthetically attractive façades have not been matched by equal concern for the rectangular street pattern and medieval burgage plots; in Warwick, new road proposals preserved, but marooned, the historic town centre, by carving through medieval and early modern ribbon development which once linked the town to its rural hinterland.[85]

Our review has been selective, indicative of our own biases, as a comparison of the topics covered here with what follows in the rest of the book will quickly reveal. But certain omissions, not the result of our own ignorance or lack of interest, deserve notice. It is evident that there have been few studies *relating* social and economic structures. Most research has been thematic, all too rarely making links between diverse urban phenomena. A focus on the relationship between work and home, and the use of more personal sources of information, would inevitably lead to a greater emphasis on the roles and experiences of women in towns. Recent years have witnessed the rise of women's history and an introductory text on feminist geography[86] but apart from the occasional study of domestic service,[87] urban historical geography has depicted a man's world, in which male household heads make journeys to work, and choose where to live and when to move. In reality, as many working-class biographies and oral histories reveal, *effective* household heads were often female. Decisions to move house, the search for new lodgings, and engagement in local social and commercial networks were all women's work in the late Victorian and Edwardian city.[88]

Structuralists have pointed to the need to situate urban studies in appropriate socio-economic contexts. We need to consider not just the mode of production or the world system in which our cities are set, but also more local contexts. The revival of regional geography and the recognition of regional identities, in the nineteenth and twentieth centuries as much as in preindustrial societies, should prompt an exploration of the regional dimension to urbanism.[89]

We have not tried to define British urban historical geography at all rigorously. We have alluded to connections between scholars in Britain, continental Europe and North America, and we have cited some research by Britons now based in America and some research on non-British cities. Ideas cannot be isolated territorially. Urban historical geography is a growth area in British geography, expanding its interests into explorations of other countries and into fields of systematic study cultivated by scholars in neighbouring disciplines. While some established lines of inquiry are being abandoned or neglected and other approaches are meeting challenges and resistance from workers from different traditions, there is a very lively and active community of scholars pursuing research in the field loosely defined as urban studies.

3
Research in German urban historical geography

DIETRICH DENECKE

The field of research and its disciplines

The task of reviewing trends in German urban historical geography is particularly difficult. First, the review cannot be entirely restricted to the contributions of historical geographers. The framework of study is instead much wider and includes contributions by archaeologists, historians and those interested in the history of architectural form. Furthermore, the themes followed by these research workers are obviously not limited to geographical aspects – however these are defined – although it is the intention of this chapter to focus on the work of historical geographers.

Secondly, in West Germany it is almost impossible to restrict such a review to a national perspective. Though more than 95% of the publications by Germans in the field of history and historical geography are published in German, the knowledge and references of studies in other languages, especially in English, are so common, and the ideas picked up in an international context are so much integrated, that these connections are difficult to exclude. Nonetheless, this chapter will not dwell too much on the parallel trends with research in other countries, but rather focus on the approaches and contributions which well represent a national standard of research progress.

Historical aspects and the historical dimension as such have long been an integrated part of traditional urban geography. In Germany there was no urban study without going back to the historical roots, and early studies were always based on the concept of a chronological urban development. Traditionally, the study of urban geography was in fact that of urban historical geography and this is well reflected in the reviews of research up to the 1960s.[1] Urban geography was closely related to the more or less descriptive regional geography. The townscape (*Stadtlandschaft*) and its development through history was described in numerous monographs, often following an outstanding model, such as Bobek's study on Innsbruck (1928) or the study by Dörries of Göttingen, Northeim and Einbeck (1925).[2] The approach in general was a retrospective one but the final description followed in many respects a chronological order. Traditional urban geography, which developed strongly during the 1920s was often generally couched within the context of cultural history (*kulturhistorische Stadtforschung*), often with the aim of providing to the public information about their town and its historical growth. This tradition changed when during the 1970s a modern analytical approach of urban geography was developed in Germany, strongly influenced by the North American theoretical, analytical and quantitative school of that time. During the same period the tradition of a genetic urban geography was largely abandoned and this opened up the way for a new era of urban geography.[3]

At the same time, however, an explicitly historical urban geography (*historische Stadtgeographie*) developed, taking up the thread of traditional urban geography with contributions by urban archaeologists (*Stadtarchäologie*), urban historians (*Stadtgeschichte*) and historical urban geographers. Urban archaeologists and urban historians in some cases moved towards geographical approaches, whilst historical geographers tried to apply aspects of contemporary and systematic urban geography to studies of the past. This field of historical urban geography in the context of interdisciplinary research is quite young and consequently there are as yet no major reviews.[4]

The different historical-based disciplines attempted to establish links with each other, especially in the context of joint conferences, and to develop interdisciplinary research. No doubt, historical geographers should have played a leading role within this movement, but instead they occupied more secondary positions rather than taking over the leadership. The reason for this may well be that there is only a very small group of academics working entirely on urban geography. Even more importantly, most of the scholars making contributions to urban geography in history did not see the necessity of developing a separate urban historical geography. They still followed the tradition of integrated historical aspects in urban geography and so felt as urban geographers or they joined the more idealist approach of a general historic background of geography. Finally, during the last 15 years research in urban historical geography has split up in a dramatic fashion. Many new general aspects have been followed, especially in local case studies, and sadly there are no long-term systematic research projects that are steered by historical geographers. However, research on urban history was organized on an interdisciplinary basis by the Institute of Comparative Urban History (Institut für vergleichende Städtegeschichte) in Münster, where standing conferences are held, research projects developed and steered, and a number of publications edited.[5]

The growing relations between different disciplines and the emphasis, especially by historical geographers, to follow an interdisciplinary approach has led to the term 'Stadtforschung' (urban studies), which describes the general field of work. Under this interdisciplinary flag more and more research will be organized in the future. The closer contact between disciplines has also led to an improvement in the exchange of information, although it still remains the case that publications are very much scattered in a great number of general and regional journals and separated by disciplines.[6] In contrast, only a relatively small number of omnibus volumes reflect the co-operation that is based on interdisciplinary conferences.

Approaches of urban historical geography

Traditional descriptive urban geography saw the town as a whole, as a complex geographical object, as an urban landscape, a townscape. Regionalism was the next step dividing up this complexity into smaller, more or less homogeneous units, which was an approach mainly followed by geographers. The new analytical approach fragmented these regional units in very different ways by encouraging the study of phenomena in more detail and the examination of processes. As such, urban topography and its components (street patterns, single streets, places, fortification), urban functions (centrality, economic sectors) and social aspects (social quarters and patterns) are researched, but with an historic perspective. In addition, historical studies are also fragmented, focussing on a single cross-section or on processes and developments within a short period of time. The more recent questions followed, more or less in an ecological framework, were mainly picked up by historians, namely the impact of human activities on urban change and development, of politics and planning, urbanism and the urban environment, and urban housing in its social context. This trend of historical urban research is well reflected in the hitherto 25 published volumes of the series *Städteforschung*, as well as in recent research projects, and in the growing number of articles to be found in current bibliographies.

In Germany these very recent trends of historical research have made it difficult for geographers to follow up such work since it is often political and social behaviour and class struggle that are emphasized and not the town itself. In this context no doubt historians have a great advantage and it will be important for geographers to find new ways of stressing geographical interpretation and analysis of the town in a spatial context.

Recent approaches in contemporary geography such as welfare geography, humanistic geography, radical geography or environmental perception are in general hard to apply in historical urban geography, mainly due to a lack of sources. But more importantly, in German historical geography these progressive experiments together with marxist idealist approaches[7] are not as yet seriously reflected in major studies.

In Germany, historical geographers do not hunt eagerly for new theories and approaches. Instead they pursue research to improve basic approaches in empirical studies based on sources and fieldwork. Reconstruction and interpretation of place and pattern, especially within the context of social topography, the comparative approach,[8] the morphogenetic approach with new functional aspects and the systems approach (urban centrality, relationships between town and countryside) have provided the main areas of research. There is, however, an urgent need for an analysis of theories and methods used in recent urban studies. But this certainly would show that most of the research in Germany is of an empirical and pragmatic nature, not following a particular school of ideology or theory.

Another major theme has been the general discussion concerning the definition of urban settlement, and has for obvious reasons focussed on terminology. In particular the periods of urban origin and the middle ages were discussed by exploring the question of what criteria should be used when attempting to define 'urban' settlement, and researchers have specifically focussed on such features as market rights, functions, centrality, social and economic structure.[9] This discussion on terminology should be broadened, on an interdisciplinary and international basis, as it helps not only to clarify the object of research but also to bring together new ideas.

Urban origins, patterns and morphogenesis

Periods and specific phases of formation of towns (*Stadtentstehungsschichten*) in Germany were investigated and defined systematically during the 1960s and 1970s mainly by the urban historian Heinz Stoob.[10] The division of medieval urban origins into distinct periods emphasized more clearly the initiatives: the political, strategic and economic aims that lay behind urban foundations and developments. The geographical aspect, however, was not followed in any detail, which means that the question of the location and distribution of towns, the choice of site and the urban pattern in a geographic and territorial context were never fully discussed.[11]

The question of the structure and function of early medieval urban settlements was discussed at a conference of the Akademie der Wissenschaften in Göttingen on 'Vor- und Frühformen der europäischen Stadt im Mittelalter' (1972).[12] This represents the findings of many different disciplines, although significantly at this time most contributions came from archaeologists.

A central theme investigated initially by historians and more recently by archaeologists is the question of the pre-urban nuclei of medieval towns (*Stadtkerne*).[13] Past research has identified three major types of pre-urban settlements. First, the village which was the pre-urban nucleus of most German towns. Very often villages remained as separate agrarian communities for a long period after the foundation and development of an urban community.[14] Secondly, are those settlements associated with castles, where a suburbium often developed in connection with a fortified feudal seat. Thirdly, research in a number of studies by historians has revealed that markets also acted as foci for early urban development.[15]

One of the very interesting geographical aspects of the early medieval period of urban development is the shifting of urban settlements and functions within a small area. Often earlier sites were deserted while new locations were adopted. Haithabu and Schleswig, Alt-Lübeck and Lübeck, Bardowiek and Lüneburg, Corvey and Höxter, Burg Spandau and Spandau, Altencelle and Celle or Alt-Rinteln and Rinteln are all outstanding examples and it seems as if this process was quite common. On the base of historical evidence, excavations and geographical analysis the question has to be raised, whether political actions or functional changes were behind this shifting of location.[16]

The expansion of a town (*Stadterweiterung*) is a spatial process operating over time, that can be followed in cross-sections and which usually has developed in specific phases of growth. Louis followed the concept of regional historical geography and of townscape history when he described and mapped the expansion of the city of Berlin in terms of historic fringes in 1936.[17] This later became a prosperous field of research and it laid the foundation for the morphogenetic approach. However, whereas in Britain Conzen was to develop this approach as an important concept of urban morphology, in Germany this research did not make the same degree of progress.[18]

Recent studies on urban growth during the nineteenth century often proceed to examine processes and to consider the political, functional, social and economic agents that lay behind such urban expansion.[19] To some extent this followed on from the work on the medieval and early modern development of suburbs (*Vorstadt*) which in a number of specific studies considered not only the legal question, but also social and functional aspects.[20] During the eighteenth and nineteenth centuries medieval suburbs were integrated in the expanding cities and new suburbs developed, quite often starting out from rural nuclei.[21] This preindustrial expansion has a quite different social and historical background from the later industrial expansion, and eighteenth-century concepts of planning are clearly evident in many examples. Unfortunately most of the research tends to be local case studies, and there is not as yet a more general or regional view of urban expansion since medieval times.

The analytic functional approach led to detailed studies of urban fragments, their morphogenetic and functional change, especially during the nineteenth and twentieth centuries. A number of local case studies were devoted to former rural villages that had become integrated into inner-urban areas.[22] In contrast other studies focussed on the old town as a specific urban quarter with new activities,[23] main streets and their city functions,[24] the urban fringe as a location of specific urban functions,[25] urban places changing their form and function[26] or the urban green in its historic development.[27] This interest in individual sections of the town is not only a fragmentation and a change in scale, but the part is thought to represent the whole; it is therefore an example or model, with which to illuminate change, processes and agents for the whole of the individual town. The processes that the town underwent are often reflected in the mirror of one of its parts, and this focus allows the researcher to go into detail and to follow threads, that finally again knit everything together on a more general and theoretical level.

It is not yet known how important the influence of building regulations, fire regulations or restrictions on certain building materials were on the development and structure of urban street patterns and buildings – not only for the last 100 years but also for the preindustrial period and even in medieval times. This is due to the fact that most of the local and regional regulations in Germany have not yet been compiled systematically. For example, there is only one general study on their development,[28] and there are only a few studies on their influence and impact on nineteenth-century urban design.[29] However, very recently planning history has become of considerable interest in Germany, particularly in the work of architectural historians. As yet most of the recent studies are devoted to urban planning and planning policies during the second half of the nineteenth century.[30] Another recently prospering field is urban planning and urban renewal during the 1930s, focussed on the continuation of earlier town planning traditions during the Third Reich, and particularly on the impact of political and ideological concepts of urban design.[31] Urban planning and ideology have also been examined in a comparison of the concepts of capitalist and socialist planning.[32]

Concepts and decisions of preindustrial town planning become especially evident in the process of defortification since the middle of the eighteenth century. Gates were demolished to open up the towns for through traffic, ring roads were designed along former ditches, and greens, parks, gardens and promenades were laid out in the areas formerly outside the defensive works. A few case studies give something of an idea of this rewarding field of research under the auspices of uncovering communal decisions that were fulfilled in the layout of German towns (*raumwirksame öffentliche Tätigkeit*), still represented in today's topography.[33] Thus an old topic of local historians becomes a new stimulating field of academic research, of modern analytical and applied urban historical geography.

Historians and architectural historians are mainly involved in these new fields of research, analysing planning decisions in history, but historical geographers are at present not that well represented. Indeed, the geographical interest in planning history is not the biography of planners, their ideas and individual concepts, but rather the resultant pattern of urban development.

Housing, housing policies and social order have become other themes of recent historical research,[34] although the regional and spatial aspect in most of these studies is very neglected. The focus is on lower-class housing and the impact of industrialization on the development of working-class quarters. Standards and deficiencies of housing and the beginning of social housing and housing societies also have a wide range of geographical aspects, and are particularly important in understanding change in the nineteenth- and early twentieth-century town. Morphogenetic studies on urban expansion have to proceed to a consideration of the agents behind this development, to politics, economic backgrounds, social concepts, models of layout and standard of housetypes; but once again in Germany these are mainly contributions made by historians.[35]

Historians have also proceeded to investigations on the living and housing standards in nineteenth-century Germany.[36] Much of the work is mainly a social history developed within the context of the reconstruction of everyday life. Even here, however, geographical aspects can be followed, especially in the context of place, environment, social patterns or spatial relations.

With the growing concern over environmental protection and pollution, historians and social historians have begun to investigate this problem in historical periods. Urban water supply, sewage, water and air pollution, often resulting in epidemics such as the Black Death or dysentery, have become topics of interest, generally in a technical or social context. Such studies now encompass the medieval period as well as preindustrial and industrial urban settlements.[37]

Historical urban centrality

Few geographers need reminding that the theory of central places was developed during the 1930s by Christaller in South Germany, although it took quite a long time before this aspect of urban functional relations and the inter-urban system were also investigated for historic periods. Since the 1950s regional and local geographical studies have been pursued.[38] Initially, the medieval period and the phase of urban origins was the focus,[39] but during the 1970s the interest shifted towards the preindustrial period.[40] Indeed, a number of special conferences devoted to this particular topic were held, and resulted in a series of publications.[41] Mention should be made of the comprehensive study by Blotevogel of central places in Westfalia which is an outstanding example because of the different ways and indices used to follow and document urban centrality and the changing urban system. This study also makes it clear that there are different aspects of centrality which should be distinguished. There are inner-urban institutions with central functions, and these were especially of interest in the early, more static, studies. A hierarchy of central places was elaborated on this basis, for medieval and modern periods.[42] Economic, cultural and social interflows between town and countryside as a process of spatial interaction and influence became foci for research, throwing more light on the dependency between town and countryside. In addition, mobility, population migration, marriage patterns and trade connections were spatial interactions that were to be documented and analysed in a number of specific studies. More recently, the regional differentiation of changes within central place systems were followed over time, especially for the period of the eighteenth and nineteenth centuries when industrialization led to a drastic remodelling of the urban hierarchy.[43]

Historians focussed initially on trade and marketing as major central functions,[44] but later political, social and cultural aspects also became important. Within the context of trade, in some respects, the model of central places was sometimes misinterpreted as a system of long-distance contacts and connections. However, a quite progressive early study was contributed by Ammann,[45] who reconstructed patterns of contact (such as invitations of guests for fairs, and provenance of journeymen) for selected dates for medieval towns. Ammann also proceeded to a consideration of the knowledge and perception of distance as well as the influence of political and economic factors over large-scale regions.

More recently, Denecke has attempted to evaluate a toll register of the late seventeenth century, in order to reconstruct a detailed pattern of the supply of agricultural products to an urban area.[46] The subject of migration to towns, especially during the late medieval period, when rural areas were partly deserted, has been followed in a number of studies, using the records of naturalized townsmen.[47] Finally, cultural and educational links between the countryside and the town have been reconstructed, evaluating for example the enrolments of students of medieval and early modern latin schools.[48]

In comparison with research in other countries there seems therefore to be a special emphasis on urban centrality studies in Germany, largely due to the long tradition and role of central place theory in this country.

Historical geography, urban renewal and conservation

There is a growing interest in and discussion of the erosion of history in German towns, or of the planned destruction of the German heritage.

This process of destruction and replacement, of urban renewal, caused by town planners during the 1950s and 1960s is well documented in the local planning programmes of that time. It might, however, be a task in the near future for historical geographers to evaluate this material not only to get a quantitative and topographic picture of the dimensions and results of this process, but also to elucidate the planning concepts and the decision-making processes that lay behind them.

In this context a rewarding contribution of historical geographers would be to reconstruct and analyse periods and processes of, and reasons for, urban destruction and renewal for individual towns or in comparative studies. Occasionally in town histories data and maps were compiled on great fires, on damage by wars, on destruction during different phases of replanning and renewal or on the damages by the bombardments during the Second World War. But as yet, there are no basic historical geography studies. However, more important than destruction is the documentation and analysis of reconstruction. There are only a few local studies on early modern rebuilding after fire or on replanning for early urban expansion.[49] Recently historians and architectural historians have become involved in examining the reconstruction of destroyed German towns after 1945.[50] However, these studies are in general still in the stage of documentation and description and have not yet proceeded to any comparative analysis.

The idea of restoration and conservation is not only a contemporary one, since in historic periods there were phases when conservation of buildings and historical remains prospered. It is a question of how these earlier activities of conservation affected the heritage of the building fabric, the street patterns or fortifications in old towns. Finally, studies of this kind tend to become a history of conservation but with an emphasis on geographical aspects.[51]

At the beginning of the 1970s there was an important shift within the concept of town planning towards conservation, and in Germany it was marked by the new Federal Building Law of 1972 (Städtebauförderungsgesetz). Aspects of conservation and restoration were discussed by art historians[52] and the general question of the meaning and perception of history in an old town was brought into a theoretical debate.[53] Social aspects, especially within the context of required planning studies, were analysed by social scientists and social geographers.[54] Most of the studies, even the theoretical ones, were biased towards the more applied and practical aspects, both as a general basis for planning decisions, as well as critically analysing the results in local case studies.[55]

Historical urban geography has not yet made significant contributions, but there are several aspects of basic research which could be pursued.[56] For example, historic-geographic building surveys, which have a long tradition in German urban historical geography,[57] may be an important contribution for conservationists and planners. The perception of historic elements in old town centres and the economic value of the historic potential for urban tourism has also not been sufficiently analysed by historical geographers.[58] Historical geography could also make a contribution to the debates concerning conservation and wholesale renewal, by investigating more thoroughly the historical background of the area under consideration. These questions have to be followed within a recently developing applied historical geography.[59]

Conclusion

From the standpoint of urban historical geography during the last ten years significant changes have occurred: in approach, in focus, in the periods investigated and in fields of interest. Moreover, traditional and progressive concepts are followed at the same time, and indeed both of them have their representatives and followers. As to the discipline itself, geographers have difficulties in coping with the immense production and the progressive approaches of urban and social historians. The individual studies of a handful of historical geographers may be compared with a great number of well-organized research projects steered by historians, largely in connection with the Sonderforschungsbereich 164. In most of these projects only a small number of historical geographers are integrated into the research teams. Nevertheless, close contact and co-operation gives the chance to bring in new ideas and concepts, mainly initiated by the progress of contemporary urban geography, influenced by British and American approaches. Unfortunately, it is unlikely that major research projects steered by geographers will occur in the near future as the group of workers is too small and much too divided. Instead a further integration into interdisciplinary work should be the aim, producing a more general field of urban historical studies. In this context the role of the historical geographer will be to develop the spatial concept and to follow spatial change over time, and also to throw more light on the agents and processes behind such changes. In this wider academic community historical urban geography does appear to have a valid and exciting future in Germany.

PART TWO

The evolution of urban settlement and the development of the medieval town

4

The town in the Norman colonisations of the British Isles

BRIAN GRAHAM

Although the origins of the medieval town in the British Isles clearly pre-date the Norman invasion of England in 1066, that event initiated a series of colonisations which had significant implications for urban development throughout the islands. William I's conquest was accompanied by that of Wales, the origins of which date to *c.* 1080. However it was only completed after a lengthy hiatus with Edward I's final subjugation of the native Welsh princes in the late thirteenth century. The Anglo-Norman colonisation of Scotland which began in the first years of the twelfth century and continued throughout the thirteenth was rather different, occurring not by conquest but at the direct behest of the Scottish kings. The culmination of Anglo-Norman expansion was the partially successful attempt to conquer Ireland which commenced in 1169 and continued until the late thirteenth century.

Rather surprisingly, given that these settlements were part of a general process of expansion and during the eleventh and twelfth centuries frequently involved the same Anglo-Norman families, the power of contemporary boundaries and nationalisms has ensured that the study of the associated towns has been circumscribed by insularity. Barrow refers to the 'malign parochialism' that typifies studies of feudalism in Scotland and England and his phrase also effectively describes the analysis of the medieval town in the British Isles.[1] The aim of this chapter is to use some of the recent and relatively well-known research on post-Conquest English medieval towns as a perspective or base-line for a discussion of the much less familiar urbanisation in Wales, Scotland and Ireland during the Middle Ages. This is not to insinuate that definitive answers can be advanced to the problems of the English town, but the arguments are more substantial, better rehearsed and oft-reviewed compared to those concerned with medieval urbanisation in the peripheries of the British Isles. The English evidence is discussed elsewhere in the volume and no claim of comprehensiveness is made for this chapter which is consciously orientated towards those peripheries and the overlapping perspectives and analogies which they provide for each other.

Several common if tentative leanings might be discerned in this brief survey. In the first instance, there is a distinct trend towards re-evaluation of previous orthodoxies concerning medieval towns. Some cognisance is being taken of the need to analyse settlement in the context of societal structure – in this case feudalism – and to develop theory and generalisation. Again there has been a marked diminution of explanation by invasion, the tendency to view the Norman colonisations as the primary explanatory process in the development of medieval settlement. Finally, there is an awareness of the insular parochialism of much previous work and ideas and rather belatedly more attention is being paid to continental studies, both as comparisons and contrasts. Oddly, however, the revisions and re-evaluations persist in their isolation of each other.

Feudalism and other approaches

The study of the post-Conquest medieval town in England has attracted some recent attention from geographers although the bulk of the considerable corpus of modern work is either historical or archaeological. Its singular defect, as Hilton observes, is that the degree of conceptualisation is low, too much research lying within a descriptive non-theoretical tradition with little attempt at generalisation.[2] A consciousness of the social and economic structures within which settlements occur means that, as in many European studies, the medieval town is placed squarely within the confines of feudalism, providing a conceptual basis which is common to England, Wales, Scotland and Ireland although the resolutions of the dialectics of the mode of production were frequently at variance with each other.

The essential feature linking feudalism and the medieval town was the relationship of subjugation and expectation called lordship. Duby stresses the role of the feudal lords in economic endeavour, constantly thinking 'in terms of ensuring new sources of profits for themselves' – mills, markets and towns.[3] The town, he argues, was a mechanism to mobilise this wealth through markets and credit, the cash that the lords took from the peasantry returning to the countryside in bourgeois or mercantile credit. This point is taken up by Hilton who notes that the medieval town is *one* expression of feudal society rather than a contradictory element within it.[4] He argues that the income of the ruling class was rent and that the village markets (*villae mercatoriae*) and seigneurial boroughs which multiplied in England in the twelfth and thirteenth centuries provided the mechanism whereby conversion of rent to cash was achieved.

If medieval towns are regarded in this way, it is quite clear that Postan's famous Pirenne-derived *dictum* that 'medieval towns were non-feudal islands in a feudal sea' is no longer tenable in its original sense.[5] Rather, towns were an intimate part of the structures of feudal agrarian society and were involved in the contradictions of that structure without, as Hilton argues in a point worthy of emphasis, 'being the principle of contradiction'.[6] Towns were set aside by law, especially the Law of Breteuil (Breteuil-sur-Iton, a small Normandy town in the Department of Eure which belonged to William fitz Osbern who, as Earl of Hereford, was one of the principal Norman adventurers in England and Wales), and there was inevitably a paradox whereby the feudal lord, dependent upon obedience, was creating freedom.[7] However, the seigneurial need to create towns was so essential to the economic conduct of feudal society that the contradictions were accepted and gradually freedom of a sort percolated the rural world.[8] Hilton divides medieval towns into two types, differentiating between those which arose from the operation of the agrarian economy, the places where the peasant surplus was converted into cash, and the large urban centres, more familiar perhaps to students of Pirenne *et al.*, which developed from the combined operations of the feudal ruling class, the state and merchant capital.[9] Two-thirds of English medieval towns belonged to the former type as did many in north-west Europe as witnessed, for example, by the plethora of *bourgs* identified by Musset in Normandy.[10] Hilton has devoted a series of papers to discussing the society of these small towns, particularly in the English Midlands, a study which unfortunately cannot be replicated in the peripheries of the British Isles because of documentary deficiencies.[11]

Urbanisation is thus increasingly interpreted as an integral part of the feudal seigneurial economy, the process of re-evaluation being part of a wider reconsideration of the nature of feudalism itself. As Dodgshon observes, feudalism and manorialism are no longer ascribed to the Normans.[12] A considerable debate on the origins of English feudalism has occurred and it is worth emphasising that explanation by invasion, so common in medieval histories of the British Isles, can no longer be regarded as acceptable. The origins of feudalism and hence, by association, the English medieval town pre-date the Conquest. The same process of feudal revisionism has been characteristic of the periphery. Barrow argues for the normality of feudalism in thirteenth-century Scotland, claiming that it was almost a copybook version of the system found in north-west Europe.[13] Again, as Frame notes, the Anglo-Norman settlement of Ireland took place within the controlling framework of lordship, the most potent social force of the time.[14] 'Anglo-Norman Ireland was less a lordship than a patchwork of lordships'[15] and it can be argued that medieval urbanisation developed in a direct relationship to this.[16]

However, it is not sufficient to dismiss the Anglo-Norman penetrations into Wales, Scotland and Ireland as an expansion of English feudalism, a parallel to the viewpoint which sees the contemporaneous Germanic expansions to the east of the Elbe in the tenth to twelfth centuries as representing the conversion of the Slavic system of government and space organisation into a feudal one, the town acting as the focus for this transformation. Some historians argue that Ireland for example was moving towards a system of feudalism prior to the arrival of the Anglo-Normans, a reassessment of the 'invasion hypothesis' which is analogous to the way in which English feudalism is now held to have pre-Conquest origins.[17] Conversely, Wales seems to fit into the concept of a feudal expansion while in Scotland, Barrow sees the Anglo-Norman colonisations as a great land-taking, not so much an expansion but more the result of the direct and deliberate importation of feudalism under David I (1123–53).

Crucially for the analysis of the town there is a trend in Irish studies to disregard the idea of a benign colonisation, an expansion of development of feudalism. Instead an interpretation of the medieval history of the island is offered which is based upon the concept of colonialism, defined as the deliberate subjugation of a periphery to a core, the towns, particularly the walled ports, being the means through which this dependent relationship was imposed.[18] The manifest hegemony of ports in medieval Ireland suggests a set of dependent linkages with the mother country as does the large-scale exportation of foodstuffs and capital to support the operations of Edward I in Wales and Scotland.[19] Davies argues that the initial central concept of feudalism gave way to colonialism in the thirteenth century when the English, deprived of alternatives after their loss of France, turned to Ireland as a provider of primary goods and instituted a state of dependence and legal dualism which was not characteristic of either Wales or Scotland.[20] Such a conceptual approach has obvious implications, yet to be worked out, for the study of urban networks, and again the legal dualism of medieval Ireland must have had significant effects upon the social geography of the towns. It does seem clear, however, that this is a conceptual approach with little relevance for Scotland or Wales.

On definitions and sources

If the answers advanced are dependent upon the conceptual approach adopted so too are they reliant upon the definitions used. The tacit assumption which characterises almost all work on medieval towns in the British Isles is that *borough* (or *burgh* in Scotland) can be equated with town and indeed relatively little discussion has taken place on the efficacy of this assumption despite the acknowledged deficiencies of legal definitions.[21] Emphasis upon them prompts the assumption that *de jure* recognition is synonymous with creation whereas frequently it must have been applied to an existing settlement; again, borough status was often a theoretical state never converted to reality. It was a concept of Norman law and undue concentration upon it emphasises explanation by invasion, a flaw apparent in Beresford's organic-plantation typology of English medieval towns, the latter term implying foundation rather than the genetic growth which now frequently seems more likely. Again, Reynolds notes that legal terms must be used with caution; the clerks of Domesday 'used the word borough to describe, not to define' and she emphasises that we must be wary of being dependent upon exact definition of terms that may have been loosely used and that changed meaning in the Middle Ages.[22] Thus, she argues that 'borough status' is a poor expression to apply to the twelfth and thirteenth centuries; all that it means is that there were certain liberties and privileges that one expected a borough to possess.[23]

Numerous attempts have been made to develop alternative definitions of towns. One of the more recent is that of Hodges who defines 'urban' as a community of some size with significant non-agricultural employment and more than one institution.[24] A similar list of criteria is used by Reynolds for English towns although it is not rigorously applied while Bradley uses a set of morphological criteria in his analysis of Irish medieval towns.[25] This type of definition may well work at the upper end of the urban scale if demographic and functional data are extant. Unfortunately, due to deficiencies of evidence, it is generally inoperable in the lower reaches of the hierarchy where town imperceptibly graded into village, precisely where the largest concentration of settlements occurred. The large majority of medieval towns in the British Isles were small and are unreliably documented and it seems pointless to adopt definitions which do not identify them. Again the metaphysical definitions occasionally favoured in Europe are singularly inappropriate for small towns.[26]

If we return somewhat reluctantly to legal definitions, certain mitigating factors occur. First and pragmatically, the equation of borough with town reflects the sources available. It must be remembered that a combination of deficient documentary sources and a lack of open-area archaeology outside England ensures that reliably consistent functional and demographic evidence is unlikely to exist. Second, as Frame notes, every burgess community contained the possibility of urban growth within it especially because of the Law of Breteuil.[27] Hodges' statement that 'it is not possible to sustain proto-urbanism: a site is either urban or it is not' clearly cannot be sustained if the expression is held to suggest a potentiality for growth and not one moment when pre-urban became urban.[28] Finally, as noted above, a borough formed an integral part of the feudal system and was thus much more than a legal institution. It was a settlement form which reflected particular needs and constraints in that society and, moreover, one that was viewed by the seigneurial class as fulfilling particular functions. As feudalism and its law was ubiquitous, the use of 'borough' permits comparability throughout the British Isles.[29]

The extant documentary sources available to do this vary in quality and quantity from area to area, a particular problem being their increase through time. There was a dramatic growth in the number of towns in England in the tenth and eleventh centuries but 'it is impossible to be sure that the simultaneous improvement in the sources does not exaggerate it'.[30] English documentary sources are, however, amongst the best in Europe and in addition there is a considerable corpus of archaeological evidence. By contrast, Wales and Scotland possess little published archaeology to add to the reviews contained in Barley's *European towns: their archaeology and early history*[31] (although there have been notable if as yet unpublished excavations at Caernarvon); however, substantial preliminary discussions of the important excavations of Anglo-Norman and Viking Dublin have recently appeared.[32] This comparative lack of archaeological data exaggerates the importance of documents which as a generalisation are poor but sufficient. For example, despite the relatively few charters extant for Irish or Welsh medieval towns, the piecemeal sources still permit the identification and comparative discussion of boroughs and large places are comparatively well documented.[33] Scottish sources are notably poor for the key twelfth century and on functional and social information generally.

Using documents Beresford and Finsberg recorded 609 boroughs in England,[34] Soulsby identified 105 medieval towns in Wales (a few of which did not hold borough status)[35] and Pryde listed over 400 burghs in Scotland.[36] However only 109 of these were founded prior to 1500, burgh foundation in Scotland being quite exceptional in the British Isles in that it continued uninterrupted into the sixteenth, seventeenth and even eighteenth centuries. Finally, in an interim listing Graham recorded just over 200 boroughs in Ireland although recent if unpublished research has increased this total to almost 300.[37] In a further listing, which requires considerable correction and editing, Martin noted about 240 Irish boroughs recorded before 1500.[38]

On origins and continuity

Re-evaluation of traditional theses extends beyond feudalism. The pre-Conquest origins of that system are now accepted for England and so too is a pre-Norman development of urbanisation. Obviously, this means that boroughs, the results of Norman law, were founded in addition to earlier towns and as a result of the grant of borough status to existing settlements. The re-evaluation of previous orthodoxies extends beyond England to Ireland and to a much lesser extent to Wales. A critical point to be remembered is that Ireland was never part of the Roman Empire while in Scotland Roman forts did not generally grow into towns. Although several urban centres developed in Wales, notably at Moridunon (Carmarthen) and Venta

Silurum (Caerwent), the intensity of Roman town foundation in England and the ensuing problems of continuity clearly demarcates it from the remainder of the British Isles. In England in the early medieval period we are dealing with continuity or revival whereas in Wales, Scotland and Ireland the discussion effectively concerns origins.

The vexed issue of Roman-Anglo-Saxon urban continuity or discontinuity in sixth- and seventh-century England is increasingly being resolved in favour of the latter stance. Life, trade and institutions in the Anglo-Saxon revival of towns are increasingly seen as coming from outside, continuity being of site alone.[39] It is generally agreed that the *burhs* noted in the *Burghal Hidage* and the *Anglo-Saxon Chronicle* represent a growth of towns long before the Norman Conquest of 1066. As Reynolds observes, the coincidence of the Norman upsurge and the flowering of towns in Western Europe is not necessarily a causative one and it is thus clear that the boroughs noted in Domesday Book represent a pre-Norman urbanisation.[40]

The origins of towns, the causative processes ascribed to the Norman conquests and the issues attending early medieval continuity are very different in the remainder of the British Isles. The traditional view was well expressed by Binchy who argued that 'urban civilisation remained quite foreign to the Celtic-speaking peoples of these islands until it was more or less imposed upon them by foreign conquerors'.[41] The viewpoint has also been individually reiterated for each of the three countries. Lewis believed that 'there were no towns of purely Welsh origin'[42] and for Jones Hughes, 'Ireland possessed no native urban tradition ... [a] ... factor largely attributable, as elsewhere in the moist, cool fringe of Atlantic Europe, to the pastoral and tribal nature of society.'[43] The same idea was expressed slightly differently in Mackenzie's statement that 'the key word to the [medieval] burghs [in Scotland] is creation, not growth'.[44] With the notable exception of Ireland, these viewpoints whilst somewhat modified have not been radically altered.

In Scotland, the issue of continuity is almost non-existent. Small for example argues that unlike Ireland, Scotland did not generate the wealth necessary to promote the growth of large Viking *emporia*.[45] Brooks, discussing the dearth of urban archaeology, observes that excavation results at St Andrews and Aberdeen imply that not all burghal settlements were creations[46] and Duncan agrees that burghs could have had a genetic growth from small but non-urban settlements of pre-burghal origin.[47] Beyond these commonsense modifications to an explanation by invasion, Adams' statement that the origins of clearly identified urbanisation lay in the twelfth century during the Norman colonisation of Scotland is generally accepted.[48]

Griffiths believes that early medieval continuity problems may exist in Wales.[49] There is a faint possibility that Carmarthen retained its urban use as a Celtic Christian Dark Age settlement although Davies is doubtful that other settlements such as Caernarvon were more than proto-urban.[50] Certainly the largest Roman town in Wales, Caerwent, was abandoned, the Norman borough being at Chepstow, and Carter argues that continuity was of tradition of settlement on a site or in an area rather than taking any direct or dynamic form.[51] A clearer but different example of continuity of site is that of Rhuddlan, the Anglo-Saxon *burh* of Clydemutha which became an Anglo-Norman borough in 1073 and was reconstituted on a different site as a castle-town by Edward I in 1277. Again, citing the instances of Nefyn and Pwllheli, Jones Pierce argued for the existence of what he called manorial boroughs, differing in origin from the Anglo-Norman plantations. These late thirteenth-century incorporations involved the enfranchisement of fully developed urban communities with roots firmly embedded in the pre-Conquest history of Gwynedd.[52] Soulsby points to further examples of the transition form *maerdref* (market) to town, noting that these native urban foundations were lesser affairs than the English boroughs on which they were modelled.[53] Thus the likelihood of genetic growth from pre-urban nuclei is high in Wales but this scarcely radically alters the conclusion that the large bulk of Welsh towns emerged from the Anglo-Norman conquest after 1080.

One possible pre-urban nucleus in Wales has assumed greater importance in recent discussions of early medieval Irish urban origins. Bowen concludes his study of Welsh Celtic monasteries with the observation that they did not possess great nucleation power in the settlement pattern although it would, conversely, be a considerable understatement to maintain that they had none.[54] In Ireland, the monasteries have been elevated from the status of pre-urban nuclei to early medieval towns although the evidence is limited to a very few sites.[55] The essence of the argument is essentially hypothetical, based upon assumptions that references to trade in the early Irish Annals can be combined with allusions to arguably urban morphological features such as streets at some monastic sites including Armagh, Glenalough and Kildare to corroborate the existence of a pre-Anglo-Norman urbanisation. In contrast to the arguments on the revival of English urbanisation in the seventh and eighth centuries in which a multiplicity of causative processes – the influence of a polity, defence, trade and the episcopal church – is stressed, the Irish argument depends substantially on economic activity although it lacks the sustained conceptual discussion on the relationship between trade, marketing and urban origins made necessary by the deficient evidence.[56]

Interestingly the concept of the monastic town partially arises from a desire to discuss early medieval Ireland in its wider European context.[57] Unfortunately, the incorporation of analogical material is too often naive and uncritical, a factor which, together with a lack of definition, is leading to the promulgation of an ill-considered and exaggerated orthodoxy of indigenous origin. Too many ambiguities exist to be easily dismissed. Clarke's judgement is that extreme caution should be exercised in considering monasteries to be urban earlier than the tenth century,[58] the development arguably being a response to the Viking Age in Ireland.[59] However, there is again a danger of assumption by coincidence. The Viking towns appear to have been *emporia* although Wallace would disagree,[60] and De Paor strongly implies that Ireland lacked a regional space-economy which could have sustained an urban network based on monastic towns.[61] Hodges also views the Viking towns as *emporia* possessing no real symbiosis with an Irish economy, noting that the most important mode of economic interaction was through warfare and raids.[62] The Viking towns of Dublin, Wexford, Waterford, Cork and Limerick formed the bridgeheads for the Anglo-Norman invasions of Ireland after 1169 and De Paor argues that Rory O Conor's surrender of them to Henry II shows how little importance the Irish placed on towns.[63] A further problem with early medieval urbanisation is that unlike Wales there is no evidence of the divided Irish political leaders founding towns nor oddly is there any real evidence of post-invasion towns apart from a few episcopal centres such as Armagh, in those parts of the island which remained beyond the ambit of Anglo-Norman control.[64] The development of the bulk of Irish medieval towns is perhaps post-Conquest but, rather like Wales, a number developed on sites of pre-urban nuclei and were clearly not plantations.[65] However, the Viking influence and the argument on monastic towns underline the quite significant variations which occur concerning the relative contribution of the Normans to the development of medieval urbanisation within the British Isles.

Comparisons and contrasts

A similar diversity characterises the evidence for the high medieval town. Although several noteworthy summaries of empirical evidence on English medieval towns have been published recently, Beresford's older work still carries the depth of conviction despite its stress on explanation by invasion.[66] With the exception of Soulsby's recent study of Wales, there are as yet no comparable attempts at synthesis for the periphery although a number of significant contrasts are still discernible. Despite the caveat about sources, the scale of borough foundation in England was quite remarkable. Compared to the Domesday total of 111, 80% of the eventual total of over 600 was in existence by 1300.[67] Dodgshon argues that this increase did not mean that England was becoming more urbanised (although certainly Wales, Scotland and Ireland were). Rather it was a function of demographic growth.[68] Population estimates are what they are but it has been calculated that English population rose by about 300% between the late eleventh and early fourteenth centuries.[69] The vast majority of the English medieval towns were small. Hilton estimates that while London had a population of 45,000–50,000 by the fourteenth century, only 39 other towns exceeded 2,000, the vast majority lying between 500 and 2,000 and the bulk being nearer the lower end of the range.[70] It is for this reason that he argues for more research into small towns, pointing out that they did contain one half of England's urban population.

In addition to the boroughs, a large number of market villages were either legally created or recognised. Not every market had burghality although every borough possessed a market. While less than 350 boroughs were created between 1199 and 1350, there were 2,000 new market grants in the same period.[71] A number of these were made by seigneurs although it was politic in England to obtain permission from the Crown. The charters sought or granted by seigneurial lords reflect their perception of boroughs and *villae mercatoriae* as a means of enhancing profit. In this context, it is probable that Beresford's distinction between organic and planted towns is somewhat ingenuous for as Slater observes, almost all successful plantations were preceded by a period of manorial growth, often with a marketing function being actively if unofficially encouraged by the lord.[72] Thus the grant of a market or borough charter was frequently a legal recognition and not a creation. A number came to nothing, for local lords were not always good judges of places to which they granted charters, the offer of urban life singularly failing to be evidence that it developed.[73] Processes of competition within marketing circuits soon induced the development of urban hierarchies as Unwin and Slater demonstrate for Nottinghamshire and Staffordshire respectively.[74]

As well as location, the status of the seigneurial lord was an important influence on the ultimate success or failure of a borough. The earliest and larger English towns tended to develop under royal or ecclesiastical patronage but seigneurial developments increased rapidly after 1200 and ultimately accounted for almost half the total.[75] However, according to Beresford by far and away the most significant contribution to success was an early arrival and as a generalisation almost all the larger towns originated prior to the mid-twelfth century.[76] Consequently, the plethora of small towns was most directly associated with local seigneurial ambitions and it is entirely possible that too many were created.

When we turn to Wales, Scotland and Ireland, significant contrasts occur both in relation to England and to each other. Obviously in absolute terms the scale of borough foundation was much less but so too were the populations. Sources do not permit anything more than the crudest of estimates, Russell assessing the Welsh, Scottish and Irish populations before the plague at around 300,000, 550,000 and 800,000 respectively.[77] It is possible that about 20% of the Welsh population lived in towns although deficiencies in data preclude similar estimates for Scotland and Ireland. Again there are few sources such as poll taxes to estimate individual town populations although the large majority of Welsh, Scottish and Irish boroughs were small. Population estimates are generally dependent upon extrapolations from burgage rents or lists of burgesses. The largest Welsh borough was Cardiff with 420 burgages in 1295, indicating a population in excess of 2,000 but the majority of towns had less than 100 burgages or burgesses.[78] Scottish boroughs were also generally small, Fox estimating that a medium-sized burgh contained around 100–120 burgages and a population of approximately 600.[79] Edinburgh with about 400 houses and 2,000 inhabitants in the fourteenth century was the leading town. Irish borough populations were quite variable, some being considerably larger than any examples in Wales or Scotland. Kilkenny for instance contained in excess of 300 burgages in 1307[80] while the burgage rent of New Ross in 1307 was £251 6s 8d, equivalent to $506\frac{1}{2}$ burgages.[81] Dublin was the dominant town by far, Hollingsworth's estimate of a population of 25,000 placing it amongst the largest medieval cities in the British Isles.[82] However, the majority of Irish boroughs were small, calculations indicating that almost half of those with extant data contained populations of less than 500.[83]

Although the small town therefore dominates in numbers throughout the British Isles, the borough was much more evident in the settlement structure of the periphery because the *villae mercatoriae* so typical of England did not occur in any significant numbers. While a few settlements in Wales such as Bridgend and Wrexham had economic functions without achieving borough status,[84] *villae mercatoriae* do not appear to have been a feature of medieval Scotland and although there were about 50 in Ireland, they were strongly outnumbered by boroughs. It is entirely possible that the legal status of borough was used as a lure to attract settlers to Wales, Scotland and Ireland,[85] a similar process being characteristic of the contemporaneous German colonisation of the lands east of the Elbe. The origins of borough populations in the periphery remain an impenetrable mystery but the bribe of a greater freedom may have been a causative process in stimulating migration. However it would be unwise to discount seigneurial ambition as a factor in large-scale borough creation. Ireland and Scotland provided new opportunities and lands for ambitious Anglo-Norman lords in the twelfth and thirteenth centuries and the borough was by then a well-tried means of increasing manorial revenue.

The relative absence of *villae mercatoriae* in Wales, Scotland and Ireland suggests that the distributions of boroughs provide a good index of the intensity of the Anglo-Norman colonisations. About a half of the Welsh boroughs were in the southern march and most of the remainder were either located in north Wales or on the English borders (Figure 4.1). By contrast, the smaller Welsh communities were largely confined to the agriculturally unattractive upland regions.[86] In Scotland, most of the burghs

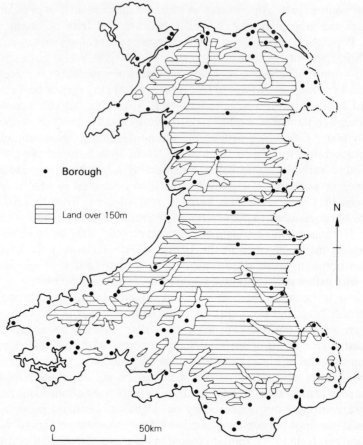

Figure 4.1   The boroughs of medieval Wales

Sources: M. W. Beresford, *New towns of the Middle Ages. Town plantation in England, Wales and Gascony* (London, 1967); I. Soulsby, *The towns of medieval Wales* (Chichester, 1983).

in existence before 1500 were located either south of the Forth–Clyde line or along the east coast (Figure 4.2) while the vast majority of Irish examples were in the south and east of the island, reflecting the areas of most intensive Anglo-Norman colonisation and the distribution of good arable land (Figure 4.3).

Turning to the relationship between borough foundation or development and the feudal structures in Wales, Scotland and Ireland, significant contrasts occurred both with England and each other. With the exception of the Anglo-Saxon *burh* of Rhuddlan, the majority of Welsh boroughs

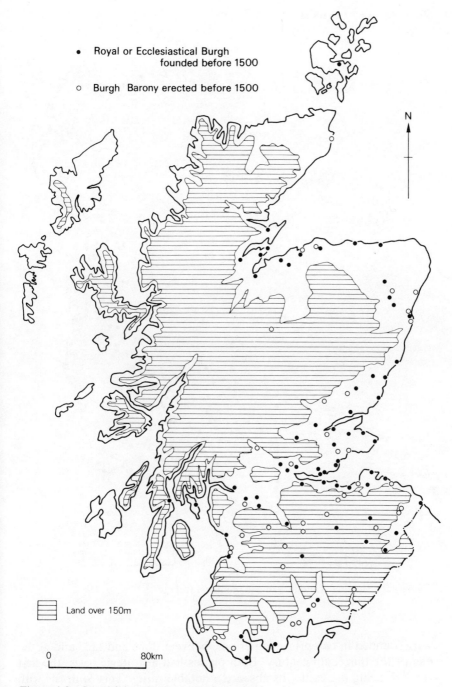

Figure 4.2   Scottish burghs erected prior to 1500
Source: G. S. Pryde, *The burghs of Scotland; a critical list* (Oxford, 1965).

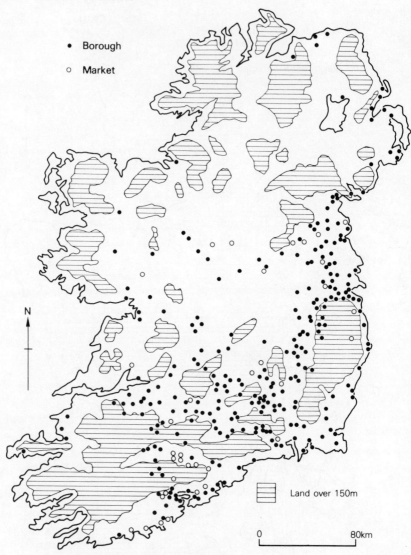

Figure 4.3   Boroughs and markets in medieval Ireland

were founded in two principal periods, between 1066 and 1135 and at the end of the thirteenth century. Both phases had a strategic basis, the first concern being the castle, its absence a notable rarity. This contrasts with England where many of the seigneurial boroughs, especially those founded after 1150, were unwalled and defended towns became increasingly rare as fewer were established by the Crown.[87] The early Welsh boroughs were planned and created not by the Crown but by the Norman marcher lords.[88] With a few exceptions, the royal borough was missing until Edward I, following his defeat of the native Welsh princes, established a succession of castle-towns in north Wales in the late thirteenth century, perhaps the only recognisable *bastides* in the British Isles.[89]

Burgh foundation in Scotland appears to have been a subdued and perhaps controlled process, reflecting the existence of a centralised Scottish polity. Between 1124 and 1153, David I created 13 royal burghs in Scotland and although these display the association of castle and town, the majority of towns were undefended. The later and subsidiary 'burghs in barony' and 'burghs of barony' were subordinate to royal burghs in economic and legal privileges and few had formal fortifications.[90] The *bastide*, Adams concludes, is an inappropriate term for medieval Scotland.[91]

In contrast to this apparent element of centralised control which may be partially responsible for the relatively small number of pre-1500 burghs in Scotland, the development of the Irish borough was a distinctly anarchistic process although it is one about which we have little direct evidence from charters. The royal borough was very much the exception. Several Viking settlements including Dublin and Waterford were initially retained by the Crown and a few towns developed under the lee of royal castles such as Dungarvan and Roscommon but seigneurial lords (including ecclesiastics) were responsible for the development of the majority of Irish boroughs including most of the ports and larger towns. The 'series of lordships' which appeared in the wake of the Anglo-Norman invasion occasioned a hierarchy of urban foundation within each lordship which paralleled the seigneurial power structure. The 'rule' of success or failure replicated that of England in that the most successful boroughs, occupying the most advantageous sites, were created early in the Anglo-Norman colonisation by the most powerful feudal lords within each lordship.[92] As in Wales, the distribution of boroughs had a strategic basis, almost all the early towns developing on sites fortified in the initial stages of the Anglo-Norman Conquest, pre-urban nuclei only being used when their sites were adaptable to these military considerations. The castle-town did occur although the term is little used in Ireland and a considerable number including some quite small examples were walled; again the term, *bastide*, is not one that would be readily applied.

Conclusions

We can therefore isolate the broad characteristics of the processes promoting the development of the town in the Anglo-Norman colonisations of

Ireland and Scotland but detailed studies do not yet exist. Wales is marginally better served with Soulsby's recent book offering an empirical synthesis. The study of the English town in the post-Conquest period is by contrast much advanced compared to the other countries and will obviously remain so, not only because of the volume of existing work but also the sources are superior and the wealth of archaeological evidence will not be replicated in the periphery. Several conclusions can be drawn from the preceding discussion. The study of the role of the town in the various colonisations has undoubtedly been hindered by the insularity bred of contemporary boundaries which has to date precluded any significant comparative dimension. Again, there is a lack of conceptualisation, most clearly in a tendency to analyse settlement as a self-contained phenomenon rather than as a component of a distinctive and constantly changing social and economic structure. When a comparative dimension does exist, it is far more likely to be in a continental context[93] and while this is obviously necessary, so too is the realisation that medieval towns were developed throughout the British Isles as part of the ubiquity of feudalism. To a very real extent, the contrasts raised here are different solutions by the same feudal elite to different problems while, conversely, similarities represent the use of familiar techniques for economic development and creation of profit by that elite. Additionally the political relationships within and between the countries were influential for the development of the medieval town as shown for example by the royal structuring of burgh development in Scotland and the possibility of analysing the urban structure of medieval Ireland from a colonial stance. The comparative study of the medieval town within the British Isles, combined with a credible theoretical structuring, offers the real possibility of substantially enhancing explanations of the issues discussed briefly in this chapter.

5

Urban archaeological research in Germany: a regional review of medieval topographic development

HANS STEPHAN

General history of research, and major foci of interest

The objects and foci of urban archaeological research have varied to an extraordinary extent. Initially, economic and topographical questions dominated the work of the first long-term project: Viking-German Haithabu/Schleswig. However, the exceptionally good state of preservation of what was found in Haithabu led into the problem areas of the design and construction of buildings. The enormous amount and variety of finds dating from the ninth to the eleventh (and thirteenth) centuries led to extensive studies in the fields of typology, chronology, area of coverage and technology of the building fabric.

In contrast, work into major Slav-German centres such as Lübeck followed a different course. First, problem-oriented excavations were undertaken in the settlement that had preceded Lübeck (which gave the town its name); the foci of research, however, were archaeological investigations into monuments that had been preserved in the historic town centre. As a general rule, this is the combination of foci that applies to German urban research generally. What was unusual at the time – but essentially a result of the nature of the existing sources – was the fact that, almost exclusively, the finds discovered dated from the late medieval and early modern periods.

These two major projects in the farthest north-east of the Federal Republic are the only ones in which archaeological research has continued from the thirties and fifties until the present day without interruption. Both as regards source materials as well as their extent, these projects have secured and provided the most extensive range of finds in the field of urban archaeology.[1]

In the centre of the Federal Republic Frankfurt was, for a long time, the only place where urban archaeological research was undertaken to any significant extent. There, the development of the area of the Pfalz (residence) since Roman times was the focus of investigation.[2] Several Rhenish and South German towns have seen extensive excavations of churches and fortifications which have resulted in important findings concerning the history of buildings, and in certain cases the structure of central feudal residential areas, nuclei of (later) urban settlements.[3] These themselves, however, were not investigated. Over a longer period, emergency salvage operations conducted in such places as Lüneburg, Goslar and Höxter-Corvey have also yielded important evidence on realia of the medieval and early modern periods.[4]

Excavations in cathedrals and cathedral fortifications, in monastery and abbey churches (less frequently in parish churches and chapels) were in part closely linked to the areas of early urban nuclei.[5] However, because these excavations were carried out by art historians (whose interest focussed on the history of building and the methods of construction), the settlement aspects received little attention. This has led to a situation in which we are relatively well informed about the Roman settlement and the history of the most important churches in places like Cologne but know little, archaeologically speaking, about the development of medieval urban settlements and realia until the early modern period.[6] Occasionally, parts of relevant feudal monumental architecture of the early and high medieval period have been researched. The most important examples of such investigations are Goslar (Salian – Staufen royal residence) and Frankfurt am Main (Carolingian – Staufen royal residence).[7]

A further factor that led to the securing and evaluation of archaeological finds in urban centres is the commitment to the preservation of local monuments and remains. In the Federal Republic this applied to very few places, whilst in the German Democratic Republic somewhat greater efforts were made to document those archaeological sources of urban history that were threatened with destruction. The lack of commitment in the Federal Republic was possibly due to the self-critical attitudes of specialists in the relatively new discipline of pre-history who did not consider themselves qualified to deal with later periods. For these reasons, the fifties saw very little attention being given to local conservation work; it is only recently that it has been hesitantly embarked upon. It has to some extent been encouraged by work in related disciplines and the interest taken by the wider general public but once again has been hampered by many an expert in prehistory. As a rule, positive exceptions were the result of the personal commitment of individual researchers, often with some training in related disciplines.[8]

In the Federal Republic, systematic research into urban centres and their nuclei – which had, at any rate, been confined to few places – mostly ceased around 1960. There were two main reasons for this; first, the increasing economic pressure for reconstruction and the use of heavy construction machinery, and secondly, the assumption that the main trends of the history

of building and construction as well as settlement had already been un-
ravelled or that any further research would be enormously expensive. At
the end of the fifties, research in the town centres of Hamburg and Hannover
was discontinued, although research in Frankfurt and Lübeck continued,
with emphasis upon conservation. In other cases – such as Haithabu, which
had always been a research project of a fundamentally different kind, being
a deserted urban site – research intensified.

During the 1950s, Germany's 'economic miracle' was causing the gradual
loss of archaeological sites and sources even in smaller towns – losses which,
by the 1980s, may well have reached levels exceeding those caused by
the destruction of the war. Neither those involved in conservation nor
those involved in research were able to take effective preventive action.

The mid-1970s and more particularly the early 1980s have seen a revival
of urban archaeology in the Federal Republic (Figure 5.1). As a rule, the
main consideration tends to be conservation; increasingly, however, urban
archaeological projects now have clearly defined research objectives. At
this time, research centres were established in Schleswig and Lübeck,[9] whilst
major conservation work is being undertaken in Braunschweig.[10] Municipal
archaeological centres have been set up in Städe, Göttingen, Konstanz
and Augsburg. In virtually all Länder, conservation efforts now increasingly
include work in town centres.[11] Such activity gives particular cause for
satisfaction in the cases of Westphalia and Bavaria where no such work
had been undertaken previously. When archaeologists at district level
ensure that intensive conservation work is carried out, and where committed
local archaeologists are at work, then important new results may be
expected in the future.

Urban archaeological research in individual regions of Germany
Schleswig-Holstein

The landscape of Schleswig-Holstein was, as far as its settlement patterns
are concerned, dominated by rural settlements until the nineteenth century.
In general, the towns are small in number and size; there were, however,
several places that counted among the most important trading centres in
Northern Europe after the early Middle Ages. Since the 1930s, Haithabu
has been the object of research; in the late 1940s, Lübeck was added;
work in both centres is still continuing and it is interesting to follow the
change in archaeological methods and research questions over this long
period.

The removal of the trading functions of Haithabu to the site of the historical centre of Lübeck after the eleventh century has been the object of
follow-up research (resulting from the original Haithabu project) since the
mid-1970s.[12] It has been possible to clarify topographical details of the

Figure 5.1   The distribution of archaeological sites in Germany

early period of Schleswig, among others the sequence of landing stages near the later Dominican Priory, the development of the secular settlement 'Am Schild' near the Rathausmärkt and the history of the Nikolai Chapel outside the town centre. A surprise discovery was that of a hitherto unknown church on the later Rathausmärkt site, dating from the eleventh and twelfth centuries.[13] Although the conclusions drawn related to an area limited in size they had such significant evidential value that it has been possible to test historical hypotheses.

Archaeological evidence of settlement in Schleswig during the eleventh century is still rare. The twelfth century saw an acceleration in construction and it was then that the foundations of the later network of roads were laid. Still, not earlier than the first half of the thirteenth century, Schleswig underwent major structural changes (e.g. the establishment of a market square, the construction of the Dominican Priory) which gave it the character of a fully developed Western European town of the late Middle Ages.

Among a number of quasi-urban settlements, Slav-Abodritic Oldenburg in Holstein deserves mention; since 1973, excavations have been in progress in the Burgwall (fortification wall).[14] At one time, the prince's palace and an episcopal church were located within the walls. At the time of the German conquest the development at the Burgwall ended for the time being. The episcopal see and trade transferred to Lübeck. Nevertheless, a German castle was built on the same site and in addition a German town with a regular grid of streets made its appearance in the thirteenth century.

Minor efforts to investigate the history of the fully developed medieval town were made in Kiel, Flensburg and Eckernförde.[15] During the next few years, local contributions towards urban archaeological research may be expected in areas of intensive conservation work and above all in areas where district archaeologists and museums are involved in relevant investigations. This applies in particular to the districts of East Holstein, Eutin, and Dithmarschen.

Lower Saxony, Hamburg, Bremen

The north-west may be divided into the north – partly maritime and with few towns, partly with major, but not always urban, trade centres – and the middle and south – more closely linked to land-based activity, with the latter having numerous medieval towns. In the 1950s, Hamburg and Hannover were among the cities in which urban archaeological research was undertaken.[16] After a break in the 1950s and 1960s, excavations have been undertaken in both cities, on a major scale, whilst Bremen has an even longer tradition of urban archaeological investigations. Unfortunately, with the exception of the excavations at the cathedral, none of the projects has led to an attempt at more systematic research; the future, however, should bring a commitment to intensive conservation work.

In all these towns and cities, large areas were devastated during the war. Consequently large-scale reconstruction between the 1950s and 1980s was in most cases undertaken without any opportunity for archaeological research. Thus, large areas have, from an archaeological point of view, been destroyed. In future, only very limited areas will be accessible to archaeological research, and those only at considerable expense. Due to intensive conservation work and detailed targeted research work in Braunschweig since 1977, it has been possible to demonstrate that important evidence on settlement and cultural history may still be gleaned even in a largely reconstructed city.[17]

Lüneburg has, since the 1950s, been the scene of emergency salvage operations during which several sewers of historical significance were discovered. Nearby Bardowick, a partially abandoned town and one of the most important North German trade centres of the ninth to the twelfth centuries, did not see any archaeological prospecting until the late 1970s.[18]

Werl, near Goslar, ranks among the typical examples of a royal residence in the tenth to the twelfth centuries (deserted). Within the extensive fortified area around the castle residence itself traces of settlement from the tenth to the thirteenth centuries were found.[19] This provides evidence that feudal and political centres became nuclei for the development of proto-urban settlements. These were distinct from rural settlements with regard to size of settled area, fortifications and presumably the occupations of the inhabitants. Yet they cannot be properly described as towns. Even more extensive research has been undertaken in the case of the residence of Tilleda, which despite having a market place did not develop into a town.[20]

Neighbouring Goslar, with the advantage of mining on the Rammelsberg and the later transfer of the central functions of the residence of Werl to Goslar, is assumed to have developed into the most important urban settlement in Lower Saxony besides Braunschweig in the twelfth to the eighteenth century. Its topography for the period 1150–1200 has been partially reconstructed by using the position of existing religious buildings in conjunction with excavations in the residence area and in several other parts of the town. However, in spite of these efforts, it has so far not been possible to form a coherent picture of the early settlement.

Since about 1950, building sites in Goslar have been under close scrutiny – the findings, however, have been largely ignored in the literature outside the region. Significant finds covering the twelfth to the eighteenth centuries were documented and salvaged there.[21] However, for several years now there has been doubt whether investigations in this important mining town and residence will be continued or even intensified in future. On the other hand, emergency salvage and, occasionally, excavations have been undertaken in several other places that had previously not seen any investigation. Among these are Jever, Verden an der Aller, Oldenburg, Wildeshausen, Meppen, Lingen, Gifhorn, Hildesheim, Einbeck, Hameln, Hozminden, Northeim, Duderstadt and Hannoverschuünden.[22]

Planning offices for urban archaeologists have been set up in Göttingen and, more recently, in Städe. In Göttingen, the focus of research has, since the late 1970s, been the development of the town of the High and Late Middle Ages, the design and construction of buildings, and the investigation of realia together with that of the environmental factors.[23]

Westphalia

Westphalia has a considerable number of towns, some of which were established quite early, due to the fact that the region forms a link between the interior of Germany and the Hanseatic trading area.[24] In Münster, valuable insights were gained into early Saxon settlement, the history of the cathedral and monastery, the fortification protecting the area enjoying immunity (*Immunitaet*) and the density of its built-up areas, extremely high in places.[25] The secular settlement areas outside remain largely unexplored and many have also largely been destroyed. During the last decade, archaeological research has been undertaken to investigate the history of the nearby church of St Lamberti in the market area.

The Carolingian period has generally occupied a central position in early medieval archaeological research in Westphalia. This also applies to Paderborn which experienced a brief period of extreme importance during that era.[26] In spite of several early attempts in the 1930s and 1950s, and in spite of isolated investigations by conservation authorities, no systematic archaeological research effort has been made in Paderborn, a town which suffered very heavy destruction during the war. Even so, it was possible to reconstruct the Carolingian fortress and the extension of the area enjoying immunity under Bishop Meinwerk (early eleventh century). The findings relating to Charlemagne's royal residence and its alterations in the early Salian period, together with more recent findings relating to the church and the cathedral, rank among the most important ones of their kind in the German-speaking area. Herford – whose archaeological source material has already been extensively destroyed – was the scene of investigations into the abbey church and the Nikolai Church.[27] One relevant finding in this context is the fact that church and market place had their origin in the period around 1100, and not significantly earlier as had previously been assumed.

In the town of Minden, besides the cathedral, the close and some churches, a number of individual building sites were investigated; among other finds, an important one of pottery wasters dating from the early modern period was made. Excavations straddling several plots of land in the Baeckerstrasse (near the Weser Bridge) and the immediate vicinity of the cathedral provided proof of settlement on those sites since the late tenth century. It was possible to reconstruct in part early timber-framed and later half-timbered buildings. In the late twelfth or early thirteenth centuries, the large plot of land was subdivided into sevesral smaller lots and at their rear, solid stone buildings were erected.[28]

In all cases, the investigation of churches has been of particular importance when seeking to clarify the history of settlement, particularly if the investigation was not exclusively oriented towards the history of a building, as is the case of the Aegidienkirche in Wiedenbrück where the scope of the investigation was widened.[29] This investigation led to the discovery of a sizeable Romanesque building (twelfth century) and an even more splendid basilica (ninth century) which may well have formed part of a royal residence or of a main estate of the Bishop of Osnabrück.

Since the Early Middle Ages, Soest had been one of the economic centres of Westphalia. Excavations were undertaken in and near some churches and in the Saelzerviertel (salters' quarter) which yielded valuable insights into salt production during the Early and High Middle Ages.[30] Werl was also an important salt-producing town. At the same time it was the centre of a fertile agricultural area and the residence of several generations of the Counts of Werl that were of intermittent local importance (and gave the town its name). Excavations revealed remains of a building, presumably dating from the Ottonian period.[31] This may have formed part of the Count's residence. It was possible to discover remains of buildings and salters' workshops in the historical town centre (twelfth century and later).[32] An important discovery was the fact that a sizeable area about 350 metres west of the late twelfth-century town appears to have been settled since the ninth century and apparently was deserted in the early thirteenth century.

Since the early 1960s, intensive archaeological research in town centres in Westphalia has been limited to Höxter and Corvey where it is pursued with limited funds by a small number of volunteers. One of the oldest quasi-urban settlement complexes of the Early and High Middle Ages in Northern Germany is gradually emerging in outline. It is there that archaeological finds from the Late Middle Ages and the modern period have been exhaustively investigated from the perspective of cultural history.[33]

From about 1981, investigations into town centres conducted by conservationists have increased in number,[34] covering such places as Dortmund (Reinoldi graveyard), Hamm, Lippstadt (St Anne's convent), Warburg (Town Hall in the new town), Billerbeck and Coesfeld (inter alia the market square).[35]

The main focus of any excavation is still the history of construction, of buildings and built-up areas (topography). Intensive or problem-oriented research into town centres is not within the realm of practicality and does not fall within the parameters of conservation work at the level of the conservation authorities of the Land.

The Rhineland and the Palatinate

Apart from some small areas at its fringes, this area was part of the Roman Empire. During the Carolingian period it formed a central area of their royal domain. It was there that a symbiosis between Roman civilisation and Germanic tradition emerged and consequently merits special attention concerning settlement history. The Rhine was of paramount importance, particularly with regard to North-South traffic. Several of Germany's most important towns developed in its catchment area. However, urban archaeological research focussing on the Middle Ages and the modern period is in its infancy in this area. This is particularly regrettable on account of the fact that towns and quasi-urban settlements existed there in ancient times which often formed the nuclei of important medieval towns. Of particular notice are the Archbishoprics of Köln, Mainz and Trier which ranked among the oldest and most important towns of the Frankish Empire and, later, the Holy Roman Empire of the German Nation.

Traditionally, research has focussed upon the period of Roman occupation with its impressive remains. The results of excavations in Köln, Trier, Mainz, Xanten and Neuss are of international significance and have been widely publicised.[36] Since the 1940s a further focus has been research into the continuity between ancient times and early medieval times. Excavations of churches[37] and burial grounds[38] with grave goods have made important contributions in this respect. Research into the history of buildings has in the Rhineland had a long tradition of using archaeological methods and tended to concern itself with the post-Carolingian Middle Ages as well. Particularly important results were achieved in most major towns,[39] as shown in Figure 5.1. Although there was religious continuity (churches) – and its cultural significance is beyond any doubt – there is clear evidence of a break in urban civilisation during the great migration of peoples (*Völkerwanderungzeit*). It would appear that new nuclei emerged during the eighth to the twelfth century which developed into medieval towns, although no attention has so far been paid to these by archaeologists. Limited investigations in Bonn and Duisburg (residence, market)[40] and lately in Worms do not invalidate this claim.

Hesse

Hesse has relatively few large cities dating from the Middle Ages but has an infinite wealth of small and medium-sized towns that were hardly affected by the destruction of war. In the Early Middle Ages, its function was that of a link between the Frankish Empire and Thuringia as well as Saxony. Initially, urban archaeological research in Hesse remained confined to Frankfurt, then severely damaged by the war.[41] The emphasis was upon the Roman period and the Early Middle Ages, particularly the investigation of the Carolingian and Staufen Pfalz (residence). The topographical development of the medieval town and its cultural history await treatment – as far as it may still be possible on the basis of the rather limited finds that were salvaged.[42]

The investigations into the cathedral area and various other sites of the historical town centre of Fulda, pioneered by Vonderau in the twenties, have not resulted in systematic research into the town centres.[43] The same is true of investigations in Lorsch, Gelnhausen and Hersfeld where research remained confined to the history of the buildings and, at most, the history of the monasteries concerned.[44]

In a wider sense, investigations into densely populated early medieval fortified areas such as Büraburg near Fritzlar, Amoneburg and Christenberg near Marburg do represent contributions towards research into proto-urban developments.[45] This is particularly true in cases like Fritzlar where, in addition to excavations in the abbey church, research involved limited observations in the town centre.

Since the mid-1970s, a Working Group on Buildings Research has been active in Marburg. It preserves detailed data on half-timbered buildings. In addition, it has conducted archaeological excavations and archival studies.[46] This has enabled it to bring into play, and relate to each other, as many available sources as possible, also helping to clarify questions of the physical environment of the late Middle Ages and early modern period. This work holds the prospect of important new conclusions, leading to further research and interpretation.

During the past few years, greater attention appears to have been paid to archaeological finds in town centres. Those actively involved are conservationists (still lacking qualified staff), scientists from various disciplines, curators of museums, archaeological working groups and interested individuals. Some important results were registered in the following places: Hofgeismar, Witzenhause, Eschwege, Rotenburg, Fulda, Hersfeld, Alsfeld, Giessen, Limburg, Wetzlar and Korbach. Altogether, it must be stated that there is a considerable need to tackle research tasks in urban archaeology in Hesse that have so far been ignored, although institutions capable of doing this do not exist on an adequate scale.

Baden-Württemberg

South-west Germany is a region with numerous towns. It was there that the first organisational unit with the remit of medieval archaeology and covering the whole region was set up within the framework of conservation planning. It is structured according to districts. The extensive excavations undertaken in churches in Esslingen am Neckar could have formed the basis of further systematic research into the town centre of this Carolingian market town – which later developed into an important Imperial town. Yet efforts to include urban archaeology among the tasks of conservation have generally remained rather modest and limited, with the possible exception of excavations in the upper suburb of Sindelfingen.[47]

During the last few years, the situation appears to have undergone a gradual change. In Freiburg's Austin Priory the discovery of a sewer/tip led to an exceptional wealth of finds.[48] A minor research project on the development of the castle and town of Marbach am Neckar has been in progress for several years now.[49] Various places have yielded larger quantities of pottery, more or less systematically collected and preserved.[50] In Konstanz, perhaps the oldest urban centre of the region, a fairly comprehensive collection of finds has been amassed over the last one hundred years or so, mainly by amateur archaeologists. Follow-up work is planned. It is also envisaged that opportunities to explore building sites should be fully exploited. These will focus on the topographical development of settlements since pre-historic times as well as building typology and the study of everyday objects. Taking into account the amount of material available and interpretation work that has already been carried out, the prospect of making a start on systematic research into town centres and their topographic development would appear to be encouraging.

Bavaria

From the point of view of historical settlement geography, Bavaria may be divided into three parts: Franconia with its numerous towns, the Oberpfalz and Altbayern, both rural areas with small market places and a small number of medium-sized or large towns. Altbayern and Bavarian Swabia did form part of the Roman Empire whilst Franconia and Oberpfalz were part of unoccupied Germania.

Until recently, no systematic archaeological research into medieval and early modern towns had been undertaken in Bavaria.[51] This is particularly regrettable in the cases of Würzburg and Nürnberg, heavily damaged during, and extensively rebuilt after, the Second World War. Larger building projects (of which there have recently been fewer) do attract the attention of conservationists and have led to remarkable discoveries concerning the construction of Würzburg's castle and defensive walls during the eleventh and twelfth centuries.[52] The situation in Nürnberg is similar and the various smaller finds that were made have not so far been evaluated.[53]

In Regensburg, Passau and Augsburg, the Roman period has received most priority. In addition, research has, in several instances, focussed on the Early Middle Ages. Among relevant projects are major ones in St Severin, the Holy Cross, in the fort of Boiotro as well as the cathedrals in Passau and Regensburg, and above all in St Ulrich and Afra in Augsburg.[54] The development of these churches and their graveyards allow important conclusions to be drawn concerning settlements that must have existed in their vicinity. Important insights are to be expected of district archaeologists in Regensburg as far as the Middle Ages are concerned; examples are the excavations in the Gerbergasse (tanners' street: development of settlement since the tenth and eleventh centuries) and the suburb of Prebrunn.[55] Similar progress may be expected in Augsburg which has had an office for town archaeology since 1981.[56] Large-scale excavations have been undertaken in the cathedrals at Eichstaett and Bamberg, which have also been important sources for the history of the towns themselves.[57] Straubing saw the discovery of several finds of pottery dating from the Renaissance, which enabled important new conclusions to be drawn for further research into the field of modern pottery production.[58]

The fact that individual finds are listed here is indicative of the backward state of urban archaeology in Bavaria. Archaeological work in the districts by both experts and amateurs will probably lead to a considerable increase in the amount of archaeological source material to become available over the next few years.[59]

German Democratic Republic and West Berlin

For more than a century, historical and archaeological research has been in progress in this former central part of Germany into early German settlements and particularly the Slav settlements that had preceded them.[60] Magdeburg, Leipzig, Dresden and Frankfurt an der Oder are places where such research has been particularly intensive especially after 1950.[61] In the abbey town of Quedlinburg archaeological research has focussed upon the history of building and construction.[62] In Halberstadt, valuable insights have been gained into the history of the settlement of the area around the cathedral.[63]

In the south-east of the Saxon tribal settlement area important contributions have been made to clarify the topography of Ottonian market places, most of which either developed into small towns or failed to grow at all. The site most thoroughly investigated has been the royal residence of Tilleda Ostharz.[64]

Brandenburg is one of the areas in which the gathering of source materials and their evaluation has been closely linked, and where intensive conservation work is being done.[65] General surveys of the archaeological evidence and a typology were elaborated covering the topographical and legal development of the castles, quasi-urban and rural settlements that achieved the full status of towns in the High and Late Middle Ages.[66]

One example of the development of a German town next to an older, Slav, regional centre is Spandau in the Greater Berlin area.[67] Since the early Slav period, a walled castle and open settlements had existed here. The town of Spandau with its regular street plan and its own fortifications sprang up some short distance from it. Around 1240, part of the earlier (1170–5) Nikolai settlement had to make way for a new and stronger wall protecting the town.

Investigations in Thuringia have taken place in Jena, Eisenach, Arnstadt and Weimar.[68] More extensive observations have been made in Erfurt. Pottery dating from the eighth and ninth centuries has occasionally been found, but as a rule only strata from the High and Late Middle Ages are extant in part; this contradicts current theories on urban developments based upon written sources.[69]

The complex of questions surrounding the gradual expansion of planned colonies (*Gruendungsstaedte*) during the High and Late Middle Ages did – in contrast to the Federal Republic – soon attract the interest of historical research in the German Democratic Republic. Results of such research have emerged in Chemnitz, Dresden, Frankfurt an der Oder, Leipzig, Mittweida (Kreis Hainichen), Zwickau and Spandau. According to these, the settled nuclei were still rather small in the thirteenth century; it was only during the fourteenth and fifteenth centuries that population density increased and that buildings covered all areas within the towns. This was followed by the addition of (or extension of already existing) suburbs.[70]

The prospect ahead

Urban archaeological research has largely been oriented towards rescue and conservation rather than towards seeking answers to specific questions. Almost all the excavators are experts in prehistory or early history, others are art historians and cultural historians without specific training in the field of archaeology; thus they first have to acquire relevant skills, which is a slow and arduous task. In addition, almost all excavations have so far been influenced by considerations of conservation. It was the imminent destruction as a result of pending construction work that usually led to investigation; this, then, had to be undertaken under pressure of time. Thus it is hardly surprising that the majority of sites and finds have not so far been fully evaluated, and that the evidential value of existing archaeological sources varies widely. The emergence of centres in Braunschweig, Göttingen, Schleswig, Lübeck, Marburg, Augsburg, Konstanz and Regensburg at which conservation is practised in conjunction with urban research of an inter-disciplinary nature is of particular importance. Yet the scale on which source materials are still being destroyed in other places must not be overlooked. What is urgently required is the application of available resources to specific, problem-oriented research and conservation.

The extrapolation of more recent conditions to more distant periods is a technique of research made necessary by the scarcity of written sources relating to the Early and High Middle Ages. This technique, however, carries with it serious risks. It is almost invariably based upon the subconscious assumption that a town that was of great importance in the Middle Ages must have held a central economic position and been of considerable size in earlier periods also. This is particularly true of towns in areas with good communications and of towns in which religious or secular institutions were permanently established.

There is no doubt that, in several respects, the development of Germany's four Roman provinces took a different course from that of Germania libera. Religious buildings in particular have been the object of archaeological investigation and have often been found to provide a link with ancient times. The present state of research, however, suggests that the degree of urban continuity during the 'migration of the peoples' and Early Middle Ages must be considered to have been limited. A more typical development seems to have been a dispersal of population, with numerous smaller settlements of an agrarian character taking the place of earlier large settlements. Late Roman churches and small forts often continued in use, albeit in reduced form, although they formed nuclei in which urbanisation was either resumed during the Carolingian period, or was intensified. Yet in Köln, one of the most important German cities, the urban nucleus lies outside the Roman walls. Thus, Roman buildings may be regarded as island of religious continuity and as representative of authority. It may be that the significance of ancient civilisation lay less in its influence upon the topography of early medieval centres than in its role as a reservoir for cultural rejuvenation. As such, it also affected the eastern, more recently conquered provinces of the Frankish Empire.

As to the Slav settlement areas, occasionally it was the case that a German town was founded during the Middle Ages on the same site as an earlier Slav centre. In many instances, however, a slight change in location occurred. What appears to be significant is the location of centres for long-distance trade; these were often situated in exposed border areas; for example, Haithabu, Lübeck, Bardowick, Magdeburg.

After the incorporation of Bavaria, Alemannia, Hesse, Thuringia, Frisia and Saxony into the Merovingian and Carolingian Empire, urbanisation advanced only slowly and hesitantly. It is not possible or appropriate to apply the fully developed legal concept of the late medieval town to early and high medieval centres. One precondition for the clarification of the genesis of towns as well as the development of different types of towns is the most detailed possible knowledge of their topographical structure. This is particularly important when dealing with the origin of towns that may be classified as pre-urban or early urban forerunners of towns.

In places such as Bremen, Hameln, Osnabruck, Verden and Erfurt the evidence for secular settlements during the eighth to the eleventh centuries outside the sacred areas has so far been largely negative. This demonstrates the unreliability of the technique of extrapolation. Even during the Middle Ages there was, during various phases, a considerable change in the pattern of settlement, with very different developments in various localities.

It is easy to exaggerate the continuity and importance of older market places and trading towns. On the other hand, archaeologists have, in a number of cases, been able to produce evidence of the importance of economic factors leading to the establishment of settlements in the Early Middle Ages and the beginnings of the High Middle Ages. In part, this has led to considerable modifications of the theory of the travelling merchant. To a hitherto unimaginable degree, archaeologists have been able to flesh out our image of what medieval towns looked like. In addition, they have added to the body of knowledge relating to farmers, craftsmen, merchants, traders and servants who had been largely ignored in the written sources produced by the literate nobility or clergy of the day.

Nevertheless, it remains true to say that archaeological research oriented towards the investigation of historical hypotheses has so far focussed upon churches, areas around cathedrals enjoying immunity (*Immunitaeten*) and castles. Up to a point, this is certainly appropriate, since it was in those centres that the accumulated wealth of feudal lords concentrated. They were also the centres to which all members of the various strata of feudal society related, be they members of a family, a parish, legal community, or subject to military service.

Archaeological discoveries have given us information that enables us to realise how different one cathedral and its area, a 'civitas', could be from any other after the Carolingian period. This was so not only in the Rhineland but also in the territories east of the Rhine that had never formed part of the Roman Empire. We have a good idea now as to how its architecture developed until the Late Middle Ages. However, it has not been possible to gain a clear picture of what buildings were erected in the immediate vicinity of cathedrals. The cathedral and monastery, extensive graveyards, perhaps one or more churches were common to all; beyond these, the infrastructure could vary widely. It may have ranged from large green areas and open courtyards used only by the clergy and with very few buildings to a dense network of buildings where craftsmen had their premises, such as were discovered in parts of the cathedral precinct in Münster.

Similarly, the foundation of churches after 1000, particularly in bishoprics, was of considerable long-term significance as far as the development of secular settlements is concerned. Generally, the main consideration appears to have been the provision of religious precincts in accordance with the Roman model. In a number of cases, these foundations were quite a distance from their mother churches and did not, at any time, lead to the setting up of a large secular settlement.

In Germania libera, episcopal sees mostly dated from between the eighth to the tenth centuries. Until the first half of the twelfth century, they, together with a number of Imperial abbeys set up in the eighth and ninth centuries, probably formed the most secure bases for the development of urban settlements. Nowhere (except in Hamburg) has it been possible to achieve an even partial clarification of the topographical structure of such settlements outside the cathedral precincts.

In the interior of Germany, Höxter–Corvey is the only quasi-urban settlement of the Early and High Middle Ages whose topography it has been possible to reconstruct to any significant extent. Several major and minor nuclei sprang up around the Imperial abbey of Corvey, at Weser crossings near Höxter and Corvey, at important roads and by the river. Extending about 2,500 metres east–west, and up to 1,000 metres north–south, this settlement is larger than any other known in North-West Germany, although Bardowick and Magdeburg might perhaps have been of similar size.

Settlements that were primarily centres of secular power showed much less stability before 1000. They had far less significance as far as the emergence of economic centres or quasi-urban settlements was concerned. Bardowick–Lüneburg, Braunschweig, Werl–Goslar, Duisburg and Frankfurt are excellent examples of urban settlements of importance that developed from such beginnings.

In future, archaeological investigations should also be undertaken into smaller places, those that obtained the right to hold markets during the tenth and eleventh centuries. As they have been built over to a lesser extent, and as they must, presumably, have been smaller in area, the prospects for further research there appear to be good. Among such settlements is the Gandersheim area, where a start was made with excavations in Brunshausen. Helmstedt, of whose size we have some idea because a register (*Urbar*) lists the houses that were liable to taxation, is a good example of a place where archaeologists might find concrete evidence.

6

Recent developments in early medieval urban history and archaeology in England

CHRIS DYER

Introduction

The title of this essay, which links history and archaeology, may imply that those who practise the two disciplines are involved in a co-operative venture. In fact studies of the urban past based on documents, and those based on the evidence of material culture, have developed along separate lines, sometimes in parallel, more often divergent. Both urban history and urban archaeology have grown rapidly in the last twenty years, as can be seen from the expansion in research expenditure and the quantity of publications. The new wave of urban studies began in the 1960s; in terms of archaeological excavations it reached a peak of activity in 1974.[1] As the acquisition of new knowledge slows down in the 1980s, there is a tendency to take stock, to reflect, and to synthesize.

To some extent the two disciplines have been concerned with different periods. The main thrust of historical research has been in the later middle ages, in the centuries after 1200 when the documents are most abundant. The main archaeological effort has been to explore the origins of urban life before 1100. The documentary evidence for this period has been known for many years; there is much scope for its reinterpretation but any major extension in the quantity of data must depend on archaeology, and consequently archaeologists have taken the lead in generating new ideas.

The differences in approach between historians and archaeologists are well illustrated by comparing their definitions of towns. Until quite recently historians worked under the influence of the great debate on English boroughs that took place in the 1930s.[2] This was a controversy about constitutional matter, and now historians have thrown off the last vestiges of legal and institutional definitions, so that there is general acceptance that a town was a centre of non-agricultural economic activities, characterized by a diversity of occupations, especially those involved in trade and industry, located in a permanent settlement of large size and high density.[3] Thus, the social and economic life of the town has been recognized as its defining characteristic. Archaeologists seem more reluctant to abandon constitutional definitions, and Biddle's 'bundle of criteria' for the recognition of a town include such institutions as a mint, legal autonomy, and courts, as well as economic, social, and topographical features.[4] There is perhaps a certain irony in the high regard paid by sudents of material culture to legal and administrative abstractions. One reason for this lies in the prominence in the material evidence of the public works, such as fortifications and streets, to which the attention of the archaeologist is inevitably drawn. Clear evidence for such social features as a diversity of occupations is less easily obtained from excavation.

In the search for the genesis of English towns some archaeologists would suggest as a starting point the hill-forts and *oppida* of the pre-Roman Iron Age. The urban nature of these important places is disputable, and we do not have incontrovertible evidence of urban life until southern Britain was brought into the Roman Empire. There is still some uncertainty in identifying the full range of the urban hierarchy of the Roman province. The large, walled, and densely built-up *civitas* capitals and *coloniae*, with their wide range of administrative, social, economic, and religious functions can be accepted by everyone as truly urban. Problems arise in assessing the urban character of the many 'lesser walled towns' and the even more numerous nucleated settlements, which in some cases covered many hectares, which sometimes were involved in industry, but which were smaller, less compact, and contained a narrower range of activities than the *civitas* capitals.[5] Opinion seems to be moving in favour of accepting the urban character of these lesser settlements, suggesting that Roman Britain was served by dozens of small market towns as well as twenty or so larger cities, not unlike the urban network of the later middle ages.

Settlement continuation

The similarity between Roman and medieval urban patterns should not be taken to mean that urban settlements continued to exist during the intervening period. For some time archaeologists looked for every type of evidence for continuity, but now there is general agreement that urban life, as normally defined, declined before 400 and ceased in the fifth century. Settlement on town sites might have continued for a time, on a small scale, and fulfilling non-urban functions. A likely explanation of the timber buildings erected in the ruins of the Baths basilica at Wroxeter (Shropshire), for example, is that they were used by the aristocracy who dominated the area after the withdrawal of Roman imperial government.[6] In other cities, such as Canterbury and Gloucester, an accumulation of soil over the rubble of collapsed Roman buildings suggests that much of the area within the walls reverted to waste or was used as agricultural land.[7] For most of the fifth and sixth centuries urban life was impossible, given the absence of a plentiful coinage, a significant level of trade, or much industrial production.

However, Romano-British towns did influence the location and topography of their medieval successors, because of the persistence of the sites as administrative, military, and religious centres. Warrior aristocrats, ultimately to become the rulers of new kingdoms, seem to have taken over such Roman cities as Canterbury and Winchester, and used them as residences and centres of political power. The mechanics of the process remain mysterious; it may have begun with the defence arrangements made by late Roman city authorities who engaged barbarians as mercenaries.[8] Also churches that had been built in extra-mural Roman cemeteries, sometimes at a saint's grave like that of St Albans, or indeed churches in town or fort centres, as at Lincoln, may have been left standing, and even continued in use, long enough to be incorporated into the religious organization of the new phase of missionary activities after 597.[9] When the rulers of the new English church founded bishoprics, half of the sees were located in or near former Roman towns because they had enough political importance to make them obvious centres for ecclesiastical government. Also, judging from the writings of Bede and others, churchmen were very conscious of the Roman past and held in high regard the material remains of the Roman province.[10] The presence of royal administrative centres, churches, or still-usable town walls all gave the former Roman town sites a good chance of acting as *nuclei* of urban growth when towns developed again in later centuries. In some cases, notably at Caistor (Norfolk) and Wroxeter (Shropshire), the Roman cities were abandoned and their medieval successors (Norwich and Shrewsbury) grew up within a few kilometres, perhaps because of shifts in road systems or centres of political power. There has been a temptation, when so many medieval towns are seen to sit on or near the ruins of Roman predecessors, to assume a continuity of urban life. It is now clear that for a long period in the early middle ages, even for as long as five centuries, such sites went through a non-urban hiatus.

The idea that Roman urban life ceased, but that the use of former Roman town sites was perpetuated by kings, nobles, and clergy, is not new – it is an adaptation to English conditions of Pirenne's theory of urban origins in continental Europe.[11] Pirenne, partly because he wrote before the modern development of medieval archaeology, paid insufficient attention to the continental trading centres of the seventh to ninth centuries at such places as Domburg, Dorestad, Quentovic, or Haithabu. Towns of similar type and date have been recognized in England, notably at Hamwih and Ipswich, where extensive excavations have been carried out, and less certainly at London, Norwich, and Sarre (Kent).[12] There is evidence of trading activity at all of these at some time within the period 650–850. Hamwih, the area of which has been estimated at more than 30 hectares, and Ipswich, with evidence of pottery-making over an area of more than 50 hectares, were very large settlements. They were apparently not defended; nor did they stand on major Roman sites. Their urban character cannot be doubted, because of the evidence for intensive occupation over large areas, and the indications of a variety of non-agricultural activities. Hamwih had a number of small-scale industries, and maintained widespread trading contacts, both within England and with the continent, especially northern Gaul. A silver sceatta coinage, ideal for use in trade in goods of moderate value, was used and indeed minted there. Pottery manufacture played a major part in the economy of Ipswich, and the products of its kilns were traded over much of eastern England. No doubt the commerce of these early emporia depended on perishable goods, such as cloth, slaves, and wine, which leave little or no trace for archaeologists to find, but are occasionally mentioned in the documentary sources.[13] In the long term some of the sites of these wics or emporia were abandoned, with a movement in the ninth century to fortified sites, though settlement apparently continued at Ipswich.

The development of burhs

A new phase in the history of English towns in the ninth and tenth centuries is marked by the development of the burhs.[14] The term originally referred to any fortification, but is customarily reserved for the large forts built by kings. The rulers of Mercia are thought to have constructed burhs in the eighth century, and they proliferated during the wars between the kings of Wessex and the Danes. The Wessex burhs of Alfred's reign (871–99) are well recorded, notably in the Burghal Hidage, a list once thought to have been compiled in the early tenth century, but now dated to the late ninth. This reveals a ring of forts round southern England, designed to defend the main routes, especially the river valleys, into Wessex. The walls of the burhs were to be manned by a levy of men, calculated according to the formula that four men should defend a pole or perch (16½ feet or 5.03 metres) of wall, each hide of land in the surrounding countryside providing one man. When Alfred's successors conquered territory outside Wessex, they set up more burhs that, besides serving the needs of defence, were eventually used as the administrative centres of a new system of shires. In the Danelaw four of the 'Five Boroughs' set up by the Danes, and also York, became shire towns.

The burhs pose great problems in explaining the origins of towns. They were defensive strongholds, and many of them acted as centres of royal administration, so they seem initially to have performed primarily military and political functions. The period of burh fortification also saw a process of urbanization, often but not always centred on burh sites. One of the symptoms of that urbanization was the growing size of the settlements affected. By plotting finds and excavated artefacts datable to the late Saxon period and any churches of pre-Conquest origin, the likely area of occupation of an individual settlement can be estimated. Such distribution maps for towns indicate that many grew to more than 30 hectares and Norwich, which had the largest urban area calculated in this way, attained 200 hectares.[15] Domesday Book gives us some figures for urban populations in 1066 and 1086, tending to underestimate, but still suggesting that nine or more towns exceeded 3,000 people, mostly in eastern England, and that there were at least another sixty places which had populations in excess of 300.[16] The high density of people and houses within one urban settlement is indicated by a document from ninth-century Canterbury which tells us of a local law that a gap of 2 feet for an eaves drip should be left between properties.[17] Preserved organic material and insect remains provide rich evidence of a fetid and unhygienic urban environment, more so than in either Roman or late medieval towns. Excavations at Durham, Lincoln, and York show houses, out-buildings, middens, and pits tightly packed into confined spaces.[18] Although many urban buildings seem indistinguishable from contemporary structures in the countryside, one type, provided with a large cellar, does seem to represent a specialized adaptation to urban needs.

Excavation of urban sites, especially those on which organic remains are preserved, gives ample evidence for a multiplicity of occupations, mainly in the form of detritus from industries as diverse as cloth-making, leather-working, potting, and the manufacture of goods in bone, glass, wood, iron, and bronze. Trade on a very local level is demonstrated by the botanical evidence from York, where there was evidently a constant traffic from the surrounding countryside in hemp, flax, reeds, rushes, and ling, as well as food plants and wood.[19] Regional and inter-regional trade is reflected by the spread of the products of English pottery kilns such as those at Stamford and Thetford, and commerce over longer distances resulted in the import of continental wares. Stone objects, such as soapstone vessels, whetstones, and millstones, can be shown to have come from Scandinavia and Germany, and there are occasional finds of exotic luxuries like ivory and silk. At London long-distance sea-borne trade on a large scale is suggested by the substantial wharfs. The gaps in the material evidence are partly filled by documents which show that, for example, in the early eleventh century merchants from northern France and Germany were visiting London: fish figured prominently among the imports.[20]

A picture then emerges of large settlements, occupied densely and intensively by a permanent population, many of whom pursued a variety of craft occupations, and who were involved in trading contacts both locally and over long distances. In other words, these places had become urban by any normal definition. In addition, both the documentary evidence of law and administration, and the archaeological evidence of an organized laying-out and maintenance of property boundaries point to some form of specialized town government.

What was the relationship between the burghal forts and the towns that developed in the tenth and eleventh centuries? One relatively simple answer is to argue, as archaeologists and a few historians have done, that the towns formed as much a part of a centrally conceived royal plan as the forts. An important study of the town plan of Winchester, the conclusions of which are to some extent applicable to other towns, has shown that the street system had been created about the time of the refurbishment of the fortifications, around 900.[21] The rectilinear pattern of streets, and streets running behind the walls, would have enabled defenders to gain ready access to any part of the circuit. The land between the streets would have been assigned to local lords, who by sub-division created building plots. The streets survived in use into the late Saxon and medieval periods, serving the artisans and traders of the growing city. Dr Hodges, employing the methods of the 'new archaeology', has developed much further the idea that kings created towns. The result is an argument that great men 'have ... altered their cultural circumstances to their own ends'.[22] He sees the wics or emporia of the seventh to ninth centuries as the inventions of the early kingdoms of Wessex, Kent, and East Anglia, and he believes that the trade passed through them was controlled by rulers who distributed the goods to their subjects. The mechanisms for exchange and distribution were not based on the market but on royal power. He also suggests that Alfred and his successors, like the Carolingians in his view on the continent a century earlier, had a concerted plan for making towns, and that an urban network and marketing system developed as a result of these royal policies.

These bold theories have stimulated debate and criticism. It is generally acknowledged that kings sought to protect and regulate trade, and that they had a special relationship with merchants.[23] By siting their mints in towns in the tenth century kings helped to stimulate them as trading centres. But to regard such policies as a coherent strategy of town planning is to misunderstand the nature of early medieval government. The English state, although unusually centralized and efficient,[24] fell far short of omnicompetent dictatorship. It lacked a salaried bureaucracy and police force, and laws cannot be assumed to have been enforced. Government depended on the delegation of authority to the nobility (both clerical and lay), who exercised much independent power. Even had Alfred or Edward the Elder wished to set up a network of new towns, it is very doubtful if their wishes could have been carried out. Medieval governments were usually concerned with fiscal policy, such as the minting of coins and the collection of taxes; they were interested in the extraction of wealth, not the organization of production. Comparison between the situation in England and on the continent suggests the minor role played by state policy in urban growth.

Emporia similar to Hamwih are found in Scandinavia, where states had reached varying stages of development, all of them less advanced than those of eighth- and ninth-century England. In the tenth and eleventh centuries towns grew all over Europe, both in centralized states and small-scale feudal principalities, showing that the political context was not of primary importance in determining social change. Orders from above, no matter whether they were given by emperors, kings, or counts, could not create a town: social and economic circumstances made town life feasible.

The argument about the relationship between early states and the wics depends very much on the evidence from Hamwih. It must be said that the excavated material from Hamwih does not seem to support its depiction by Hodges as a regulated trade centre. The many crafts practised there look like unspecialized and unco-ordinated responses to demand. Its trade contacts ranged widely, not in set channels. The imported goods originated mainly in northern France, but there were other sources of supply in the Rhineland and further north, and it has been shown that the routes from Hamwih inland carried goods into Mercia as well as Wessex.[25]

The idea that trade was limited to a few controlled ports seems unlikely to be true of Kent. Besides Sarre there were Fordwich, Sandwich, and probably southern ports, notably Dover, which must have served a rich rural hinterland. The distribution of ports and traded goods, reflecting the patterns of wealth rather than power, could point to the existence of a market system in the eighth and ninth centuries. An obstacle to a resolution of the problem is the uncertainty among numismatists as to whether the silver sceatta coinage was being used in trade or in some non-commercial exchange system.[26]

The burhs do not seem to fit into a simple pattern of a royal plan either. They were not a single system of fortifications, but an emergency stitching together of refortified prehistoric hill-forts, burhs built before the crisis of the late ninth century, and new constructions. Some of the sites, like the hill-forts, were not suited to urban development, nor was, for example, the burh that occupied the island of Sashes in the Thames. In some cases a town grew up at a more suitable nearby site, as at Cookham (Berkshire) near Sashes.[27] Whether the town grew in or near the burh walls there might still be a lengthy interval between the building of the fortifications and the growth of the town. Growth might be slow and uncertain: Cricklade (Wiltshire), to name one, is unlikely to have ever filled its fortified area.

It is indeed possible that the burh building was no more than an episode in the history of a place, and not the main impetus for urbanization. Most burhs were built around existing settlements, usually of high status with a centre of royal administration, an important church, and even a community of developing urban character. There is evidence of late eighth- and ninth-century occupation at Oxford, including a trench for flax retting which might indicate a settlement involved in industrial activities. Ninth-century Canterbury was already densely occupied and had a guild. A Worcester charter granted at the time of the building of the burh in the 890s implies that the market and streets already existed of a town involved in the salt trade from nearby Droitwich. At Gloucester a layer of wood-trimmings, bones, and other organic material suggests a phase of intensive, if not very sophisticated, occupation in the ninth century before the refurbishing of the fortifications. All of these places possessed major churches, either monasteries or cathedrals, which could have served as nucleii around which towns developed in the eight and ninth centuries before the burh policy was initiated.[28]

Reconstructions of early street plans show that the Winchester example is by no means typical. The streets of Northampton seem to have been laid out in a piecemeal fashion as they were needed, and the excavated part of Thetford had a relatively open plan.[29]

To sum up, it seems unlikely that town growth resulted from a conscious royal policy. The wics' relationship with emergent states is neither proven nor plausible. The fortifications of burhs were sometimes built around places that were already showing signs of urban growth. The towns that grew up in burhs do not always show signs of planning, and of course some burhs did not become towns at all. The study of individual towns, which shows them all to have had different characteristics, makes any single explanation of their origins unlikely. This does not mean that we should abandon attempts at generalization, but rather that we should examine explanatory theories that are more flexible than the 'great men' hypotheses.

The relationship between town and country

If the origins and early growth of English towns is examined as a long-term historical process, we need to look at developments in rural society. Here the work on the continent by such scholars as Duby and Fossier points the way to understanding the interaction between town and country.[30] They see the tenth and eleventh centuries as a period of economic take-off, beginning in the countryside. Duby stresses the introduction of new forms of seignoral exploitation, which stimulated the market by forcing peasants to sell produce, and gave the lords greater purchasing power. English lords did not enjoy the powers of justice available to their continental contemporaries, but they had opportunities to gain more from their peasants.

Expansion in the countryside is indicated by the appearance of nucleated villages and open-field systems, which suggests a growth in population and the intensity of cultivation from the ninth century onwards.[31] In Norfolk, where field work has shown that the settlement sites marked by scatters of late Saxon (ninth- to eleventh-century) pottery are larger and more numerous than those producing middle Saxon (seventh- to ninth-century) wares, the implication is that the population grew, and contacts with urban markets (where the pottery was made) were maintained or increased.[32] Among the landlords the main trend of the late Saxon period was the acquisition of relatively modest estates (5 hides or less) by thegns. At the same time many of the very large land units granted to church landowners in earlier generations were being fragmented. It would appear that a more numerous aristocracy were living off individual estates that were smaller than those enjoyed by their predecessors. In order to maintain a decent style of life landlords would have needed to extract more from their peasant tenants, and to maximize the income from their demesnes. The methods by which this intensification of estate exploitation was carried out are hidden from us. It may have been associated with the gradual abandonment of slave labour, notorious for its low productivity, and the conversion of some peasant dues and services into cash rents. The involvement of landlords in commodity production by the eleventh century is suggested by charters recording a market for land in eastern England, the abundant evidence for cash renders in Domesday Book, and the same source's record of demesne sheep flocks which provided wool in marketable quantities.[33]

Rural society was evolving in a way which provided the towns both with surplus produce for sale, and with consumers able to buy traded and manufactured goods. This evolution must in turn have been stimulated as townsmen grew in numbers, needing more foodstuffs and raw materials, and also tempting their rural customers with a wider range of goods. Country and town came into contact in a number of different ways. The townsmen may have included the agents of landlords (resembling the continental *negotiators*) who sold estate produce and bought goods on behalf of their masters. Their presence is indicated by the numerous references in documents, and especially in Domesday, to urban houses being attached to rural manors. Ultimately, the agents became independent, and perhaps provide one line of descent for the merchants of the developed medieval towns.

Another group of early townsmen were the craftsmen. There is abundant evidence that pottery manufacture became an urban industry at such places as Stafford, Stamford, and Thetford. Stamford also had a large-scale iron industry at a very early stage of its development. Cloth, previously made in peasant households or in seignoral workshops, seems to have been made increasingly in towns coinciding with a technical innovation, the introduction of the horizontal loom.[34] Craftsmen, no doubt a numerous group of townsmen, are likely to have been recruited from among the peasantry. Perhaps artisans were initially subordinated to lords, but if late Anglo-Saxon towns in any way resembled their successors in the better-documented thirteenth century, their populations were built up by waves of rural immigrants (including many women), who found employment initially as servants, and in the less-skilled occupations such as small-scale trading in foodstuffs.[35]

Once the economic trends outlined here were set in motion, certain sites clearly enjoyed advantages as potential urban centres. A number of types of settlement could act as pre-urban nucleii – burhs, royal tuns (residences and centres of local administration), and important churches.[36] All three functions might be combined, as burh fortifications were often built round an existing royal tun, which would commonly be served by a minster church. People were accustomed to travel to such centres to pay dues, to attend courts, and to worship in the church. Markets would have developed naturally at large gatherings, for example on Sundays in churchyards. Agricultural surpluses would have been exchanged to obtain the cash to pay in rents, taxes, and church dues. The visiting peasants, as well as the resident wealthy clergy and officials, would have needed to buy goods and services from craftsmen and other specialists. An example of manufacturing activities at such a centre is provided by the iron-smelting and iron-working complex at Ramsbury (Wiltshire) that was active in c. 800. It is assumed that it had been set up to serve the needs of a large royal estate, and it could also have developed to supply the local market for iron goods.[37]

Not all royal tuns, minster churches or burhs acted as pre-urban nuclei. Sawyer has listed almost 200 known royal tuns, and the existence of many more can be deduced from post-Conquest evidence; only a fraction of them became towns.[38] Similarly many minster churches did not attract urban settlements. Some places were favoured for growth because they had high grade administrative functions, as shire towns or hundred centres, for example. Or in the case of churches large and wealthy monasteries like Malmesbury or St Albans were more likely to act as a focus for an urban community than an ordinary minster church. A potential town site might have a good chance of success if it lay on a frontier between differing ecological zones, for example a wood-pasture and a champion district – differences in landscape and economy that we now know to have existed in the Anglo-Saxon period. Finally, acts of rulers, like a king designating a town as a place for minting coins, or the deliberate founding of a market by a monastic lord, as happened at Evesham (Worcestershire) just before the Conquest, could help a town's growth.[39]

English historians and archaeologists do not commonly use the phrase 'pre-urban nucleus', though, as the foregoing discussion shows, they make use of the concept. It must be stressed that not every town appears to have had a royal or ecclesiastical site that can be designated as such a nucleus. This may be because places like Ipswich and Norwich are not well-provided with documentary evidence in their early phases, but it is also possible that in some cases communities developed because of the natural advantages of the site for trade or industry; the political and ecclesiastical authorities recognized the importance of the places at a later stage. Again such a model of urban origins, for which a later analogy might be the mushrooming of the town of Ravenserodd on a sand bank in the Humber estuary, would allow for the role of the townsmen taking the initiative under economic stimuli.

Conclusion

Much remains to be known about the origins and early growth of towns. Although there may be agreement between scholars over the interaction between town and country which spiralled into a process of urbanization, the first cause of expansion still eludes us. Climatic change, trends in state policy, the social upheaval caused by the decline of the Carolingian Empire and the Viking invasions have all been suggested, but all seem insufficient as single explanations. Recent research may not have solved this conundrum, but it has advanced our appreciation of the past history of towns in three important ways. First, archaeology has given us the ability to measure and quantify our early towns – the size of the occupied areas, the productive capacity of some of their industries, and the extent of their trade contacts. Secondly, archaeological analysis has taught us to recognize order and organization in towns. The frequently close relationship between centres of royal power and urbanization has only recently been fully recognized; the regularity of town plans and the durability of property boundaries are also relatively new discoveries. Thirdly, historians have re-assessed the place of towns in the aristocratic and agrarian social formation that is summed up by the term 'feudalism'. The traditional view has been to see towns as alien growths, ultimately corrosive of the feudal social order because their economic organization and mental outlook were incompatible with feudal lordship and aristocratic values. Now, as has been outlined above, commerce and towns are seen as fulfilling the needs of the landlords, and they are recognized as integral parts of developed feudal society. If they posed any threat to aristocratic control, why did so many lords acquire property within the larger towns, and encourage the growth of towns on their estates? If the townsmen were in any sense subversive of the feudal order, why did they hesitate so long before challenging the power of the lords?

There is a good deal of common ground among historians and archaeologists in recognizing the close connection between the exercise of power in early medieval society and the creation of a climate conducive to urbanization. The differences in interpretation lie mainly in the degree to which the beginnings of towns can be regarded as deliberately planned with a political and economic background.

7

Urban archaeology in Germany and the study of topographic, functional and social structures

HEIKO STEUER

During the last few decades, archaeology has added greatly to the fund of source materials on such matters as the origin of towns, their topographical organisation and function and their social structure. This enables us to attempt an initial summary of certain regular developments as well as to draw attention to specific aspects of individual towns.[1] Archaeology, together with urban historical geography, gives us an insight into the new form of social organisation of larger numbers of people, and into the various forms that this new pattern could assume. Furthermore, archaeology can go far beyond written and illustrative material in describing and evaluating daily life, urban culture and the everyday environment.[2] An excavated living room in a wattle or stone building with its fireplace,[3] the insulation of a medieval chamber by means of a floor of spherical pots with their openings pointing downward[4] or the parasitic organisms found when a sewer is investigated[5] are of far more immediate value than any written sources. This is a totally convincing argument and probably the reason why nowadays important historical exhibitions seek to re-construct buildings or even whole streets.[6]

What follows is an attempt to summarise the results of urban archaeology in Germany – defined as the political and economic region of the German Empire, Roman Germany, or the Holy Roman Empire, viz. its territories north of the Alps.[7]

The medieval history of German towns comprises several phases:

1. The condition of Roman towns in the eighth and ninth centuries, linked to the question of a possible continuity between the Roman period and the Middle Ages especially along the Rhine and the Danube.
2. The origin and development of trading centres and market towns in the border areas along the North Sea coast and along the Elbe in the ninth and tenth centuries.
3. The emergence of extensive suburban areas alongside a concentration of trade and, above all, craft activities around episcopal sees or royal

81

residences. (2) and (3) are often considered to be precursors or early forms of medieval towns, sometimes characterised as early conurbations.

4. The peak period of Ottonian–Salian towns in the tenth and eleventh centuries.
5. The full development of existing towns and the main phase of town foundations during the Stauffen period, *ca.* 1200, accompanied by the establishment of towns (with charters and privileges similar to those west of the Elbe) in territories beyond the Elbe as part of the German colonisation of the east.
6. It is in the east that we encounter the fully developed Slav town which has, since the ninth or the tenth centuries, seen a development similar to, but by no means identical to, that in phases (2) and (3) above.

If we do not look at individual towns but the distribution of urban settlements, then, according to Stoob, the following types can be discerned:[8]

1. Regional centres.
2. Chains of towns along overland routes or along borders.
3. Networks of towns in individual regions.
4. Isolated towns on the edge of territories or at the border.
5. Leagues of towns such as the Hanseatic League or the various leagues of South German towns.

The location of towns and early topographical development

The street plans of present-day towns often enable us to trace earlier basic layout and subsequent stages of expansion. However, as had long been suspected,[9] these plans do not take us back to the original plan of a town at its foundation but usually reflect and preserve the medieval position which, in itself, had often been the result of various fundamental changes. It is important to differentiate between a town that had existed in classical Roman times, had then disappeared and finally been re-established in the Middle Ages, a town that developed around a castle or fortress and its suburbs and a town that was planned and established as a foundation in open fields, as it were, even if it may often be assumed that such a town may have had a forerunner in an economically favourable location. Such differences may be highlighted by some major examples.

Dorestadt am Krummen Rhein has its origins in the systematic parcelling out of the riverbank sites. Each plot consisted of a strip of riverbank (with the main building), where landing stages were built later, and a further strip beyond which accommodated further buildings.[10] The original layout of Haithabu was one of rectangular plots and paths, which remained virtually unchanged between about 800 and the end of the eleventh century, although there were changes in the nature of the buildings occupying the sites. Fences surrounded the plots, often in such a way that there were two fences immediately next to each other, with minimal space between them, where two plots shared a boundary.[11]

The younger settlement of Schleswig[12] also started with the systematic parcelling out of land, with the inclusion of riverside and landing stage sites. A roughly rectangular grid of paths linked the landing stages and the adjoining areas. The individual plots were roughly equal in width, almost completely covered by one building, with the narrow side facing the path. Farther away from the water, in the area of the later market, the individual plots were larger and accommodated several buildings; residential buildings as well as stables, etc. The layout of the plots there was less regular than in the port area. This structure remained unchanged from the eleventh until the thirteenth centuries. Early in, or towards the middle of, the thirteenth century, however, a completely new pattern of plots was introduced; the new street plan showed long, narrow plots whose front areas were occupied by gabled houses.

In Hamburg, the reorganisation of the pattern of plots beginning in the eleventh, but mainly carried out in the twelfth, century coincided with the introduction of a new type of house in all the areas that were investigated; this structure was then maintained until the modern period. As in Schleswig, traces of earlier residential buildings were discovered below the later Fischmarkt.

It is frequently possible for the archaeologist to provide evidence of later structural changes, particularly in connection with the establishment of market places; this is the case in the whole of the area bordered by Bonn in the west – where earlier Carolingian buildings were located below the market and cathedral square (Münsterplatz) – and by Magdeburg in the east where Carolingian defences (ditches) and a later Carolingian settlement were discovered below Ottonian and more recent structures.[13]

The old market (Alte Markt) in Magdeburg, presumed to date from the Ottonian period, was established in the second half of the twelfth century after the removal of older buildings on the site.[14] The market place in Verden was established on a site previously occupied by buildings. In Kiel, too, founded some time between 1233 and 1242, i.e. relatively late, all the indications are that the Alte Markt was established only when a reorganisation of the town was undertaken.[15]

Archaeological excavations – in addition to the evidence provided by town plans – have frequently shown that, even in the more modern period, market sites were smaller, i.e. that more space was then occupied by buildings than is now. Examples are the Münsterplatz in Neuss,[16] or the Kohlmark in Braunschweig,[17] where the market area was considerably smaller, accommodating, as it did until its demolition in 1544, the church of St Ulrich as well as a guardhouse.

Archaeological investigation has thus enabled us to identify a secondary creation of 'old' markets as a fairly typical development. It has also been able to establish that business in these markets was chiefly done in booths, stalls and similarly unsubstantial structures. Known as 'Gaddemen' from written sources relating to Köln, these have also been discovered and archaeologically evaluated as to their extent and development in Magdeburg and Lübeck.[18]

During the twelfth and thirteenth centuries, a period of numerous town foundations, older urban settlements often went through a period of a second 'foundation' and were reorganised. Freiburg im Breisgau is one of the foundations of the Dukes of Zähringen, in the south-west of the Empire. The charter establishing it as a market town dates from 1120. Two main streets, crossing each other virtually at right angles, served as the starting point for a roughly rectangular town plan, consisting of plots of 50 by 100 ft (15.2 by 30.4 m) each. These plots were then rented out at a fixed rate. Older structures on the site were modified so as to fit into the new pattern of plots. New buildings gradually filled in the gaps in the town that had been 'founded'.[19] One major conclusion that may be drawn from the archaeological evidence is that today's plans and the structure of plots usually reflect an older state of affairs but do by no means invariably reflect the layout at the town's foundation.

Archaeologists and conservationists have also undertaken research into cellars in an attempt to reconstruct the structure of towns in the medieval and early modern periods. Comprehensive plans of cellars have been compiled for various towns, e.g. Berne, Freiburg im Breisgau, the residence of Wimpfen, Marbach am Neckar, Ladenburg; there are partial plans also for Zürich, Göttingen and Lübeck.[20]

Once again cellars reflect an earlier stage of development of streets but not the earliest layout. Whereas dendrochronology has made it possible to date cellars in Freiburg to the thirteenth or even the late twelfth century, cellars in other towns are often of later origin (fourteenth to sixteenth centuries). Often cellars were, in fact, added to a building during its later life.

Future excavations in partially or completely abandoned settlements may well yield further evidence as to the basic structure of towns. To be included with these towns are ones that were relocated to a site offering better communications, such as Celle/Altencelle, Uelzen/Oldendorp, Villingen/Alt-Villingen, together with towns that lost their function, e.g. Bardowiek. During the Carolingian period Bardowiek served a useful function as a trade centre, and grew as a result, whereas the northward and eastward expansion of the Empire eventually reduced it to an insignificant town. Deserted mining towns such as Münster im Münstertal/Black Forest and Prinzbach in the Black Forest should also be mentioned in this context.

In addition to numerous lesser towns that declined into villages, a number of failures of foundations occurred where towns were established in positions such as at the very edge of an economic area or in an exposed and vulnerable position. Plans of such towns, which include their fortifications and numerous built-up sites, have been compiled for the deserted settlements of Landsberg near Wolfshagen/Hesse, Blankenrode, Kreis Büren/ Westfalen, or Rockesberg/Landkreis and Freudenstadt/Baden-Württemberg. All these appear to have been abandoned at an early stage and have thus preserved evidence relating to their initial phase of development.[21]

Fortifications and stages of growth

Fortifications were not a feature of the original development of most towns. For example, the early trading centres of Dorestadt am Niederrhein and Haithabu near Schleswig were not fortified at all. Only during the final phase of Haithabu's existence, in the late tenth century, was the settlement protected by a ring wall and palisade. As towns developed, fortifications such as walls and ditches, wooden palisades, even stone walls (tenth century) were constructed. The only earlier fortifications were the large hilltop castles established by royal authority in the Frankish-Saxon border areas, e.g. the Büraburg near Fritzlar, or the Christenburg/Kersterburg near Marburg (eighth century). There is archaeological evidence to this military function (strong fortifications, frequently rebuilt, and reinforced walls, towers and gates) as well as to their urban functions (sizeable population, traces of trading and craft activities). This line of development does, however, peter out.[22]

There are numerous examples of castles established by bishops becoming nuclei of urban development even though the archaeological evidence has sometimes been limited to the discovery of a defensive line formed by ditches. In Köln and Magdeburg, Münster, Paderborn and Hamburg, Halberstadt, Verden an der Aller and Osnabrück such basic fortifications have been identified. Ditches and walls surrounded the site of the church and the bishop's residence, which themselves are in locations that have some form of natural defences, i.e. on hilltops or flanked by rivers. As early as the tenth century some of the walls were partly built of stone.[23]

The lines formed by defences also allow us to trace various stages of urban expansion. Thus, across Germany, from Köln to Basel, from Magdeburg to Aachen, the remains of walls, written evidence in archives and the evidence furnished by archaeologists enable us to arrive at a description of the growth of towns from their nuclei at foundation to their apex in the thirteenth or fourteenth centuries. Two parallel developments may be discerned. First, the growth of the nucleus itself, secondly, the incorporation of areas that had developed independently – either suburban developments, or monasteries and religious foundations, with their immunities and privileges.[24]

Whereas the more recent phases of expansion had long been known, the oldest fortifications in towns like Köln, Magdeburg and most other towns have only been discovered relatively recently (and their existence proven) through archaeological research.[25]

Excavations of the residence of Tilleda am Kyffhaeuser and the Stauffen residence of Wimpfen am Berg/Württemberg illustrate the possible range of urban features within a royal residence. The history of Tilleda is known in detail for the period from the eighth to the fourteenth centuries. From the ninth or tenth to the twelfth centuries, it saw increased activity by various craftsmen in the areas at the periphery, but within the outer defences. Traces of their activities were analysed in more than 200 houses.[26]

When the Imperial residence of Wimpfen was built around 1200, it gave added impetus to the growth of the town that had developed to the west of it. Both areas were fortified, had coalesced by 1300, and incorporated further ground to the south into the town. Additional space was needed for further development as the original site could accommodate only about 100 houses. It was secured by the addition of a new ring wall. The area of the former residence itself – which had been abandoned soon after 1300 – saw the development of a new, built-up, urban area with numerous buildings (of whose cellars forty have been the target of intensive archaeological research).[27]

Harbours and urban infrastructure

Over a period of about 150 years, between the end of the seventh and the early ninth centuries, a number of landing stages were built along the Rhine in Dorestadt. As the river gradually receded from the old settlement, these bridge-like structures had to be extended at frequent intervals. These structures, about 26 ft (8 m) wide, eventually reached a length of some 656 ft (200 m) and extended along a stretch of the river about 1 kilometre in length.[28]

Landing stages have also been excavated in the trading town of Haithabu near Schleswig. In addition, semicircular lines formed by palisades protecting the seaward side of the town have been discovered, as well as the substructures of bridges that extended as far as 131 ft (40 m) out into open water. Nothing is known about the superstructures, although they may have formed a continuous area for trading activities.[29]

In Schleswig, the settlement that succeeded Haithabu, seven bridges were discovered across a front of 492 ft (150 m). They had been buried under rubble. Further bridges appear to have existed to either side of these seven. The landing stages were up to 33 ft (10 m) wide and so close together as to leave sufficient room only for rowing boats. Larger ships could tie up only alongside the ends of the landing stages. Dendrochronology has been able to prove that all the bridges were extended at the same time. The area that was created could have been used as a market place. It is not possible yet to establish whether individually owned stages were extended under the control of some authority (which could have involved the raising of a large labour force and a considerable amount of building materials) – for example, whether the expansion was controlled by the town authorities, or whether the planning and construction of the extension to these bridges was a purely cooperative venture.[30]

In prints of the early modern period, the large medieval town of Köln is shown to have had a riverside quay with landing stages leading out into the river at right angles.[31] In Konstanz am Bodensee, excavations in the area of the Fischmarkt have brought to light structures made of boards which extended out into the lake and served both as a framework for new building land and as a landing area for ships.[32]

Starting around 1230, additional land was created through landfill along the banks of the Trave in Lübeck in order to add to the harbour facilities. The roads leading to the Trave were extended in length by raising the level of the muddy stretches of the river banks (thorough archaeological research has been undertaken in the Grosse Petersgrube).[33] A similar method was adopted in Hamburg, where in the late ninth and tenth centuries the original settlement with the bishop's castle and suburbium was extended to the south and the west into the marshy areas along the river; and large-scale landfill virtually doubled its area.[34] Certain knowledge on the creation of new building land has also been gained in Braunschweig where 56% of the town's area of 114 hectares was added, probably on the initiative of Heinrich the Lion.[35]

As long ago as the early Roman period, the harbour and the arm of the Rhine between the rectangular Roman settlement and an island in the river had been filled in to link the economically useful area of the island with its stores directly with the town of Köln. These landfill activities for the purpose of creating new land for trading and building in the so-called Rhenish suburb (Rheinvorstadt) were resumed in the tenth century and helped to create the new centre of the medieval town, fortified as early as the first half of the tenth century.[36] Street names such as Langedamm-strasse (Long Dam Street) or Bohlweg (Timber Path) in Braunschweig or Brückengasse (Bridge Street) in Köln are all indicative of the transformation of such previously marshy areas.

Archaeologists have also been able to disprove previously held views on the paving of streets. Thus, it has been shown that central areas in towns were paved quite early, either with timbers or crushed stones. Evidence to both has been obtained for Hannover from as early as the thirteenth and even the twelfth centuries.[37] In many towns consecutive layers of paved street surfaces, up to a depth of 10–13 ft (3–4 m), have been discovered.[38] Other infrastructure has also been revealed. For example, a network of channels of running water along the edges of streets, supplied by a leat or a natural brook, has been discovered in numerous towns right across Germany (Basel, Strassburg, Speyer, Erfurt, Goslar, Quedlinburg). Piped systems such as the monasteries had had for centuries were only gradually introduced in towns, starting in the thirteenth century.[39] There is evidence of piped systems in Goslar, Stralsund and Basel, where instead of the lead pipes used in monasteries, hollowed out tree trunks were used as pipes.

Craftsmen's workshops and their location

The great variety of urban craft activities has been reflected in the discovery of large amounts of discarded materials, waste, craft refuse which had, however, as a rule been moved from its original location. Thus, it has been easy to obtain evidence of the existence of a number of crafts but considerably more difficult and often impossible to gain hard facts on the location of the craft workshops and their nature and equipment. It is possible, however, to give a general indication of the location of various crafts and to trace changes in their distribution over the centuries with some certainty.

Archaeologists have been able to show, for example in Hamburg, that one site may, in succession, have been the workshop of a comb-maker, a bone-carver, a butcher and finally a cooper.[40] It has been shown that around 1300 one building in Göttingen was used by a craftsman who produced bone-carvings as well as iron and other metalwork and he may even have been involved in enamelwork.[41]

It would seem that any specialisation of craftsmen in German towns in any one particular craft does not appear to have occurred until the twelfth or the thirteenth centuries. Furthermore, during this period craftsmen of the most varied trades obviously lived and worked next door to each other, with their houses distributed at random across the whole town. This random distribution, 'mixed location', of crafts is particularly well documented in the St Kolumba district of Köln (1286). We also know the occupations of houseowners in various districts of Lübeck in the fourteenth century and it is in Kiel that there is early evidence of a concentration of individual crafts in particular streets, e.g. smiths, shoemakers, woodturners, bakers, or tailors during the fifteenth century.[42]

Archaeologists have not always been able to prove the existence of a workshop on the basis of discarded materials or waste. In most cases, such waste materials had been carefully removed from the workshop and either used in road repairs or landfill – leather, shoemakers' discarded materials, waste from bone-carving workshops and iron slag have all been found in Haithabu, dating from the ninth to the eleventh centuries – or taken away some distance from the town altogether. In Konstanz, for example, enormous quantities of material discarded by the paternoster makers were used, together with other refuse from the town itself, to create new land on the town site of the monastery of Salem by being tipped into Lake Constance (late fourteenth and fifteenth centuries).[43] In the immediate vicinity of the riverbanks, between the previous Hafenstrasse and the riverside quay in Köln, numerous tools used by shipwrights were discovered: axes, hammers, caulkers' rivets, boat hooks; but mixed in among them were quantities of waste brass and waste discarded by the needlemakers frequently referred to in written sources.[44]

In other studies, numerous salters' workshops have been excavated; those in Bad Nauheim and Bad Hersfeld date from the Carolingian period, whilst in Soest they originated in the eleventh or twelfth centuries. Related trades probably existed in Lüneburg and Werl.[45] Potteries, even with their attendant risk of fire, were initially seldom concentrated at the edge of towns; an example would be Siegburg, a potters' town, where both potteries and deposits of shards were excavated in the Aulgasse.[46] In Köln, on the other hand, groups of potters' kilns were discovered in scattered locations in the high medieval and early modern town, although some of these date from a period in which written sources testify to the authorities' attempts to ban the trade within the town because of the smoke nuisance it created.

Building sites and construction methods

Archaeological research into town centres has resulted in radically new insights into residential building. In small and medium-sized towns houses built of wattle and daub predominated, and stone buildings usually merit a specific mention well into the High Middle Ages, but apparently small stone turrets and ladies' bowers were much more common during the High Middle Ages than in later periods.[47] The increased use of stone, at the social level of the patricians and administrators living in towns, starting in the south and gradually advancing northward, is first evidenced in towns such as Basel and Zürich by 1100.[48]

Whereas the example of Italian towns may be claimed to have been influential in the South German towns, developments elsewhere in Germany seem to have followed the example of the 'immunity area' of episcopal sees, of the residence, in the adoption of stone buildings. We may, therefore, assume that stone buildings of a similar nature existed in Köln, Mainz, Trier and other Rhenish towns after the middle of the twelfth century.

Square towers measuring about 33 by 33 ft (10 by 10 m) and rectangular buildings of about 33 by 66 ft (10 by 20 m) appear to have been developed side by side until the fully developed Romanesque house, built of stone and having a representative façade, finally emerged.[49] More than in the south, where the stone house appears to have existed from the very beginning (e.g. in Zürich, Basel and probably also Freiburg), further north – where there was a long-standing tradition of building in timber – the appearance and spread of the stone house reflects the social topography of the residences of the urban upper classes, patricians and administrators, merchants and nobility residing in town.

Houses built around a framework of upright posts were superseded in the second half of the twelfth century by houses erected on a horizontal base formed by timbers and stones to support the walls. This made possible the construction of houses of several floors. Concurrent with this development, the urban upper classes adopted stone turrets, and stone towers behind the main building which served as fireproof stores or as heated living quarters. Urban archaeology has shown that such 'Turres' – be they in the South German/Swiss region, North Germany (Minden 1180, Osnabrück 1177, Braunschweig, ca. 1200, Goslar, first half of the thirteenth century) or built in fired brick (Lübeck, Stettin, from Thorn to Riga and Reval, second half of the thirteenth century) – were scattered throughout the centres of old towns rather than limited to certain streets. The adoption of the stone house by the upper classes occurred wherever this class had the financial resources to do so.[50] In this sense it provides an important and early indicator of social topography in many towns.

As with other aspects of urban life and culture, archaeology has been able to prove that a phase of accelerated development occurred in the field of construction between 1150 and 1250. However, because of the limitations imposed by present dating methods it has not been possible to establish a starting date in the second half of the eleventh century of this pattern of an urban, tower-like structure used either for protection or as a residential building, nor to date its spread. It does, however, appear to have spread very quickly – possibly because it became the fashion – over a few decades, throughout the whole Empire.

In less prosperous towns, the thirteenth century saw the construction of houses on stone foundations (well documented in Minden/Westfalen), houses with a ground floor built of stone with half-timbered upper storeys or houses entirely half-timbered, standing on foundations of boulders. Dendrochronology has yielded remarkable results as to their construction and history; it has been possible to prove the existence of half-timbered houses dating from the thirteenth century in numerous German towns.[51]

The German colonisation of the East (late twelfth to mid-fourteenth centuries) meant the spread eastward of settlements with the status of towns as well as the layout of urban buildings and their construction methods. The town as a specific form of settlement and economic activity, however, was not 'transplanted'. The new German towns were simply superimposed upon older German towns (which had originated in the ninth and tenth centuries, like the western towns of traders and craftsmen but, being forward outposts in Slav territory, had followed a different course of development). Regular grids, a tightly-knit structure of plots, fairly uniformly built on (timber-built, square houses) are characteristic of these towns. As a rule, a high density of uniform timber buildings is typical of the Slav towns, whereas towns within the German Empire covered a larger area which allowed the development of a settlement of lesser density, with many different buildings offering a variety of functions, although these towns also developed from an initially fairly uniform pattern of plots. The continuous front formed by the gable ends of buildings developed only very gradually, as a result of a lengthy development and of an ever-increasing density of settlement in the restricted area within the town's fortifications.[52]

Conclusion

Current trends in German urban archaeology may roughly be summarised as follows. Early interest – down to the first few years after 1945 – focussed upon the development of towns as single entities. Without archaeological and historical investigation, a number of theses were advanced as to the reasons why a particular location had been selected for the establishment of a town, e.g. favourable location in relation to communication networks beyond the immediate region, development of a town in a centre of political power, towns as outposts of an episcopal see, a secular residence or a castle. Town plans and written historical sources supported the theory of a polycentric development with its starting points in a number of monasteries and religious foundations, or monasteries and castles. The town plans provided evidence of various phases of expansion, from the nuclei to extensions and the incorporation of suburbs; they also made possible an analysis of the succession of various rings of fortifications.[53] In this respect, each town has its own history and there are particular reasons for each town's establishment.

The next phase focussed above all on the 'roots' of towns. Urban archaeologists attempt to track down the very earliest traces of urban development; this had often become possible as a by-product of reconstruction following wartime destruction. This line of investigation was followed when old Roman towns on the Rhine and the Danube were the targets of research, e.g. Köln, Mainz, Regensburg. It also governed research into the past of Hamburg, Hannover and Magdeburg, towns that had been established outside the former boundaries of the Roman Empire.[54]

The third phase – which was closely linked with the 'rehabilitation' of inner city/town centre areas since the 1960s – was one in which virtually any evidence that came to light was collected. Excavations yielded a great variety of source materials illustrating various aspects of all the phases in the development of a town; it proved impossible, however, to assemble the evidence into a coherent picture.

The 1970s saw the first planned programmes. In many cases these were triggered by the 'rehabilitation' of urban areas, and these programmes aimed at the exploration of whole town centres together with the systematic evaluation of the evidence obtained. Among the examples of such archaeological investigations are Schleswig and Lübeck.[55]

One result was that the established theory that town plans permitted us to discern the very early stages of development had to be abandoned. Even as the results of these large-scale projects are being prepared for publication, a tremendous impetus has been given to medieval urban archaeology in Germany, and also to the work of urban historical geographers.

The most recent phase started in the late 1970s. While its results have so far remained largely unpublished and have mainly been subjects of discussion in various expert circles (such as the Arbeitsgemeinschaft für Mittelalterarchaeologie of the Deutsche Verbände für Altertumsforschung), new aspects have become the targets of research.[56] Thus, it is no longer the town as a physical entity, with its ring of fortifications and its plan, that is the focus of investigation but the history of its inhabitants, its burghers and craftsmen, traders and patricians, throughout the Middle Ages and the modern period, as represented by the variations in the occupation of the various plots and sites. Large areas in town centres are examined, whole plots with all their buildings, wells and sewers, etc., are excavated, investigated and analysed, from the roof ridge to the very foundations. The medieval town plan, the structure of the plots (established at the town's foundation), is investigated; other themes worked on are the process by which the density of buildings increased, the adoption of stone as a building material and the distribution of craftsmen's workshops across the whole town. Cultural aspects of town life are explored archaeologically, parallel to the development of thought and attitudes in the field of history and to some extent historical geography.[57] Clearly, the degree of progress made is not the same in all towns. Much still depends on coincidence or good fortune, on archaeologists who, within the framework of their tasks as conservationists, have put and are continuing to put their emphasis on urban archaeological research. There is clearly considerable scope, however, for archaeologists and urban historical geographers to work closely together, especially in the attempts to reconstruct past social topographies.

8

English medieval town planning

TERRY SLATER

The past ten years have seen an upsurge of interest in medieval urban history in England.[1] This has resulted, at least partly, from the recent developments in urban archaeology following the redevelopment of many English town centres in the 1960s and early 1970s. This renewed interest in medieval urban history and archaeology, however, has not as yet resulted in a similar resurgence of interest on the part of historical geographers in Britain and, consequently, investigations of the topography of medieval towns have not been prominent in the geographical literature of the past decade. Conzen's eloquent plea to the first meeting of the Urban History Group, in 1966,[2] for more detailed investigation of medieval English plan 'families' remains as relevant today as then, since most of the topographical work that has been generated, either by archaeologists or by inter-disciplinary teams, has been concerned with individual towns rather than with comparative studies.

Beresford's work on the medieval new towns of England, Wales and Gascony[3] provides the only notable exception to this lacuna but even this study is not characterised by a depth of plan analysis. County survey volumes of urban archaeological potential, written for planners, are notable for their lack of urban topographical comparison,[4] though they provide much of the necessary data. Similarly a recent survey of the medieval boroughs of Wales, while excellent in other respects, is distinguished by the poverty of its cartographic representation and lack of comparative analysis of the town plans.[5] Much more satisfactory in this respect is Haslam's stimulating survey of Anglo-Saxon towns in the south of England.[6]

More general surveys of British urban development have included comment on medieval town planning; they include books by Platt on England,[7] Adams on Scotland[8] and Carter on Wales.[9] The most detailed comparative survey in this general category is Aston and Bond's volume on the landscape of towns[10] in which, unusually, the principal elements of the tenement pattern are shown on the town plans. A more serious attempt at comparative analysis, using the terminology developed by Conzen, was made by White-hand and Alauddin in their preliminary survey of the whole of Scotland,[11] and this emphasised some of the difficulties in attempting such comparative surveys. More recently, Slater has focussed on two counties in the English Midlands,[12] but this survey did not attempt a comprehensive analysis of all town plans, only of particular plan elements; in this instance market places and burgages.

No studies published in the past two decades analysing the plans of individual towns and cities have begun to approach the analytical depth and conceptual richness of M.R.G. Conzen's studies of Alnwick[13] and central Newcastle.[14] Whitehand has recently attempted to trace the intellectual origins of Conzen's ideas and to show how they have been subsequently developed by others, primarily in Britain, rather than his native Germany.[15] The two most detailed town-plan analyses drawing upon Conzenian techniques have been the study of the Scottish burgh of St Andrews by Brooks and Whittington[16] and an analysis of Pershore by Bond.[17] Both are limited to a consideration of the medieval period and add little to the conceptual framework developed by Conzen. Nonetheless they show an unusual sensitivity to the burgage pattern and the fine grain of the town plan.

Conzenian ideas have also begun to filter out to historians and archaeologists who are now less prone to earlier simplistic assumptions about plan development.[18] Archaeologists in particular have begun to recognise the importance of the composite nature of the plans of even quite small towns. Large-scale inter-disciplinary studies of the major British towns, such as London,[19] York,[20] Lincoln,[21] Winchester,[22] Canterbury[23] and Southampton,[24] most of which were initiated by archaeological excavations, have also begun to provide a richness of data which points to the complexity of urban development in the medieval centuries. The historical town plan atlas project, of which two volumes have thus far been published,[25] has been a valuable stimulus, though the British volumes have been severely criticised for their lack of analytical maps in the commentaries.

Town planning

The interest in Britain in medieval town planning arose with the development of modern planning in the early twentieth century. This interest was generally limited to consideration of sixteenth- and seventeenth-century cartographic representations of planned medieval towns and, subsequently, to the categorisation of planned towns according to their street plans.[26] Some planned medieval towns were subjected to more detailed studies, especially those with rectangular grid plans. Hope's study of Ludlow[27] was one such investigation remarkable for its more detailed consideration of the plan evidence. The Welsh bastide boroughs of Edward I also attracted more detailed historical consideration,[28] as did the new, grid-planned towns of Salisbury and Winchelsea[29] where episcopal and royal sponsorship respectively meant a wealth of surviving documentation.

These local historical studies culminated in 1967 with Beresford's massive comparative analysis of medieval new-town foundations and the planning practices associated with them.[30] Three chapters are devoted to various aspects of medieval new-town planning but only in the introductory section, which uses the detailed research on Winchelsea, Salisbury and the Edwardian Welsh bastides, does this consideration extend beyond the basic layout of streets, market place and boundaries to the details of plot layout. A decade later, a comparative survey of medieval planned towns by Butler[31] demonstrated a regression in analytical capability in its inadequate sketch illustrations of street plans. However, the volume in which Butler's essay appeared was important in other respects, particularly for its comparative survey of medieval urban defences by Barley[32] and for Keene's stimulating essay on extra-mural suburbs.[33]

Conzen's plan analyses of Alnwick and central Newcastle had little to say about medieval planning practices since both were essentially unplanned towns growing by means of successive, relatively small-scale additions to the town plan. However, his consideration of plot dimensions in the old-town cores of these two towns, and his concept of the burgage cycle, are fundamental to any appreciation of the reality of medieval planning practice. He attempted to demonstrate this himself in his well-known study of Ludlow and Conway.[34] In Ludlow (Shropshire) plan analysis demonstrated that Hope's earlier, and long-accepted, interpretation of the town as having been created by a single act of planning at its foundation was untenable. Conzen's interpretation suggested at least six plan units, necessarily laid out at different times and adapting to different circumstances and planning ideals. The consideration of the North Wales bastide at Conway is even more interesting since it attempts to uncover the underlying planning ideals of the medieval urban surveyor and the related practical outcome of his solutions on the ground. Although the town was planned as a single entity it is revealed as a complex 'best-fit' solution to a variety of planning problems.

Subsequent development of Conzen's work on the fine grain of the plot patterns of town plans has had to wait until comparatively recently. It has taken two directions. One, burgage analysis, involves the measurement and analysis of modern plot frontages in the light of surviving cartographic sources and basic medieval documentation of particular towns,[35] and the second, which might be characterised as 'total plot history', involves the painstaking reconstruction of the individual histories of particular plots in terms of area, building fabric, land use, ownership and occupation from deeds, directories, rentals, surviving building fabric and, sometimes, archaeology. Such plot history work is extremely time-consuming, can only be successfully completed on a large scale where there is extensive documentation, and normally requires a team of people with a variety of expertise in the different sources of evidence. Nonetheless, a number of such studies have been undertaken and others are in progress. One of the earliest and most remarkable is Urry's reconstruction of medieval Canterbury from surviving rentals,[36] but the most comprehensive reconstruction published thus far is Biddle and Keene's study of twelfth-century Winchester.[37] The techniques developed here are now being put to use in studies of medieval London and York but they have also been utilised by local groups in the analysis of smaller towns. The unpublished retrogressive reconstruction of plots lining some of the principal streets of Stratford-on-Avon[38] was one of the first such local studies, but a better-known analysis is being undertaken at Ludlow by the Ludlow Historical Research Group under the direction of David Lloyd.[39]

Burgage analysis

The metrological analysis of burgage series based on modern plot frontage measurements has been developed by Slater using towns in the West Midlands and Devon as case studies. The work began with an examination of plot series in Stratford-on-Avon,[40] one of relatively few British towns where burgage dimensions are specified in the foundation charter. The specified width is 3.5 perches (57.75 feet, 18 m) and metrological analysis of present-day frontages confirmed that the great majority of modern plot boundaries conformed to some fractional measure of this documented width. With the technique justified with a properly documented example, similar analysis was then extended to other towns where the original burgage dimensions were not documented. Published case studies include the Fore Street suburb of Totnes (Devon).[41] Here a 3.5 perch frontage width was suggested as an original standard for the whole street, suggesting that it had been developed as a planned entity. Similarly at Ashburton (Devon), developed by the Bishops of Exeter (but like Totnes having a composite town plan), analysis of the burgage series along East Street suggested an initial layout of plots 3.5 × 9 perches in size which were still perfectly preserved in the modern townscape. In the south-east of England, Wood's topographical analysis of East Grinstead suggested that the original burgages had been 2 perches wide.[42] Still more interesting was the metrological analysis of the plot series on either side of the Bridge Street–High Street axis of Pershore (Worcestershire).[43] Two plot series on the west side suggested common dimensions of 4 × 10 perches, despite a division of manorial lordship between the two measured lengths, while the east side of the street had a different base measure of either 2.5 or 5 perches width. The details of this case study suggested that the west side of the street had been replanned at some time, possibly following a fire in 1233.

A more recent case study in a different region, that of Hedon, a medieval new town and port in East Yorkshire,[44] has been able to add an archaeological dimension to the metrological evidence, besides suggesting a more complex developmental history for the town than that provided by Beresford.[45] The only documentation of plot dimensions at Hedon is of land given to St Leonards' Hospital, York, in the mid-twelfth century, which was 1 acre in size. The planned new town at Hedon had been largely abandoned by the sixteenth century and had reverted to pasture closes. However, the field boundaries continued to reflect the earlier plots and cartographic analysis suggested plots 20 perches long (330 feet, 100.6 m) by 8 perches wide (132 feet, 39.6 m), which is exactly 1 statute acre, the documented size of the St Leonards' Hospital plot. A substantial length of one side of the planned street layout has been excavated and these excavations, to the west of Middle Lane, uncovered a series of ditches at right angles to the road that almost certainly represent the medieval plot boundaries. The ditches of six out of a possible nine plots within the excavated area were approximately 4 perches (66 feet, 20 m) apart, while another plot was 6 perches (99 feet, 30 m) wide.[46] It may be that the estimates made from the relict plot boundaries represent an amalgamation of plots in the later medieval period and that the original planning module at Hedon was 4 × 20 perches, giving half-acre plots. Alternatively the excavation evidence might represent the second stage of the planning process whereby the original burgages were subdivided and sub-let by their first owners. Such a process is well evidenced in the first borough rental at Stratford-on-Avon,[47] where a very large proportion of the plots had already been divided longitudinally into halves or thirds only fifty years after the foundation of the borough.

Burgage-series analysis in three different English regions has suggested a common planning dimension in the layout of new, properly planned areas of medieval towns; namely the use of the statute perch and the statute acre as the unit of measurement by medieval urban surveyors. That the measure was often the areal one, rather than the more precisely specified length and breadth in perches, is shown by surviving borough charters. Besides Stratford, only New Sarum (Salisbury), with plots specified as 3 × 7 perches, Altrincham (Cheshire) – 2 × 5 perches and Burton-upon-Trent (Staffordshire) – 4 × 24 perches, have plot dimensions recorded in this way,[48] whereas in the single county of Oxfordshire the Bishop of Lincoln's new town at Thame was planned with one-acre plots and extensions to Eynsham with quarter-acre plots, and to Witney with very large two-acre plots.[49]

The results thus far obtained have important implications for our understanding of the medieval town plan, and, indeed, for present-day townscape management practice. They suggest that the great majority of planned urban developments in the medieval period were based upon statutorily laid down measurements which were utilised over the whole of England. This realisation does not, of course, detract from Conzen's empirically derived 'standard' burgage width in Alnwick of 28–32 feet.[50] First, because such a standard is remarkably close to the 33 feet of 2 statute perches; secondly, because he was concerned with building widths rather than original plot widths, indeed, the explanation of his 'standard' is couched in terms of a two-bay medieval house arranged with its long axis parallel to the plot frontage; and, thirdly, because Alnwick was not a planned town in the way that the towns more recently subjected to burgage analysis were.

Burgage analysis has not yet been undertaken for an unplanned town, partly because such analysis is likely to be inherently less useful. However, if a suitable exemplar could be found it would be interesting to measure a town known to have been developed over open field land, or from village tofts, on a feudal holding where customary measures were known to have been in use in an agricultural context. Local customary acres and perches are known from a number of areas but as yet no urban plots have been shown to have been laid out to such dimensions.

Nash's work on perch and acre sizes in medieval Sussex[51] suggests that Battle might be a suitable case study since a perch of 16 feet is recorded on the estates of Battle Abbey at a time contemporary with the laying out of the town in the late eleventh century. Similarly, in Romney Marsh (Kent) a 20 foot perch was commonly utilised and New Romney town would thus again be suitable for study. Homan's work in reconstructing the original layout of New Winchelsea[52] suggested a perch size of 16.25 feet but Beresford believes the layout to have been based on the statute perch[53] and in view of its royal ownership this seems inherently more likely. However, Homan's work is valuable not just for its reconstruction but for revealing the differences between ideal and reality in medieval town planning. He shows, as did Conzen in Conway, that existing landscape features were incorporated into the new town plan, that the varied topography of the site had its effect, and, most important, that the detailed requirements of the first occupants of burgages did not necessarily coincide with the ideal plan in the mind of the surveyor, a point to which we shall return.

Ludlow: a case study of burgage analysis

Burgage analysis, then, is not a simple mechanistic exercise. It is especially complex in larger medieval towns where plot amalgamation and plot subdivision through the centuries have often caused considerable disruption

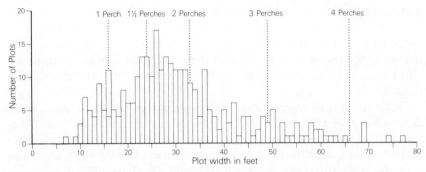

Figure 8.1   Modern plot widths in the medieval streets of Ludlow (Shropshire)

to the plot pattern. Stratford-on-Avon is exceptional in the degree of preservation of its first plot boundaries,[54] which is partly a consequence of its unitary layout. Ludlow, in contrast, provides an excellent example of the complexities of burgage analysis in a composite plan town and, since Conzen has already provided a plan analysis,[55] it is possible to proceed directly to the burgage measures. All the principal streets of the medieval town have been measured according to the techniques described elsewhere.[56] A frequency graph of these measures demonstrates the enormous variety of plot widths (Figure 8.1). The great majority are between 22 and 32 feet wide, though there are significant numbers of narrow plots between 11 and 17 feet wide and, equally, of plots much wider than 32 feet, not all of which are the result of modern plot amalgamation. The modal plot width is 26 feet (seventeen occurrences) and the average plot width is a little over 30 feet if plots greater than 70 feet wide are excluded.

If the graph is examined for plots which conform to multiples of the statute perch it is striking that they are so inconspicuous. Plots roughly 1 perch wide are perhaps most prominent (eleven occurrences) and there are similarly some plots 1.5 and 2 perches wide. However, they are certainly not sufficiently prominent to account them as the initial planning module for Ludlow. Even when the plot widths are graphed for individual streets in the town, perch-based measures are no more significant, though there are interesting variations between streets. High Street, which is primarily commercial, has very few broad plots, for instance, whereas the largely residential Broad Street has a substantial number of plots of above average width. Such results are entirely consistent with those collected in other towns, though there are variations in median plot widths, and in the range of plot widths.[57]

It is only when such initial plot measures are combined within the framework of the primary plot boundaries[58] of the town plan that a perch-based pattern begins to emerge. Indeed, the whole medieval area of the town seems to have been laid out on the basis on the statute 16.5 feet perch despite the variety of plan-units apparent in the town plan, and despite the disruption caused to some areas of the town by the subsequent insertion into earlier burgage series of the castle, town walls and two large friaries (Figure 8.2).

Given that the town was developed in a number of discrete and clearly discernible phases, it should not be expected that each plan-unit was developed to the same standard burgage size. Indeed, given the topography of the borough, with the land sloping steeply away to both north and south from the High Street east–west axis, it would have been difficult to ensure a rigid rectangularity. This is most clearly seen in the subtle curves and indentations of the four street blocks between Mill Street and Broad Street. Each of the Mill Street–Broad Street frontages of these blocks is slightly different; the blocks are wider at their southern ends than at their northern, though all are a specific number of perches. In so far as a common frontage width in this plan-unit can be discerned, then 3.5 perches (57.75 feet, 18 m) is the most satisfactory. Since the plots are some 12.5 perches deep they would have been a little over a quarter of an acre in area.

In High Street and in Lower Broad Street a 2 or 4 perch width seems a more probable base width. Since the plots in both plan-units are rather deeper, the smaller width is perhaps the more likely. The long north–south axial road of Corve Street and Old Street contains rather more than half the 3 perch plot combinations recorded and this would seem to be the most likely base for this part of the town. The obviously planned burgages in Corve Street are exactly 18 perches deep (Figure 8.2).

Though far from conclusive, burgage analysis in Ludlow has confirmed the complexity of the plan outlined by Conzen and has suggested the planning module upon which the various plan-units were based. Documentary work by the Ludlow Historical Research Group has taken these suggestions much further and the evolution of the plots lining particular streets can now be traced in great detail.[59] Nonetheless, even in a town as well documented as Ludlow it is impossible to return to the initial conception of the town plan without an understanding of burgage analysis.

Ideal and reality in the planning process

The very early stages in the evolution of a burgage series can perhaps best be traced in a town plan which is less complex then Ludlow, and by examining a single street block in greater detail. Lichfield, the largest town in medieval Staffordshire,[60] has a planned, rectangular grid of streets at its core which was laid out by Bishop Roger de Clinton towards the

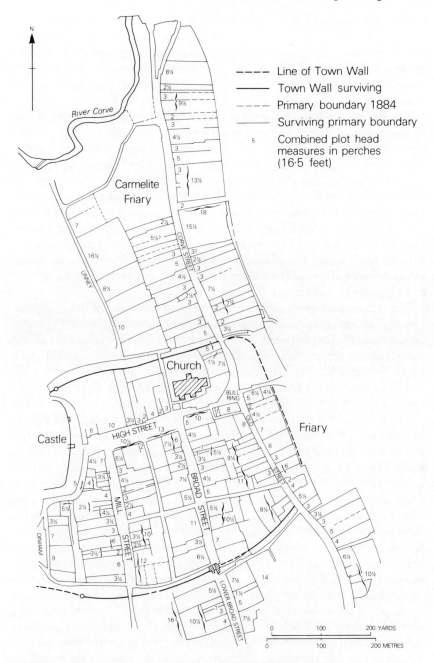

Figure 8.2   Primary plot boundaries and composite plot widths based on the statute perch in Ludlow

end of his episcopacy in *c.* 1150.[61] The town is remarkable for the number and variety of historical and topographical studies that have been published[62] but the complexities of its plan have yet to be properly elucidated.[63] However, the planned core of the town is clear and provides an excellent example of the difference between ideal and reality in medieval planning practice.

The street plan was conceived as four parallel streets running north-east to south-west linking the two main routeways through the town, which run north-west to south-east. As such, the street plan falls into a rather uncommon category of town plans which earlier writers have characterised as 'ladder plans', the streets of the town appearing like the rungs of a ladder between two roughly parallel through routes.[64] The trapezoid market place is inserted asymmetrically in the northern corner of this ladder plan. The asymmetry ensured that traffic using all but one of the through routes had to pass through the market place, and that exception included an inconvenient ferry across the Bishop's fish pond.[65] Bore Street was conceived as the primary street of the ladder and was laid out correspondingly wider to emphasise its 'high street' function (Figure 8.3).

The rectangular street blocks of the planned borough are unusually narrow and, though they were probably initially planned to be some 13 perches (214.5 feet, 65.4 m) between streets,[66] they narrow progressively towards the north-east (Figure 8.3) because of the containing town ditch. The street block between Market Street and Bore Street is altogether smaller and is 11 perches (181.5 feet, 55.3 m) wide at the Market Place end and 9 perches (148.5 feet, 45.3 m) wide at the Bird Street end.

The relict primary plot boundaries suggest the way in which these street blocks were subdivided into the first burgage series. North-west of Market Street were plots 13 perches deep and probably 4 perches (66 feet, 20.1 m) wide. Since the widths of the remaining street blocks were only as great as the depth of this Market Street series, only the block between Frog Lane and the city ditch could be, and was, similarly divided into plots 13 × 4 perches in size (Figure 8.3). The Bore Street–Wade Street and Wade Street–Frog Lane blocks could have been so subdivided if Wade Street had been relegated functionally to a back lane giving access only to the rear of plots fronting Bore Street and Frog Lane. However, the town planner clearly wished to avoid this since both blocks are divided transversely by boundaries which remained almost continuous until the late nineteenth century.[67] They show that burgages were intended to front both sides of all three streets. The solution to this planning problem is ingenious in its subtlety. The transverse boundary dividing the two street blocks in question are placed so that the blocks divide irregularly; the plots on the south-east sides of Bore Street and Wade Street being roughly two-thirds the depth of the large plots fronting the north-west side of Market Street, while those

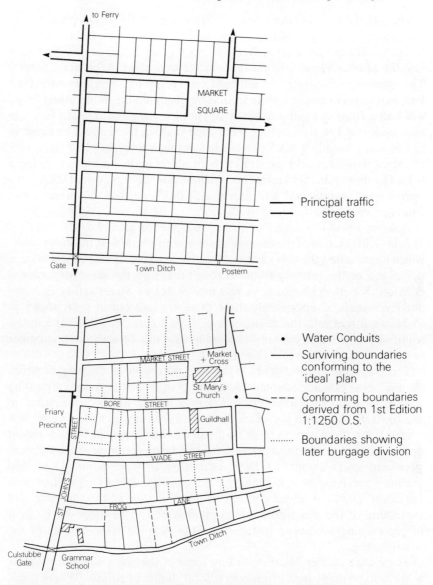

Figure 8.3   The 'ideal' plan of central Lichfield (Staffordshire) and relict plan features illustrating the actual development of this ideal

plots on the north-west sides of Wade Street and Frog Lane are roughly one third the depth but much wider so that their long axis was parallel to the street. In this way the status of Wade Street and Frog Lane was equalised and the importance of Bore Street maintained.

The street block between Market Street and Bore Street provided an even more difficult planning problem as these streets were clearly destined to become the most important in the planned new town since they disgorged into the Market Place; and yet this was the narrowest of the street blocks. The planning solution again adopted was to lay out burgages with their long axis parallel to the streets so that burgage holders in this street block still had a roughly similar quantity of land for their 12d rent. In fact, the dimensions of the street block were such that six plots could be fitted in in this way (roughly 9 × 4.5 perches in size) with a seventh laid out across the block with its short axis parallel to the street in the normal way (Figure 8.3). The plot boundary and measurement evidence suggest that these plots were rapidly subdivided into halves and thirds so that the prime street frontages could be effectively used.

A second problem faced by the town surveyor at Lichfield concerned St John's Street, one of the existing north-east to south-west through routes, which approached the town at an obtuse angle to the 'ladder' streets. Since it was one of the primary routes through the town the surveyor took the decision that plots should generally face St John's Street rather than the 'ladder' streets. Consequently these plots are laid out at right angles to St John's Street and the alignments of Frog Lane, Wade Street and the south side of Bore Street are deflected northwards by some seven degrees to accommodate this layout (Figure 8.3).

The trapezoid market place is another reflection of the way in which the medieval planner adapted his 'ideal' plan to fit the frame of existing townscape features. However, sufficient evidence has been provided to demonstrate the ingenuity of medieval town surveyors and to show that a search for the planning basis of medieval new towns in Britain should not be reduced to seeking a mechanistic regularity in burgage-series dimensions and street layout.[68] Where sufficient plan, documentary and field evidence survives, as at Lichfield, it becomes possible to appreciate both the 'ideal' plan, conceived perhaps only in the mind of the surveyor, and something of the practical adaptations that had to be made in the light of pre-existing landscape features and the detailed requirements of the first occupiers.

These case studies illustrate briefly some of the ways in which progress is likely to be made in urban topographical studies in Britain. Where documentary sources are profuse then the 'total plot history' approach will always pay substantial dividends. However, the number of towns where such studies can be undertaken is strictly limited and they are generally places which were both large and economically successful. For the hundreds of smaller market boroughs in England, as well as for the great majority of towns in Wales and Scotland, the necessary sources do not exist. If the substantial contribution to the economy made by such towns is ever to be properly appreciated, and if the full richness of urban plan types in Britain is ever to be understood, then the techniques of comparative town-plan analysis and of burgage-series analysis must be more widely employed. Perhaps the time is not far off when some part of England will at last have a comprehensive, comparative, historical town-plan atlas.

PART THREE

Social areas and social patterns

9

Economy and society in eighteenth-century English towns: Bristol in the 1770s

ELIZABETH BAIGENT

Introduction

The eighteenth century has long been a neglected period in English urban history and historical geography. By comparison interest in the early modern period has been fostered by both geographers and historians.[1] Similarly, there is a plethora of studies on the social and economic structures of many English industrial cities.[2] Such activity makes even more striking the absence of any detailed work on the historical geography of eighteenth-century towns. Indeed, the first general survey of such settlements only appeared in 1982, since which there has been some growing interest in the eighteenth-century way of life.[3] Unfortunately, there are relatively few case studies which investigate the economic and social composition of specific towns. The research of George for London remains a classic work, along with other notable studies by Rogers, Rudé, Schwarz and Jones on the same city.[4] Bath has received some attention from Neale and McIntyre, whilst Wilson and Money have carried out investigations of Leeds and Birmingham respectively.[5] Such work, however, appears to have benefited little from the general upsurge of interest in urban history compared with the study of the nineteenth century. In particular the ideas and perspectives of the Annales school and the possibilities afforded by sophisticated computer techniques have impinged little on eighteenth-century historians. It is regrettable, too, that geographers, with a few exceptions such as Langton and Laxton, have contributed little to the study of the period, knowledge of which is surely a prerequisite to the fuller understanding of the patterns of social and economic change during the nineteenth century.[6] Theoretical work also jumps from the pre-industrial or pre-capitalist city to the modern one, giving no theoretical cohesion to work on this phase of transition.[7]

Probably the single most important reason for the paucity of research is the intractability of eighteenth-century sources. These, like those for the early modern period, are inconsistent and partial and at the same time one is dealing with populations of the size normally associated with nine-teenth-century studies. Bristol, for example, had a population of about 55,000 in 1770 and no single satisfactory source covers more than 4,000 of them.[8] The sources used so productively in historical demography, the parish registers, are often seriously incomplete for rapidly growing eighteenth-century cities, many of which in any case had very fragmented parish structures. Norwich is the obvious case in point, but Bristol too had many city parishes. The growing non-conformist and Roman Catholic populations, which escaped registration to varying degrees, add to the un-reliability of the registers.[9]

Because the sources are so fragmentary, research tends also to be particu-lar rather than comprehensive. We know much of individual religious sects and merchant elites, but lack comprehensive studies to allow us to put these small studies in context. This is especially regrettable in view of advances in computing which allow large sets of information to be stored and manipulated and because in a period of change such as the eighteenth century it is important to know what was happening to whole populations, not just notable groups or eminent individuals, if we are fully to understand the nature of the transition.

The following study attempts to bring some of the methods and ideas of the Annales school to eighteenth-century urban history, first to examine the usefulness of some neglected eighteenth-century sources, secondly to investigate the social structure of Bristol in the later eighteenth century and thirdly to try to set this in the context of wider research on the nature of the *Gemeinschaft-Gesellschaft* transition.[10]

Bristol in the eighteenth century: sources and methods

There is no source for eighteenth-century Bristol that is not partial, frag-mented, unreliable or a combination of these. The Bristol city boundary had within it sixteen parishes ranging in size from the huge to the tiny, together with the liberty of Castle Precincts, the site of the old castle, and Temple Ward. In addition the *de facto* city extended into a number of rural parishes, but conversely some parishes extended beyond the city boundaries to include suburbs and rural areas. This fragmentation, together with the fact that the city had a strong and growing tradition of non-conformity, made the use of the parish registers a daunting prospect.

Other fairly comprehensive sources for eighteenth-century cities are guides and directories. These have been successfully utilised in several coun-tries including England and Canada and the similar *Addressbücher* are used in Germany.[11] The first directory for Bristol was compiled by James Sketchley in 1775 and contains the names of some 4,200 eminent and gentle residents, listed simply by right of their gentility, and retail tradesmen and craftsmen who hoped to gain custom through this type of publicity.[12]

Poll Books, lists of voters and the votes they cast in Parliamentary elections, are well known as a source for eighteenth- and nineteenth-century political and social history, but, with the notable exception of Rudé's work on the Wilkite elections in Middlesex, research has been concentrated overwhelmingly on the nineteenth century.[13] This is for the obvious reason that before the 1832 Reform Act electorates were often small, and under the control of a local magnate. However, this was not always the case, since Bristol had a particularly large electorate.

Other fairly comprehensive sources of data for many eighteenth-century towns are rate and tax returns. City rates covered such expenses as maintenance of the poor and provision of a night watch, and varied from town to town. National taxes were raised on windows and land throughout the country. With the exception of the use of Poor Rate returns to investigate the specific question of urban poverty, such fiscal returns have been little used.[14] The returns in general and Land Tax returns in particular seem to find as little favour today as historical sources as the taxes themselves did in the eighteenth century as a means of raising money. The returns are seen as poor documentary evidence of a procedure which was corrupt, partial, reliant on outdated estimates of rateable value and, perhaps most serious of all for our purposes, which differed from one area to another, so that comparison amongst areas is impossible.

This criticism, however, stems too much from knowledge of the legal, fiscal and administrative difficulties associated with rating and taxing and not enough from the consideration of the returns as historical sources. Simply because the collection of the Land Tax was an administrative shambles and socially inequitable, the use of returns as historical sources is not precluded.

It was decided, as a basis for an *histoire globale* of Bristol in the later eighteenth century, to try to combine some of these sources to form a surrogate census for investigation of the economy and society of the city. The sources chosen for the study were Sketchley's directory, the Poll Book and all the extant rate and tax returns for Bristol in 1774/5.[15]

Table 9.1 shows the information contained in the chosen sources and the potential for amalgamating these data using nominal record linkage (the joining of two or more pieces of information ascribed to named individuals) is immediately apparent. A nominal record link would provide a single body of wide-ranging information useful in itself and as a means by which to check the reliability and representativeness of the individual sources. This latter use is one which has to date been overlooked, since linkage has been very largely confined to demographic studies in which just one type of source, parish registers, is used. The link in this study was undertaken in two stages: first, the 405 extant city rate and national

Table 9.1 *Information available from Sketchley's directory, the 1774 Poll Book and rate and tax returns*

Information	Source		
	Directory	Poll Book	Rate returns
Surname	Yes	Yes	Yes
Forename	Yes	Yes	Usually
Sex	Yes	Yes	Usually
Occupation	Yes	Usually	Rarely
Status	Sometimes	Sometimes	Sometimes
Votes cast	No	Yes	No
Street of res.	Yes	No	Yes
Parish of res.	No	Yes	Yes
Building type	Sometimes	No	Often
Rateable value	No	No	Yes

Table 9.2 *Rate and tax returns used*

Rates and taxes	1	2	3	4	5	6	7	8	9	10	11	12	13	14	15	16	17	18	19
Poor	R		R	R	R	R	R								R	R			
Lamp	R	R	R	R	R	R	R				R	R	R		R				
Pitch				R															
Watch	R	R		R				R	R						R	R		R	R
Sewer											R				R		R		
Widow										R				R	R				
Land	R	R		R	R	R	R	R	R		R	R	R	R	R	R	R		

Parish numbers

1 All Saints	8 St Leonard	15 St Stephen
2 Castle Precincts	9 St Mary le Port	16 St Thomas
3 Christ Church	10 St Mary Redcliff	17 St Werburgh
4 St Augustine	11 St Michael	18 Temple Ward
5 St Ewen	12 St Nicholas	19 St James Outparish
6 St James City	13 St Peter	R = Rate/tax return(s) extant
7 St John	14 SS Philip and Jacob	and used in study

tax returns for Bristol in the year 1774/5 (Table 9.2) were linked by hand at the record office as the data were collected. This presented a number of difficulties as the collectors of the various rates missed out parts of streets, were unsure where one street ended and another began, and were in some cases reluctant to venture into unsavoury back courts. Generally, however, the records were easily linked and so it could be seen how much a man's house had been assessed for under a number of different rates.

The main difficulty arose when it was realised just how incompatible the various assessments were. Table 9.3 presents one of the worst cases from which it is evident that there was no immediate way of comparing the wealth of one man for whom there exists only a Poor Rate assessment with another for whom there is only a Pitching Rate assessment, since the assessments are not the same and neither do they vary in constant proportion to one another. Contrary to established thought, however, they did bear some relation to known levels of wealth in the city: houses in streets known to be elegant thoroughfares had consistently higher assessments than those in courts, alleys, lanes and ditches. Given that there was no alternative source of information on wealth, it was decided to estimate the missing data using two- and three-step regression procedures which calculated values for missing cases of one variable using the whole array of available data. Finally a single rateable value for each property was calculated as the mean of all values, real and estimated, for that property. Given the degree of manipulation and estimation which the data had undergone, the final figures can be used only to suggest broad bands of wealth and poverty within the city: any further degree of accuracy would be entirely spurious. Nevertheless, this is important as it turned a large number of returns, which individually were more misleading than useful, into a single source which proved itself subsequently a valuable indicator of wealth patterns in Bristol. Further, linkage analysis proved itself as a source testing procedure. The Land Tax returns, in which one would initially have least confidence and which are almost universally discarded as useless, proved in fact very useful. They were by far the most socially comprehensive of all the returns and covered many of the poor who occupied houses assessed at £1, 10s or simply marked 'under the rate'. Geographically, too, it was the most comprehensive tax and its collectors were the most conscientious of all such men. They visited the worst courts and alleys, noted the names rather than just the presence of many of those exempt from payment and gave useful information as to the nature of the buildings they visited.

The combined fiscal information was then merged with Sketchley's directory and the Poll Book. A weighting procedure, in which points were awarded for coincidence of information on name, sex, address and occupation, was used to determine whether individuals with the same name were in fact different people and conversely whether people with different names were in fact the same person. Figure 9.1 shows the remarkably small overlap amongst the sources. Only 1,064 people were in both the Poll Book and the directory. Some difference was expected: the 300 women in the directory could not be included amongst the voters; but one would nevertheless have expected both sources to list the wealthier and more established members of the community and hence to have a large number of common entries. Similarly, it is surprising that only 1,200 men were in the Poll

Table 9.3 *The incompatibility of rateable values in Castle Street, Castle Precincts*

Name	Lamp and Scavenging Rate 1774/5	Watching Rate 1774/5	Land Tax 1775
Dagg, Abel	16	14	6
Chambers, Charles	12	12	5
Bray, Robert	16	12	9
Lawson, Robert	21	20	9
Taylor, Thomas	14	14	6

All figures represent rateable values in pounds.

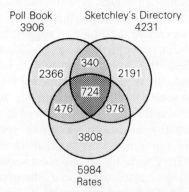

Figure 9.1   The overlap between different data sources used in Bristol

Book and the rate returns and only 1,700 people were in both the directory and the rate returns. Some of the women in the directory would perhaps not have been the heads of their households and some parishes (Clifton and Bedminster) are not covered by all three sources. Of the 10,872 people mentioned in the sources, only 724 were in all three. The rigorous linking method under- rather than over-estimated the number of common entries. Nonetheless, the overlap is surprisingly small and vindicates the decision to use all three sources to gain as full and as impartial a picture of Bristol society as possible.

With the use of PDS, a database management package which can select and combine material and which performs simple arithmetic functions, the information in the three sources was analysed to investigate the economic and social composition of Bristol at the end of the eighteenth century.[16]

Table 9.4 *Classification of occupations in Sketchley's directory and Poll Book under scheme 1*

Class	Number	%
A Gentry & Prof.	847	12.1
B Personal services	270	3.9
C Textiles	435	6.2
D Earthenware	229	3.3
E Wood	461	6.6
F Metal	613	8.7
G Leather	535	7.6
H Food & drink	853	12.2
I Glue & wax	90	1.3
J Clothing	500	7.1
K Mixed materials	129	1.8
L Building	549	7.8
M Agriculture	151	2.2
N Transport	125	1.8
O Shipping	764	10.9
P Seagoing	245	3.5
Q Miscellaneous	214	3.0
Total	7,010	100.0

The structure of occupations

Using three classifications the data on occupation given in the Poll Book and the directory were examined. The first classification (Table 9.4), designed to identify the sectors of the economy, showed that Bristol's economy at this date was very broadly based and included the traditional productive base of any sizeable town: textiles, earthenware, wood, metal, leather, glue and wax, mixed materials, food and drink, and clothing. Superimposed on this traditional base were some distinct specialisations. The first of these was the Gentry and Professional class. The sources used overstate the numbers in this class, but it is clear that the traditional urban patriciate of merchants and gentlefolk, such as the clergymen of the city, had been augmented by the many Customs and Excise men, bankers, lawyers and brokers all directly involved in the commercial life of the town and by the doctors, who had increased in number as the Hotwells spa prospered, to make the class of Gentry and Professional disproportionately large (12.1%).

The next specialisation – that of shipping – revealed that 10.9% of the men and women listed in the Poll Book and directory were ships' craftsmen or ships' suppliers and a further 3.5% were seagoers. This was one speciali-

Table 9.5 *Classification of occupa-tions in Sketchley's directory and Poll Book under scheme 2*

Class	Number	%
A Clergy & Gentry	181	2.6
B Profs. & Services	936	13.4
C Distributors	1,487	21.2
D Artisans	3,395	48.4
E Builders	534	7.6
F Labourers	93	1.3
G Rural	139	2.0
H Seagoing	245	3.5
Total	7,010	100.0

sation within a very broadly based economy and the degree of specialisation does not compare with that in many port towns, where shipping trades could employ 73% of all adult males.[17]

A second classification (Table 9.5) breaks down the economy not in terms of production sectors, but by looking at the pattern of work for the individual. It shows that the number of true gentry was surprisingly small (2.6%), but the number of professional men, men of the new middle classes, and those in personal services, was large (13.4%). Distributors, traditionally some of the wealthiest citizens, were numerous (21.2%) and although some of these people were petty traders of ill repute, most were substantial mercers, drapers, grocers and the like. Artisans still accounted for 48.4% of the population under consideration. However, eighteenth-century occupation titles conceal much information on the condition of the man (was a 'potter' an independent artisan, the owner of a large works or an employee in one?) and despite the fact that 'artisans' could be sweated workers as well as independent masters, this figure still says much about the organisation of work and the fragmented production pattern in Bristol at this date.

A third classification (Table 9.6) groups the population according to the status which attached to their occupation. It was devised using two mid-eighteenth-century guides to trades and uses the information on appren-ticeship fines, journeymen's wages and the amount of capital a master would need to set up in business to draw up three classes of status.[18] Those with occupations of high status formed 13.6% of the population under consideration; this was a very sizeable percent and re-enforces the sugges-tion that the gentry, and particularly the professional element in the popula-tion, was both important and growing. The proportion in high status callings

Table 9.6 *Classification of occupations in Sketchley's directory and Poll Book under scheme 3*

Class	Number	%
A High status	953	13.6
B Middle status	1,994	28.4
C Low status	2,199	31.4
X Not classified	1,864	26.6
Total	7,010	100.0

is particularly large in view of the fact that this is an examination of those *with occupations* so the true gentry, unless they were clergymen, members of the corporation or some such, were excluded from the discussion. Those 28.4% in employments of middle satus were solid, decent but by no means prosperous tradesmen who formed the backbone of the city economy.

Those in employments of low esteem (31.4%) may be considered in relation to those who are not included in the sources. The poor may be divided into *pauvres de structure*, the aged, lame, sick and young children who were unable to support themselves in even the most favourable economic conditions, and *pauvres de conjoncture*, men and·women with a trade and a few possessions, critically the tools of their trade, who could support themselves in times of economic expansion and low food prices, but who could be forced into the class of the desperately poor in a *conjoncture* or year with a bad harvest.[19]

The sample considered here is 7,000 of a population of about 56,000 or 1:8 people or 1:2 heads of households. If we consider those in Class C (about a third of those listed or 15% of all heads of households) to have been *pauvres de conjoncture* and the bulk of the population not included to have been poor in some measure, we conclude that 65% of the population must have been actually or potentially poor. This is to interpret *pauvres de conjoncture* rather broadly, as *conjonctures* obviously vary in intensity and duration, affecting varying numbers of people; but the figure of 65% is not far from Corfield's 60% poor in Norwich in the late seventeenth century and it does serve to remind us just how precarious was the lot of the majority of the population.[20]

The occupational structure of men and women was compared and the results showed that women were active in all sectors of the economy, except for obvious cases such as seagoing in which no women were employed. In the traditional trades they concentrated in food and drink (21.9% compared with 13.3% men) and clothing (13.8% women, 8.1% men), and they were disproportionately important in the newer sectors of the economy: distribution (38.4% women, 28.3% men) and personal services (24.4% women, 4.4% men). These sectors were expanding rapidly and would continue to do so into the nineteenth century. Women remained, however, most often in low status trades which employed 47.2% of women compared with 30.7% of men.

Social topography

Occupation and place of residence were compared using each of the three classifications and the results are summarised in Figure 9.2. The city was fairly sharply divided into four types of parish. First, were the central commercial parishes which had high numbers of professional men, distributors and those in high and middle status trades in general. This fits the picture of a pre-industrial city and shows that eighteenth-century expansion had not radically altered the economic composition of this key area of the city.

Secondly, there were the artisan parishes which were largely on the periphery of the city, especially on the unfashionable southern and eastern sides, although the large parish of St James is the exception to this rule. Craftsmen in all sectors, artisans and those in low and middle status trades predominated in these areas and this again suggests that the rich core and poor periphery of the pre-industrial city were still to be seen in Bristol at this date.

The suburban residential parishes on the fashionable northern and western sides of the city formed the third distinct area. The most famous of these was Clifton, which included the Hotwells spa, but St Michael's and St Augustine's parishes and St James Outparish also had notable concentrations of the gentry, professional men and those in high status employments. They differed quite sharply from the central parishes, in which were concentrated professional men and those in traditional trades. In the suburban parishes were greater percentages of gentry and those who were excluded from the third (Status) scheme since they followed new callings which could not be classified in traditional eighteenth-century terms.

The fourth group of parishes is termed 'transitional' as they fell into no simple type. Some, such as Castle Precincts, had been areas of ill-repute and were gaining in respectability, whilst at the same time they kept vestiges of their old artisan structure. St Augustine's parish might be said only just to have moved out of this semi-peripheral transitional class to join the genteel parishes, as it too had many artisans, particularly ships' craftsmen, but was increasingly dominated by merchants and wealthy ships' captains. Other transitional parishes were declining in status. As far as can be inferred from mid-sixteenth- and seventeenth-century data, St Leonard's parish had once been amongst the wealthiest in the city, but by the later

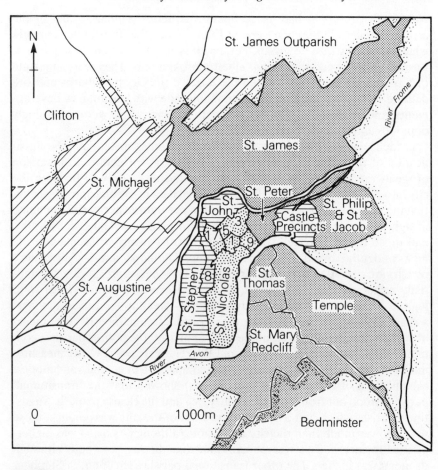

N

St. James Outparish

Clifton

St. Michael

St. James

River Frome

St. Peter

St. John

St. Philip
& St.
Jacob

Castle
Precincts

3

17 5

1 9

St. Augustine

St. Stephen

St. Leonard

8

St. Nicholas

St.
Thomas

Temple

St. Mary
Redcliff

River Avon

0   1000m

Bedminster

:::::: Wealthy trading parishes

▓▓▓ Artisan parishes

≡≡≡ Transitional parishes

/// Genteel suburban parishes

····· City boundary

—— Parish boundary

‒‒‒‒ Limit of built-up area in outparishes

1 All Saints
3 Christ Church
5 St. Ewen
8 St. Leonard
9 St. Mary le Port
17 St. Werburgh

Figure 9.2   The social topography of eighteenth-century Bristol

eighteenth century it had an occupation structure similar to that of the artisan parishes. St Stephen's and St John's were other transitional parishes which fell easily into no group. Perhaps it is significant that these parishes formed an inner suburban ring, albeit a broken one. They were in a state of flux, having been replaced on the edge of the city by suburbs of more definite character, more on the fashionable side with elegant new developments, and on the unfashionable side with parishes which were increasingly populous and with noisome, low status trades.

Evidence on wealth patterns from the rate returns substantiates the classification of the city parishes in terms of occupation structure. Comparison of mean rateable values proved a simple and direct way of dividing the city into rich and poor (Figure 9.3). The fiscal data re-enforce the suggestion that the rich core and poor periphery of the pre-industrial city still remained in eighteenth-century Bristol, although there are no usable data for Clifton, and those for St Michael's parish seem untrustworthy; consequently the new residential areas, other than St James Outparish and St Augustine's parish, are excluded from the discussion. The central areas were substantially richer than the peripheral areas; their mean rateable values were high not because a very few extraordinarily wealthy men lived amongst a mass of paupers, but because these parishes contained large numbers of rich and moderately well-off people. Similarly, the poorer parishes contained large numbers of the poor and the relatively poor. Other measurements of the distribution of wealth (e.g. comparison of medians and modes, classification of the data into four groups) showed that the 'transitional' parishes stood out from both the clearly rich and the clearly poor. St Augustine's parish, which had only just moved out of the ring was amongst those with a lower mode than the city as a whole, although its mean was higher. Castle Precincts had a lower median value than the city as a whole, although its mean was higher. The other transitional parishes (St John, St Stephen, St Leonard) all had patterns of wealth which were not readily classifiable and this substantiates the suggestion that the inner suburban ring of parishes was a zone of transition.

One striking feature of the distribution of wealth was that all parishes had properties of the highest and the lowest values. Each parish had its share of the poor and even the parishes with the lowest mean values (St Mary Redcliff and St James City parishes and Temple Ward) had their wealthy residents. It was noticeable too in the classification of occupations that no parish was without its gentlefolk or its low status artisans. This suggests a pre-industrial pattern of social mixing at the parish level combined with sharp segregation at the street level. It was evident from the rate returns that the rich lived on the main throroughfares and the poor in the back houses, courts, alleys and ditches immediately adjacent to them. This pre-industrial pattern contrasts with the modern pattern of more homo-

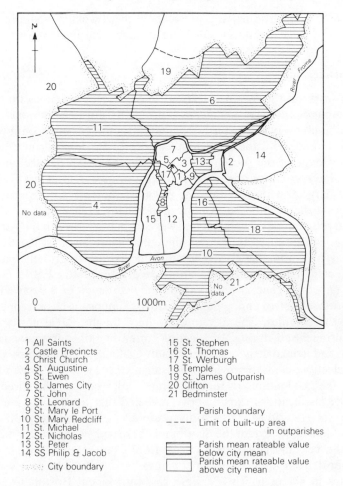

1 All Saints
2 Castle Precincts
3 Christ Church
4 St. Augustine
5 St. Ewen
6 St. James City
7 St. John
8 St. Leonard
9 St. Mary le Port
10 St. Mary Redcliff
11 St. Michael
12 St. Nicholas
13 St. Peter
14 SS Philip & Jacob

15 St. Stephen
16 St. Thomas
17 St. Werburgh
18 Temple
19 St. James Outparish
20 Clifton
21 Bedminster

——— Parish boundary
– – – – Limit of built-up area
     in outparishes
▤ Parish mean rateable value
 below city mean
▢ Parish mean rateable value
 above city mean

City boundary

Figure 9.3 Distribution of parishes in eighteenth-century Bristol

geneous areas and sorting at the parish rather than the street level.

 Examination of the wealth of men and women showed that women in general were the heads of households which occupied properties of middle value. They were not occupants of the very poorest or the very richest properties. Whilst it is not surprising that they did not head households which lived in the best houses, and this result corroborates evidence from occupation data which suggested that many women had occupations of low status, it is surprising that they were not concentrated amongst the poorest in the source. This is probably because they were simply too poor. It is well established that women outnumbered men amongst paupers, as opposed to poor artisans, and presumably these women would have had no fixed residence and thus would have escaped inclusion in the returns.

Political allegiance

Rudé's work on the Wilkite elections in Middlesex examines the wealth and occupations of voters and in this study the Bristol electorate was investigated in similar way, not to further our understanding of eighteenth-century politics, but so see if the political allegiance of Bristolians contributed to our knowledge of the social divisions within the city. The election seems a particularly promising one. The Bristol electorate was, after that of Middlesex, the largest in the country and 3,906 of the voters were resident in the city. At the election, an American merchant, Henry Cruger, who had a radical programme of demands and was conciliatory towards the American colonies, and Edmund Burke, an influential figure amongst the Rockinghamite Whigs who was also generally conciliatory towards the colonies, were elected. They defeated the sitting candidates Matthew Brickdale and Lord Clare, who generally supported the government of the day and who had made themselves unpopular in Bristol by supporting coercive measures against the colonies. The election was hard fought; 2,000 new freemen were enfranchised during the election, often in rather irregular circumstances, and Brickdale later unsuccessfully challenged the result.

The election seems to provide promising material for study, but examination of the occupations of the electorate under each of the three occupational classifications shown above revealed that it was only the upper strata of society who had clear voting preferences. The gentry, professional men and to a lesser extent the distributors gave some support to Brickdale, and had a very marked preference for Lord Clare. He derived almost all his support from upper rank Bristolians, for example, he received only 283 votes in all, of which 237 were cast by resident Bristolians, 46.8% of whom were gentry and professional. To say that Lord Clare and to a lesser extent Brickdale derived support from the upper strata is not to imply that they received no support from ordinary tradesmen, nor that the radical Cruger and the conciliatory Whig Burke received overwhelming support from the common folk. Each candidate received support from some of the highest and some of the lowest ranking members of society.

There were no marked differences in voting patterns amongst trade groups; rather the reverse. Each candidate was supported by tradesmen from each sector of the economy roughly in the same proportion as that group held in the whole city. Thus, 6.9% of all voters were employed in textiles and of Cruger's supporters 7.0%, of Burke's supporters 6.5% and of Brickdale's supporters 7.0% were in the textile trades. Sectional trade interests are held to be significant in a pre-industrial society, but the only clear division shown in the 1774 election was a distinctly modern horizontal or class-type divide.

When the voting patterns were analysed by parish no very clear pattern emerged. Some wealthier parishes with concentrations of those in higher status trades (St Augustine, All Saints, St Nicholas) supported the losing gentle candidates, but others (St Mary le Port, Christ Church) supported the radical and Burke and others still (Clifton) had a mixed response. Some poorer artisan parishes supported the victorious Cruger and Burke (St Philip and St Jacob, St James) but others (St Mary Redcliff) were mixed in their response. The transitional parishes again stand out: poor St Leonard's parish supported the gentle candidates, richer Castle Precincts the radical and Burke, and St John's parish had a mixed pattern. We have seen that rich and poor were present in all parishes and since the only criteria influencing voting seem to be those of status and wealth the confused parish voting patterns reflect this intra-parish mixing. The lack of any clear parish pattern is also in part due to the sudden increase in the electorate during the polling. The 2,000 freemen who were enrolled at the candidates' expense would have expressed not their own views, but those of the committees who were paying them, so patterns of allegiance are inevitably rather blurred.

It will be remembered that 1,200 men were in both the Poll Book and the rate returns and the voting patterns of these men were measured against their wealth. The picture of support by the wealthiest for Brickdale and to a much greater extent Lord Clare superimposed on a broad base of support from all wealth groups for each candidate is again apparent and confirms the suggestion that voting allegiances, as far as they can be said to exist for the mass of the voters, were on horizontal class-type lines in which men of the same wealth and status tended to vote together without regard for sectional or trade interests.

These results point to the uniqueness of the Middlesex election where a political issue, rather than the amount of beer provided by the committees, dominated the poll. By comparison the Bristol election tells us relatively little. Nonetheless, the results do contribute to our understanding of Bristol society at this date and temper the inferences drawn from the topography of the city that pre-class divides were still most important there.

Conclusion

The use of these rather neglected sources has thrown some light on the nature of economy and society in eighteenth-century Bristol. The city as a whole was in a period of change and flux: its occupation structure showed the continued importance of traditional trades, but also the emergence of new middle-class professions which were to grow in importance in the next century. Voting patterns within it showed that society could be divided quite sharply on horizontal lines, where wealth and status were more important criteria than trade or sector of the economy. Within the city the parishes were in a state of change. Some, on the edge of the city, were being built upon for the first time and were changing from rural to suburban, whether genteel suburban, as in the case of Clifton, or poor suburban as in the case of Bedminster to the south. The central parishes were wealthy and housed many commercial and professional men as they always had done, but they were being eclipsed as the highest status areas of the city by the new residential suburbs. The populous artisan parishes were much as they always had been and still retained some rich and gentle people within them; but they stood out increasingly from the genteel parishes which had only a very limited craft sector, if they had one at all. Finally, there were the parishes which we have described as transitional, which formed a heterogeneous group. They were difficult to categorise and were transitional both in the sense of being located between parishes of more distinct character and in the sense of being themselves in a state of change, whether upward in status (St Augustine, Castle Precincts) or downwards (St Leonard).

As much as contributing to our knowledge of eighteenth-century Bristol the study shows the value of some neglected eighteenth-century sources. It can be dangerous to generalise from one study, we do not know for example how representative Bristol's rate returns are; but it seems clear that, using computer techniques which can handle large amounts of poor quality data, more use could be made of these comprehensive sources. The inferences which can be drawn for them are inevitably limited, but provide a vital background and a context for the studies of particular groups on which our knowledge of eighteenth-century society too much relies. The eighteenth century was a critical period in the move to a *Gesellschaft* or class society and it is not unreasonable to suggest that change would be most apparent where growth was concentrated – in the town.[21] Knowledge of eighteenth-century urban society is thus vital to our understanding of social change beyond the century and in English society as a whole.[22]

Acknowledgements

I should like to thank the staff of St Hugh's College, the School of Geography and the Computing Services of the University of Oxford; those of the Historisches Seminar of the University of Münster and those of the Bristol Record Office for their help; the E.S.R.C., Bryce Research Fund and the King Edward VII British–German Foundation for their financial support; and my supervisor Jack Langton for all his valuable advice and help.

10

Social status and place of residence in preindustrial German towns: recent studies in social topography

DIETRICH DENECKE

Research in social topography

Since the 1940s a lively discussion has been carried on between historians and social historians concerning the theory and reality of social stratification and its variation through time.[1] In Germany this discussion came to a peak during the 1960s and 1970s when historians emphasized substantial changes in the historicity of social stratification and social indicators, changes which were related to the development in the political organization of society.[2]

However, social stratification is not only a vertical differentiation of urban social hierarchy or a question of social mobility, but is also related to a spatial differentiation of social indicators, and a regionalization or segregation of the urban community. Thus, place of residence reflects social status, and social indicators are organized in specific patterns giving distinctive social topographies. During the period of regionalization in geography, in the 1950s and 1960s, social areas were defined and mapped for individual towns, especially in a cross-sectional fashion.[3] Social area analysis, based on urban social indicators, was elaborated to reflect the regional differentiation of the internal social structure of a city. This is still a rewarding line of investigation although, when generalized too much by postulating simple homogeneous social quarters, it can obscure the actual social patterns. In order to avoid such generalizations, more detailed research is required, and in particular an examination of the place of residence at the level of the family and household, their social status and social structure. Analysis must descend to the most basic levels of social structure, which might be assembled by mapping social indicators house by house, family by family and also separately indicator by indicator. Social topography attempts to answer the question: who is who and where and why? Within the study of social topography a number of key indicators or indices can be recognized:

1. Density of population: residents/households per building.
2. Housing standard: building classification, size, quality, value of residence.
3. Type of residence: owner occupier, tenant, sub-tenant, lodger, etc.
4. Occupations and trade.
5. Income and property ownership.

Historical social topography (*Sozialtopographie*),[4] which aims to reconstruct distribution patterns of social indicators in towns, has to rely on
statistical data at a household basis. Another precondition for such research
is the availability of the personal data for the entire urban community
and that addresses allow one to locate information on a town plan as accurately as possible. Quite often substantial statistical material is available
for a complete urban population, but an address or topographic reference
is unfortunately missing. Furthermore, there is often a lack of any contemporary large-scale town plans with a numbered key relating to the statistical
material, and this condition will generally restrict this approach to a few
possible selected case studies and cross-sections for earlier periods, or from
the nineteenth century onwards.

As early as 1857 Wilhelm Heinrich Riehl, in his studies on Augsburg,
wrote a chapter entitled: 'The townplan as a layout plan of society'.[5] In
addition, in 1933 Karl Friedrich Leonhardt, a German historian, was the
first to compile a detailed and complete map of occupations in the town
of Hannover for the year 1435, based on the evaluation of tax assessments.[6]
His new approach made him a pioneer, but – as happens quite often to
unexpected progress – nobody followed up this innovation. Nearly forty
years passed before interest in the reconstruction and analysis of detailed
social patterns emerged. Thus, it was during the 1970s that a number of
contributions were made for different towns, so that regularities or similarities in social patterns began to be established, which in turn led to a series
of comparative studies.[7]

The approach that most of the research in Germany has followed is
an empirical one, based on the topographic reconstructions of residential
and occupational locations and resulting distribution patterns; evaluating
various written sources and only then proceeding to an analysis of the
social meaning of place, distance or spatial relations. In addition, attempts
were made to derive base models of social ecology from theories of social
stratification. Studies by Sjoberg[8] should be mentioned in this connection,
but Langton,[9] raising persuasive arguments, came to the conclusion that
most of these theories have nothing to do with the social reality at all and
that they construct a social hierarchy and stratification which did not exist.
In this respect there is no doubt that empirical, inductive work must come
first, based on the evaluation and mapping of statistical source material.

Social stratification certainly was a factor which contributed to the spatial differentiation of a society, but one must also consider a number of other aspects of social indicators, such as occupation (within the context of social status), ability, skill, political status, wealth, general economic development, regulations or dependencies directing place of residence and work. Finally, simple pragmatic needs also have to be taken into account, which formed and changed the pattern of residence and place of work in medieval as well as in modern towns.

Statistical techniques have so far only been used in a limited way, since most of the studies are dealing with periods before 1850 and with small towns with a limited amount of data. For the development of meaningful models more case studies on a comparable basis are needed, as results are not yet sufficient to produce any overall conclusions.

Against this background the focus of this chapter will be on research in Germany and on German towns. However, within this context it becomes difficult to follow a strictly national view or standpoint, since much of the research reflects a growing tendency towards an international debate.

Social indicators and their patterns

Population density, households per building and interior size of dwelling

Simple distribution patterns of population in medieval and early modern towns show that there were usually remarkable differences in density (*Bevölkerungsdichte*). Along main streets, around the market place and in bigger towns in specific districts low densities may be observed, whereas high densities were quite often concentrated in peripheral quarters. This was not associated with any use of space for retail business or with a city development, as these factors did not play a great role in medieval towns, but was related to social status. Thus, there was a correlation between the interior size of the dwelling and the social status of a family. There were already in medieval times large buildings in central parts of the town and smaller, more modest dwellings on the periphery. The pattern of available housing space was therefore inversely proportional to the density of households or the number of residents.[10] The small houses were, especially since early modern times, overcrowded with tenants and lodgers, whereas the more spacious houses situated in the central streets of the town offered far more square metres per head. The owners or occupants were able to pay for this standard of housing and living. Unfortunately it is difficult to obtain any detailed data on living space per head for a medieval town, because the complete number of heads per family is rarely given before about 1750 and furthermore there is rarely any data on dwelling space per house.[11]

The pattern of heads per house (*Behausungsdichte*) or at least households per house (*Parteienziffer*) is a very distinctive one, increasing as one moves from central locations to the periphery. Braunschweig in 1758 (one of the bigger towns in northern Germany with 22,000 inhabitants) is a good example for the modern period. The town had developed since the middle ages out of a number of nuclei or primarily separated settlements, which also differed in their social and economic structure. They were finally combined in the late middle ages into the city of Braunschweig, with the result that the population density in 1758 was a mosaic of a number of genetic quarters.[12]

In contrast to a number of other social indicators, a low density is generally related to high status areas, and high density to low status areas. This may not be very surprising, but if we succeed in reconstructing detailed proportions of high and low density for a greater number of towns or their quarters, this might give, within the frame of comparative regional studies, some further insight into standards of living within regional urban systems.

Building classification

It is well known that the standard and quality of a house reflects the social and economic status of its owner or resident. Many studies following social regionalization of nineteenth- and twentieth-century towns drew their conclusions from a qualitative analysis of the existing building fabric.[13] However, for earlier historical periods very often buildings have not survived, although classifications in quality and status exist, which allow a reconstruction of detailed distribution patterns of housing standards. For taxation and also for fire insurance purposes during the seventeenth and eighteenth centuries the building fabric of many German towns was divided into three, four or sometimes even more classes of quality (*Häuserklassen*). Usually we do not know the criteria used, but generally it was the number of storeys, the size of the house, the space available, the building material, the actual condition and perhaps also the size of the plot. Reconstructed patterns of any building classifications or standards of construction clearly show a social hierarchy from principal streets to by-lanes and finally to small lanes at the periphery along the town walls.[14] No doubt this pattern also reflected a classification of the value of house and property.[15]

But how, when and why did such a pattern develop? After all, there are examples of planned medieval towns that show the opposite in the hierarchy of this core-periphery pattern. Rinteln, Stadthagen and a number of other, especially thirteenth-century, planned towns in Germany were laid out in one or two parallel main streets, surrounded by an oval of mansions with large properties. This fringe belt of mansions of feudal landlords (*Burgsitze*, *Freihöfe*) was attached directly to the town wall, and it appears that the function of defence was behind this concept, as the back of the fortified stone buildings formed a main part of the town wall. However, these towns are the exceptions, although in some instances they are probably primary stages of urban development, for which there is evidence in most planned feudal towns. Usually, however, a clear hierarchical ranking of the streets existed, arranged from the centre (the high street, or a number of main streets) to the periphery. These main streets, usually the genetic nuclei of a town, always had the advantage in development since they were highly preferred sites. This was a matter of prestige, status and social order in the medieval urban society of patricians, merchants and upper-class craftsmen, organized in gilds, all of whom wanted to be represented in the centre of the city. This pattern and spatial order demonstrated and reflected the hierarchy of the urban society, and also led to a hierarchy of property values. There is also evidence that in many cases this hierarchy of place was and had to be accepted. There was a social law and order that directed the market of real estate and the place of residence according to rank in the medieval urban society. This began to change slowly from the seventeenth century, but, in general, especially in smaller towns, the pattern survived up to the nineteenth century.

In German medieval towns there was also a very important legal distinction between houses with brewing rights (*Brauhäuser*) and those without these rights (*Buden*). The ideal quality value of a house was raised by these rights, as the rights were attached to the house and plot, and not to the owner himself. Houses with brewing rights (generally 30% to 50% of all the houses of a town) were always concentrated along the main streets.[16]

Patterns of owner occupants and tenants

A very important indicator of a social structure of a town is the proportion of owner occupants on the one hand and tenants and sub-tenants on the other. By the late middle ages there were already enormous differences among German towns, with a broad increase in tenants during the sixteenth century (Table 10.1).

A complete map of medieval Germany giving the proportions of owner occupants and tenant households would clearly show that towns with a high percentage of tenants and sub-tenants were those with increasing immigration and modern urban production. These towns had the first beginnings of manufacturing and 'industrial' production together with communities of consumers, who had no means of subsistence. These settlements were unlike the small agricultural towns where houseownership usually also meant ownership of land and agricultural production at least for subsistence. Dresden, Augsburg and Leipzig no doubt were such progressive cities during late medieval times. There were also remarkable differences between

Table 10.1 *Variations in levels of owner occu-pants in selected German towns*

Town	Period	% of tenants
Rostock	1404	17
	1430	19
Mühlhausen	1418	20
	1552	28
Leipzig	1554/6	23/65
Dresden	1488	44
	1562	52
Augsburg	1498	44
	1554	55

different quarters within a single town (see Leipzig, Table 10.1).

The highest proportions of tenants were usually found in the suburbs or in the periphery of the inner town, whereas in the inner-urban quarters or in central areas there was a minimum of tenant households. A differentiated pattern would certainly show up within each district or even within each street. Unfortunately, for the medieval and even for the early modern period, the lack of sources does not allow detailed household studies. We may presume, however, that tenants and lodgers were concentrated in the back lanes and that they were far more segregated than in the smaller towns. From the middle of the nineteenth century onwards there is sufficient data, particularly to be found in directories, for it to be possible to reconstruct the distribution pattern of tenants, but as yet these studies have not been undertaken for many settlements.

Patterns of occupations and trades

Occupations and trades were linked directly with the social hierarchy, especially in the medieval society, and so they form an important indicator in the context of social topography, though their pattern of location also reflects economic needs. Thus, research on occupational patterns (*Gewerbe-topographie*) has tended to become a special field of interest.

It is commonly suggested that in a medieval town occupational groups were separated and clustered in specific streets (*Handwerkergassen*) or quarters (*Handwerkerviertel*).[17] This pattern would seem to be documented by street names which were present in nearly every medieval town, such as 'Baker Street', 'Butcher Lane' or 'Coppersmith Street'.[18] These names imply a clear segregation and accumulation of occupations similar to the bazaars in oriental cities.[19] However, it must be questioned whether this suggestion coincides with the historic reality, either in all types of European towns or for different periods. Most of the recent studies suggest that a clustered pattern rarely occurred or that it only existed in an early or later stage of development under special circumstances.[20]

There tended to be specific patterns for distinctive occupations, trades or crafts. The reasons for the development of any specific pattern might vary (special needs, regulations, spatial regulations to customers, etc.) Quite often a remarkable persistence in the type of pattern can be observed, but on the other hand the patterns often underwent substantial changes and variations, influenced by economic and social development.

No doubt the site of a number of trades was predetermined by the special needs for production, such as a waterflow, or by measures of fire precautions. This is the case with fishermen, shipwrights, millers, tanners and dyers as well as potters and founders.[21] They were relegated to the waterfront, to the waterflow or to the periphery of the built-up area. There is also a suggestion that regulations against pollution in medieval times, which ordered certain trades and crafts to settle in distinct locations, may have been of some importance.[22] Tanners nearly always lived in comparable quarters, next to a waterflow going out of a town, and even today many of these tanners' quarters are well known as such, for example in Strassburg, Colmar, Ulm and Freiburg.[23] However, crafts which used open fires or which caused pollution of water or air were not always clustered or located in peripheral areas.[24] It would seem that where such a cluster did exist it was often as a result of the passing of new regulations, necessitated, for example, by fire damage or by general urban reorganization. In many instances, these regulations tended to fall into disuse, whilst in other cases, regulations were not enforced at all.

The location of other trades and occupations was clearly determined by their customers. Thus cartwrights, wheelwrights or farriers were often located near the town-gates; sometimes also in suburban extensions, where the waggons entered the town, thus producing a place of immediate demand.[25] Butchers, bakers and often tailors were dispersed throughout the town, in order to accommodate the daily needs of nearby customers.[26] This sales-oriented pattern generally shows a further internal differentiation by standard, that is by social areas (documented for example by differences in wealth or tax rates and their distribution patterns).

However, among butchers, and to a lesser extent bakers, clustered patterns were sometimes observed.[27] Butchery was one of the few crafts where production and sales quite often were separated. The residences of the butchers, together with the slaughterhouses, therefore might have been dispersed, whereas the special stalls and shambles (*Scharren*, *Metzig*) were located at the market or at a special site in the centre of the town – usually by order of the town authorities, in an attempt to control the sale of products. In these circumstances the houses of the butchers may have been oriented towards these central stalls. This was also the case with the bakers in some larger cities, as for example in Lübeck.[28] The bakeries and bakers' homes were dispersed throughout the town, whereas the bread was sold in a central place (*Brotscharren*) from medieval times up to the seventeenth century.

Related to social stratification or to the social hierarchy of occupations was the centralized pattern of merchants and upper-class craftsmen. They owned houses around the market place or along the central parts of the main streets of a town. Textile workers, weavers, cloth makers, workmen, day labourers or unskilled craftsmen on the other hand clustered around small streets or lanes and accumulated towards the periphery along the town walls, living in between their workshops.[29]

Research on the spatial pattern of trade and retailing in preindustrial German towns as yet remains limited, although some projects have been started. The merchants' trading house (*Kaufhaus, Kophus*) was situated in a central position in the town and some of their trade was conducted there.[30] Other merchants had temporary stalls on market or fair days near the market place or along some of the main streets.[31]

Miners, tanners and sometimes also wine-dressers formed specific social and communal groups. They very often lived in distinct quarters, clearly dominating all other occupations, and gave these quarters a special character. This is evident from the type and size of house, more or less standardized, adapted to their needs. Culture and daily life was also characterized by their specific occupation and habits. For example, in the mining town of Goslar there even existed a separate settlement for the miners (Bergdorf) with its own wall, attached to the main town of Goslar. When this separate town was destroyed during the fifteenth century, the miners moved into a special quarter in the west of the town (Frankenberger Viertel), occupying most of the houses in this area, until the nineteenth century.[32]

The wine-dressers in Stuttgart formed a similar dominating group, where, for example, in the late eighteenth century 23% of all houses in the Esslinger Vorstadt were occupied by families engaged in this occupation. There were also two other similar clusters, one in the southern part of the central town, the other in the Reiche Vorstadt.[33]

The persistence of these patterns, usually only elaborated in one or two cross-sections, is difficult to determine because of the limited number of case studies. It seems as if, however, in some respects there was a remarkable persistence of location and types of distribution patterns. Conversely, there were also changes which related to the variations in the number of craftsmen, the efficiency of regulations and the changed economic importance of specific trades. Gild regulations may also have influenced the locational pattern of crafts and shops as also did changes in the inner-urban building fabric, caused by fires, urban expansion and changes in the defence system.

An exploratory attempt to follow an unbroken line of development of houseownership and occupations house by house for a complete town has been made for Seesen between 1670 to 1950.[34] In this study, persistence and change may be followed in detail and the unbroken record allows conclusions to be drawn regarding the mobility of property ownership, and the stability or change in social ecology (Figure 10.1). This longitudinal study also reflects periods of drastic change or of stagnation. Thus, for example, it might be seen that the pursuit of agriculture, where it existed at all, came to an end in the town during the second half of the nineteenth century. The same is true for weaving and cloth making, which were previously well represented. This approach could be very fruitful and in addition promises to answer numerous questions relating to the dynamics of urban social ecology. It means going beyond cross-sections and proceeding to study longitudinal lines of development, which finally leads to a consideration of residential occupational mobility and property inheritance.

Occupational and social status

In medieval times and up to the beginning of the nineteenth century, a social hierarchy of occupations and gilds was essential. Merchant, baker, shoemaker, butcher, smith, tailor and weaver was a common hierarchy in German towns, although there were also many individual variations from town to town as well as historical changes. Significantly, this hierarchy of occupations is closely related to the hierarchy of social stratification, which is the main agent behind any occupational grouping.

However, within each stratum of this social hierarchy of occupation there is another stratification, a hierarchy in wealth. A number of studies have focussed on this question with regard to social stratification and its relation to trade or craft, as well as the hierarchy of place of residence.[35] The differentiation in wealth of any occupational group shows quite often that there were poor and rich members together in a group of craftsmen or gild, although there were differences in proportion relating to the kind of craft. The question is whether it was the status determined by occupation or the status based on wealth which had priority in determining the place of residence within a town.

There is evidence for some occupations, for example, merchants, leatherworkers, metalworkers, etc., that the rich as well as the poor of each group were represented together within particular inner-urban quarters. In such circumstances there was a mixture in wealth and not a spatial differentiation from the centre to the periphery or main street to side street. This situation was different with lower-class craftsmen and workers, such as weavers, who formed groups of mainly poor people, often living in the inner-urban periphery or in suburbs.

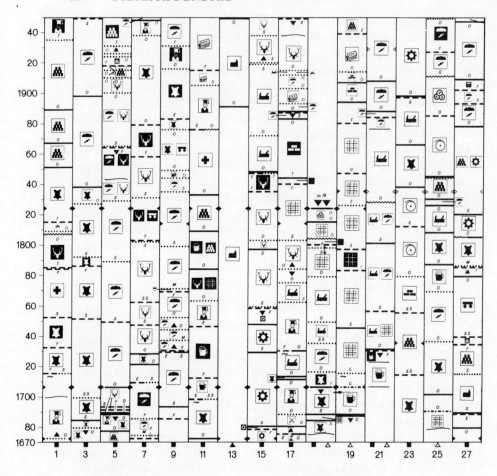

Groups of occupations/ production

Primary production
- agriculture, forestry
- mining

Crafts
- construction
- ironwork and metalwork
- woodwork
- leather and fur production
- textile production
- food
- paper and printing
- other crafts

Trade and transport
- wholesale and retailing
- transport

Administration, public service
- administration
- church, school
- military

Private service
- catering trade, hotel
- hygiene, medical service
- day labourer

Private maintenance
- funds, rent
- two different occupations at the same time
- continuation of trade by widow

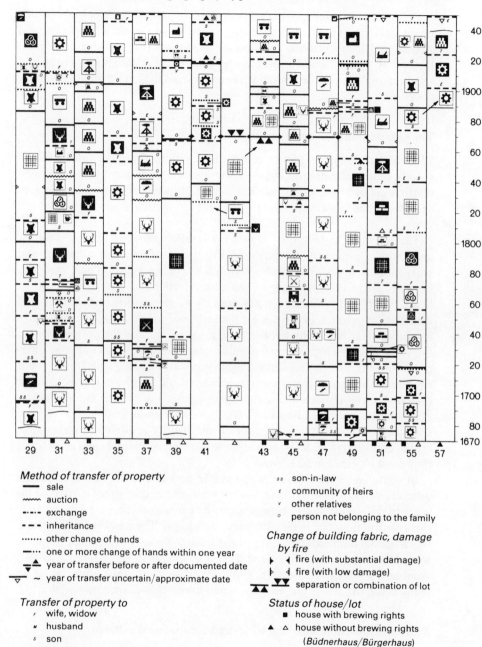

Figure 10.1 The continuity of property transfer and the occupation of house owners in Seesen, 1670–1950

Complicated social and spatial processes lie behind these patterns which might only be explained sufficiently on the basis of more cross-sectional studies and also by more detailed local analysis of economic and social factors. A general conclusion may be that when occupational status and status in wealth coincide, a spatial hierarchy from the centre to the periphery develops.

The distribution pattern of wealth

Wealth was the main agent in competition with the hierarchy of the feudal society during the middle ages. In some cases there may even have been restrictions of a real estate market, based on political or social influences or power, but these were often overt and are consequently hard to determine.

The statistical evidence of wealth is revealed mainly in tax assessments, and there are numerous studies on the social structure of medieval and early modern cities using such data on a broader scale. It is only recently, however, that tax rates have been plotted on maps house by house or hearth by hearth. Through these studies we get an idea of the detailed distribution patterns of wealth for a number of towns, and generally there is a quite clear hierarchy between the town centre and the periphery near the town walls.[36] However, we should not over-generalize the spatial interpretation, but use the advantage that comes from being able to represent each household in a social topographic map. At this level it is noticeable that within the clusters of wealthy people there were also numerous low tax payers, sometimes houseowners, but more often tenants. There was, therefore, not an explicit segregation of wealthy residents in the centre, but, in contrast, rich and poor people were often neighbours and sometimes they lived together in one house.

In some cases there were high taxable households located in a distant quarter, and quite often these houses were situated at street corners. This is a general and frequent observation, which is also expressed in the size, the construction and value of these buildings. The reason is that there was a special demand for corner plots, since the owner of a corner property was able to present his house with two frontages to the public, and thus dominate a street crossing. In addition, these plots were often taken up earlier than the rest of the vicinity, when lower-class people moved in.

Acts and regulations affecting social and occupational patterns

The general influence of regulations on urban social topography has to be investigated more closely. Unfortunately, little systematic work has been carried out on the early urban regulations and their impact on social topography. We know about numerous fire precautions of the seventeenth and eighteenth centuries, although most of them did not affect to any great extent the locations of crafts or trades. It was only orders or plans introduced after fire that in most cases led to a new arrangement of the street pattern and a new planned social topography.[37] We also know of a few local acts that were especially concerned with restrictions for noisome, odorous or perilous crafts, which were in some cases ordered expicitly to move out of town or to withdraw to a distant quarter in the periphery. In Strassburg at the end of the fifteenth century the bakers were ordered to move and settle beyond the town walls. The same happened to the 'Bender' (wood-workers who produced bent timbers) in Rothenburg; similarly in Würzburg the potters were moved out to the suburbs at the end of the fourteenth century because of fire precautions. An exclusive concentration within a distinct quarter or street was ordered by an act in 1402 in Frankfurt for the 'Bender' and during the sixteenth century in Siegen for the blacksmiths and the locksmiths as well as for the butchers and the tanners.

It is also documented that soapmakers, candlemakers, dyers, potters, limeburners, tile and brickmakers had to have their workshops, yards or kilns out of town, separated from any residential areas. This means that, at least in certain towns, sites of workshops and places of residence might have been separated at an early date. This fact needs therefore to be taken into account when mapping occupations, since the past understanding has been that place of residence, place of production and even place of sale were identical from medieval times up to the nineteenth century. However, it should also be stressed that though these regulations were enacted, they then generally fell into disuse, as did most medieval laws, for want and will of power to execute them. The medieval way was to understand very clearly what ought to be done, then to pass a law commanding that thing to be, but after that the power of execution was often never pursued. Unfortunately in towns for which regulations are known it is not possible to reconstruct past distribution patterns and so we cannot directly prove the effectiveness of these regulations.

Another question which is not yet sufficiently resolved is whether the gilds enacted regulations which led especially to the clustering of their members, as reflected in so many occupational street names. It is, no doubt, plausible that the gilds had an interest in concentrating their members and also the production as far as possible in a distinct quarter, in order to have a better control of work and price levels. Mutual assistance and sound competition might have been further reasons for working and living closely together. We may presume this, knowing about the general aims of the medieval gilds, but the analysis of the documents and the enormous amount of studies devoted to the history and organization of the gilds have yielded little that might prove the above suggestions.

It seems possible that in many cases regulations existed and that they indeed resulted in distinct locational patterns, but that on the other hand in many towns some gilds did not exist, or they had lost power and influence to stabilize a concentration of related activities. Moreover, there were a number of forces operating against this segregation of crafts, such as prices of property, inheritance and marriage patterns. These factors very often led to the abandonment of a segregated pattern, as is shown in a number of studies.

There were also idealized, imaginary land use patterns in a medieval town, such as the model of an ideal city, which Albrecht Dürer, the famous German artist of Nürnberg, drew up in 1527.[38] The ground plan is a totally geometric one, consisting of rectangles and quadrangles with all the occupations and crafts concentrated in distinct quarters (see Figure 10.2). The concept of social stratification may be proved by the inner ring of servants of court and the mansions and residences of noblemen around the large central place. The idea of fire precautions may be evident in that the quarter containing founders and smiths is in the one corner of the town away from other activities. Interesting and hard to explain is the fact that the church is not located in the centre of the town but in an outer corner, surrounded by tradesmen. The ideal model may give an idea of a theoretical order that might have existed in late medieval times, but the reality usually differed greatly as is shown by studies of social topography.

Patterns of intra-urban residential mobility

Intra-urban moves today are a most general phenomenon and many social and geographical studies have already been devoted to this process. In historic periods, prior to industrialization, this residential mobility within the town walls was quite limited, as there were few moves to locations beyond the walls, except in the very large towns, where suburbs had already developed.

One reason for a limited intra-urban mobility, especially in small towns, was the relatively high proportion of houseownership. On the other hand, there were also in earlier times a number of determinants of residential mobility. Hitherto, observations have shown that the patterns of intra-urban mobility in medieval towns were closely related to the patterns of social areas. This meant that the move was usually over a short distance, quite often to a near neighbourhood or quarter. For the preindustrial town no fundamental research has yet been carried out, but there are some initial results for the nineteenth- and early twentieth-centuries.[39]

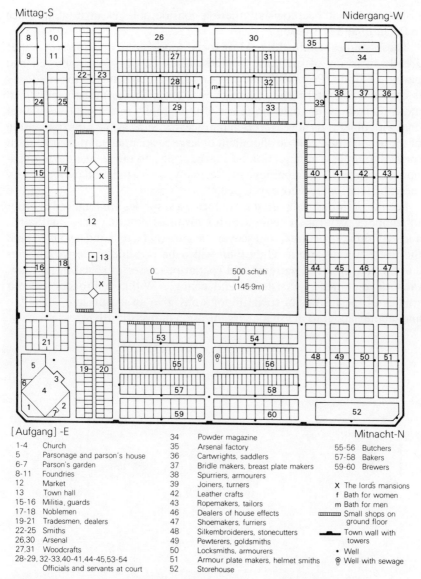

Figure 10.2   Land use patterns of a model medieval town by Dürer (1527)

Mittag-S

Nidergang-W

[Aufgang] -E

Mitnacht-N

1-4	Church	34	Powder magazine
5	Parsonage and parson's house	35	Arsenal factory
6-7	Parson's garden	36	Cartwrights, saddlers
8-11	Foundries	37	Bridle makers, breast plate makers
12	Market	38	Spurriers, armourers
13	Town hall	39	Joiners, turners
15-16	Militia, guards	42	Leather crafts
17-18	Noblemen	43	Ropemakers, tailors
19-21	Tradesmen, dealers	46	Dealers of house effects
22-25	Smiths	47	Shoemakers, furriers
26,30	Arsenal	48	Silkembroiderers, stonecutters
27,31	Woodcrafts	49	Pewterers, goldsmiths
28-29, 32-33,40-41,44-45,53-54		50	Locksmiths, armourers
	Officials and servants at court	51	Armour plate makers, helmet smiths
		52	Storehouse

55-56	Butchers
57-58	Bakers
59-60	Brewers

X	The lord's mansions
f	Bath for women
m	Bath for men
▥	Small shops on ground floor
▬	Town wall with towers
•	Well
◉	Well with sewage

Conclusion

The reconstruction and interpretation of the social topography of pre-industrial towns have only recently become of general interest. Apart from the studies in Germany, which were taken up by historical geographers, historians and archaeologists,[40] there is considerable research taking place in Poland[41] and in Sweden.[42]

These studies within the field of social topography do, however, differ greatly in terms of methods, sources, research questions followed and period of study. For the medieval period the feudal hierarchy of society is essential for interpreting place of residence. In the modern period of industrialization the question of social topography or social ecology must deal with numerous new aspects and processes, such as the rapid expansion of the urban fringe, the development of large residential quarters of explicit social differences, immigration on a large scale and the residential segregation of migrant communities. In Germany such studies have only very recently been extensively developed.[43]

For the preindustrial period more local case studies are required in order to compare patterns or sequences for towns of differing sizes, and social and economic structures, to discover the general factors and agents behind the distribution pattern. Only then will it be possible to derive theories and models of social patterns and spatial processes of social interaction, their development, persistence and change. Within a broader context studies of the history of social topography give an insight into social life and labour, and into the spatial organization of historic urban societies.

11

The economic and social spatial structure of an early industrial town: Aachen

CLAUDIA ERDMANN

Introduction

French rule over the left bank of the Rhineland did not extend beyond two decades (1794–1814), yet this period was sufficient to bring about important changes in the economic and social structure of the region. Furthermore, due to fundamental political and technical innovations the pre-industrial phase was brought to its conclusion, and early industrialisation could take its course without much obstruction.

The former Free Imperial City of Aachen played a special role in this respect as it was designated the capital of the new Roer-Department under its Prefect. Geopolitically, Aachen thus gained a decisive advantage over the Rhenish towns of Köln and Bonn which were situated at the border.[1] This pre-eminent administrative position tended to favour and strengthen its previous urban functions: the traditional trade in cloth and needles. The example of this town therefore lends itself particularly well to the process of tracing the transition from the pre-industrial to the industrial era. An additional factor is the existence of reliable sources, in particular a complete population census which covered the entire population (1812: approximately 30,000) and categorised it individually according to residence, marital status, age, occupation and religion.[2]

Not only does this enable us to investigate the contemporary urban structure within Aachen but also to point out characteristic features that might be typical of early industrial towns generally. In this field of geographical research, however, the situation as regards published material is not at all favourable. Whereas contemporary urban geography is usually well served with sufficient information and statistics, the sparse number of publications covering the historical dimension is explained by the scarcity of relevant data and sources. Recently a number of studies concerning Victorian towns have been published in Great Britain;[3] their results, however, are exclusively based upon the census results between 1851 and 1871. In doing so, such studies deal with economic and socio-geographical conditions in well-developed industrial towns. However, as regards the middle and end of the eighteenth century, in Britain, source material relevant to spatial analysis is somewhat problematical.[4] Yet from an urban-geographical perspective this period is a crucial one since it was in the course of early industrialisation that Europe's towns experienced a decisive structural change that pointed the way to further developments.

Thus, the type of early industrial town has much more frequently aroused the interest of the economic or social historian than that of the historical geographer. The city of Aachen therefore offers the opportunity to throw some light on this aspect, particularly as it followed a development which appears to be comparable to that of other European towns. During the Middle Ages it was one of Europe's trading centres for long-distance trade. Later, it shared the fate of many other economic foci, a continued decline in importance, until it was able to move forward into a new age based on early industrialisation due to French political initiative. Before considering such changes, however, it is necessary to define typical features for both pre-industrial and industrial towns. Bearing in mind that any over-simplification produces its problems, one nevertheless may use Sjoberg's concept (as a working hypothesis) to categorise types of towns according to the degree of technical development.[5] The main criteria applied are technology, economic organisation, social organisation and use of space.

Technological and economic change

According to Sjoberg, technology – the most important feature in determining economic change – is reduced to human and animal power in a pre-industrial town. Inevitably, production is thereby limited in quantity. In an industrial town, on the other hand, full mechanisation means infinitely greater production of goods which are, in addition, standardised.

Sjoberg's criteria of a pre-industrial town apply fully to the town of Aachen. This can be clearly demonstrated with regard to Aachen's main products: cloth and needles. The medieval cloth trade, based upon small local streams and hot springs, was stimulated further through a privilege granted by Barbarossa in 1166. It soon developed into an important long-distance trade, although until the French period it was entirely dependent upon human labour. The same applies to the needle trade which from the early seventeenth century had taken over from the previously significant metal trade (brass). Technical innovation started in these two leading trades during the Napoleonic period. The manual production of cloth was successively displaced by the use of machinery. Typically, this amelioration first occurred in the capital-intensive firms of the most prosperous cloth manufacturers.[6] As recorded in a report of the Prefect dated 1807, steam engines were already employed for dyeing cloth whereas most other machines were driven either by water-power or operated by hand.[7] A similar development occurred in the needle trade, since its early mechanisation and concomitant economic success also started in Napoleonic times.

These innovations caused a significant increase in production, clearly to be seen from the total value of goods produced. Thus, total cloth production in 1806 was valued at 9m frs, whilst four years later the value had risen to 11m frs.[8] Considering that the total value of production was 15m frs the tremendous significance of the highly specialised cloth trade to the economy becomes apparent and reveals the lesser importance of needle manufacturing. Nevertheless, both trades could, as they became increasingly mechanised, raise their production to a significant extent. A further criterion of early industrialisation is thereby met.

The causes of this development are by no means only technological, however; without changes in both economic as well as social organisation (some of which started prior to the French period) these innovations could not have been nearly as successful. Consequently, our attention must now be directed to forms of organisation.

Economy in the pre-industrial town is, according to Sjoberg, dominated by the guilds, division of labour practised according to age, sex and occupation; and as a rule the worker's home contains also his workplace. A further characteristic is that there is little standardisation of price, measures, weights, currency and quality beyond the immediate locality.

In contrast, freedom of trade in the industrial town results in greater independence of the individual, hand in hand with division of labour, according to the degree of specialisation. Thus production is separated from sale and the home is no longer also the workplace. This process results in the phenonemon of the factory. Mass production also requires, in addition, the introduction of standardised prices, measures, weights and quality.

It is possible in this respect also to cite the development of Aachen. A number of street names, particularly in the vicinity of the market, have left traces of the former concentration of certain medieval guilds in the area; of these, the most important one was beyond any doubt that of the clothiers. This trade which had already reached a high degree of specialisation and division of labour in the Middle Ages required, earlier than others, a tight organisation. Therefore, it is not possible to agree with Sjoberg when he stipulates the absence of such diversified trades as typical of the pre-industrial town.[9] In Aachen as in other towns the economic, social and political status of the members of the guild were determined by the strict rules of the craft court.[10]

This organisation experienced its first changes after the fifteenth century, although their full impact was not felt until the seventeenth century, coming first within the needle trade, and then spreading into other economic activities. Thus, the transition from production by craftsmen to the decentralised putting-out system marked a decisive turning point.[11] There were two distinct processes in the needle trade: the 'Rauhwirker' had the task of cutting the needles, pointing them and making the eye; the finishing process was done by the 'Schönmeister' or the agent who was also responsible for the packing and sale.[12] Thus, the independent master of the Middle Ages became the wage employee of the agent who may, therefore, be regarded as a forerunner of the new capitalist economic system.[13] This structural change led to a significant increase in production which, in turn, caused the number of masters in the trade to rise from about 100 needle masters in 1660 to 200 by 1700.[14]

The guild regulations proved a good deal more long-lived as regards Aachen's cloth trade. Protestant clothiers in particular were compelled to leave the town, so that any expansion of their firms by the putting-out system had to take place in the neighbouring villages of Burtscheid, Vaals, Verviers and Monschau during the seventeenth and eighteenth centuries. There they were not restricted by guild regulations and succeeded in establishing a flourishing cloth trade. Within the Free Imperial City of Aachen, however, the final dismantling of the old economic organisation did not occur until the French period. It was then that the customs barriers which restricted trade on the left bank of the Rhine were abolished by the Treaty of Lunéville (1801). The political unity of the left bank decisively favoured the trading role: to compensate for the loss of markets on the right bank of the Rhine new markets opened up, e.g. the Levant and Turkey which were supported by customs policy.[15] In addition, the Continental Blockade (1806/7–12) resulted in the elimination of powerful English economic competition and further concentration of the French trading area. While it is true to say that these measures led to economic prosperity an even greater stimulus was provided by a thoroughgoing internal reorganisation of administration. The standardisation of the law and of taxation, religious liberty and social equality between town and country within the French sphere provided a firm foundation for the establishment of flourishing trade.

The most decisive act, however, was probably the introduction of freedom of trade (Law of 26 March 1798) which lifted all restrictions imposed by guilds and thus stimulated individual enterprise based upon the factors of production: capital and labour. Nevertheless, private enterprise was henceforth controlled by the Chambers of Trade and trade 'courts'.[16] Official quality regulations for goods destined for the long-distance markets had been introduced; these were based on standardised units of measures and weights, applied throughout the whole French Empire. A further condition indicating the change from the pre-industrial to the industrial period had been met. Similar to the practice during the economic heyday of the guilds the cloth was stamped and the best quality goods awarded prizes at industrial exhibitions, three of which took place in Aachen (1807, 1810, 1813). State awards for newly developed machinery offered a further incentive to mechanisation in the various trades.

Thus, the economic organisation of Aachen in 1812 was characterised by the putting-out system in trades that were export-orientated. Closely linked to this had been the rise of manufacturing firms since the middle of the eighteenth century. The commercial tracts were located vertical to the street on either side, whereas the dwelling-house of the manufacturer and his family connected these two wings in the back of the courtyard. According to Fischer these developments dominated early industrial enterprise in Aachen.[17] In contrast, the high industrial period in the mid-nineteenth century was characterised by the regional separation of factory and residence of the factory owner.

Even for the French period, however, there are examples of such physical separation; it occurred wherever monastic buildings were secularised and placed at the disposal of manufacturers. Organisational and technical innovations were reflected in the emergence of new occupational terms such as 'fileur à la mécanique', 'contre-maître', 'chef ouvrier'. Overseers and foremen took the place of the master. These changes were the first indication of a growing decline of the hierarchic putting-out system: apprentice/journeyman – master – merchant (agent).

In conclusion, it may be said that the economic system, whose medieval structure had already been significantly modified by the putting-out system, received its decisive legal impetus in the French period by which it was propelled into the early industrial period. The decentralised organisation, with masters working for other firms, accounted for the majority of Aachen's production of cloth and needles, yet at the same time the demand for progressive physical concentration of production was already being voiced. Thus, it was that manufacturers gained in importance, both in number and economically, supported by technical developments.

Social organisation

It is self-evident that the technical and economic changes affected the social structure of the town of Aachen as it then was. In several respects it did not conform to Sjoberg's criteria typical of a pre-industrial town (rigid class system, ethnic-religious education limited to the elite, dominance of religion and personal unity of legislative and executive). The theory that the pre-industrial town was dominated by a two-class system has no validity as far as Europe is concerned; for the medieval town contained the numerically significant class of the burghers and thus had a three-class society.[18]

Any attempt to deal with social classes, particularly in their historical dimensions, presents a serious problem; once again, the situation with regard to sources is decisive. Studies often confine themselves to a mere listing of various occupations within the population without explaining what the social status was that a particular occupation conferred.[19] There are reservations too arising from the possibility that the structure within a certain trade was heterogeneous. It is essential therefore that further criteria must be used, quantifiable and able to develop an objective social stratification expressing inter-human dependency, distance and hierarchy. One such criterion is income, which during the first phase of industrialisation mirrors fairly accurately the various social differentiations. Fortunately, Aachen's contemporary tax returns have been preserved. This fiscal evidence allows us to reconstruct the relative incomes of the population.

The hypothesis that the personal tax – a kind of earnings/income tax – permits us to reach conclusions as to social stratification is tested by its correlation with demographic variables. Often there is a close relationship between the relative importance of variables and the total amount of tax paid. The values arrived at by means of applying Spearman's correlation (ts) indicate either high positive or high negative correlations. High positive values are typical of the lower class whereas high negative values are characteristic of the upper classes. There are further variables with low values of correlation as their upper ranks fall into the middle category of taxation groups. They provide additional information on the middle classes because of proved similarities. The original eleven taxation groups were reduced to five. On the basis of these data, the social distribution of Aachen's population at the time was as follows: 80% belonged to the lower class, 13% were lower middle class, 5% upper middle class, with the remaining 2% forming the upper class.

The upper class is defined by those variables with a minimum correlation factor of -0.9. This social class includes high administrative officials with the highest income. The trade function is indicated by the fact that a majority of clothiers and needle manufacturers belong to this group. What is also striking is the relatively high proportion of non-Catholics among the total population. It was only during the French period that this group was permitted to live and work in Aachen again. As a rule – comparable to the City of Cologne – the individuals were protestant entrepreneurs who moved into the town from the surrounding area or from the right bank of the Rhine and soon succeeded there. The prosperity of the upper class is well documented by its sizeable share of immovable property and by the number of domestic staff employed, which resulted in larger households when compared with other social groups.

Further contemporary sources confirm this social categorisation. Thus, in 1803 members of the upper class described as 'notables de cette commune' held a collection for a newly established welfare office.[20] To a large extent this group approach coincides with that nine years later. The social status of wealthy factory owners is also indicated by the fact that they held leading positions in administration, for example, the needle manufacturer de Guaita was Mayor of Aachen for many years. Interestingly, the highest positions in the Prefect's administration were, however, held exclusively by Frenchmen.

The middle class basically comprised the large group of people that produced goods for the local market and/or sold them. A representative group would be employees in the food sector. In contrast to those in the hotel and restaurant trade they would mainly be counted among the lower middle class. The middle class shows variables in the middle range of both positive and negative, providing further criteria for our classification.

The large body of employed persons belonging to the lower classes typified as wage earners such as journeymen, labourers hired by the day in trades both local and otherwise. They provided the entire workforce in the lower textile trades, whilst child labour was particularly widespread in the needle trade. Further evidence is provided by a list of persons receiving support from the Poor Administration in 1820, as shown in Table 11.2. Most of the people listed belonged to those occupations that had already, eight years earlier, been typical members of the lower class. A further social indicator was the spread of vaccination against smallpox which was also introduced in Aachen during the French period. The proportion of two- to four-year-old children that had not been vaccinated was significantly higher in lower-class households than among other social classes.

First indications of an early proletariat, directly linked to pauperism, which had been present since the Middle Ages, emerge from the social stratification of Aachen in 1812.[21] A similar analysis of tax returns for Augsburg (1396–1712) by Blendinger yielded a structure of lower ('have-nots'), middle and upper class.[22] At the beginning of the eighteenth century, he detected an increase in the proportion formed by the middle class, whilst it was often the merchants and traders that joined the ranks of the upper class. We do not have comparable analyses for Aachen, but at the beginning of the nineteenth century the proportion of the lower classes significantly increased in relation to the middle classes. This is another indicator of its early industrial structure, whose roots went back to the days when it was a Free Imperial City. Towards the end of the eighteenth century, it was the auxiliary trades of spoolers, combers and fullers that formed the beginnings of a proletariat, a development which was intensified during the French period due to technological advances. Significantly, similar observations for the area of Baden have been made by Fischer and for Barmen by Köllmann.[23]

The social criteria of the pre-industrial town as described by Sjoberg

Table 11.1 *A comparison of Sjoberg's model and the Aachen case study*

	Pre-industrial town	Early industrial town	Industrial town
Technology	Human and animal sources of power – limited production	Partial use of machinery – increased production	Mechanisation – mass production
Economic organisation	Guilds[1]	Introduction of freedom of trade	Freedom of trade
	Division of labour according to age, sex and occupation[2]	Division of labour partly according to age and sex, partly by degree of specialisation	Division of labour according to degree of specialisation of labour force
	Craftsman produces and sells[3]	Part-separation of production and sale	Separation of production and sale
	Little standardisation of price, measures, weights, currency and quality	Standardisation of price, measures, weights, currency and quality	Standardisation
	Home and workplace identical[4]	Partial separation of home and workplace	Separation of home and workplace
Social organisation	Two-class system:[5] rigid class system with lifestyle typical of class	Three-class system: relatively rigid class system	Three-class system: 'permeable' class system
	Education limited to upper class, ethical-religious basis	Education still basically limited to upper class; partly including natural sciences	Education for all classes; natural-science content
	Dominant role of religion	Subordinate role of religion	Subordinate role of religion
	Personal unity of legislative and executive	Separation of legislative and executive	Separation of legislative and executive

Table 11.1 (*cont.*)

	Pre-industrial town	Early industrial town	Industrial town
Utilisation of space	Low degree of urbanisation	Growing degree of urbanisation	High degree of urbanisation
	Differentiation within towns according to occupational and ethnic groups	Beginning of differentiation within towns according to financial potential	Differentiation according to financial potential
	Centre: administrative and religious institutions; residential areas of upper class[6]	Centre: commercial and administrative areas; residences of middle class, adjoining residential areas of upper class	Centre: business district, adjoining residential areas of lower class
	Periphery: residential areas of lower class	Periphery: residential areas of lower class	Periphery: residential areas of middle and upper classes

Characteristic features of the European pre-industrial town (deviation from Sjoberg's model):
[1] Middle Ages: guilds and/or *Verlagswesen*
[2] Partially already high degree of specialisation, e.g. cloth trade
[3] *Verlagswesen*: different persons involved in production and sale
[4] *Verlagswesen*: manufacture, i.e. separation of home and workplace
[5] Three-class society, cf. among others Jecht, 'Studien zur gesellschaftlichen Struktur der mittelalterlichen Städte'
[6] Centre: residential areas of middle and upper classes
Sources: pre-industrial and industrial town: Sjoberg, *The preindustrial city*; early industrial town: case study, Aachen

mainly seem to apply to the oriental type.[24] In contrast, the European town witnessed a change affecting the middle class in particular. On the one hand there was social decline, such as that of journeyman, who was in general unable to achieve the status of master, on the other there was social advance.[25] The early industrial proletariat was therefore composed of former members of the middle class as well as those that had already formed the lower class of both urban and rural society in the pre-industrial period.

In Napoleon's time the class system, with regard to education, remained relatively rigid in Aachen. Schooling of any kind was de facto limited to members of the higher social groups. However, state education, differentiated according to level of skill and intended to further the transmission of natural-scientific concepts, was introduced by law and took its place alongside those church institutions that had previously had a monopoly of higher education, orientated towards the humanities. Indeed, during the French period state control was extended over large areas of church

Table 11.2 *Employed persons being supported by the Poor Administration in Aachen, 1820*

Occupation		Number/percentage of persons
1 Textile manufacture and processing		783 (72.9%)
Among them: Spinners	281	
Wool carders	51	
Weavers	85	
Dyers	10	
Knitters	108	
Sewers	35	
Washers	53	
2 Metal processing		64 (6.0%)
Among them: Needlemakers	46	
3 Timber and leather trades		53 (5.0%)
Among them: Cobblers	15	
Shoemakers	13	
Wood carriers/gatherers	9	
4 Other trades		118 (11.0%)
Among them: Day labourers	40	
Charcoal burners	15	
Bleachers	12	
5 Personal services		56 (5.1%)
Domestic staff	11	
Total		1,074 (100%)

power, which received its most severe blow from the secularisation of the monasteries.

The economic and social organisation of Aachen in 1812 show important characteristics of the transition from pre-industrial to industrial town; further evidence is given by data regarding the utilisation of urban space. This analysis is particularly important because spatial variations provide a further important variable capable of explaining changes in economic and social structures.

The utilisation of urban areas

A comparison on the basis of those characteristics that Sjoberg regards as typical of pre-industrial towns (such as a relatively low degree of urbanisation, differentiation within towns according to occupational and ethnic groups' polarization between the core with its administrative and religious institutions including the elite's residences and the periphery with the space of the lower classes) yields clear differences when made with early industrial

Aachen in the French period; on the other hand, similarities to its pre-industrial condition also emerge. Despite the fact that the socio-economic spatial structure of the medieval period can only be described imperfectly (on account of the sparsity of source material), some significant statements of general validity can still be made. When the cloth trade flourished in the middle of the fourteenth century the Market Hill became the economic and social centre of the town. Merchants from far afield were accommodated in fifteen superior inns, mentioned in the wine tax register of 1438. The positioning of the monasteries founded in Aachen during the thirteenth and fourteenth centuries further underlines the significance of the town centre. They are all situated within, or adjoining, the inner – i.e. Barbarossa's – wall. The same applies to the residences of the nobility that can only be traced back for the later period after 1656, following the great fire. The medieval patrician houses may have been fewer in number, but as their sites were mainly unaffected by the catastrophe, their positions remained more or less the same. In contrast to Sjoberg's model, the town centre also housed the urban middle classes. The Krämviertel, south-east of the market and north-east of the cathedral, indicates the presence of a specific social group, the small merchants, already established in medieval times. However, the outer areas of the streets leading to the town gates were, as a rule, the location not of religious, administrative or guild buildings, but of the lower-class craftsmen, ancillary workers in the various trades and arable farmers.

However, this division of pre-industrial Aachen into an economically and socially superior centre, housing the middle and upper classes, and an inferior periphery, with its lower class, no longer existed at the beginning of the nineteenth century. One of the most significant factors creating such change was the incipient and later accelerating rate of urbanisation, triggered by mechanisation. The population increase may be described as enormous, since between 1782 and 1815 it went up by 53% from 21,000 to 32,000, most of which occurred in the period after 1801.

How can this demographically unusual development be explained? Natural population growth does not provide a satisfactory explanation, even though it can be shown that, on account of the introduction of vaccination, the death rate fell. The real cause of the increase was a migration of people from the vicinity of Aachen, within a radius of some 20–30 kilometres, into the town itself.[26] Using the registers of births and deaths and the annual population figures, we may calculate the percentage that migration contributed to the population increase for 1799 and 1812, which was 82% and 86% respectively. Subsequent years do not show such high levels.

The extent and nature of migration was determined by the expansion of Aachen's functions and importance which greatly increased during this

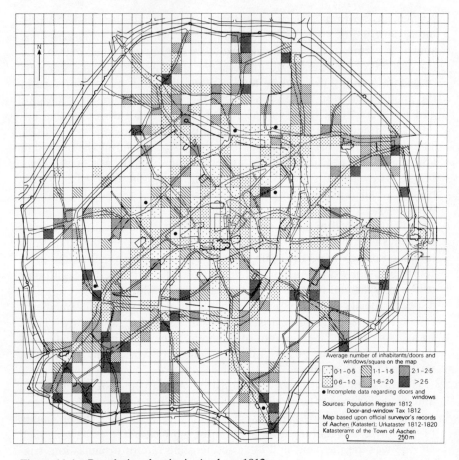

Figure 11.1   Population density in Aachen, 1812

period. The flourishing trades needed labour to such an extent that the town's own potential was totally insufficient, and this stimulated in-migration. Increasing urbanisation linked to a large population increase preceded the processes of segregation within the town that occurred during early industrialisation. As the area of the town was then still largely determined by the line previously formed by its late medieval walls, the population growth led to an accelerating density (Figure 11.1). Particularly affected were the streets leading to the gates which, as lower-class areas, became the chief 'targets' of immigration.

The change in Aachen's functions, however, had been already initiated in the eighteenth century when hot springs were developed in the north-eastern area within the inner town wall. Numerous new bath-houses caused a switch of 'tourism' functions from the market towards the eastern centre; this went hand-in-hand with social 'appreciation', as wealthy retired merchants increasingly settled in the area of the Seilgraben. This location had one further advantage that may have been decisive as far as cloth manufacturers were concerned in that it was close to the various brooks. It can also be shown that such locational advantages prompted some other well-to-do textile manufacturers to move into this part of the town.

This natural factor alone, however, is insufficient to explain the functional-spatial structure of Aachen during the Napoleonic period, for only some sections of Aachen's brooks were affected. The most successful clothier, for example, moved his residence from the Jakobstrasse, near the market, to the Karlsgraben, near the western part of Barbarossa's wall. Both residences were situated near to a brook, but as the Karlsgraben was less densely built up it offered better conditions for an expansion of the firm. In many other cases there is no spatial coincidence between running water and cloth manufacture. What was decisive as far as these merchant manufacturers were concerned was the fact that the new sites were in the wide, spacious 'Grabenstrassen' (streets next to the moat), of which the Komphausbadstrasse is representative. It was there that they commissioned Aachen's famous town architects Johann Joseph Couven (and his son Jakob) to build them town residences ('Höfe').

The changes that contributed to these developments explain the economic and social spatial structure of Aachen in 1812 as shown in Figure 11.2.

Basically, it is possible to distinguish three zones:

1. The centre was dominated by residents of the middle-income groups. The area of Büchel and the market, however, retained highly ranked (III) areas on account of its 'tourism' function as well as important trades being located there. The other sectors (II) accommodated, as they had done since the Middle Ages, local trades such as small shopkeepers, weavers' and grocers' shops ('Krämviertel' within Krämergasse).

2. Adjoining the centre were areas of highest social rank (IV). However, because of the insufficient number of this class, the area does not form a complete ring. On the whole it coincides with the 'Grabenstrassen' (streets next to the moat) and their immediate vicinity. This was mostly inhabited by protestant manufacturers, wealthy retired people. The average density of this area (0.5 persons/door and window-unit) is the lowest density of any area in the town. It should be noted that there are no data on floor areas, but data on door and window taxes have provided a meaningful and valid alternative.

3. The highest densities (more than 2 persons/door and window-unit) are to be found on the periphery of the town, particularly along the streets leading to the gates. These areas were mainly inhabited by members

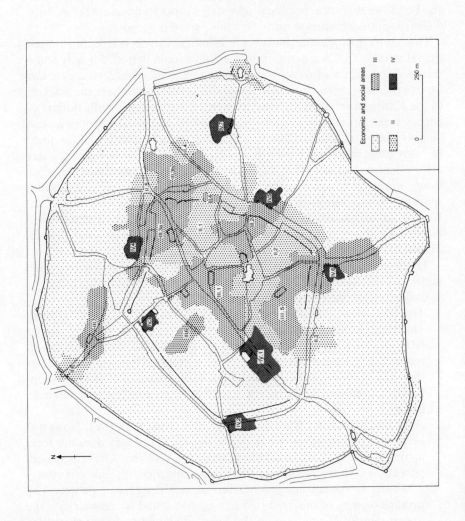

Area	Centre	Streets leading to gates	Periphery
I (up to 1Fr)			**3-6** B: Lower textile trade Occasional processing of textiles D: More than 1·6 persons
II (up to 2Fr)	**1-2** B: Local trade (shopkeepers, weavers, grocers) Administration Retired people D: 1-1·5 persons		**7** B: Textile processing Occasional lower textile trades D: Up to 1·5 persons **5-6** B: Retired people Farming D: Up to 1 person
III (up to 8Fr)	**1-2** B: Local trade Administration Retired people D: Up to 1 person **3a** B: Local trade Textile processing D: Up to 1 person	**3b** B: Inns etc. D: Up to 1 person **4** B: Retired people Textile processing D: Up to 0·5 persons	**7** B: Textile processing Manufacturers Retired people D: Up to 1 person B: Textile processing Manufacturers Retired people D: Up to 1·5 persons
IV (above 8Fr)	**1** B: Manufacturers with local firm D: Up to 0·5	**2-6** B: Manufacturers Retired people D: Up to 0·5	**7** B: Manufacturers Retired people D: Up to 0·5 persons

B = Occupation

Figure 11.2 The economic and social spatial structure of Aachen, 1812

of the lowest income groups, predominantly employed in manufacturing trades. The percentage of day labourers, journeymen, workers in the low textile and needle trades, working children and children that had not been vaccinated was particularly high here. In addition, small farmers, mainly in market gardening, cultivated small plots away from the streets leading to the gates.

In its economic and social spatial structure, Aachen during the Napoleonic Age shows the gradient from centre towards periphery which is typical of pre-industrial towns. In addition, Aachen contains a further zone adjoining the centre which developed into areas dominated by the urban upper class. This happened partly as a result of people leaving the centre, and partly as a result of people moving into town. This utilisation of space within the town is indicative of the economic and social forms of organisation during the period. In a settlement such as Aachen, a manufacturing and trading town, this pattern was mainly determined by the state of technology. An additional factor of great significance would have been tourism, certainly during the eighteenth century, with its increased building activity, possibly attracting wealthy merchants and high-ranking administrators.

A comparison between pre-industrial and industrial models and this case study shows that the town was going through a phase in which traditional structural elements were being dissolved by technical, social and economic innovations. This transitional period from pre-industrial to industrial town may perhaps be taken as typical of the early industrial town in Europe generally. This may be illustrated by making comparisions with the urban patterns of European pre-industrial and industrial towns. In the pre-industrial town, with its limited technical potential, the paramount principle was that of minimum spatial separation; thus, the town centre, the market square and the immediate vicinity were reserved for the middle and upper classes. The periphery, particularly the streets to the gates, were left to the lower classes. In contrast to the industrial town, living areas coincided with workplaces.

As the population grew in the age of mechanisation, new residential areas within the town were opened up. This led on the one hand to a decline, socially, of some existing areas, and on the other to a comparable rise in areas where new building occurred. The opening up of new residential areas was generally undertaken by the urban upper class. In Aachen this resulted in the emergence of a third area between town centre and periphery (Figure 11.2). Thus, the economic and social spatial structure of Aachen during its early industrial phase may be fitted in with the geographical development of other European towns. However, in the absence of comparable research data it is impossible to answer the question as to whether the results of this case study are also applicable to other towns of similar structure.

This case study undoubtedly confirms the main features of both the pre-industrial and the industrial city as postulated by Sjoberg; and the general influence of technical innovation on urban socio-economic structures is clear to see. Nevertheless, in Aachen one can also see a multiplicity of historical influences, which throw into question the use of a simple, twofold, 'pre-industrial – industrial' subdivision. It has been demonstrated on many previous occasions how unsatisfactory it is to rely on a single pre-industrial model for the whole of the European region.[27] Here, and to a limited extent in North America as well, empirical studies indicate that at least a three-stage scale ought to be applied.

The first stage, which may be characterised as pre-industrial and pre-capitalist, found its most widespread expression in Europe in the towns of the Middle Ages – ignoring the influences from the Roman period. This accords with some aspects of the Sjoberg model.[28] By and large the city walls defined the limits of both the plan and the economic structure. The main streets ran from the city gates to the economic centre, the market place. The market place and its surrounding area contained not only the upper classes, but also the middle-class burghers. The main streets were relatively densely built-up towards the outskirts and housed the lower classes.[29] In general the social position of an individual depended entirely on whether or not he was a member of one of the guilds, the contrasting features of these being reflected spatially in the infrastructure of the city centre.

This structure underwent significant change with the rise of mercantilism after the sixteenth century. Thus the early capitalist, proto-industrial town must be viewed as a second stage within the overall process of development. With the introduction of the putting-out system there emerged a class of business entrepreneurs, who can be considered the 'forerunners of a new capitalist economic system'.[30] They had the effect of modifying, or rather raising, the level of sophistication of the existing order based on craft industries. For this reason Vance quite rightly sees the growing emphasis on trade and private investment as a decisive turning point in the evolution of the economic and social structure of European cities.[31] Naturally these new developments were more important in the metropolitan centres of London and Paris than in settlements lower down the hierarchy. It needs to be stressed that the mercantile city was in no sense feudal, as Sjoberg postulated in his conception of the pre-industrial era. Rather the elites in both Europe and the USA were made up primarily of a group of able entrepreneurs and businessmen residing principally in the city centre.[32] Another apparently typical feature of this period is that the nobility and burghers living off their capital were no longer confined exclusively to the city centre, but sought out residential areas on the outskirts, because they could now afford to live away from the economic heart. They thus precipitated the first deviation from the vertically graded scale of prestige, in favour of an horizontal one. Swauger writing about Pittsburgh in 1815 points out that the town periphery, even before the introduction of modern forms of transportation during the process of industrialisation, was more attractive for some sections of the upper class than the historic central area.[33] The same was also true of Charleston in 1860.[34] These results are especially useful in explaining the location of some of the palaces of the nobility in Europe in the eighteenth century, notably those in Vienna, St Petersberg and Koblenz.[35] It also explains the location of monasteries in cities high up in the urban hierarchy like Florence.[36] In the same way, when Amsterdam was undergoing a period of rapid growth during the seventeenth century, many people and the well-off merchants in particular were rehoused in the new developments on the outskirts (*Herengracht*). The middle classes on the other hand stayed in the city centres, while the lowest social classes were still confined to houses in back streets and along the city walls.[37] For this restructuring to become the norm it was necessary for the elite of this period to become more segregated horizontally, at least in comparison with the Middle Ages. The change was brought about primarily by the arrival of main factories, for their arrival also acted as a spur to the relocation of mercantile businesses. This new influence also led simultaneously to the beginnings of the spatial separation of home and place of work, due to the greater degree of specialisation within the production process itself.

All the main diagnostic features of this early capitalist, pre-industrial phase can be identified in the case of Aachen in 1812. In this particular case another important influence was religious intolerance, which, from the beginning of the sixteenth century, forced protestant entrepreneurs to locate new industrial enterprises outside the city gates, thus transferring economic functions of a high order away from the cities and into the countryside. The trend towards creating cottage industries outside the medieval trade centres was typical of large parts of Europe, and is yet another characteristic of the proto-industrial era[38]

Finally, it needs to be emphasised, therefore, that models can only realistically have any geographic relevance when they are linked closely to the prevailing levels of urban development. An urban historical geography of this kind leads one inevitably to the conclusion that inner-city land use systems need to be studied from many more points of view than is allowed for in the better-known general models.

12

The social geography of nineteenth-century British cities: a review

COLIN POOLEY and RICHARD LAWTON

Definition, concepts and approaches

It can be argued that modern social geography began in the slums of nine-teenth-century British cities. Writers such as Engels, Mayhew, Booth and many lesser-known authors produced comprehensive works of empirical sociology or descriptive social geography which accurately portrayed the social topography of the cities they described, and which have become important historical documents for later generations.[1] In the twentieth century the tradition was continued by researchers such as Bowley, Jones and Burnett-Hurst, the inter-war years of economic depression stimulating a particularly large number of social enquiries.[2] Modern social geography has largely sprung from this empirical sociology and, although in the post-war years social geographers attempted to create a more coherent theoretical framework for research, often drawing on American sociology of the 1920s and 30s, the empirical study of spatial variations in social phenomena remained prominent.[3]

A second major influence on modern social geography was the French tradition of human geography, in particular Jean Brunhe's ideas on the organisation and livelihood of social groups ('Geographie Humaine') and the concepts of 'genres de vie' developed by Vidal de la Blache. A prominent part of such studies, the concept of social organisation of space, was well developed in the French geographical and sociological literature but until recently has been relatively neglected in studies of society by British historical geographers.[4]

From the 1960s social geography has begun to change in a number of ways. In particular the philosophical basis of analysis has increasingly emphasised behavioural, humanistic, structuralist and Marxist approaches, and the importance of many issues studied by social geographers for the solution of social problems has been fully recognised.[5] A review of recent work might suggest that social geography is concerned with spatial variations in social phenomena, with the interaction between social relations and spatial form and with the study of social processes which have spatial manifestations. Research has been carried out at a variety of spatial scales (ranging from individual perceptions, through group experiences to the study of wider social patterns), has been approached from a variety of philosophical and theoretical perspectives and is increasingly oriented towards the solution of practical social problems.[6]

However, few studies in the historical geography of urban society over the last two decades have fully assimilated changes that have taken place in the mainstream of the discipline. Research has had more in common with empirical social investigators of the nineteenth century than with contemporary social science, leading to a predominantly positivist-empiricist approach which either has a limited theoretical basis or is tied almost exclusively to social ecology. Historical geographers have only slowly assimilated changes in cognate disciplines, leading to justified criticism by urban historians that geographers describe social patterns without attempting to understand the society that creates those spatial forms.[7] The desire accurately to describe spatial variations in social phenomena – derived from a limited and outdated view of the scope of social geography – coupled with the availability of easily computerised census enumerators' books, led to a spate of large-scale quantitative studies in the 1970s.[8] These have been valuable in providing detailed studies of the social and spatial structure of a range of British cities, which have posed important questions for further investigation but have rarely moved beyond basic description: few have attempted to assimilate recent philosophical and theoretical debates in urban history or modern social geography. Moreover, most have focussed on medium-sized industrial towns, and although the geographical distribution of published and unpublished work is widespread, the degree to which this represents the full range of British urban experience can be questioned.

Often outside the mainstream of urban social geography, some historical geographers have attempted to break out of the positivistic, classical ecological mould. Gregory, for instance, presents his analysis of industrial change in the West Riding in the early nineteenth century within the framework of the theory of structuration which draws on both humanistic and functional structuralist and Marxist structuralist analysis.[9] The book provides a stimulating framework for studying social change that could be applied to nineteenth-century cities, whilst Harvey has attempted to apply Marxist theory to studies of residential change in urban areas, though he presents little empirical historical evidence.[10] Other work has begun to move away from aggregate spatial analysis of urban areas towards a more behavioural approach to the study of community formation, social networks, individual action spaces and images of the city, all of which are related in various ways to the Gestalt psychology of Wertheimer which stressed the importance of the perceived environment.[11] In attempts to bridge the gap between social geography and urban history a few historical geographers have also begun to tackle political issues such as social protest and class relations in Victorian society.[12] However, with notable exceptions, most studies of nineteenth-century British cities have been immune from theoretical and philosophical discussions in the social sciences; for example Ward's recent theoretical discussions of nineteenth-century urbanisation remain remarkably tied to aggregate neo-classical analysis.[13]

Themes in the social geography of nineteenth-century British cities

As in other branches of geography most historical studies in social geography incorporate three elements of description, explanation and interpretation, although the balance between these three has been uneven. Description, tied to a limited theoretical framework, has thus far formed one of the main preoccupations of many studies of nineteenth-century towns.[14] The explanation of processes of change has been limited, but has been successfully tackled in studies of population mobility and the housing market.[15] The interpretation of spatial form and study of the implications of particular patterns and processes for individuals and society has rarely been attempted.[16] The three themes of description, explanation and interpretation will now be discussed and illustrated by selected case studies drawn from the authors' work on nineteenth-century Liverpool and from published and unpublished research on other towns.

The description of social patterns

One starting point for many recent geographical studies of nineteenth-century towns has been the hypothesised continuum of spatial change within the city from the pre-industrial urban form idealised by Sjoberg to the so-called 'modern' urban structure identified in Chicago by Burgess. It has been tacitly assumed that during the nineteenth century industrialising cities became progressively segregated with the poor at the centre and the rich on the periphery; most geographical studies of nineteenth-century towns have tried to assess the extent to which such structure had been attained.[17] However, the debate over the 'modernity' of nineteenth-century cities may be both illusory and distracting,[18] leading to an over-emphasis on pattern at the expense of process, and to a reification of ecological social theory. As several authors have already shown, different spatial patterns will inevitably emerge if different variables are mapped at varying spatial scales. Thus segregation and intermixing may be identified within the same town if different criteria of analysis are used.[19]

Despite the dubious theoretical and methodological validity of descriptive

ecological studies, they do provide a framework on which more sophisticated and illuminating analyses may be based. The spatial characteristics
of three industrial Lancashire towns of different size illustrate the value
and limitations of such approaches. In a spatial analysis of Chorley (population *ca.* 12,000) Warnes used 21 variables taken from the census enumerators' books for 1851, rate books for 1848 and map evidence of 1844–7
in a principal components analysis within a framework of 58 small spatial
units based on streets.[20] Although spatially confused due to the discontinous
built-up area, Warnes was able to conclude that by 1851 groupings based
on status and occupational skill were beginning to replace individual occupations as the basis for residential location. New streets which were added
to early clusters of houses based around employment were often single
class, though there was little segregation into larger social areas, and high-
status occupations continued to concentrate near the town centre. In 1851
Chorley retained a spatial form similar to that associated with pre-industrial
towns (Figure 12.1A).

Chorley's close neighbour, Preston, was much larger (population
c. 70,000 in 1851), had undergone a greater degree of industrialisation and
might be expected to have a more clearly defined social and spatial structure.
Bristow's study of residential structure based on a principal components
analysis of 33 variables from the 1851 census enumerators' books and other
sources,[21] used a spatial framework of 240 units based on 100m grid
squares.[22] The main dimension of urban structure revealed by his analysis
was socio-economic, picking out the skilled working-class element of the
population and clearly separating it from those of higher and lower social
status. Subsidiary components measuring elements of stages in the family
life-cycle and ethnic/migrant status suggest that Preston's population was
more clearly differentiated than Chorley's. However, spatial differences
were not so great: while skilled working-class families clustered in a series
of peripheral suburbs close to places of work, the core retained many high-
status residents, though they lived close to a low-status area of sub-standard
housing and a growing Irish population. Preston was clearly transitional
between pre-industrial and industrial urban forms (Figure 12.1B).

Liverpool, one of the few large nineteenth-century towns to have been
studied from this viewpoint[23] had a population of 493,405 in 1871. A 10
per cent sample from the census enumerators' books of 1871 produced
35 variables for a principal components analysis within a spatial framework
of 394 units derived from census enumeration districts. The main components of urban structure identified were measures of housing quality and
density and social status, with an Irish dimension strongly associated with
both components. The analysis demonstrated a high degree of spatial separation between social groups, a lesser degree of segregation by family status,
and clusters of Irish ethnicity overlapping these areas. The segregation

of different social and ethnic components of the population is confirmed by more detailed analysis of individual distributions, and the general pattern of low-status core and high-status periphery conforms to the ideal-type of the modern city (Figure 12.1C).

However, few areas of Liverpool were homogeneous: no enumeration districts were exclusively occupied by semi-skilled and unskilled workers, and skilled manual workers were found in all but one enumeration district. Such small-scale mixing within sub-areas, which have clear majority social characteristics but were not exclusively occupied by one class, is emphasised by Ward in a study of Leeds.[24] Ward argues that whilst the extremes of society were segregated, there was ample opportunity for most people to mix together in a city where limited transport restricted dispersion from centralised employment opportunities. However, differences in the actual levels of segregation in Liverpool and Leeds are small and owe as much to methods of analysis and interpretation as to significant differences in their spatial structure.[25] These and other studies of the spatial structure of nineteenth-century towns suggest that residential segregation and the development of social areas as defined by measures of social status, ethnicity, housing quality and family status did occur but, not surprisingly, the level and nature of differentiation varied considerably. Quite apart from the influence of local topography on the layout of the town, and contrasting economic and political conditions, large towns seem to have developed measurable levels of segregation earlier than small towns, which were characterised by clustering within small areas based principally on occupation. However, all towns exhibited some intermixing of population, the degree of separation identified being partly dependent on the scale at which analysis is undertaken.

The explanation of social processes

The description of spatial patterns in nineteenth-century cities begins to take on real significance only when linked to the processes which produce particular spatial arrangements. Carter and Lewis suggest a number of social, economic and political processes which had important spatial implications in the nineteenth-century city,[26] including the evolving class structure, population movement, changing land ownership and building development, and the effects of central and local government legislation. While, with a number of notable exceptions, geographers have been slow to move from the description of spatial patterns to the investigation and explanation of processes, social historians have focussed on process but rarely make explicit links to spatial form.[27]

Historical geographers have probably devoted most attention to the study of population movements, ranging from long-distance migration to short-

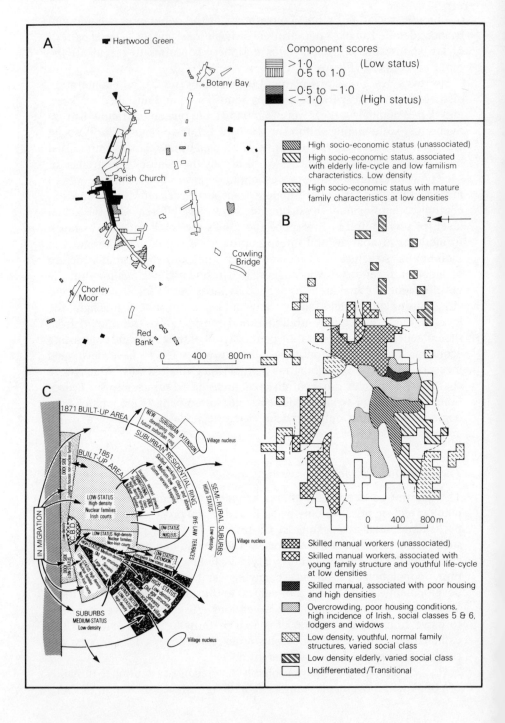

A

Hartwood Green

Botany Bay

Parish Church

Cowling Bridge

Chorley Moor

Red Bank

0   400   800m

Component scores

>1·0 (Low status)
0·5 to 1·0
−0·5 to −1·0
<−1·0 (High status)

High socio-economic status (unassociated)

High socio-economic status, associated with elderly life-cycle and low familism characteristics. Low density

High socio-economic status with mature family characteristics at low densities

B

N

0   400   800m

Skilled manual workers (unassociated)

Skilled manual workers, associated with young family structure and youthful life-cycle at low densities

Skilled manual, associated with poor housing and high densities

Overcrowding, poor housing conditions, high incidence of Irish., social classes 5 & 6, lodgers and widows

Low density, youthful, normal family structures, varied social class

Low density elderly, varied social class

Undifferentiated/Transitional

C

1871 BUILT-UP AREA

NEW SUBURBAN EXTENSION developing into future suburban ring

SUBURBAN RESIDENTIAL RING

1851 BUILT-UP AREA

Village nucleus

SEMI-RURAL SUBURBS

LOW STATUS High-density Nuclear families Irish courts

LOW STATUS High-density Nuclear families Non-Irish courts

BYE-LAW TERRACES

IN MIGRATION

Village nucleus

SUBURBS MEDIUM-STATUS Low-density

Village nucleus

distance intra-urban mobility.[28] Migration directly affects the social geography of towns through the origins and composition of its population, whilst
the process of intra-urban mobility represents the constant reappraisal of
the urban environment through the residential decisions of the population
which reshape the spatial structure of towns. However, many studies of
migration and mobility have been limited to static descriptions of the
mobility process, usually using data in census enumerators' books: only
rarely have they sought to explore the motives behind moves and the implications of mobility for everyday life.[29]

The nature and extent of residential mobility in nineteenth-century towns
has been demonstrated in a number of studies: for example, Dennis found
that 58 per cent of his sample persisted within Huddersfield 1851–61,[30]
whilst in Liverpool 46 per cent remained within the city averaged over
two decades 1851–61 and 1871–81.[31] Many writers have commented on
both the short distance of most intra-urban moves[32] and the tendency for
a general out-movement of population, with the highest rates of mobility
from old slum areas towards new residential suburbs linked to changes
in housing provision. Studies of Leicester, Huddersfield and Liverpool suggest that the most mobile households in nineteenth-century cities were
young, in lower social groups and in rented accommodation (with few constraints on short-distance movement); the wealthy moved less often but
usually over longer distances towards the suburbs[33] (Figure 12.2). The spatial impact of different levels of mobility was limited, with notable short-
term stability reflecting the dominant short distance, circulatory movements, though in the longer term these produced a significant overall shift
of population towards the periphery (Figure 12.3).

While such studies accurately describe processes of population change,
for the most part they fail to identify the reasons for movement and the
impact of mobility on people's everyday lives, mainly because aggregate
descriptive studies demand the large-scale linkage of evidence from sources
such as rate books, directories and census enumerators' books, whilst other
evidence of a more individual and behavioural natural has been passed
over. Although requiring careful interpretation, the evidence of contempor-

Figure 12.1   Spatial pattern of social status components in three nineteenth-century
towns: (A) Chorley 1851; (B) Preston 1851; (C) Liverpool 1871
Sources: (A) after A. M. Warnes, 'Residential patterns in an emerging industrial
town', in B. D. Clark and M. B. Gleave (eds.), *Social patterns in cities* (IBG Special
Publications, 5, London, 1973); (B) after B. R. Bristow, 'Residential differentiation
in mid-nineteenth century Preston', unpublished PhD thesis, University of Lancaster, 1982; (C) after R. Lawton and C. G. Pooley, 'Problems and potentialities
for the study of internal population mobility in nineteenth-century England', *Canadian Studies in Population*, 5 (1978, Special Issue, 1980).

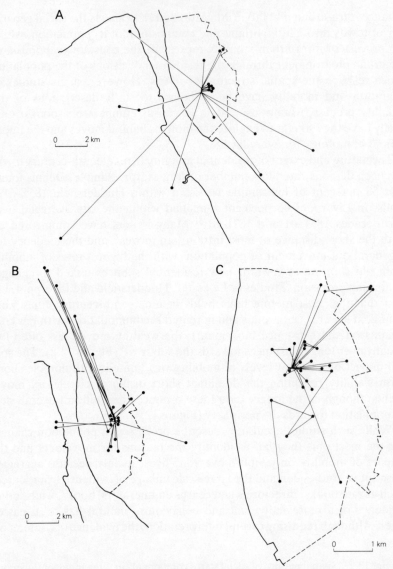

Figure 12.2 Residential mobility from three streets in Liverpool: (A) Rodney Street 1851–61; (B) Shaw Street 1871–81; (C) Virgil Street 1871–81

ary accounts, diaries and oral history can aid explanation of the processes described in aggregate studies.[34]

One diary, written by a migrant to Liverpool in the 1880s, suggests a typical working-class mobility pattern[35] and provides insights into why the

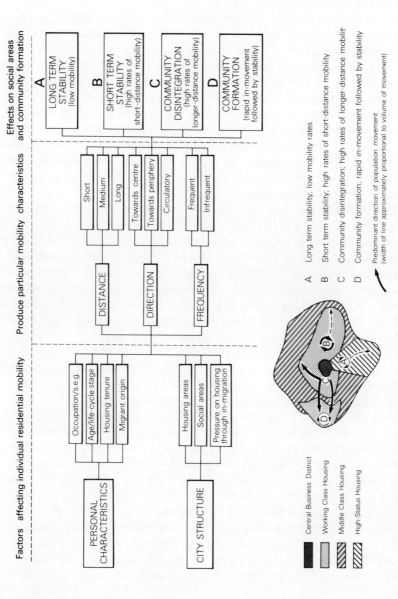

Figure 12.3 The mobility process in nineteenth-century cities

Factors affecting individual residential mobility

Produce particular mobility characteristics

Effects on social areas and community formation

PERSONAL CHARACTERISTICS
- Occupation/s.e.g.
- Age/life-cycle stage
- Housing tenure
- Migrant origin

CITY STRUCTURE
- Housing areas
- Social areas
- Pressure on housing through in-migration

DISTANCE
- Short
- Medium
- Long

DIRECTION
- Towards centre
- Towards periphery
- Circulatory

FREQUENCY
- Frequent
- Infrequent

A LONG TERM STABILITY (low mobility)

B SHORT TERM STABILITY (high rates of short-distance mobility)

C COMMUNITY DISINTEGRATION (high rates of longer-distance mobility)

D COMMUNITY FORMATION (rapid in-movement followed by stability)

A Long term stability: low mobility rates
B Short term stability: high rates of short-distance mobility
C Community disintegration: high rates of longer-distance mobilit
D Community formation: rapid in-movement followed by stability

Predominant direction of population movement (width of line approximately proportional to volume of movement)

Central Business District
Working Class Housing
Middle Class Housing
High-Status Housing

diarist should have moved twelve times in eight years within the same area of the city. David Brindley moved to Liverpool from rural Staffordshire and first lodged and worked with an urban cowkeeper. After ten months he became a porter at the Canada Dock Goods Railway Station and lived in a series of bachelor lodgings, for part of the time with relatives who themselves moved three times in one year, mobility that was possibly stimulated by an accident to the household head. Following marriage to his cousin, Annie, the couple initially took lodgings in the same area of Everton (moving to an adjacent street after only two weeks because they were 'besieged by bugs'), and four months later they rented a newly built two-up, two-down terrace house at 5s 6d per week, also in the expanding working-class suburb of Everton. They moved after only six months to an identical house across the road, probably because their first home was next door to a public house which doubtless generated noise and offended Brindley who disapproved of excessive drinking. Their next move, to an older but slightly larger house, was prompted by the impending birth of their first child and possibly a desire to be close to relatives. Moving house, a relatively trivial occurrence, causing little disruption and with no significant effect on income, expenditure, friends and contact patterns, was clearly stimulated by a combination of minor inconveniences and life-cycle stage factors, which saw a progression from lodging in rooms to renting a house suitable for family life. Such insights into the reasons behind individual residential mobility flesh out the bare bones of aggregate patterns and suggest the variety of familial, economic and social factors at work.

The urban housing market was closely linked to and constrained the mobility process. However, the ways in which the housing market operated in nineteenth-century cities to create housing areas which helped to sort the population into distinctive groupings in different parts of the city have rarely been studied by geographers.[36] Moreover, despite a considerable body of literature on nineteenth-century housing from social and economic historians, this seldom explicitly explores the relationships between the housing market and the social and spatial form of the city.[37] Geographers have made some notable contributions to our knowledge about the provision of new housing, ranging from studies of the economic and social factors affecting decisions to release land for building, to the structure of the building industry and the influences on house construction and other land uses at the urban fringe.[38] They have also contributed to morphological studies of urban areas, including analysis of housing types and the nature of nineteenth-century slums.[39] However, such studies do not always link the processes of housing provision, both in the form of new construction and the resale and letting of the established housing stock, to the socio-spatial structure of the city; while they rarely consider the constraints imposed and opportunities offered by the nineteenth-century housing market for individual residential mobility.[40] Some geographers have recognised the need to link social and spatial form through detailed analyses of housing and other aspects of the physical environment, but such studies are still in their infancy and frequently remain linked to aggregate concepts of social area analysis.[41]

Jackson's examination of the private housing market of two south Lancashire towns goes further than most in relating housing-market change to urban social and spatial structure and residential mobility.[42] In St Helens most bye-law terrace housing was owned by small landlords (47 per cent of landlords had only one or two houses in 1871), while small shareholders predominated in local building societies: in the Second St Helens Building Society (1836–9) almost half the shareholders had only two shares (enough for one average house) and the society's shareholders included a range of skilled workers such as engineers, iron-founders and watch-makers. In the second half of the century a small number of larger builders each built an average of 45 houses per year in regularly laid-out residential estates to the north west of the town, which were particularly attractive to such skilled manual workers as glass-workers who were encouraged to move from older company housing near the Pilkington Glassworks from the 1840s. Other workers followed, including watch-makers, iron-founders, carriage-builders and coopers, to form a residentially stable skilled working-class residential area by mid-century. Further from the town centre newly developing white-collar estates at Cropper's Hill and Cowley Hill represented a significant social grading in terms of the attitudes and respectability of their inhabitants. There was little mobility between these two social areas, but within each housing sub-market short-distance movement was common (Figure 12.4). Such a study clearly demonstrates the interplay between the decisions and aspirations of individual entrepreneurs and workers and the broader social and economic forces which, transcending conventional aggregate social area analysis, shaped the nature and form of housing development in nineteenth-century towns.

Except for housebuilding, there have been a few studies of the effect of economic factors on the social geography of nineteenth-century cities. The structure and location of employment in individual towns and the operation of their labour markets had significant effects on the aspirations, social characteristics and residential choice of the population, yet geographers have seldom explicitly linked the social characteristics of a town and the nature of employment. Vance's study of housing and employment in Birmingham almost 20 years ago generated surprisingly little interest amongst geographers,[43] although Ward has stressed the importance of employment linkages in shaping the social characteristics of different neighbourhoods[44] and social historians have devoted considerable attention to the labour process, often also highlighting its spatial implications.[45] The

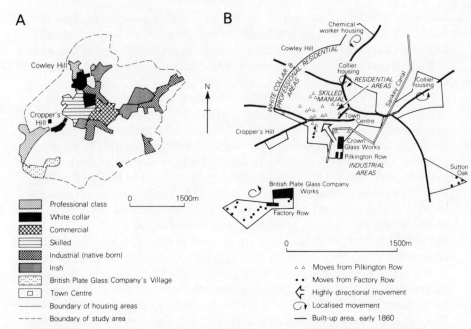

A

B

Professional class
White collar
Commercial
Skilled
Industrial (native born)
Irish
British Plate Glass Company's Village
Town Centre
——— Boundary of housing areas
– – – Boundary of study area

0 ——— 1500m

△ △ Moves from Pilkington Row
• • Moves from Factory Row
⟨ Highly directional movement
⟳ Localised movement
—— Built-up area, early 1860

Figure 12.4   (A) Housing areas in St Helens 1871; (B) Residential mobility in St Helens 1851–61

Source: after J. T. Jackson, 'Housing areas in mid-Victorian Wigan and St Helens', *Transactions of the Institute of British Geographers*, NS, 6 (1981).

nature of casual employment on the Liverpool docks had a profound influence on the residential preferences of dock workers.[46] Despite reasonable wages in times of full employment, the casual nature of dock work limited earnings and restricted dockers to cheap sub-standard housing close to the dockside because of the need to be close to the stands at which workers were hired on a half-day basis. Within dockside residential areas, dominated by unskilled working-class families, enclaves of 'respectable' dock workers separated themselves out from other unskilled households, particularly from the Irish. But for all such workers the nature and place of employment dominated where they could live.

In London, the city with the largest casual labour force in the nineteenth century, dock workers, building workers, drivers and cab men, many employees in manufacture of metal, food and clothing and other unskilled labourers were joined by a wide variety of hawkers, costermongers and other street traders.[47] Green's detailed analysis of street traders in the St Giles district of London emphasises their fluctuating numbers, acute poverty, unlicensed operations and spatial impact.[48] While some saw street trading as their sole occupation, for others it formed an alternative to which they turned because of underemployment elsewhere in the labour market: for example, as unemployment in building, metal working, clothing and shoe making rose in the 1840s, so the numbers engaged in street trading also increased leading in turn to considerable distress amongst established hawkers and costermongers. Their increased numbers, coupled with legal action against street traders in traditional central locations and the expansion of permanent markets, forced many street traders to become more mobile. In the 1850s they moved into the respectable suburbs in an attempt to retain trade and escape legal action. Street traders thus became a marginal group within the city with no area in which they could work unharassed. Forced out of low-status central areas they attempted to penetrate middle-class districts necessitating a high degree of daily mobility and leading to great hostility from local residents. Although continuing to live in the 'rookeries' of such districts as St Giles, the nature of their trade meant that they did not fully identify with any area of the city. Further analyses of specific trades and occupations are undoubtedly needed before the interactions between the labour market and the social and spatial structure of nineteenth-century cities are understood.

Progressive control of urban land use by national and local legislation affected the construction and layout of residential areas, the location and nature of employment, and most aspects of the urban environment and landscape. Thus nineteenth-century towns were increasingly shaped by political processes. Although historians have extensively researched the operation and effects of national and local government on urban life,[49] geographers have been slow either to draw on this work or to initiate their own research into the influence of political processes on the social geography of the city. However, geographers have contributed to studies of the development of the town planning movement – though mostly this has been researched by historians, architects and planners – and the growth of public intervention in health, sanitation and other aspects of the urban environment, although much of this work has been more descriptive than explanatory in nature.[50] Research on nineteenth-century Liverpool, Manchester and Birmingham has attempted to explain spatial variations in disease-specific mortality by analysing changes in the physical and social environment and the development of the public health movement,[51] whilst research by Kearns on the impact of cholera on parts of London in the 1830s and 1840s demonstrates the close interplay between the political process and the measures adopted to counter problems of disease and public health.[52] The intervention of local authorities in the provision of working-class housing clearly demonstrates the way in which political factors interact with economic and social forces to shape the social geography of the city. There is now an expanding historical literature on this topic,[53] although most of it concentrates on the twentieth-century experience. In the nineteenth century, Liverpool corporation built the largest stock of working-class housing of any British city apart from London, with 783 units opened before 1900 and a total of 2,895 flats and houses by the end of the First World War.[54] Analysis of the arguments surrounding the provision of these early corporation properties suggests that although the council often divided on political lines, with Conservative councillors strongly opposed to corporation involvement in housing, and arguing instead for slum-clearance sites to be sold to private enterprise for rebuilding, it was first-hand experience of inner-city housing conditions and the opportunity for personal political or economic gain which most often swayed councillors' opinions. Thus whilst some members of the city council representing central wards, such as the Irish Nationalist Pat Byrne, seemed genuinely concerned to improve working-class housing conditions, others were recommending a halt to slum-clearance and the construction of corporation tenements on existing sites so that population loss from central areas would be minimised and the income of local merchants and traders (the principal ratepayers and electors) could be protected. The intervention of central government in the form of the Local Government Board finally swayed the issue: in 1892 the Board refused to sanction further loans for slum-clearance unless suitable schemes were proposed for housing the dispossessed. Schemes built under the 1890 Act consisted entirely of tenement blocks built on slum-clearance sites, with tenants carefully selected on social and economic grounds. Those families who could not pay corporation rents, or who failed to conform to corporation standards of behaviour, were excluded from the flats which increasingly housed a working-class elite. Although the total impact of such schemes was small in relation to the housing problem, the history of Liverpool's involvement in municipal housing demonstrates the way in which local and national political processes influenced the social geography of the city and can help explain the patterns so frequently described by geographers.

Interpreting the social geography of nineteenth-century cities

In 1980 Richard Dennis posed the question 'Why study segregation?', arguing that geographers needed to focus more attention on the interpretation of spatial patterns and processes and, in particular, to relate these to the perceptions of contemporaries.[55] Martin Daunton makes a similar criticism of the work of historical geographers in stating that the 'meaning attached to the use of space does not emerge as a self-evident truth from the maps of historical geographers';[56] views on which other historians and geographers have recently elaborated.[57] The basic criticism is that while urban historical geographers have accurately described spatial patterns of social phenomena, and in some cases have probed the social, economic and political processes underlying these patterns, they seldom attempt to assess the implications and meanings of these processes and patterns for everyday life. There is little point in describing levels of segregation or measuring rates of residential mobility without assessing their impact on the individuals and families involved or on the wider structural processes which shaped nineteenth-century cities. Greater understanding of nineteenth-century society will require investigations of the significant and important, rather than concentration on what is easily measured from readily available data.

For instance, changes in the location and composition of social areas in towns can only be fully interpreted through detailed studies of the structure and organisation of communities. Where the pattern of local contacts and community organisation cuts across social areas identified from census variables, the usefulness of such ecological measures in the understanding and interpretation of nineteenth-century urban society is brought into question. Some studies have begun to move in this direction: for example, Dennis has used such indicators as marriage distances, church membership and residential mobility to assess patterns of interaction within neighbourhood communities in Huddersfield,[58] whilst a number of studies of the Irish and other minority groups have highlighted the role of locality-based communities in aiding assimilation to urban life.[59] But this sort of interpretation still needs to be developed further and extended to other studies of urban social and spatial structure. The careful integration of data on individuals from censuses, rate books and similar sources with qualitative accounts, diaries and oral reminiscences can provide a fuller and more satisfactory assessment of the meaning and significance of both the patterns and processes of urban life.[60]

The significance of residential segregation can be assessed on at least three different levels: from the perspective of the individual living in a particular neighbourhood; from the point of view of other citizens, not least politicians and entrepreneurs with power to manipulate urban society and environment; and from the perspective of nineteenth-century urban society as a whole.[61] Segregation, and the processes causing spatial differentiation, also influenced and were affected by a wide spectrum of processes encompassing the urban economy, environment and social and political structures. For instance, the development of neighbourhoods with distinctive social, ethnic or religious characteristics not only affected individual perceptions and aided identification and orientation within the urban environment, but also influenced the decisions of builders, landlords and others who controlled the nineteenth-century housing market. Investment and development would be closely linked to the existing characteristics of areas and the types of tenants that a developer could realistically expect to attract, whilst at the societal level residential separation affected class relationships, though the precise nature of this interaction is confused. Much work remains to be done in this field, with behavioural and humanistic studies of nine-teenth-century towns particularly poorly developed, but by paying greater attention to the interpretation of pattern and process new life may be breathed into existing descriptive social geographies of towns.

Conclusions

Even a brief review of recent research on the social geography of nineteenth-century British cities demonstrates that, although, we now know a great deal about spatial variations in such social indicators as occupation, social status, ethnicity, mortality and housing quality, and their combined effects on social areas, there is much that we do not understand about the relation-ship between pattern and the underlying social, economic and political processes. Not only are more studies of process needed, but pattern and process must be more fully interpreted and integrated in studies of the significance of such phenomena as community formation and residential mobility in nineteenth-century urban society. Still in its infancy, such work requires a much wider range of quantitative and qualitative sources than have been conventionally used by social geographers, and should bring the interests of historical geographers and social historians much closer together.

Utilisation of a wider range of sources should also encourage historical social geographers to move outside the confines of the period for which manuscript census enumerators' books are available, into studies of the social geography of the eighteenth and early nineteenth centuries and of the late nineteenth and early twentieth centuries. Some studies are begin-ning to move in this direction,[62] but there is scope for more work of this nature. In the mid-1970s research on the social geography – especially the social ecology – of nineteenth-century cities was at the forefront of British historical geography, generating frequent conferences and copious publication.[63] There has since been a hiatus, as the limitations of much early work have been realised but relatively little that is innovative has been attempted. The stage is now set for research on the social geography of nineteenth-century cities to enter a new era of growth and vitality, build-ing on the description of spatial patterns but using these as the basis for generating philosophical and theoretical structures which enable both the explanation of process and the interpretation of meaning at a variety of spatial scales. Much of this work will be interdisciplinary in nature, drawing on resources and techniques used throughout the social sciences, and may help to bring together the research of social historians, economic historians and historical geographers in a more effective study of urban history.[64]

13

Patrician urban landlords: research on patronal relations in nineteenth-century 'estate towns' in the British Isles

LINDSAY PROUDFOOT

Introduction

Aristocratic involvement in the development of towns and cities in nineteenth-century Britain has long been recognised,[1] but much less attention has been paid to the character of the patronal relationships which existed between aristocratic urban landlords and their tenantry. The importance of these relationships and of the way they developed during the century has only recently found emphasis, notably in Davies's work on Cardiff, in Cannadine's studies of Eastbourne and Edgbaston and in his recent volume of collected essays.[2] Much of the potential for research identified by Cannadine in his earlier review essay in 1978 remains unexploited.[3] In Ireland, similar studies have yet to appear. Published discussion of aristocratic urban patronage has concentrated either on the role of landlords in promoting townscape change,[4] or if it has commented on landlord–tenant relations, has done so as part of some more specific theme, such as the growth of Dublin or Belfast.[5]

This chapter examines some recent research findings on the changing nature of aristocratic urban patronage in nineteenth-century Britain and Ireland. The emphasis is as much political as social, and this reflects the recent awareness among workers of the importance of political goals in accounting for patronal decision-making. The first two sections discuss the evidence as it relates to two aspects of urban patronal relations which have received most attention in recent studies: the idiosyncratic nature of aristocratic social and political patronage in estate towns, and the variable but sustained challenge to patrician authority posed by the growth of middle-class political assertiveness. The concluding section considers the applicability to selected Irish estate towns of Cannadine's recent attempt to formulate a model of urban patronal relations in nineteenth-century Britain.

This Irish evidence is based on the author's previously unpublished research on the Duke of Devonshire's estate towns in southern Ireland

175

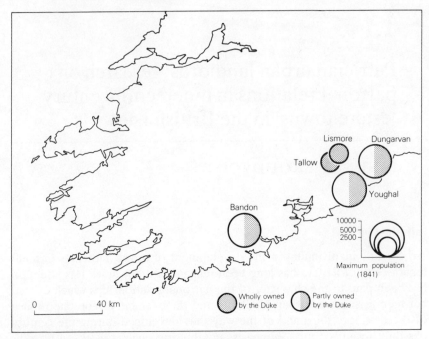

Figure 13.1　The Duke of Devonshire's Irish estate towns

(Figure 13.1). As part of the vast Burlington inheritance, these towns passed to the Duke of Devonshire in 1748, when Lady Charlotte Boyle, heiress of the fourth Earl of Cork and third Earl of Burlington, married William Cavendish, the future fourth Duke. Lismore and Tallow were owned outright, along with the old town at Bandon. At Youghal the Devonshires' property was equalled by that of the Corporation and the Earl of Shannon, but had the advantage of comprising most of the centre of the town. In Dungarvan, the Devonshires initially owned about one third of the town,[6] but extended their holdings in 1808 by the purchase of the Osborne estate.[7] Such emphasis on the Devonshire property permits comparisons to be drawn between English and Irish experience within the context of a single aristocratic family, since the Devonshires were also involved at this time in developments at Barrow-in-Furness[8] and Eastbourne,[9] and owned property at Buxton.[10] Moreover, Cannadine has recently argued that the time has now come when further progress in the study of urban patronal relations must depend on such individual case studies.[11] Consequently, the demerits of this particularist type of approach should be offset by the detailed understanding it provides of local patronal relations set in their national context.

Even so, the pursuit of such Anglo-Irish comparisons requires caution. One consequence of the socio-economic differences which invite comparison between Britain and Ireland was the creation of urban systems which differed enormously in scale and importance. In Ireland, the demographic decline of the immediate pre- and post-Famine years[12] combined with the failure to develop a significant heavy industrial sector (save in the north-east)[13] and the deepening divisions within a plural society[14] to form a unique context for urban development. Away from the major regional centres, such as Dublin, Belfast, Cork and Limerick, the urban network was characterised by relatively small and functionally simple towns.[15] Between 1841, when the total population of Ireland was nearing its peak of *ca.* 8.2 million, and 1901, when the combined effects of famine, disease, disease, emigration and family limitation had reduced it to *ca.* 4.45 million,[16] the country's urban population barely changed, growing by 1.8 per cent to 1.25 million.[17] By contrast, between 1801 and 1901 the total population of England and Wales grew from *ca.* 8.9 million to 32.5 million, with the urban proportion rising from 17 per cent to 78 per cent.[18] Clearly, with such contextual contrasts, the potential for individual landlord patronage is likely to have differed fundamentally between the two countries.

Social and political patronage in nineteenth-century estate towns

The distinguishing feature of estate towns and urban estates lay in the opportunities they offered individual landowners to direct the social, economic and morphological development of the community in accordance with their own ideals and objectives. Obviously, these opportunities were not unlimited. Entails and financial encumbrances could limit both the landlord's scope for unilateral action and his means to pursue it, while even on the best-run urban estates, patronal enterprise could be limited by a wide variety of external factors, including, for example, the demand for housing, the cost of borrowing, the topography within the town and the locational attributes of its site. Indeed, Cannadine argues that it was factors such as these, rather than patronal decision-making as such, which ultimately determined the relative importance of aristocratic influence in towns such as Belfast, Cardiff or Nottingham.[19] Nevertheless, the fact remains that many urban aristocratic landlords enjoyed financial resources and monopolistic rights of ownership which permitted them to optimise their developmental response to these external factors in ways which remained consonant with their political and social principles and long-term economic objectives. In short, it was this potential for sustained, coherent yet essentially idiosyncratic planning of both the community and its environment in the face of external change which set the 'estate town' apart from its neighbour.

Where aristocratic urban initiatives did occur, the attitude of successive heirs was of major importance in determining not only whether the initial developmental impetus was maintained, modified or abandoned but also the nature of the social relations which emerged as the town prospered or stagnated. Social relations between patron and tenant, and between different classes of tenant, were influenced by the extent of the landlord's informed interest in the town's welfare, his willingness to invest in its improvement, the consideration he was prepared to give to his tenant's problems and aspirations where they affected his interests' and the degree to which he wished to exercise a politicial influence over the community.

The attitude of successive Dukes of Devonshire to their estate towns in Britain and Ireland amply illustrates these themes. The four incumbents who held the title during the nineteenth century each perceived the rewards and responsibilities of urban patronage very differently. The fifth Duke (1748–1811), a man remarkable for his lethargy and indolence,[20] displayed a general disinterest in estate management similar to that of the first Marquis of Bute at Cardiff.[21] In Ireland, the fifth Duke was a complete absentee,[22] which permitted his agents there a great deal of autonomy in their management of his affairs, and offered them the opportunity to extend their personal influence at the Duke's expense. Moreover, the Duke's continued absence from his Irish estates allowed his Irish relatives, notably the Earl of Shannon, to continue their inroads into his urban political influence, which they had begun while acting as trustees during his minority (1764–9).[23] Writing in 1792, Thomas Garde, the Duke's Irish law agent, recalled that prior to 1748 the Burlington family 'nominated for Bandon, Dungarvan, Tallow and Lismore. On the late election (in 1790) it cannot be said that the Duke's interest returned a single member.'[24] As far as the generality of the Duke's urban tenantry were concerned, the reason for this decline was quite clear. As their ultimate but absentee landlord, he was a distant figure to whom they owned no political allegiance and from whom they received no favours, least of all their tenancies. These they had obtained from the immediate tenants to the Duke, and it was according to their instructions that most undertenants voted.[25]

The fifth Duke's indolence and disinterest thus effectively minimised his patronal role in his Irish towns. When the sixth Duke (1790–1858) succeeded in 1811, the parlous state of the Devonshires' political influence in their Irish boroughs, and the corrupt management associated with it, had both been largely remedied. Interestingly, the improvement resulted from initiatives taken not by the fifth Duke, who wished that his political influence should be exercised in 'as quiet and conciliatory a fashion as possible',[26] but by his English auditor, John Heaton. Even then, Heaton was prompted by the growing protests of Irish tenants disadvantaged by the increasingly blatant corruption of the agent, William Connor.[27] Faced with mounting evidence of nepotism, financial mismanagement, political self-aggrandisement, and with the distinct taint of embezzlement in the air, Connor was forced to resign in 1792.[28] By 1811 his English replacements, Henry Bowman and Thomas Knowlton, had succeeded in re-establishing the Devonshires' political control over Dungarvan,[29] and in forcing Lord Bandon, the Duke's main political rival in Bandon, to abide by an agreement his father had signed with the Duke's trustees in 1767, whereby each should have the alternate nomination for the borough.[30]

Conventional opinion would have it that the sixth Duke was not the man to capitalise on these early political successes. Dismissed by a biographer of the eighth Duke as a lightweight figure,[31] the sixth Duke's reputation still remains that of a compulsive collector, ambitious rebuilder of houses, and financial incompetent, whose extravagance compounded the existing family debt (already running at over £500,000 in 1811), and contributed largely to the Devonshires' worsening financial crisis in the second half of the century. Recently discovered correspondence makes it clear, however, that though largely absent from Ireland prior to 1840, the sixth Duke played an active and hitherto unsuspected proxy role in Irish politics. By 1822 he had regained control of the Corporation and Parliamentary representation of Youghal,[32] both of which had been usurped by the Earl of Shannon. At Dungarvan, the uneasy alliance between Liberals and Radicals on the strength of their mutual detestation of the Conservative Beresford interest ensured the successive return of the Duke's candidates, General Walpole, Capt. A. W. Clifford and George Lamb, until 1834.[33] At Bandon, the Bernard family (Lord Bandon) continued to acquiesce in the alternate nomination until 1831, when a revolt by some of the ultra-Conservative members of the Corporation against the election of the Duke's nominee, Capt. A. W. Clifford,[34] led to the withdrawal of Lord Bandon's financial support for the Corporation.

The 1832 Irish Reform Act marked the virtual end of the sixth Duke's borough-mongering and his adoption of a lower political profile. This was continued by the seventh Duke, until the boroughs were either disposed of in 1860 or incorporated within the enlarged county constituencies in 1885. An active supporter of Parliamentary and Muncipal Reform, the sixth Duke felt that to exercise anything more than what he considered 'the legitimate interest afforded to him by his property', would be inconsistent with the principles of the Reform Act. Moreover, the Duke was becoming alarmed at the increasing violence attending Irish elections, and the growing threat and expense they posed to his urban property.[35] Although his Irish agent at the time, F. E. Currey, was well aware that 'management for political power invariably entailed some sacrifice of property', this was a sacrifice the Duke was increasingly loath to make.[36] Accordingly, during the remainder of his life, and that of the seventh Duke (1808–91), agents in Ireland were normally instructed to do no more than request tenants to vote for the Duke's preferred candidate, who was almost invariably a Liberal. On the three occasions when the sixth Duke's relatives took the field, W. G. Cavendish for Bandon and F. J. Howard for Youghal in 1837, and C. C. Cavendish for Youghal in 1841, they did so on the strict understanding that his support would amount to no more than that given to any other Liberal candidate.[37]

This less active political role did not betoken any general lessening of the sixth Duke's interest in his Irish towns or tenants. Indeed, it is a curious paradox that it was only in the 1840s, somewhat after this transition had been accomplished, and after an absence of at least twenty years, that he became a regular visitor to his property in Ireland. The re-establishment of this personal contact was warmly welcomed by the tenants, and the first fruits of the closer relationship were not long in forthcoming. Between 1840 and 1858, the annual expenditure on schools, subscriptions and charities, a reasonable index of ducal liberality, averaged £2,215, over one third more than it had been in the preceding twenty years. Between 1840 and 1858, capital expenditure on the Lismore, Tallow and Kinnatoloon estates alone totalled £110,515, including £34,059 spent rebuilding Lismore Castle. In the previous twenty years, the total capital expenditure on this sort of improvement on these estates had been £53,872, less than half the later sum.[38] The tenants were duly grateful. Successive visits by the Duke to Lismore, and other parts of the estate were marked by general festivities as the tenantry professed themselves suitably conscious of the Duke's benevolence.[39] In fact the Duke never subscribed more than 8 per cent of his local rent income to charitable causes in his Irish towns, but this formed part of total recurrent expenditure amounting to more than 50 per cent of his Irish income.[40]

As Cannadine demonstrates, on the Devonshire estates at large, the inevitable financial crisis was looming. As early as 1844, in the wake of the auditor, Benjamin Currey's, bleak assessment of the state of the sixth Duke's finances, consideration had been given to extensive sales of Irish property as a means of paying off the family debt, which had risen to just under £1,000,000.[41] Despite the Duke's initial inclination to sell in Ireland,[42] and Joseph Paxton's enthusiastic endorsement of the idea,[43] Benjamin Currey and his nephew, Francis Currey, the resident agent, were able to dissuade the Duke from doing so, on the grounds that such a sale would injure the interests of the Duke's tenants, fail to realise the full value of the property and diminish the family's social and political standing.[44] Paxton was not convinced, and when the whole issue was raised once more in 1858, on the seventh Duke's succession, he reiterated his belief that an extensive Irish sale was the only convenient way to raise the necessary sum.[45] Again, the Curreys protested, using the same paternalistic and financial arguments as before.[46] This time, despite similarly cautious advice from the Duke of Bedford,[47] the Duke decided to press ahead and attempt to raise £200,000 by the sale of his urban property at Dungarvan and Youghal, and the detached portions of his agricultural estate in Co. Tipperary. Moreover, the Duke made it clear to the Curreys that he expected management costs to be substantially reduced on the Lismore and Bandon estates which he intended to retain, and to receive in future a nett annual income of at least £25,000.[48]

These sales mark a significant change in the Devonshires' attitude to their towns in Ireland, and an important stage in the long process of patronal disengagement which, by the end of the century, had left them with urban property in Lismore and Tallow alone. For the seventh Duke, the sales provided an opportunity of reducing some of the heavy management costs incurred on the Irish estate, and of ridding himself of two communities where political opposition and social antagonism towards his interests had always been most pronounced. To the predominantly Catholic tenantry in Dungarvan, the Duke's political stance had appeared suspiciously inconsistent. A supporter of Catholic emancipation in 1828,[49] he was nevertheless opposed to the radical nationalism embodied in O'Connell's Repeal movement, and had remained neutral in the Waterford election in 1830.[50] In Youghal, where emancipation and the changes in the franchise in 1832 had strengthened the Catholic challenge to the traditional Protestant domination of borough politics, successive elections had become more venal and violent.[51] For the tenants in both towns, the sales provided differing opportunities. At Dungarvan, where the Duke was prepared to accept private offers from occupiers,[52] before putting the remainder up for sale in larger lots through the Landed Estates Court, the more substantial tenants could seize the opportunity to become owner-occupiers or rentiers in their own right, free of the last traces of patronal influence. At Youghal, where the Duke's entire estate was sold in one lot, his tenants merely exchanged one landlord for another.[53] The consequences for the Duke's social patronage were equally immediate. Like his predecessor, the seventh Duke restricted his charitable patronage to those localities where he possessed property.[54] Accordingly, the extinction of his property interests in Youghal and Dungarvan led to the progressive reduction in his financial patronage there.[55]

The seventh Duke remained an annual visitor to his towns in Ireland until the assassination in 1882 of his second son, Lord Frederick Cavendish, in Phoenix Park, Dublin. His role as patron during these years is recorded in his diaries and in the correspondence of his agents and auditor. The picture which emerges is one of financially limited but socially even-handed patronage of schools and churches of all denominations,[56] civic societies[57] and urban improvements begun on local initiative or under the provisions of the Town Improvement Act of 1854 or the 1878 Public Health (Ireland) Act.[58] These included the improvement or construction of a piped water supply[59] and gasworks[60] at Lismore, and of a reservoir[61] and town hall[62] at Bandon. Between 1858 and 1890 the sums involved averaged £3,564 per annum, which still represented only about 8 per cent of the rent income due each year.[63] Moreover, when expenditure on repairing tenants' houses in Bandon began to rise in the late 1870s and again in the 1880s, the Irish agent was quick to ensure that the local sub-agent in the town was made aware of the need to reduce such spending to a more acceptable level.[64] At the same time, the Duke was also willing, albeit with increasing reluctance, to continue his predecessor's investment in Cork and Waterford railways. By 1890, he had invested some £200,000 of his English revenue in their construction,[65] in an attempt to improve the region's economy and promote urban growth.[66]

Compared to the sums the seventh Duke invested at Barrow-in-Furness and Eastbourne, the amount he spent on Irish railways was small and on his Irish towns, infinitesimal. At Barrow, the Duke's indefatigable promotion of the iron and steel works, shipyard and Furness railway prior to the slump of 1874, and his enforced role as their financial saviour thereafter, resulted in an expenditure by the mid-1880s exceeding £2,000,000.[67] At Eastbourne, the sums involved were not so large, but since the development was designed to be self-financing, by 1893 it had returned a surplus of barely £36,000 over an investment of £748,000.[68] This disparity in the Duke's spending on his English and Irish towns reflects the fundamental difference in his attitude towards them. A sombre, business-like figure, the seventh Duke looked to his Barrow investments to pay off his inherited legacy of debt, and on Eastbourne as an exercise in legitimate estate development which promised, too, to be profitable. He had begun work there in 1849, while still the second Earl of Burlington, and during his lifetime his influence dominated the town. Enjoying an exalted social status and a princely patrimony, he was a larger than life figure in Eastbourne. Hailed as its creator and major benefactor, he was also, wrongly, thought to be its main beneficiary.[69] Despite the lack of an immediate financial return, and possibly at the overzealous promptings of the Curreys and the local agent, R. A. Wallis,[70] the seventh Duke continued to finance the provision of amenities and infrastructural improvements alike. After a reduction in the rate of expansion in the 1860s, he was ultimately rewarded by what Cannadine describes as 'an orgy of building' in the 1870s and early 1880s and again in the late 1890s.[71] Southern Irish towns in the post-Famine period offered no such prospect of major growth. The continuing slow haemorrhage of population, the vulnerability of agriculture to periodic harvest failure and growing foreign competition and the accelerated penetration of the provincial Irish market by British goods, all combined to place severe limits on the potential for urban expansion. In seeking to maintain a low patronal profile in his Irish towns, the seventh Duke was doing no more than circumstances warranted.

But even this level of patronage could not be maintained indefinitely. The collapse of the seventh Duke's investments at Barrow meant the ultimate failure of his attempt to restore the family's fortunes. As Cannadine demonstrates, it was not until the eighth Duke (1833–1908) began his programme of sales and financial retrenchment that the debt, now exceeding £2,000,000, began to be significantly reduced.[72] Among the assets liquidated were extensive parts of the Derbyshire and Irish estates, which realised £1,450,000 by 1914, and included the town of Bandon, sold to Sir John Arnott[73] in 1894. This retrenchment also affected Eastbourne. Cannadine's research shows that by dint of a sustained reduction in capital expenditure, the eighth and ninth Dukes derived a disposable surplus of over £236,000 from the town between 1894 and 1914,[74] but only at some cost to their real influence there. As the family's financial patronage declined and their financial expectations from the town increased, so the Corporation began to take a more active and independent role in Eastbourne's affairs. The election in 1897 of the eighth Duke as Eastbourne's mayor was, as he himself recognised, a 'purely ornamental affair'.[75]

The progressive disengagement by the Dukes of Devonshire from their Irish urban property, and the gradual decline in their influence at Eastbourne, provides a theme which can be amplified from elsewhere. In Cardiff, Davies demonstrates that successive Marquesses of Bute varied greatly in the extent of their participation in the development of the property and, accordingly, enjoyed very different relationships with their urban tenantry.[76] The passive disinterest of the generally absentee first Marquess (1744–1814) permitted the local agents the same high level of autonomy enjoyed by Connor at Lismore, and contrasted strongly with the active intervention of the second Marquess (1793–1848), who was responsible for the first major industrial and urban development of the Cardiff property. The second Marquess was also a much more active philanthropist than his grandfather, but had more cause to be so. The £25,000 he spent on various charitable causes on the Cardiff and Glamorgan estates between 1821 and 1848[77] was essentially political philanthropy, designed to ensure the continued loyalty of voters to Bute nominees at elections. Paradoxically, the need for this investment had arisen from the second Marquess's success in developing the estate. The radical changes in estate management which necessarily accompanied its transformation had given rise to resentment among local estate officials. Allying themselves with an existing anti-Bute political faction, the Bute's local solicitors, the Woods, fomented outright opposition to the Bute candidate at the election in 1818.[78] Although successful in returning his candidate, the second Marquis took care that his philanthropy aided the successful exercise of his political influence.

The third Marquess (1847–1900) was the antithesis of his father. Following his succession in 1868, the third Marquess accepted the role of a mere figurehead on his urban estate. Mayor of Cardiff in 1890, dignitary in various local clubs and societies, he continued his father's philanthropic activities in the town without concerning himself more than necessary with the management of the estate.[79] This remained in the hands of a trust established by the second Marquess. The third Marquess's real interests lay elsewhere in religion and medievalism, and consequently he appeared a more distant figure to his Cardiff tenantry; interested in the revenue from the estate, but not in the patronal responsibilities its personal management would have entailed.

Political assertiveness and the middle classes in estate towns

Whatever the attitudes of individual patrons and the immediate circumstances in which they operated, it is clear that on many urban estates in Britain, the nineteenth century saw the sustained erosion of aristocratic power in the face of a growing challenge from middle-class elites. Recent research has shown that this was as characteristic of industrial estate towns such as Dudley and West Bromwich as of exclusive residential suburbs or seaside resorts such as Edgbaston or Southport.[80] Typically, the decline in aristocratic authority was signalled by an initial weakening in and subsequent loss of control over both Parliamentary representation and municipal bodies, leading ultimately in some cases to territorial withdrawal by the family. Trainor's work on Dudley and West Bromwich indicates that the political decline of the towns' owners, the Earls Dudley and Dartmouth, had already begun by 1850 and continued virtually unabated throughout the century as both working-class radicalism and middle-class liberalism mobilised.[81] Their only success was the return of Conservative candidates for the towns in the election of 1886, and Trainor concludes that even this owned more to the candidates' policies than to their aristocratic support. The real strength of the two families' political interest, Trainor argues, was seen at the 1906 election, when members of each stood for Dudley and West Bromwich, and were soundly defeated.[82] This political decline was matched by an equal decline in the Earls' power on local representative bodies, and by the 1880s their role was reduced to that of locally important philanthropists, primarily concerned with funding church and school improvement.[83]

A similar picture of a gradual decline in political influence emerges from Cannadine's work on the Calthorpe estate in Birmingham, but here matters were complicated by changes in the Calthorpes' political allegiance. Between 1810 and the Municipal Reform Act of 1832, the Whiggish sympathies of the third Lord Calthorpe and the civic aspirations and muted radicalism of Birmingham's middle class were well matched. Calthorpe played an attentive Parliamentary role in the furtherance of Birmingham's commercial interests, and was generous in his patronage of local improvement.[84] Thereafter the situation changed. Calthorpe's initial opposition to municipal reform heralded his growing alignment with traditional Conservatism, and consequently the eclipse in ever-radical Birmingham of his family's real political power. Moreover, although the Calthorpes continued to be fêted as important benefactors of the town in the 1840s and 1850s, Cannadine argues that this was only because of the miserable investment record of the town council prior to Chamberlain's reforms of the 1870s. The massive public expenditure on the city's improvement, begun during the Chamberlain era, exposed the real parsimony of the Calthorpes' contributions under the earlier, voluntary system of improvement. Social relations between the Calthorpes and the Corporation reached a nadir in 1880. Already strained by the fifth Lord's tactless assertion of his property rights in the city, they were exacerbated by the defeat of his brother, Augustus, as Conservative candidate for Birmingham in the general election of that year. Although the relationship improved after Augustus's succession to the title in 1893, he and his successor rarely visited Birmingham and when they did so, took little part in public life.[85]

In the Devonshires' Irish towns, political consciousness developed along sectarian lines rather than on the basis of social class, and among the Catholic community at least, was mobilised by the clergy on national issues such as Repeal.[86] Accordingly, the Duke's towns do not display evidence of the same protracted middle-class challenge to patrician authority which occurred in England. Instead, they figure periodically as arenas in which local battles over national issues were fought, during the course of which the Devonshires' role as largely absentee Liberal landlords was challenged as much by the Catholic clergy as by nationalist politicians. As early as 1829, the then agent in Ireland, Col. W. S. Currey, confided in his brother Benjamin, the Devonshires' auditor, that he could only hope to influence the Duke's freeholders at the forthcoming Waterford election 'if the priests do not put forward their power ... in case the same influence is used as at former elections, I fear I must fail'.[87] The exercise of that power helped enforce the use of Lismore as site for one of O'Connell's Repeal meetings against the Duke's wishes[88] and to defeat his preferred candidate, Sir Nugent Humble, at the Dungarvan election in 1857.[89] So great was the feeling engendered against the Duke's espousal of the liberal Conservative cause at this election, that his agent was physically assaulted by the tenants. In subsequent correspondence with the auditor, the resident agent, Francis Currey (Col. Currey's son), gives a fascinating insight into what he thought the Duke could legitimately expect in the way of political loyalty from his urban tenants, and what he should do when it was not forthcoming. Commenting on the Dungarvan parish priest Dr Halley's active role in fomenting opposition to Humble, Currey writes:

Dr Halley's duplicity and ungratitude is unmasked, he is wholly unmindful of the many favours given to him by the Duke. ... Some future remonstrance may be necessary against those freeholders who have allowed themselves to be entrapped and voted against the Duke's wishes. They should not continue to receive the full measure of indulgence (in rent and rates relief) they have had before. ... There are also a few persons who made themselves conspicuously obnoxious amongst the mob, who are holding small houses from the Duke and they ought to be made to pay up all the arrears or be turned out.[90]

But the political tide was running against such attempts to demonstrate patronal displeasure. The sixth Duke's active espousal of Humbold's candidacy was in itself unusual, and had been occasioned by the Duke's prior commitment to support any moderate candidate put forward by the Government of the day. The roundness of his defeat was a measure of the Devonshires' declining real influence in Irish urban politics in the face of the rising tide of nationalism. It is probable that had the seventh Duke not willingly adopted an equally low political profile, it would have been forced on him. The eighth Duke played even less of a political role in the Irish boroughs. Lismore and Tallow had been disenfranchised at the Act of Union in 1801,[91] and Bandon (along with Dungarvan and Youghal) lost its independent representation in 1885.[92] Moreover, since 1874, both Dungarvan and Youghal had returned Home Rulers,[93], and it is doubtful whether the Devonshires' political influence would have survived long in either town, even had they retained ownership. It is a curious irony that when the seventh Duke's heir, Lord Hartington, split the Liberal party and defeated Gladstone's Home Rule Bill in 1886, he was acting directly contrary to the wishes of the majority of his family's erstwhile urban tenants in Ireland.

A model for withdrawal?

In the only published attempt to provide a coherent conceptual framework for the process of aristocratic withdrawal in British towns, Cannadine summarises it in terms of six consecutive stages: 'power then conflict, influence then confrontation, ornamental impotence then territorial abdication'.[94] Cannadine stresses the tentative nature of the model and its variable applicability to individual cases, but argues nevertheless that much of aristocratic involvement in nineteenth-century urban growth in Britain can be encompassed within its terms. How applicable is the model to the Duke of Devonshire's towns in Ireland?

In Britain, Cannadine argues that the initial period of aristocratic power which lasted from *ca.* 1800 to *ca.* 1820 or 1840, was made possible by the survival of archaic administrative structures which favoured entrenched landlord power. Until the 1832 Reform Act, similarly archaic systems survived on the Duke's Irish estates at Bandon, Youghal and Dungarvan. As in England, the existence of these Corporations, with their limited elective franchise, offered the Duke both the opportunity to regain political control of the town and the means to keep it. For example, it was the Duke's successful action against Youghal Corporation's encroachment on his rights to the bed of the River Blackwater, by which he established title to much of the property occupied by members of the Corporation, that enabled him to regain control of both Corporation and borough representation.[95] Similarly, the fifth Duke's political success at Dungarvan was the result of a judicious mixture of liberal patronage for urban improvement and the wholesale creation of additional freeholders, with which to dominate borough elections.[96]

Subsequent stages in Cannadine's model trace successive phases in the changing balance of power between aristocratic patrons and middle-class civic leadership in the nineteenth century. Municipal and Parliamentary Reform in the 1830s ushered in a period of middle-class assertiveness, which petered out as many of the new municipal authorities failed to establish their independence from patronal influence. The resulting compromise between aristocratic and middle-class interests lasted until the 1870s, when legislative strengthening of municipal authority encouraged attempts to annex remaining patronal rights and property during the 1880s. The closing decade of the century saw renewed rapprochement, as the by-now dominant middle classes could safely afford to lionise the aristocracy as suitably elevated patrons for various forms of civic endeavour. For many aristocratic families, this 'ornamental' patronal role presaged their final territorial abdication. On the Calthorpe estate this was complete by 1918, and on the Ramsden estate in Huddersfield, by 1920. In Bournemouth and Southport, aristocratic connections with the towns had been severed by the late 1920s, and in West Bromwich and Dudley by 1947.[97]

In Ireland, the sequence and causation of the Devonshires' withdrawal from their urban interests differed, but ultimately achieved the same end: patronal disengagement from towns once dominated financially, politically and socially. The course of the Devonshires' political withdrawal from their boroughs, and the reasons for it, have already been shown to have had little to do with the growth of middle-class opposition. Much more was it the result of the growth of sectarian nationalism, itself a consequence of the emancipation of the Catholic majority within the population at large. Moreover, the close association between middle-class leadership and the creation and subsequent strengthening of municipal bodies does not, on current evidence, appear to have developed to the same extent on the Duke's towns as in Cannadine's English examples. The framework for such a development certainly existed. The Act for Lighting, Cleansing and Watching of the Towns of 1828, the Municipal Corporations of Ireland

Act of 1840, the Town Improvement Act of 1854 and the Public Health (Ireland) Act of 1878, all provided the means whereby municipal authorities could assert for themselves an independent managerial role free from patronal interference. This did not happen in the Duke's towns, largely because of his continuing monopolistic ownership of the sites required for urban improvement. Accordingly, surviving correspondence with the Duke's agents indicates a relatively acquiescent attitude on the part of the municipal authorities, with only an occasional dispute, as for example, over the repair of the quays at Youghal in 1842,[98] or the provision of labourers' houses in Lismore in 1874[99] or improvement of market facilities there in 1885.[100] Indeed, major attempts at civic improvement invariably seem to have required as much financial assistance as the Duke was prepared to give, and frequently, the active participation of one or other of the Duke's agents.

If the assertion of middle-class independence does not provide a useful theme with which to characterise the patronal relations between the Devonshires and their urban tenants in the later nineteenth century, then their progressive territorial withdrawal does. At the beginning of the nineteenth century, their urban inheritance was virtually intact, and was capable, where necessary, of being extended. By 1860, the worsening financial crisis facing the seventh Duke, coupled with his increasingly ambivalent attitude towards Irish property[101] and the social and political problems involved in its management, led to withdrawal from two of his larger urban properties, Youghal and Dungarvan. In 1894, the process was repeated by the eighth Duke at Bandon. Although as at Youghal, the outright sale of the entire estate to a single purchaser meant that for the Bandon tenants, very little changed, for the Devonshires, the liquidation of one more piece of Irish property signalled a further step in their retreat from a role as absentee landlords in Ireland. It is this retreat from power and property which characterises the Devonshires' patronal role in their Irish towns after ca. 1837, in each case for reasons which are peculiar either to Ireland or to the family itself. It is a process which is not yet complete. Although Tallow was sold in the 1920s,[102] the Duke of Devonshire remains ground landlord of Lismore.

Acknowledgements

The author wishes to acknowledge the following for permission to use manuscript material in their ownership or care: His Grace the Duke of Devonshire and the Trustees of the Chatsworth Settlement; Mr Peter Day at Chatsworth; Mr Paul Burton at Lismore Castle; the Director of the National Library of Ireland, Dublin; and Dr Anthony Malcomson, Public Record Office of Northern Ireland.

Urban functional change

14

The development of urban centrality in England and Wales

HAROLD CARTER

Introduction: some general principles

The most useful approach to consideration of the development of urban centrality in England and Wales within a very limited compass is to establish at the beginning the sets of general principles which can be considered as being of some relevance. Two implications follow from the phrase 'the development of urban centrality'. The first is that there has been a process of evolution and, in so far as increasing mobility and the consequent easing of the friction of distance were progressively characteristic over most of historic times, this can be accepted as axiomatic. There are some reservations which have to be made even here, however, for highly specialised activities create urban settlements where centrality, in its classic sense, has little part to play and more specialised functions were far more significant in the genesis of towns than more generalised central place roles.

The second implication is that centrality is historically a uniform concept, but here real difficulties arise for centrality can be based on principles which although related are, nevertheless, substantially different. It is worth noting that Christaller when interpreting contemporary centrality had perforce to invoke three principles, market, transport and administrative, in order to explain the varying 'k ratios', so that it is not surprising to find a similar necessity when reviewing historical changes. The first principle is primarily a military one when walled or defended towns acted as central points in processes of occupation and subjugation. The second is administrative when the town, after the necessary pacification of its surrounding countryside, became the centre of the necessary administration, mainly though not exclusively legal, of that countryside. It should be noted that more than one administrative system can be established. Thus in medieval Britain along with the secular system of government arose also an ecclesiastic system based on parish and diocese. The systems, especially at the parish level, were interlinked but were nevertheless separate. It can be argued that in the nineteenth century as new demands were created by industrialisation whole series of ad hoc systems were created overlapping and conflicting so that eventually they had to be, or at least partially, resolved into coherence by local government reform towards the end of the century. The third principle is economic when the town functions as the market centre for its hinterland, freed from the restrictions of control by crown or overlord and responding to those forces which because of their nature are called market forces, collecting and exporting the produce of the surrounding countryside and importing and distributing demanded goods and providing services.

The way in which the three principles have been enunciated suggests that they constitute discrete, successive developmental phases. But that would be far too simplistic a view for they overlap and their separation can only be based on differences in emphasis. There is, also, a further qualification which needs to be made. Whereas the three principles can be applied to the earliest phases of town founding and growth from the Iron Age to the Norman Conquest, subsequently a military principle becomes manifestly inappropriate and has to be replaced, for later towns came into being for very different purposes. The most obvious example is the 'Industrial Revolution' when very special functions led to town generation. But the fundamental principle remains constant for these were towns dependent on highly specialised roles rather than the more ubiquitious functions of government and marketing.

Closely related to these characteristics of urban roles and relations is the basic form of the economic process itself, which is more complex than the market designation already given and has been seen as taking three forms. The first is 'reciprocity' which has been defined as movements between correlated points of symmetrical groupings. The second is 'redistribution' where there are appropriational movements towards a dominant centre and out of it again although this must be taken as identifying the process rather than necessarily describing actual operational movements. The third process is 'exchange', which operates in a market system where price making takes place within an institutionalised setting.

It is not easy to relate these three processes just described to the three principles which were previously identified; they do not form neat and comfortable associations. Reciprocity is least easy to establish and can be considered as largely related to pre-urban situations. It would be straining credulity to argue that such was the arrangement in early times when towns were separated the one from the other without competitive interaction, and no association can be justified. Redistribution, however, would logically seem to be properly characteristic of the phase of administrative priority for it is necessarily associated with an allocative procedure. Indeed, many early town charters were also concerned with economic control and the exclusive allocation of surrounding territory to a market centre enforced by military and political control; centrality was decreed. Exchange under a free market competition is readily associated with the principle of competition between centres. Free from feudal restrictions, central places could develop in the manner envisaged by Christaller; market towns gave way to shopping centres and although administration partly held to its older given patterning, more and more it became an adjunct to the success a city derived from its economic role as a central place.

All these generalisations imply that the city system is built up by a series of superimposed layers corresponding to well-defined periods of town foundation. This is fully justifiable since town creation is characteristically not a process of continuous generation but rather occurs in a series of distinct phases; most histories of town plan are structured on the basis of these phases. Each phase is separately characterised by the principles and processes which have been put forward. But that does not imply that the genetic layers remain discrete and undated for the pre-existing pattern plays a substantial role in moulding and modifying the subsequent pattern. Thus one of the major debates on medieval urbanism in Britain has revolved around the degree of continuity from the past. Indeed, Pred, treating the growth of the city system in the U.S.A., has elevated this into the major principle arguing for cumulative causation and hence long-term stability in the most important metropolitan complexes.[1] That is, that vertical stabilities project upward through the superimposed layers of urban genesis, locking, as it were, the city system together, but also making it a highly complex amalgam in which the past makes a significant contribution. These vertical continuities, revolving about the longest metropolis, would be regarded as the most significant structuring elements in Pred's interpretation.

It is possible to represent the characterisation of city system growth which has been presented in the form of a diagram (Figure 14.1). Stripped to its essentials the study of the growth of the city system in Britain, as indeed in any country or region, consists of identifying, in detail, the processes implied in the figure and unravelling the complex of dislocations and continuities from which the eventual pattern is built. Even within this procedure, however, there are two contrasted methods of approach. The first is idiomatic and process based. Each successive period is interpreted in the light of its own detail and its own 'historical' circumstances. The second can somewhat pretentiously be called economic for the form of the city system – size against rank – is established for a series of periods and the changing condition used to establish generalisation. This second approach makes major demands, however, in terms of data before national censuses and in this review the first will be adopted.

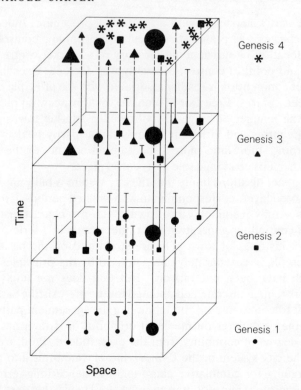

Figure 14.1   The development of centrality.
In this diagram time is represented vertically and the distribution of towns horizontally. Each 'plate' represents a phase of urban genesis based on the proposition
that towns were not continuously generated but were the production of distinctive
creative periods. In those periods origins were largely due to special functions,
such as military control, mineral extraction, manufacturing or the provision of lei-
sure services. Initially, because of the nature of origin, the functional role was
'allocated' or related to non-central place operations. Only as the conditions of
creation became relaxed did competition between towns over the share in the available centrality they could acquire become dominant. But no phase was separate
from a preceding one and in some cases cumulative causation led to strong vertical
continuities. Thus, on the diagram, the largest circle in Phase 4 might be London
with its roots going back to its Roman past and being the most significant centre
at all times. Others failed to survive once the special role was attenuated. The
decayed bastide and the distressed mining community because of pit closures are,
in basic principle, of the same nature. No attempt has been made to suggest an
ordering of towns or the relative numbers in an order on each 'plate'. The representation is purely notional (but see R. J. Johnston, *City and society. An outline for
urban geography* (London, 1980), pp. 51–120). Integral to the development of
centrality is the tension between newly generated centres, forming the horizontal
additions and the continuing centres of the vertical element.

The development of centrality: the point of departure

The initial problem is to establish a base from which a realistic analysis of centrality can begin. The whole trend of historical investigation over the last decade has been to reject earlier views of an Anglo-Norman foundation of the British city system and to emphasise continuity.[2] This extends the beginnings back at least into the Iron Age, for the hill forts of the British were translated into the 'civitas capitals' under Roman occupation. Although in most cases this meant local movement, that is a change of site, in some cases it did not. Canterbury is a good example where the movement from the hill fort at Bigbury had taken place in pre-Roman times.[3] The base layer in a meaningful study of the development of centrality must, therefore, be the Iron Age hill forts, though even in that case it would be wrong to assume no relationship with earlier settlement patterns. But the derivation of any systematic relationship between centres from the Iron Age evidence, other than one of separation, is difficult. The first clear emergence of a central place system comes with Roman occupation.

Under Roman control that section of the country under civil government was endowed with a system of cities (Figure 14.2). The 'career grade' was the 'civitas capital' which was derived from the *oppida*, the central settlements of the Iron Age tribal groupings via that continuity already noted. Below them were the *vici*, a term used to include a variety of small settlements, and the military forts, around some of which small towns had developed. Above the civitas capitals were the *colonia* (Gloucester, Lincoln, York, Colchester), settlements of time-expired soldiers, together with the only municipium for which there is evidence, Verulamium (St Albans). But these titles referred to chartered status rather than to hierarchical rank.[4]

Two critical questions as to centrality arise from this situation. The first relates to the degree of superiority exercised by the highest ranks and the second to the relationship between the civitas capitals and their inferiors.

The reference to the highest rank settlement introduces the status of London. Wacher writes:

while there is no epigraphic evidence relating to its civic status, it would seem inconceivable that . . . one of the largest towns in the western Empire, which, from about AD 60 became the headquarters of the imperial procurator, which, by the early second century at latest, had become the seat of the provincial governor, and which had a fort specially provided for soldiers attached to the governor's staff, should not have received a 'charter'.[5]

From the viewpoint of centrality the emphasis must be placed on the itemisation of London's general role and superiority rather than the charter. Whether by virtue of its geographical location, or its ebullient merchant

Figure 14.2   The Roman towns of England and Wales
Source: after J. Wacher, *The towns of Roman Britain* (London, 1974).

class, London, as provincial capital, became under Rome the head of the urban hierarchy, a position it was never to lose.

The level below London is less easily identified. Under Diocletian, Britain became one of the dioceses into which the Empire was divided and was itself divided into four provinces. There is some doubt over the capitals, however. London was most certainly the diocesan capital and the other three were probably York, Lincoln and Cirencester. If so, the *colonia* of Gloucester and Colchester had lost status but can be conceived as forming, with the four provincial centres, a layer of settlements below London but above the civitas capitals.[6]

The second question, that of the relationship between the civitas capitals and the smaller towns is even more difficult to elucidate. The primarily military role, usually ascribed to the latter, presumably dominated over standard central place functions. Hodder, however, has argued that an analysis of distribution reveals that the smaller towns occupied locations peripheral to the territories of the civitas capitals.[7] Such a situation he maintains was due either to the need for centres in areas poorly served from distant large towns or to the tendency for markets to develop at the margins of tribal territories, especially where bartering or haggling took place. These are not exclusive interpretations and can be collapsed into one.

If the views advanced in relation to these two questions are accepted then Roman Britain revealed an ordering of settlements and a hierarchical disposition of centrality even if its basis was government, for it would be pushing Hodder's case too far to imply the operation of a market principle of any significance. The problem that immediately follows is the extent to which the Roman system was bequeathed to Anglo-Saxon England. This raises the greatly complex issue of continuity between Roman town and Saxon burh. There was certainly a clear hiatus when the collapse of the imperial system and the urban needs it generated meant that any idea of the existence or the application of centrality in the conventional sense must be abandoned in face of disruption, localism and separation during the early Saxon period. But revival in later Saxon times, accompanied by new urban foundations, produced a structured system well before the Norman Conquest.[8] Presumably that system was the expression of political unification and the amalgamation of the various Saxon kingdoms and the Danelaw into one English kingdom.

Urban centrality: *adventus saxonum*

Centrality within the emerging Saxon system was in consequence most certainly dependent on administrative rather than economic bases. In spite of a peripatetic court some centre of territorial organisation was essential and part of the evolving political process. As the Saxon kingdoms grew from the phases of occupation so did their central settlements become the major towns. Many of these were the Roman civitas capitals readopted and reinvigorated. Such were Winchester and Canterbury. There were minor reorientations. The capital of the 'north folk' of East Anglia became Norwich, removed just a few miles from Caistor (Venta Icenorum) the former central settlement of the Iceni. In the Midlands, the shires (literally the divisions) established both by the English Kings, especially Edward the Elder, and by the Danes were based on newly created burhs such as Nottingham and Derby, as well as in Roman towns such as Lincoln or Leicester. The best example of a Danish creation which reached significant status was Thetford which became the sixth ranked settlement measured by the moneyers of its mint. By estimated population it was amongst the second order towns below London. Yet its existence seems to date to the wintering of the Danish army on the site in 869. Yet other emergent towns were ports of trade, such as Hamwih (Southampton), or the later cinque ports. Administration was not only secular for the Church also developed its system of government and the centres of the bishops' sees, the cathedral cities, played a significant promotional role, and new towns grew about monasteries, as at Bury St Edmunds. At this earliest period, therefore, a familiar dualism appears which recurs in periods of urban development. The largest and most significant of the pre-existing settlements achieve a further leap forward in size and significance, while the number of towns is increased by new formation.

At this stage, however, the measurement of centrality is both difficult and unreliable. Susan Reynolds writes: 'information comes from the growing quantity of documentary material, culminating in 1086 with Domesday Book, which casts a valuable but flickering light backwards into the late Anglo-Saxon period'.[9] But she also notes that 'all users of Domesday Book feel tempted to use its complex, obscure and incomplete data to produce more exact statistics than they will really bear, and notably to concoct estimates of population'.[10] If populations are not effective measures of centrality an alternative exists in the minting of coinage. 'The velocity of circulation of coinage in Anglo-Saxon England was remarkable, indicating a very brisk interchange of money, constant travel around the country and a national currency. It should not be thought that at this period the multiplicity of mints indicates purely localized coinages or localized areas of circulation.'[11] Hill has produced a map of mints (Figure 14.3) in England between 973 and 1066 based on the numbers of moneyers and expressed for each town as a percentage of total known moneyers, a method similar in principle to modern centrality indices.[12] Hill clearly infers a hierarchical structure:

there is a ranking which would seem to reflect the role of the various mints: thus there are the great national mints at London, Lincoln and York; there would appear to be provincial centres at Exeter, Winchester, Stamford and Chester; shire centres such as Shrewsbury and Oxford; down to the minor mints and secondary market centres at such sites as Steyning and Frome.[13]

In subsequent maps Hill implies a lower level still marking market centres where mints were not located but as he admits, 'the function of market cannot really be shown satisfactorily due to the haphazard nature of the evidence'.[14] These are the towns which Everitt calls 'the Banburys of

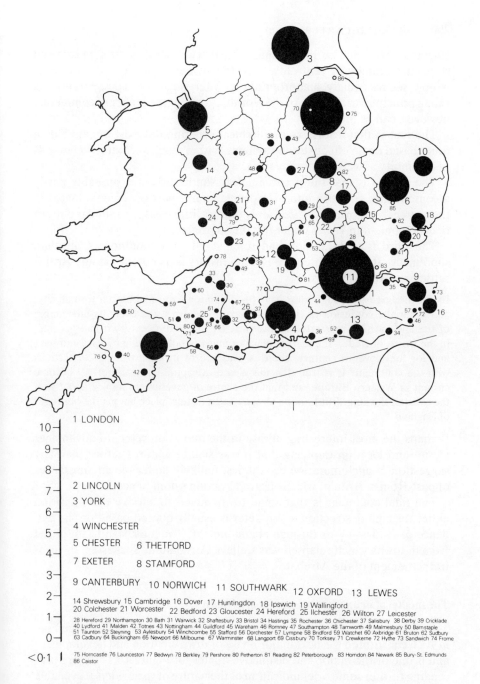

Figure 14.3   The ranking of mints as a percentage of total known moneyers, 973–1066

Source: after D. Hill, *An atlas of Anglo-Saxon England* (Oxford, 1981).

England'.[15] It would be quite indefensible to try to derive some sophisticated stepped hierarchy of centrality from this evidence but at the same time it now seems equally inappropriate to infer isolation and separation as ruling principles at the time of the Norman coming. A number of comments, however, can be made.

The first is that a form of hierarchical ordering did exist by late Saxon times based on an effective road system. Within these were strong elements of continuity as well as of innovation.

The second is that the predominantly southern bias is probably partly a consequence of more intensive development, part of regional biases in the sources of information. Certainly there is little basis for a similar pattern of development in Wales under the Welsh princes.

The third is that London had re-emerged to a condition of absolute supremacy. Its immediate post-Roman history is as obscure as any British settlement. Darby writes:

By far the largest borough must have been London ... it had been a Roman city, and, after the confusion of the Anglo-Saxon invasions was over, its advantages of site and location reasserted themselves. By the eighth century it had become, in the words of Bede, 'the market place of many people coming by land and sea'; and for the eleventh century, there is evidence of its wide trading connections with the continent. It is true that the idea of a capital city had not yet become current in Western Europe, and that the centre of government moved about with the court of the king. But London already had a distinct place among the boroughs of England.[16]

Perhaps the most interesting phrase in the quotation refers to advantages of site and location implying that it was spatial features rather than any suggestion of agglomeration economies, unlikely under the circumstances of post-Roman Britain, which ensured London's dominance.

The final comment is that some towns failed to survive the transition either through destruction – Wroxeter is usually quoted based on the evidence of Gildas – [17] or through abandonment. The most significant of the Roman towns which relapsed was Calleva Atrebatum, Silchester, the central settlement of the Atrebates.[18]

The medieval urban system and its aftermath

The Norman Conquest and occupation of England and Wales beginning in 1066 constituted the next major phase of town creation and development and is one of the major and distinctive 'plates' of Figure 14.1. Before proceeding further some brief indication of the nature of the evidence available needs to be given. Most attempts to measure the relative ranks of towns are based simply on population figures rather than more intricate assessments of centrality. But the first census was not taken until 1801 and most

1154–89	1334	1525	1660–70
London	London	London	London
York	Bristol	Norwich	Norwich
Norwich	York	Bristol	York
Lincoln	Newcastle	Newcastle	Bristol
Northampton	Boston	Coventry	Newcastle
Dunwich	Yarmouth	Salisbury	Exeter
Exeter	Lincoln	Exeter	Cambridge
Winchester	Norwich	Ipswich	Yarmouth
Gloucester	Oxford	Canterbury	Oxford
Oxford	Shrewsbury	Kings Lynn	Ipswich
Canterbury	Kings Lynn	Reading	Canterbury
Cambridge	Salisbury	Colchester	Worcester
Grimsby	Coventry	York	Shrewsbury
Newcastle	Ipswich	Lavenham	Salisbury
Doncaster	Hereford	Bury St Edmunds	Colchester
Berkhamstead	Canterbury	Worcester	Hull
Nottingham	Gloucester	Lincoln	Coventry
Bedford	Winchester	Totnes	Chester
Worcester	Southampton	Gloucester	Kings Lynn
Scarborough	Beverley	Hull	Portsmouth
Carlisle	Cambridge	Hereford	Rochester
Ipswich	Newbury	Yarmouth	Nottingham
Colbridge	Plymouth	Newbury	Gloucester
Shrewsbury	Newark	Boston	Dover
Southampton	Portsmouth	Hadleigh	Bury St Edmunds

Figure 14.4   Ranking of the largest twenty-five towns in England, 1154–89, 1334, 1525 and 1660–70

attempts to establish urban populations, especially in the earlier period, must rely on indirect and manifestly unreliable evidence. Foremost amongst the sources are taxation lists. There is no space here to enter into a discussion of the inadequacies of and difficulties in using these records, other than to indicate their unreliability. The major attempt to employ them by Russell in his book *British medieval population*[19] has been subject to considerable reservation. Figure 14.4 sets out a ranking of the largest twenty-five towns of four dates. They are based respectively on the average of 'aids' under Henry II (1154–89) and the lay subsidies of 1334 and 1525. The unreliability of the evidence is compounded by setting it out in the manner of Figure 14.4 where rank comparisons over some 400 years are indicated. At least no attempt to work out a rank correlation coefficient has been made! But when no other data are available then these which are usable can be cited, but with the considerable caution already mentioned.

The evidence of the 1154–89 listing suggests a strong element of continuity from pre-Conquest times. Bristol, in baronial hands, did not appear at all, neither did Chester and Leicester,[20] but in spite of these omissions, of the first ten ranked towns in Figure 14.3, all but Chester, already noted, and Thetford and Stamford appear in the first ten in the late twelfth century. Although a large number of settlements of varied origin appear at lower levels, a predominant continuity can be argued. Nowhere is this more significant than in the status of London. Throughout the medieval period not only did it grow in size but manifestly outgrew all other cities. By the sixteenth century estimates unanimously place it as some sixteen times the size of the next largest city, Norwich.[21] That indicates unequivocal primacy, and it appears from whatever source is used that primacy increased during the medieval period to reach its peak in early modern times. The standard bases of London's dominance can be easily rehearsed. It occupied the most significant location, at the lowest bridging point of the Thames, in the richest section of the country. Its situation on the largest navigable river made it the largest port and trading centre. It was the centre of government and administration which was increasingly complex, effective and centred on the capital, for the concept of a capital city itself had become meaningful. Increasing primacy is, therefore, as much part of the pattern of political evolution as peripheral, self-centred and autarkic systems are gathered into an ultimate dependence on the capital of a 'United Kingdom'.

Against this basis of stability, however, there was an increasing pattern of change, especially at the lower levels. This must be related in the first place to the massive creation of new towns which makes this a major genetic phase. These new towns were an integral part of the Norman process of conquest, occupation and exploitation. Beresford identifies some 160 planted towns in England and 80 in Wales between 1066 and 1334.[22] The Welsh urban system was virtually created during that period. But although they were new foundations the element of continuity was not unimportant. Carmarthen, which was to be the regional centre for south-west Wales and among the largest Welsh towns until the growth of industry in the late eighteenth and nineteenth centuries, was developed on a site adjacent to Moridunum, the civitas capital of the Demetae under Roman occupation.[23] The continuity between Roman town and Norman borough was but a thin thread of occupancy, certainly not urban in character, but the old location of authority, the tradition of centrality was revived and presumably exploited.

The creation of these new towns, whether by royal authority or by feudal lord, lay or ecclesiastic, was motivated by three purposes: first, the military pre-requisites of conquest and control; secondly, the need for cultural change and reorientation; and thirdly, the economic possibility of exploiting the market role via toll and taxation as well as to provide the stimulus to growth. To a degree it can be argued that these towns filled in the unserved interstices of a fragmentary system, but inevitably a period of competition was initiated as the newcomers sought to establish themselves and take on the role of regional service centres. Nowhere is this clearer than in the ports of trade which as the economy developed became dominant features of the hierarchy of towns. As examples, King's Lynn and Newcastle-on-Tyne were founded about 1100; Harwich, Liverpool and Portsmouth about 1200; Kingston-upon-Hull about 1300.[24] The names are in themselves indicative, King's Lynn, the King's town upon Hull and the new castle on the Tyne.

This process of competition, especially the strength of the ports of the east coast, is the main reason for the fall in rank of the late twelfth-century leaders, Exeter, Winchester, Gloucester, Canterbury and Cambridge, as well as of towns like Worcester, Nottingham and Colchester. Those increasing were Bristol, Newcastle, Boston, Yarmouth and King's Lynn. In some cases rise and decline can be clearly related. Thus the decline of Winchester is a corollary of the rise of Southampton as the capital of the Hampshire basin. Competition also marks the change from an allocative to a market basis. By their charters many towns were allocated a market area within which all exchange had to take place at the designated borough. But this soon gave way to free competition where success depended on how effectively location was exploited. Many towns failed completely and relapsed into the state of small village or hamlet or, indeed, disappeared as settlements. In some cases the change was no more than a limited locational shift, paralleling the movement in earlier times from Caistor to Norwich. Such was the replacement of Old Sarum by Salisbury.

It is difficult to establish these patterns of change in any detail but the clearest exposition is that by John Patten.[25] Given the difficulties of data his study is confined to East Anglia, but he is able to use both population figures and a measure of the range of economic activities present in the various settlements. Patten presents urban hierarchies for three periods, the sixteenth, the early seventeenth and the late seventeenth centuries. He asserts that a clear fourfold ranking of towns can be established for East Anglia in the sixteenth century. Norwich was the clearly dominant centre and a major provincial capital. Thus in Figure 14.4 it appears as next largest after London and York in 1154–89, slips somewhat by 1334 but is next largest after London in 1525. The level below was made up of the four county and/or port towns of King's Lynn and Great Yarmouth in Norfolk, and Ipswich and Bury St Edmunds in Suffolk. All four appear amongst the top thirty towns in both 1334 and 1525. They represent the devolution of government to the county level and correspond to the distinctive layer of county towns in England, and the new ports which had come into the rankings. Below these top two levels of centrality, Patten identifies some forty lesser towns divided into two further levels but with the admission that it is not easy to draw a distinctive line between them. But Patten concludes: 'The four county towns and ports remained clearly differentiated from Norwich, and from the major and minor local towns that lay below them in the urban system.'[26] A similar situation holds at the later dates although Norwich had distanced itself more clearly from the four second order towns.

A study of the towns of Wales carried out some thirteen years earlier, although using much less specific criteria, can be set alongside the East Anglian work.[27] Three grades of towns for about 1600 were identified in the Welsh study, although in each grade there were some settlements showing a tendency to rise, others to fall. The first level was made up of the four regional capitals each controlling a quadrant of the country, Caernarfon in the north-west, Denbigh in the north-east, Carmarthen in the southwest and Brecon in the south-east. Though these were relatively thriving centres their dominance was largely based on the role given by the legal and administrative framework provided under the Act of Union of 1536. Below them was a second level mainly comprised of the county towns whilst a third level, which given the nature of the data could not be subdivided, was made up of local market towns. Thus the succession, regional centre, county centre, market town parallels that, *mutatis mutandis*, which Patten established. But the necessary changes which need to be made are substantial, and it is in no way possible simply to mesh these rankings. East Anglia was one of the richest areas of the country whereas Wales was a poor, undeveloped and peripheral section. Thus the populations of the regional capitals were no more than half those of the second level in East Anglia; a whole downward shift has to be envisaged in the Welsh towns although this could be obviated by looking to the English border towns, such as Chester, Shrewsbury and Hereford as the proper regional capitals and partly meeting the needed shift in that way. Moreover, although Patten argues for considerable stability in his array, the Welsh system was still experiencing change; even so a similar stability had apparently become characteristic by the beginning of the eighteenth century.

The implication from the two examples is that under the primate dominance of London there was a series of regional systems with their own regional capitals. But they were not meshed or integrated with each other and reflected the wealth and economic development of their own areas. Centrality becomes locally and regionally organised in the first instance, but always under the dominance of the primate city.

The stability of the hierarchy, and of the distribution of centrality, should not be overemphasised by the identification of major genetic phases. There were continual readjustments but they, too, were most often related to special functions and consequent adjustments in centrality. The appearance of Lavenham and Hadleigh in the 1525 listing (Figure 14.4) indicates the importance of the broadcloth industry in promoting their growth and their significant entry into the central place system based on that industry. But with its decline they too fell away against the established superiority of the traditional central places. Moreover, towns were much more susceptible to single events, such as plague or fire, so that considerable volatility can be expected. Thus Baker summarises the changes between the 1334 and the 1525 listings by noting that:

the fortunes of English towns during this period were very varied and were character-ised by great diversity, both in time and place. Even so some general changes can be discerned, such as the relative decline and later recovery of the old corporate towns, the close association of the condition of towns with the state of trade and the increasing economic upsurge of towns and of London in particular.[28]

The interpretation advanced so far makes no allowance for the view of the late medieval decline of towns, though it is partly reflected in the 1525 rankings. Clark and Slack in their study of *English towns in transition 1500–1700* state: 'What is clear is that by the middle of the sixteenth century urban decay was widespread and affected most aspects of town life, and that recovery was often slow and never certain.'[29] Although this must be related to conditions in the country at large, to a degree it was part of the process of competition and perhaps that is why there is disagreement over the interpretation. That competition was highlighted by the threat posed to the older corporate towns by the rising prosperity of the new market towns. Clark and Slack discern by the second half of the seventeenth century 'a new urban stability'[30] representing the working out of all the competing forces.

Industrialism and the urban system

The next major insertion of new towns into the system, the next 'plate' in sequence, must of course be related to the industrial revolution of the mid-eighteenth century and lasting through much of the nineteenth. But although correct in the broadest of interpretations, it is far too simplistic. Prefacing the so-called revolution in industrial technology there was the growth of mercantilism which particularly affected the ports. The early development of the east coast ports has already been noted. Both military and commercial reasons lay behind the growth of the southern ports, includ-ing Rochester and Dover. With the discovery and development of the New World, the Atlantic ports began a major phase of growth. Bristol was already high in the hierarchy, but Liverpool also grew so that Defoe as early as the 1720s could write that it was 'one of the wonders of Britain'. 'Manchester, too, was "much encreased within these thirty or forty years". Sheffield now had "at least as many, if not more people in it than the city of York"; Coventry was "a large and populous city"; so were Leeds and Leicester. Hull was a substantial centre of commerce.'[31] The major generalisation that can be derived is that the direct relation between industry and urban growth which is often implicitly accepted was never so; urbanisation and industrialisation were mutually reinforcing.

But however much one rejects the concept of an urban and industrial revolution in favour of an elongated process of transition, it is surely proper to identify a distinctive phase of urban genesis. It has been widely studied from Weber's classic published before the end of the nineteenth century,[32] but the most apposite work with reference to centrality must be Robson's book on *Urban growth*.[33] It is a vast topic and only a limited number of specific issues which have arisen in debates on nineteenth-century urbanisation can be reviewed.

The first must be the appropriateness of Pred's conclusions from his analysis of city system growth in the U.S.A. He there refers to 'the onset of this rank-stability phenomenon, and more generally, early city system development in the U.S. and other advanced economies'.[34] He relates it to the circulation of specialised economic information which was spatially biased in such a manner that it was most readily available in the nationally largest cities, and to the two-way significant economic interdependencies which had manifested themselves between the largest cities. The result is that a rank stability set in amongst the largest units of a national or regional city system during a relatively early period of system development. Now this must depend on what is meant by 'an early period'. If it refers to a relatively discrete genetic-cum-growth phase then, with some reservations, it is true. The reservations are necessary as has been seen. London was the major centre neither in the initial phase of Roman occupation nor of the early Saxon kingdoms, although in both cases it quickly attained its dominant role. If Pred refers to a much longer period then it is manifestly not true, as the many lapsed great cities of the past attest. Even on a British scale only five out of the fifteen largest cities in 1660–1700 (based on the hearth tax returns) retained that position at the first census of 1801. And all but London had declined in rank. It is true that if the initial period of change in the eighteenth century is ignored and rankings in 1801 and 1901 be compared such stability can be maintained. But it is a contrived rather than a real situation. That innovation operated in a hierarchical way was effectively demonstrated by Robson,[35] but it was by no means universal. The largest town in Wales in 1801 was Merthyr Tydfil, nothing more than a hamlet in 1750. It was the earliest centre of the coke and blast furnace based iron industry in Wales and owed its growth solely to that stimulus. It became a centre for innovation both in the iron industry and transportation. But it failed to meet the exhaustion of local iron ore and those technological changes which made its inland location uneconomic. Size does initiate self-generating growth and Merthyr remained a service centre (though subsequently greatly depressed), but it could not compete on that basis with Cardiff and fell away as that city grew. Special-ised functions generate cities but when they decline, as so often they do, local and regional service must take over; industrial and mining towns faced exactly the same challenge as medieval bastions. There was, there-fore, an elongated phase of competition and sorting before something approaching the stability Pred postulates came into being.

The second feature is that the substantial growth of the provincial centres of industry drove them into sizes quite different from the modest popula-tions accumulated in pre-industrial times, even in the largest cities. London grew strongly, and it can be argued that its wealth generated provincial development, but nevertheless it lost its primacy.

A third characteristic is the widening functional range of towns during the eighteenth and nineteenth centuries. Ports and spas had already demon-strated distinctive growth in the eighteenth century but in the nineteenth, manufacturing towns of greatly diversified specialisms, mining towns, rail-way centres and seaside resorts were added. In consequence, the numbers of towns greatly increased. In 1801 some 32.8 per cent of the population was urban and there was only 1 city (London) with a population of over 100,000 and 253 over 2,500. By 1901, 78 per cent of the population was urban and there were 33 towns over 100,000 and 908 over 2,500.[36] However, the greatest growth had been in the largest cities. The smallest sized group, towns between 2,500 and 10,000, accounted for 29.1 per cent of the urban population in 1801 but only 11.4 per cent in 1901. The over 100,000 group made up 32.6 per cent in 1801 (London alone) but 56 per cent in 1901.

A fourth characteristic is that within the general pattern of change an enormous amount of local sorting and re-ordering had taken place related to the way in which effective service for the newly emergent industrial populations was organised. Local hierarchies, the lowest level of the distri-bution of centrality, were created in the way in which W. K. D. Davies has analysed in detail for the Rhondda valleys in South Wales.[37] But these were closely related to local potential, as had been the emergent hierarchies of earlier periods, even though they were tied into a nationally integrating system by a national transport system and the nationwide distribution of goods. But the merging of local hierarchies produced overall a national system more akin to the rank-size rule.

A fifth comment can be added. Robson's review of the series of rank-size arrays during the nineteenth century led to the identification of a consistent slope but one shifting progressively to the right.[38] As long ago as 1956 Madden had identified a similar characteristic for U.S. cities, concluding: 'The apparent conformity of the number and size of cities to the rank-size rule during the period under study portrays vividly the sense in which the growth of the system of cities in the United States can be viewed in one of its aspects as having been accompanied by stabilities or regularities.'[39]

Robson proposed the operation of an allometric principle by which the increased number of smaller sized settlements is balanced by the increased size of the smaller number of large settlements. It is difficult to propose reasons for such an observed relationship other than those which Zipf originally set out in terms of the rank-size rule itself where forces of diversification (localisation) were balanced by forces of unification (agglomeration).[40] Thus the demands set up by the vastly increased populations sent a reacting wave through the whole of the system, gathering strength as each 'level' amalgamated demand finally to project it onto the largest cities at a greatly heightened state, the whole being made possible in an integrated and interactive system.

Conclusions: the development of centrality

A broad review of the development of centrality in England and Wales to 1900 has been presented and some conclusions need to be drawn from it. The central issue in any such review is the evaluation of centrality since it is only too easy to relapse into a general narrative of urban growth at a broad and necessarily superficial level. That relapse is in itself partly due to the intractable nature of the data and of the enterprise.

At the outset the notion of development was accepted and there is no need to revise that acceptance. The lubrication of the friction of distance through more and more efficient transport and effective mobility has brought about an increasing integration within the city system. This is most effectively demonstrated by the replacement of a system with centrality overwhelmingly concentrated at one point, London, with a series of inarticulated regional systems below, by one where an approximation to the rank-size rule applies. Such a statement implies that the most attractive interpretation of change is of the order just employed where different forms of the graph of rank against size are identified as characteristic of contrasted developmental situations. There is a major problem, however, in operationalising such an approach for, before the first censuses, the data are inadequate and whereas comments on relative rank order in the highest reaches are permissible, to put any analytical weight on the figures is barely justifiable. Moreover, comparatively little basic progress has been made. Robson's analysis of nineteenth-century England and Wales led to his admitting that 'there is little in the spatial pattern which has been studied which could be interpreted better by a geographer than by the descriptive expertise of the historian'.[41] At a very much larger scale analyses have been set out by Rozman[42] and de Vries.[43] Their bases are similar, involving an early period of separation or of autarkic provincial systems being gathered together under a primate city before industrialisation transformed the system and gave rise to a quasi-hierarchical organisation of centrality.

There have been comparatively few attempts to provide a Marxist inter-pretation, although Johnston in his book *City and society* deals with the evolution of urban systems from the viewpoint of changing economic organi-sation.[44] The earlier phase is seen as pre-industrial, or perhaps the word feudal can be legitimately introduced. The city under such a condition is essentially a centre of redistribution under a politically ordered system. Mercantilism is seen as breaking across this imposed order to introduce a market based exchange system dominated especially by ports of trade or gateway cities, hence the pattern of the primate city with provincial systems below. Modern capitalism penetrated this system and the city was transformed from the means by which the feudal order controlled society to the means by which capitalism manipulated those flows essential to the creation and acquisition of surplus value. Along with this went a transfer from a primate to an extended hierarchical system, and a worldwide exten-sion also, but one only partially achieved in colonial territories where primacy still remains.

There is much in common between all these general interpretations of the movement of centrality but they are possibly on too large a scale to be applied to England and Wales at a detailed level, although their relevance to the feudal, mercantile, industrial progression is evident. At the national scale the development of centrality seems to be related more closely to the increases in the number of towns and increasing interaction between them, but that did not occur in a process of steady evolution but via a series of more or less well-defined phases, the 'plates' of Figure 14.1, which have been used in this essay. Each of these phases sees the adoption and adaptation of evolving settlements which benefit both from inherited tra-dition and actual established size. Each phase also sees new towns added to the array. All these settlements have to interact either with their imme-diate localities or with other towns before a settled system develops. In the process some are eliminated. This is a consequence of a change in role, for the creative phase is characterised by specialised functions whereas the interactive phase is dominated by the share out of centrality on which the town must ultimately depend. That centrality includes administration for the necessity of government and its organisation usually takes prece-dence. But ultimately in a free market economy the market principle will dominate in the way which Christaller was to identify. If Hodder's views are accepted then this can be applied, at least partially, to the Roman phase of occupation of England. But some specialised towns will remain unintegrated within the system. For example, nearly all large cities in Eng-land and Wales are centres of dioceses, but not all centres of dioceses are large centres for they retain their early Christian significance over and above later economic changes.

It is now possible to propose that within each of the phases of Figure

14.1 a similar pattern of development took place. It can be set out in tabular form.

Genesis: special roles	Adaptation of existing settlement pattern	Emergence of special territories, e.g. politico-religious
Administrative priority	Organise to provide control and/or government allocation	Gateway communities or ports of trade stand outside system
Economic competition	Sorting and ranking on market principles. Re-allocation of administration	Integration of ports of trade
Administrative– economic convergence	Development of a central place system – nature varies by phase	Unintegrated elements remain outside the system

The sequence is repeated for each phase although there are obvious differences in the nature of that repetition as evident in that contrasted arrays, primate or hierarchical, can result. This interpretation of the evolution of centrality is manifestly descriptive, at the best heuristic. But more enlightenment is likely to come from such an approach than from more rigorous attempts to manipulate unreliable data. Moreover it adds understanding, if not solution, to contemporary difficulties. Castle towns of the middle ages which failed to acquire more general service functions atrophied and decayed. Mining towns of the nineteenth century under present economic conditions, unless they can broaden their functional range, face the same fate. Perhaps the one universal aspect which comes through is the necessity for towns created for very specific purposes, even endowed with centrality, to establish their share of regional centrality, in competition with other towns, in order to survive and prosper.

15

The persistence and dynamics of office functions in West German cities since the late nineteenth century

HEINZ HEINEBERG and NORBERT DE LANGE

Introduction

In the English-speaking world considerable research has already been published on the dynamics of office location.[1] This contrasts with the situation in German-speaking countries, where work on the locational behaviour of offices has only been slightly developed.[2] Many of these studies have been part of wider research themes concerned with general aspects of city centre development and in some instances the changing nature of retailing structures. It is, however, within these general studies that research in German-speaking countries has taken an historical approach to the analysis of commercial activities. Some of this work has focussed on the evolution of individual streets,[3] whilst other studies have examined larger functional areas within cities, such as Wolcke's study of Bochum in 1968.[4]

Specific work on office development was for some time limited to the early study carried out by Gad on the central area of Nürnberg.[5] His approach was strongly linked to the work of geographers in Britain and North America, since it included the analysis of interactions and communications between office locations. More recent research has highlighted the processes of office decentralisation in West German cities, through the work of Dach on Düsseldorf and Hartwieg in the Munich region.[6] Unfortunately, all of these studies are focussed on contemporary processes and consequently have paid very little attention to the historical evolution of office functions or their locations.

The recent research and publications by Heineberg and de Lange have attempted to rectify this situation, through an examination of office developments from the late nineteenth century in the city centres of Dortmund, Düsseldorf, Munich, Münster and Hannover.[7] This work is part of a larger project on 'Comparative Historical City Research' analysing inner city areas and the development of quaternary functions.[8] The basic aims of the study are to ascertain the long-term persistence of office locations in a variety of urban environments. The work is based on a variety of sources, including:

1. An analysis of classified trade and city directories to enable historical cross-sections to be constructed. These data are also supplemented with archival material.
2. Complete empirical field studies in the central areas of the selected cities, listing all land use types.
3. Interviewing key decision makers in selected office sectors.

Given this background the aim of this chapter is to present some results from the research project, particularly those that highlight the locational behaviour of office functions. The examples are drawn from the cities of Dortmund and Münster, and focus on three types of office functions, namely public institutions, lawyers and doctors.

Trends in the development of office functions in German cities since the late nineteenth century

It was only after 1850 that the dynamic expansion of office functions and the modern processes of city centre development, the so-called 'Citybild-ung' began in German towns. This concept of 'Citybildung' was named after the early phases of population decentralisation experienced in the City of London, due to the expansion of banking and insurance functions.[9] In German cities the expansion of the banking system occurred somewhat later, as did the corresponding changes in city centres. For example, in the important, old business centre and former free imperial town ('Freie Reichstadt') of Nürnberg, there was only one major bank (the Royal Bank) and a few small private bankers as well as one unimportant savings bank.[10] A similar situation existed in the regional capitals, such as Hannover, where the Hannoversche Bank (an issuing bank) was founded in 1856. The territorial fragmentation and the lack of a primate metropolis caused a dispersed location of important central functions to the various regional capitals. This stands in contrast to the situation within Britain and the concentration of capital functions in London.

When the German Reich was founded in 1871 there were still thirty-one different issuing banks in existence. Indeed, it was only in 1875 that the Prussian Bank in Berlin became the 'Reichsbank', after which time the number of issuing banks steadily decreased to ten in 1893.[11]

The foundation of the Reich also gave added impetus to the development of the capital, Berlin, as the major economic and cultural centre, encouraging the spatial segregation of functions in central Berlin during the second part of the nineteenth century. Thus, in the western part of the city centre a government quarter grew up, based on the government offices of both the German Reich and Prussia. A new banking area extended to the east of this government sector, on both sides of the Behrenstrasse. However, it was only at the start of the twentieth century that the larger head offices of leading German banks were established here. Directly associated with this banking quarter was an area of insurance offices and related commercial functions.

There were also further functional areas, for museums, for exporting firms and also two major shopping streets, Friedrichstrasse and Leipziger Strasse – the latter having two large department stores built at the turn of the century. At this time the process of city centre development and the formation of functional quarters was most advanced in Berlin. This tendency was due to a great number of locational advantages, especially the outstanding position of Berlin within the national and international traffic system together with its capital functions.

The position of Berlin in the urban hierarchy of Germany became even more outstanding with the formation of Greater Berlin in 1920. Understandably, the political divisions of Germany and Berlin after World War II have caused radical change in urban system, with Berlin losing its function as a national capital for West Germany. Central functions which had formerly located in Berlin are now distributed within a group of eight to twelve regional centres, frequently capitals of the Bündeslander of the FRG.[12]

Case studies of Münster and Dortmund

The dynamics and the tradition of selected office locations in provincial West German cities can be well demonstrated by the examples of Münster and Dortmund, both situated in the Westphalian part of Northrhine-Westphalia. The cities possess historical cores of considerable size (Münster's is 103 ha, delimited now by a promenade, and Dortmund's is 81 ha and marked by a ring road), due to their historical importance. Thus, from the Middle Ages to the beginning of the nineteenth century Münster was the seat of the prince-bishop of Münster, whilst Dortmund was a free imperial town. Furthermore, both cities were members of the Hanseatic League.

After the Thirty Years War, in which Dortmund was considerably damaged, the city lost not only many inhabitants, but also a number of central, economic functions. Indeed, before the start of industrialisation processes in the nineteenth century, Dortmund had declined to a rather insignificant agrarian centre, a so-called 'Ackerburgerstadt'. In contrast, Münster's growth continued almost uninterrupted up to the nineteenth century and it became the most important city in Westphalia. In 1780, for example, a regional university was founded and, more importantly, by 1816 Münster had become the capital of the newly established Prussian province of Westphalia. This led to more important regional administrative functions being located in the city; for example, the Oberpräsident of

Westphalia, regional courts and military establishments. At this time Dortmund was incorporated into the Prussian administrative district Arnsberg (Arnsberg being a small provincial town, located in the nearby 'Sauerland'), and only received the offices of the Inspectorate of Mines ('Oberbergamt') as a regional function. In the first half of the nineteenth century the difference in the importance of the two cities was reflected in their populations, with Münster having 18,371 inhabitants in 1831 and Dortmund only 6,121. The arrival of the railways, Münster being connected in 1848 and Dortmund in 1847, had a greater impact on the latter city, with the development of mining, iron and steel, brewing and engineering in the eastern Ruhr. In contrast, the functions of Münster remained very largely confined to services.

The historical cores of both cities were substantially damaged during World War II, and it is therefore important to consider how far historical patterns of office location have survived despite such extensive destruction. Despite such problems, Münster and Dortmund remain the most important centres in Westphalia due to the concentration of quaternary institutions in both cities. Within today's urban hierarchy, the service and administrative centre of Münster can be classified as a regional centre of medium rank; whereas the larger industrial and service metropolis of Dortmund is only a minor ranking regional centre.[13] Such differences are a direct result of the individual historical heritage of both cities.

The expansion of the public office sector and its impact on city centre development

The significance of the expansion of public institutions for city centre development in the nineteenth century applied not only to Berlin, and territorial capitals, but also to subordinate administrative centres. This is illustrated by the example of Münster, where the development of the Prussian government in the decades following 1816 was characterised by the construction of many public buildings within the old core. For example, the Prussian regional administration, the Regional Postal Directorate and the Royal Bank all selected prestigious sites in close proximity to the cathedral. Similarly, the most high ranking administrative functions of the province of Westphalia, the so-called Oberpräsident and the Kommandierende General, were located in one of the most important buildings, the former palace of the prince-bishop at the western side of the old core.

After the foundation of the Reich, German cities experienced a rapid expansion in public administration and related public buildings. The representatively designed larger public buildings of the so-called 'Gründerzeit' were mainly set up in peripheral locations at the urban fringe, often where the land belonged to the public. Such developments also marked the early processes of office decentralisation. For example, in Münster the law courts were built along the former lines of the fortifications, on the western out-skirts of the old core. Up to World War I, further extensive public institutions, such as hospitals and central administration as well as military establishments, were built at the then boundary of the town. This phenomenon of the suburban orientation of public institutions reached its height in Berlin.[14]

It should also be pointed out that whilst these suburban developments were taking place, the city centres were being filled with public institutions. In Münster this process can be shown with the development of a university sector in the western part of the inner city after 1902 (this being a reopening of the university after its closure in 1818). Furthermore, most of the larger public institutions, which were established from the late nineteenth century up to World War II, are characterised by considerable locational persistence in spite of the heavy war damage within the city centre.

Despite the fact that Münster had to transfer important regional government functions to Düsseldorf after 1945, some of the former central administrative functions have remained, whilst others were introduced to counterbalance the loss of capital functions. Thus, the city today performs partly capital functions for Northrhine-Westphalia, (e.g. the constitutional court). The example of Münster also reveals how important public buildings direct the agglomeration of specific private services, a feature discussed in the next section of this chapter. However, before examining these trends it is necessary to describe some of the general features of city centre growth in the two examples of Münster and Dortmund.

During the first important phase of city centre development in Münster, after 1875, a larger central area could not be delimited, only the main shopping areas could be defined with any precision (Figure 15.1). Up to the 1930s, an area between the historical core, around the cathedral, and the railway station was developed as a city centre sector. The railways presented a main traffic axis, as well as the crucial barrier limiting central area development in the east. The location of the university sector to the west of the city centre added further limitations of growth, leaving only for the most part the north and south for expansion.

In contrast, the expansion of Dortmund's city centre functions has occupied the entire old inner core. The developments of the late nineteenth century are characterised by far less public institutions compared with Münster, a feature that can be identified as early as 1886 (Figure 15.2). In Dortmund the general expansion of the public sector and the need for larger administrative buildings from the end of the nineteenth century can be observed by a deconcentration at the former urban fringe. The city centre expanded towards the higher class residential areas in the south and east of the old core, where public ownership of sites along the former

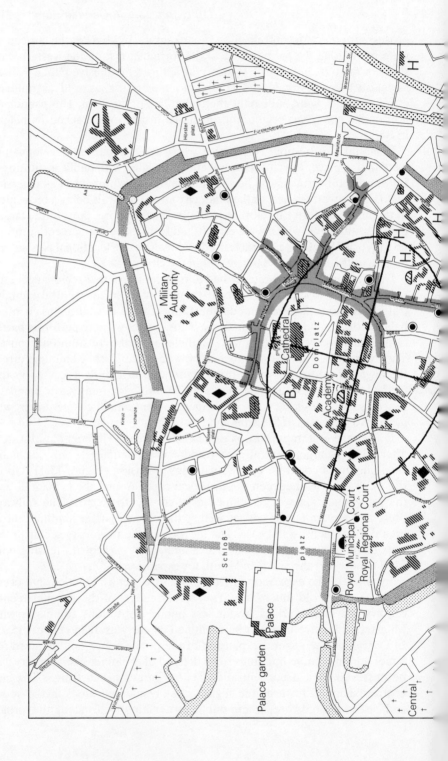

For the standard deviation ellipse see text

- • Lawyer
- ◉ Lawyer and Notary
- ◖ Court
- ◢ Former location of a Court
- ◖ Prison
- B Bishop's Seat
- H Hospital
- ◆ Ration Depot

Promenade

Areas of water

Railway

Main shopping area

Public building

Barrack

0   50 100 150 200m

Figure 15.1 The development of the public office sector in Münster, 1875

fortifications offered suitable locational advantages. This spatial expansion of hospitals, courts and schools has continued up to the present day. In the north and south the expansion of the city centre was restricted by the railways, giving further impetus to the west–east spreading of the central area.

The severe destruction in World War II, and the comprehensive recon-structional changes after that time, particularly the extension of streets and the amalgamation of building plots, have contributed to the recent expansion of public institutions in Dortmund. Münster, on the other hand, has largely reconstructed its buildings and street layout along traditional lines; indeed its individuality and outstanding image as an historic city has had positive effects on the locational development of high ranking private services.

An example of office development: the growth of legal services in Germany

The dynamics and the locational behaviour of legal services in German cities was often dependent on the general legal conditions prevailing in the nineteenth century. After the Prussian Act of 1849, the old division into representation of litigant parties at court (so-called justice commissioners) and legal advisers (advocates) was dissolved. Thus, the term 'lawyer' for both legal advisers and representatives was introduced for the largest of the German states. In Prussia, the functions of the lawyer and the notary were combined, in contrast to the situation in other German states. Further-more, it is important to remember that through the Lawyers Act of the German Reich in 1878, the civil servant status of the lawyer was terminated and an unrestricted admission to the courts was given. This led to a sharp increase in the number of such lawyers as shown in Table 15.1. Such growth rates have been even higher in the Federal Republic, a trend which coincides with the general development of the quaternary sector.

The expansion of the judicial system in the Federal Republic has had two important consequences. First, there has been a considerable increase of office concentrations, of group practices or co-operatives. Secondly, an increase in the specialisation of individual lawyers and lawyers' offices has taken place. Both processes have influenced locational behaviour; with, for example, the larger legal co-operatives specialising in business law and therefore mainly expanding in the largest economic centres such as Düssel-dorf.[15]

The locational behaviour of legal services in Münster and Dortmund from the late nineteenth century

In both cities by the 1880s there was only a relatively small number of lawyers and notaries. However, the growth rates in the following decades were substantial, and far higher than the average for the Reich (Table 15.2). Such growth produced trends in the locational behaviour of legal offices in the two cities.

The locations of lawyers and notaries in Münster by 1887 was characterised by a relatively dispersed pattern within the old core; a feature highlighted by the use of spatial statistics in Figure 15.1. However, some locational principles become apparent, as the lawyers' offices revealed a tendency towards accessible sites on main arterial roads, or close to the courts. It should be noted, though, that the court at the western edge of the old core was newly built in the 1870s and until 1875 there were no legal offices in this part of Münster (Figure 15.1).

The relationship between the locations of lawyers and courts is easier to see in the case of Dortmund, which in 1886 showed two notable concentrations of offices around both courts (Figure 15.2). The locational factors which were relevant in Münster also applied in Dortmund. In addition, the lack of locations within extended areas outside the old core reveal that there was little attraction towards residential areas.

Between the end of the nineteenth century and the inter-war period, the development of the judicial system was not only marked by an increase in the number of lawyers and of the size of the offices, but also by important locational changes. Despite the different rates of urban growth between the two cities, certain common locational patterns can be identified by 1900.[16] Some of these may be seen in the directional shifts of the standard deviation ellipsis towards more accessible sites. This concerns first the significant agglomeration of lawyers and notaries' offices within main shopping streets, which had high levels of pedestrian movement and a central position relative to public transport, and secondly the concentration of lawyers within the area of the railway station, caused by the increasing importance of railway traffic. Agglomerations of lawyers' offices were also situated at other transport junctions, such as arterial roads. The factor of proximity to courts also became important. In Dortmund the removal of the municipal court from the southern part of the old town to the east of the core led to shifts in lawyers' offices, with the former concentration around the old court being dissolved. The string of office locations between the courts and the centre of the old core demonstrate that a combination of locational factors were operating in Dortmund.

Despite the different pattern of main shopping streets and the different position of the railway station, the same locational factors appear to have operated in Münster, where a concentration of lawyers was found towards the main station. Similarly, the orientation towards residential areas was insignificant in late nineteenth-century Münster. Indeed, in both cities *ca.* 75% of legal offices were concentrated within the inner urban core (Table 15.2).

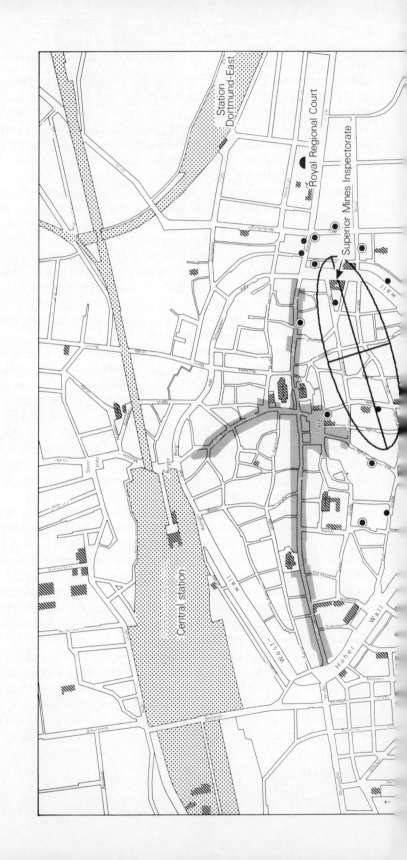

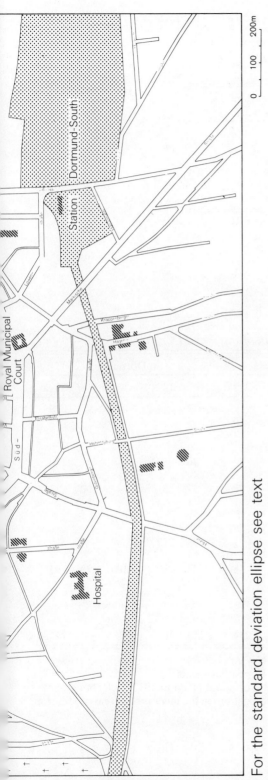

For the standard deviation ellipse see text

- Lawyer
- Lawyer and Notary
- Court

Public building
Main shopping area
Railway

Figure 15.2   The public office sector in Dortmund, 1886

Table 15.1 *Number of lawyers in the German Reich and in the Federal Republic of Germany*

	German Reich	Federal Republic of Germany
1907	8,608	
1924	13,500	
1931		(8,809)[1]
1950		11,818
1961		18,720
1980		36,081

[1] Based on the present area of the FRG.

Table 15.2 *Lawyers and notaries in Münster and Dortmund, 1886/7–1980/1*

	Münster				Dortmund				
	L	L/N	P	Total	L	L/N	N	P	Total
1886					7	11	—	—	18
1887	7	13	—	20					
1932	21	51	—	72	46	80	—	4	130
Percentage in central area	67	80	—	76	57	81	—	100	73
1980	109	136	3	248					
1981					98	212	2	4	316
Percentage in central area	28	65	—	48	27	80	100	75	63
Percentage increase 1932–1980/1	419	167	—	244	113	105	—	—	143

L   = lawyers   N = notaries
L/N = lawyers with notaries   P = patent agents
Sources: Directories of Münster and Dortmund (1886 to 1932); telephone books and yellow pages for 1980/1; own investigations in the inner urban areas of Münster and Dortmund (1980/1).

In spite of large war damage of both city centres and the considerable changes brought about during reconstruction, clear agglomerations of lawyers' and notaries' offices have been sustained in post-war years (Figures 15.5 and 15.6). The differences in the locational patterns of the 1930s, as shown in Figures 15.3 and 15.4, and those of today are due to a combination of factors. First, the significant growth in the number and size of offices. Secondly, the re-location of courts in both cities, and in the case of Dortmund, changes in street patterns. Other modifying factors consist of changes in locational opportunities. For example, the building of new department stores in the traditional central shopping street of Dortmund has led to changes in micro-level locations. The pattern of office agglomerations in eastern, central Dortmund is now far more dispersed and contrasts to the more linear patterns of the inter-war period.

Trends in the locational behaviour of doctors' surgeries in Münster and Dortmund

Doctors, as another rapidly expanding service group, have also experienced a professional development which was defined by decisive legal acts in the nineteenth century. During the period before 1850, the health system in Germany was characterised by the assistance of the poor (poor relief), and medical functions were exercised by qualified, general practitioners as well as barber surgeons, so-called 'Wundärzte'. It was only after the Prussian medical reforms in 1852 that professional medical services developed. The information from Münster shows that the number of doctors only increased during the last two decades of the nineteenth century (Table 15.3).

During the second half of the nineteenth century the medical profession was characterised by two further changes, which affected locational structures. First, consultation rooms and consulting hours were introduced, which increased the importance of accessibility to the practice. Secondly, the number of medical specialists rose, especially after 1900 (Table 15.3). Generally, it was the university towns with a medical faculty which had the largest number of specialists. In 1904, for example, Berlin had the largest number, with 799 doctors. The relatively small number of specialists in Münster apparently was caused by the later re-opening of the university in 1902.

Figure 15.7 presents a synthesis of the most important locational factors together with their changing historical importance since 1880. This diagram shows that, as for the lawyers, the locational factors of 'central location', 'favourable transport facilities', 'agglomeration advantages' and the supply of office space for doctors' practices are all of increasing significance. This increase in importance does not apply, however, to all medical specialists.

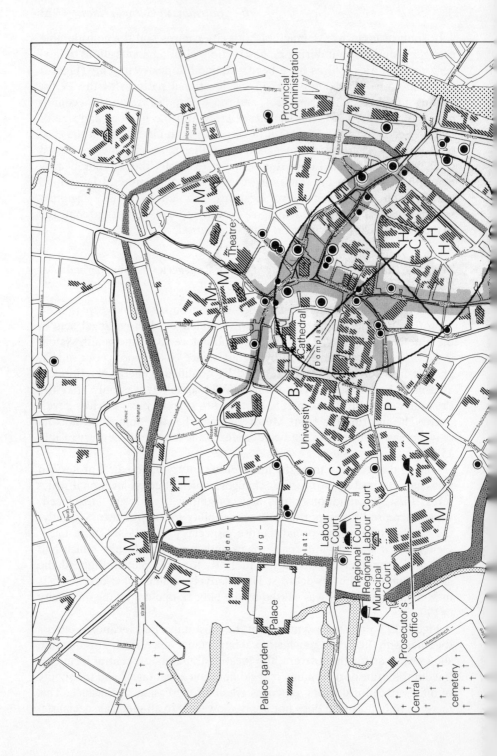

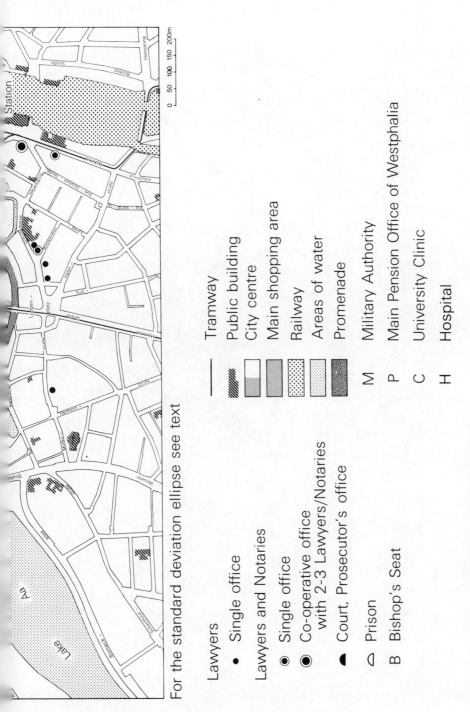

For the standard deviation ellipse see text

Lawyers
• Single office

Lawyers and Notaries
◉ Single office
◉ Co-operative office
   with 2-3 Lawyers/Notaries
◗ Court, Prosecutor's office

◖ Prison
B Bishop's Seat

——— Tramway
▨   Public building
▢   City centre
▨   Main shopping area
⠂⠂   Railway
⠂⠂   Areas of water
▩   Promenade

M   Military Authority
P   Main Pension Office of Westphalia
C   University Clinic
H   Hospital

Figure 15.3 The public office sector in Münster, 1930

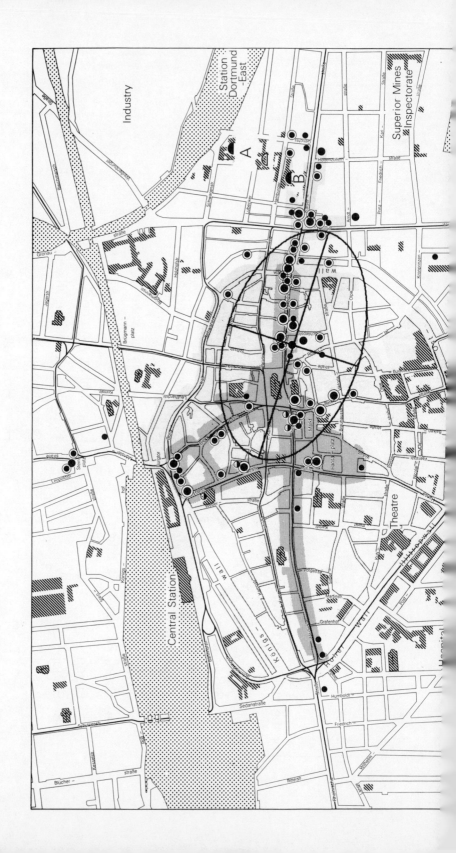

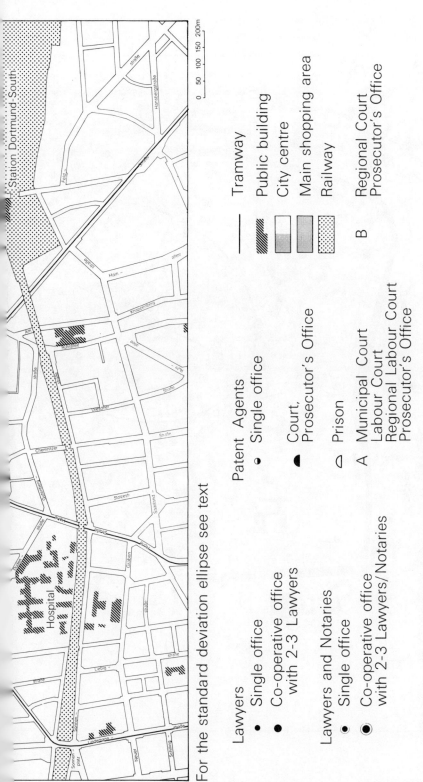

For the standard deviation ellipse see text

Lawyers

● Single office

● Co-operative office
with 2-3 Lawyers

Lawyers and Notaries

◉ Single office

◉ Co-operative office
with 2-3 Lawyers/Notaries

Patent Agents

◑ Single office

◐ Court,
Prosecutor's Office

◖ Prison

A Municipal Court
Labour Court
Regional Labour Court
Prosecutor's Office

—— Tramway

▨ Public building

City centre

Main shopping area

▧ Railway

B Regional Court
Prosecutor's Office

0 50 100 150 200m

Figure 15.4 The public office sector in Dortmund, 1930

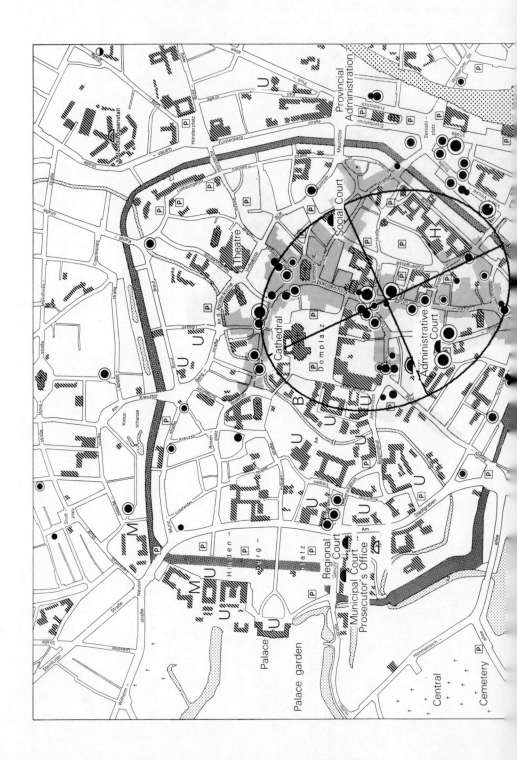

For the standard deviation ellipse see text

Lawyers
- Single office
- Co-operative office
  with 2-3 Lawyers

Lawyers and Notaries
- Single office
- Co-operative office
  with 2-3 Lawyers/Notaries
- Co-operative office
  with 4 or more Lawyers/Notaries

Patent agents
- Single office
- Co-operative office
  with 2-3 Patent Agents

H Hospital
M Military Authority

Court Authorities
- Superior Administrative Court
  of North-Rhine-Westphalia
- Other Courts/Prosecutor's office
- Prison
  Public building
  City centre
  Main shopping area
  Railway
  Areas of water
  Promenade
  Car parking
U University
B Bishop's Seat

Figure 15.5 The post-war public office sector in Münster

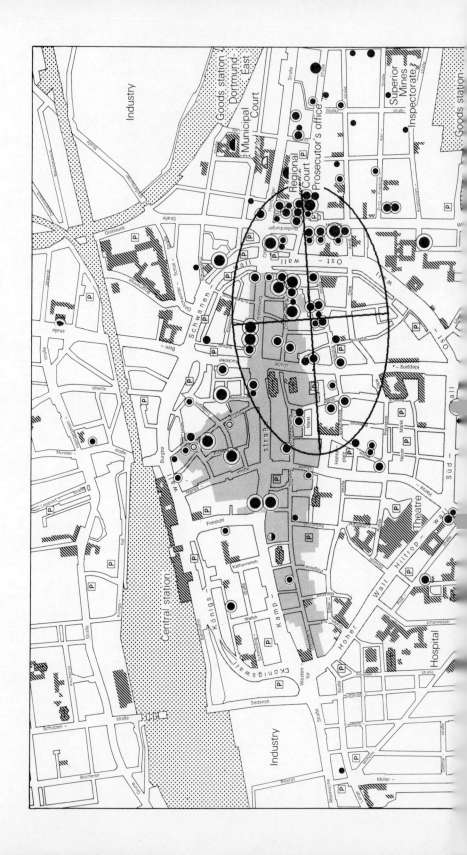

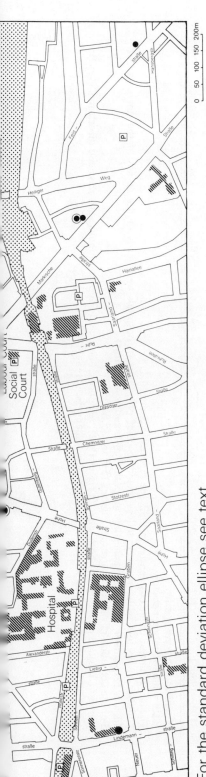

For the standard deviation ellipse see text

Lawyers

• Single office

● Co-operative office
with 2-3 Lawyers

● Co-operative office
with 4 or more
Lawyers

Notaries

◎ Single office

Lawyers and Notaries

◉ Single office

◉ Co-operative office
with 2-3 Lawyers/Notaries

◉ Co-operative office
with 4 or more
Lawyers/Notaries

Patent Agents

◖ Single office

◑ Co-operative office
with 2-3 Patent Agents

 Court/Prosecutor's office
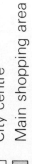 Prison
Public building
City centre
Main shopping area
Railway
 P Car parking

Figure 15.6 The post-war public office sector in Dortmund

Table 15.3 *Doctors (human medicine)[1] in Münster and Dortmund, 1875, 1886/7–1980/1*

	Münster					Dortmund				
	General practitioners	Specialists	Dentists	Total doctor[2]	Pop./Total doctor[2]	General practitioners	Specialists	Dentists	Total doctor[2]	Pop./Total doctor[2]
1875	24	1	2	27			—	—	—	—
1886	28	4	3	35	1,300					
1887						31	1	3	35	2,370
1906	38	19	9	66	1,270					
1907						53	45	10	109	1,800
1932	41	71	30	142	870	151	133	85	369	1,450
Percentage in central area[3]	20	66	67	53		15	56	47	37	
1980[4]	89	277	170	536	500					
1981[4]						214	404	228	846	720
Percentage in central area[5]	12	42	32	34		7	20	15	15	
Percentage increase 1932–1980/1	117	290	467	277		42	204	168	129	

[1] Not including homeopaths.
[2] Rate = inhabitants per doctor.
[3] For the definition of the city centres in 1932, see Figures 15.3 and 15.4.
[4] Number of doctors with private practices including chief physicians of hospitals and heads of the clinics of the university of Münster respectively (excluding anaesthetists, pathologists and homeopaths).
[5] For the definition of the city centres see Figures 15.5 and 15.6.
Sources: Classified directories of both cities (1875 to 1932); telephone books and telephone books with classified directories (1982); listings of the local medical society; own inquiries in the inner urban areas (1980/1).

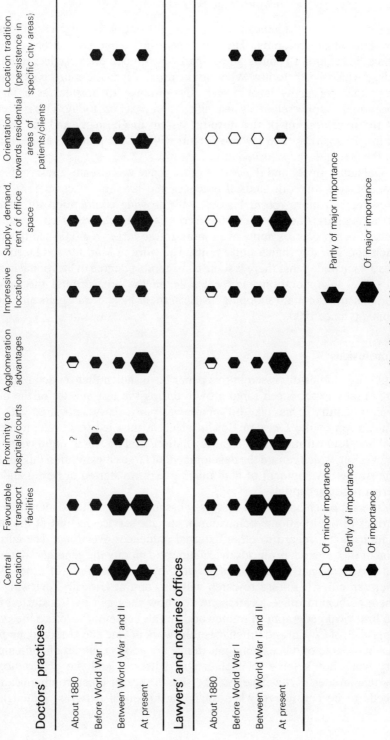

Figure 15.7 The changing influence of locational factors on the distribution of legal firms

For example, the significance of a central location has decreased mainly for general practitioners. The differences in spatial associations of legal offices in relation to courts, in comparison with doctors' practices to hospitals, are also worth noting. Whereas the proximity to the courts is extremely important for many legal offices, the distance to hospital as a micro-locational factor is relatively insignificant for practices today. This is a result of the development of the hospital system in Germany and the decline of the 'Belegarztsystem', where doctors with private practices located close by the hospitals they worked in.

Demand, supply and the cost of office space was already a relevant locational factor for both medical practices and lawyers' offices before 1914. However, in more recent history, with growing competition for sites in attractive parts of city centres, these criteria have achieved decisive importance. Such processes apply even more to the larger regional capitals with their considerably higher office rents. The work in Münster and Dortmund has also revealed that there is some considerable degree of locational inertia in office agglomerations. For example, in the area around the railway stations and the main shopping districts, there have been significant developments since 1900.

Conclusions

The case studies discussed in this paper have shown that service functions only really experienced rapid growth during the last quarter of the nineteenth century. This 'take-off' phase was particularly associated with the foundation of the German Reich, which in turn led to developments in public administration, new legal regulations and above all rapid economic expansion, which caused the development of large cities. Within this context the strong development of high ranking services started in Berlin and the larger regional capitals.

The approach adopted in this essay has made it possible to identify regularities in the locational behaviour of specific services, whilst at the same time having a regard to other external influences over time. The current aim of the research project is to examine and modify the general statements on the locational behaviour of services by a closer study of other West German cities.[17] Future research will also aim at critically reviewing the theories behind office location, to see how they can be transferred into an historical-geographical framework. In this context, the 'office life cycle' approach of Cowan and Pritchard or the work of Gad and Goddard, emphasising the role of office communications, are good examples of contemporary work not helping to explain past patterns, and the persistence of particular sites.[18] Nevertheless, the significance of office communications needs to be considered when analysing historical patterns, although its importance can probably only be deduced from locational connections and insights into the historical development of office communications. Finally, one important aspect that historical studies have shown is the locational persistence of service functions in German cities from at least the end of the nineteenth century.

16

Recent research on the commercial structure of nineteenth-century British cities

GARETH SHAW

The urban economy: a neglected research area

Few people would deny that the study of the nineteenth-century city has been one of the major growth points in historical geography over the last twenty years. The origins of such interests have been well discussed elsewhere, especially the part played by the availability of small area census data.[1] Such key data sources, together with a general upsurge of interest in social history, dictated many of the questions asked by those geographers studying the nineteenth-century British city. Unfortunately, this has led to a concentration of research concerned with social structures at the expense of other equally important features: most notably the urban economy.

Research on the urban economy of nineteenth-century Britain has been somewhat fragmented, with many themes receiving little or no attention. In some areas, particularly on commercial patterns and market centres, recent work has made some steady progress, and has gone a considerable way towards explaining past trends. In contrast, much work remains to be done on the industrial structure of nineteenth-century cities, as well as the growing service-type of activities found in most urban centres. The limited research that has been published is often not by historical geographers, but rather by economic historians. Some, such as Lee's extensive work on the service sector, has tended to develop from more traditional approaches that traced the evolution of manufacturing industries.[2] In this sense these studies are often at an inter-regional scale, and have contributed little to our understanding of intra-urban patterns. However, even at the urban scale of study economic historians have pushed ahead in territory that was traditionally the domain of historical geographers. Thus, the earlier studies of urban economic patterns by Hall and Martin in London have received little recent attention from historical geographers.[3] Such studies may, however, be compared to Forsyth's recent work on nineteenth-century

Glasgow, which uses spatial analysis to discuss the changing economic morphology of the city.[4]

The response from historical geographers to such studies has been rather slow to materialise, and the impact of industrial location on the internal structure of urban areas is mentioned in only a handful of recent publications. There remains, therefore, considerable scope for far more studies on the urban economy of industrialising cities; and in particular on the relationship between economic change and urban form.

The remainder of this chapter will focus on the retail sector of the urban economy and explore three overlapping research themes: first, structural changes in the distribution system; secondly, the study of locational change; and thirdly, the relationship between retail growth and the form of British city centres.

The transformation of the distribution system

The evolution of retail facilities during the transition from a pre-industrial to an industrial economy has formed a point of debate in much of the early literature on retail change. Initial views, with the exception of Clapham's general review, suggested that Britain's distribution system prior to 1850 was rather primitive and that major changes occurred only after this date.[5] This opinion was, however, challenged in a number of detailed studies carried out by Blackman, Burnett and Alexander, which argued that the timing of changes could be pushed back to the second part of the eighteenth century.[6] This discussion, although of a relatively limited nature, has nevertheless been important since it focussed interest on both the chronology and nature of retail change. Historical geographers have made significant contributions to both these themes, through two main areas of research.

The first concerns the timing of retail change, and in particular the relative growth of shops and markets. These studies have extended earlier work by economic historians and demonstrated the growth of fixed shop retailing in the early nineteenth century.[7] From this evidence it would seem that the highest rates of shop growth occurred between the end of the eighteenth century to about 1820. However, the pattern of change throughout the urban hierarchy was by no means straightforward, as Table 16.1 shows. It can be seen that changes in shop provision occurred in a fairly erratic fashion as population and shops increased at different rates. It is also significant that in the early part of the nineteenth century levels of shop provision were highest in the established market towns of York and Beverley, compared with industrial settlements such as Leeds and Halifax.[8] However, by 1851 and after, shop provision had become far more equalised in the different types and sizes of settlements (Table 16.1).

The recognition that changes in retail structure are stimulated by changes

Table 16.1 *Variations in shop provision for selected settlements, 1801–81*

| | Population per shop | | | |
	1801	1821	1851	1881
Leeds	340	89	61	51
Hull	97	73	60	72
Halifax	742	105	87	67
Huddersfield	429	103	69	53
York	57	70	83	48
Wakefield	115	55	62	60
Beverley	36	36	30	33

Settlements are ranked to population size, and shop data have been interpolated to the nearest census date, i.e. 1798 to 1801 and 1823 to 1821.

in population, per capita income and consumer mobility has led to a second area of research into a simple, stage type model of retail development (Figure 16.1). In this, the lowest levels of economic development are characterised by diffuse and small-scale purchasing power, with the distribution system being dominated by periodic fairs and markets, which had the lowest operating costs in such conditions. Increasing economic and urban growth leads to the concentration of purchasing power, favouring the growth of permanent markets and craftsmen-retailers, operating from fixed locations. The latter group develop primarily because poor levels of inter-urban transport limit areas of supply, thus promoting the production of consumer goods on a small and localised scale. Finally, as transport improves and more sophisticated manufacturing technology allows the production of more and varied consumer products, the distribution system becomes re-organised into distinct producers, wholesalers and retailers; and finally large-scale retail institutions begin to emerge.

By the beginning of the nineteenth century many of the initial stages suggested in Figure 16.1 had been completed. Periodic markets and fairs had ceased to be major centres of exchange, and craft guilds had lost all power over the rapidly emerging class of shopkeepers.[9] There seems no doubt from available evidence that by the first quarter of the nineteenth century, shops had become the major form of retail outlet in a wide range of settlements.[10] Concealed behind the growth in shops, however, are other important changes in the retail system. Some of these involved the redevelopment and extension of traditional elements such as the market place, together with a changed role for itinerant traders in the urban economy.

The main retail forms had therefore all undergone some degree of growth during the first half of the nineteenth century; and in this respect the views presented by Blackman and others were correct in suggesting an early transformation of Britain's retail system. However, if attention is focussed

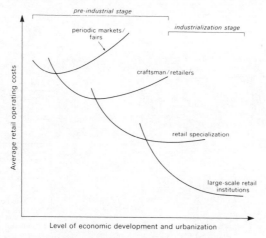

Figure 16.1   Stages of retail change in Britain

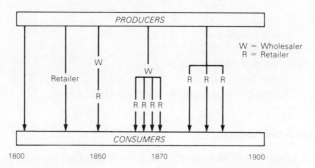

Figure 16.2   Changing marketing channels in the distribution of meat

on major organisational changes then it appears that this early period witnessed far fewer significant transformations. Indeed, recent research on the nature of urban food supply has shown that in many types of food retailing, marketing channels and organisation remained rather basic prior to 1850/60.[11] For example, as Figure 16.2 shows in terms of meat marketing, traditional producer-retailers, who also acted as wholesalers for smaller firms, were dominant before 1850/60. It was only in the last quarter of the century that new organisations emerged. These were initially based on the growth of specialist wholesalers and then followed by the creation of radically new marketing channels, controlled by multiple retail organisations largely supplying imported meat. In respect of organisational changes, Jefferys' views seem therefore equally valid, since major new retail organisations only emerged in the second half of the nineteenth century.

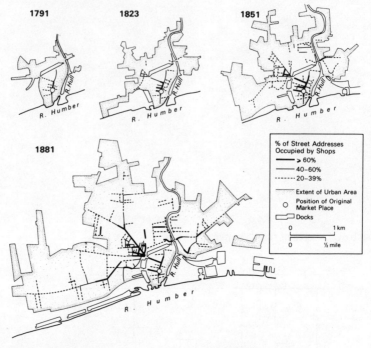

Figure 16.3   Development of shopping streets in Hull

Intra-urban retail patterns

Patterns of urban retail change can best be illustrated by taking a detailed example of one particular city. Figure 16.3 shows that the development of shopping streets in Hull was restricted to the central area and immediately around the market place in the late eighteenth century. However, by the first quarter of the nineteenth century small suburban centres had started to emerge on the immediate edge of the city centre. By 1851 the original suburban centres had developed into fairly extensive shopping areas as the number of streets containing shops continued to expand. The greatest changes were, however, to occur in the second half of the century and were marked by a rapid spread of suburban shopping streets. It was largely through improvements in urban transport, especially the development of tramways which allowed greater rates of population dispersal, that suburban retail facilities grew so rapidly. Indeed, we can recognise by 1881 the early development of linear shopping areas that form such a characteristic feature of the late Victorian city.

The picture suggested by this city-wide study of Hull indicates that the suburbanisation of shops was a relatively early phenomenon in British cities.

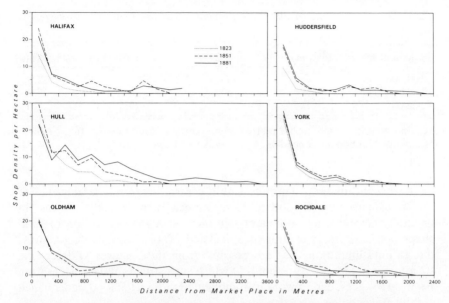

Figure 16.4   The suburbanisation of shops in different sizes of settlements

Indeed, the evidence obtained by trade directories for a range of settlements confirms this view, and shows that even in smaller cities an increasing proportion of shops were occupying suburban locations (Figure 16.4). From this information on changes in shop densities it becomes clear that the extension of retailing away from the established central shopping areas was a dominant trend in most towns. The pace and extent of change obviously varied depending on city size; although, all the settlements in Figure 16.4 show similar breaks in shop densities at a distance of about 300–400 metres away from the central market place. This line of demarcation gives some general idea of the average size of central retail areas.

Two other important features are revealed in Figure 16.4. The first is that between 1823 and 1851 shop densities in the central areas of all the sample towns increased, although the scale of change did vary. For example, established market centres such as York experienced only small changes in the city centre, compared with newer, industrial towns represented by Oldham and Rochdale. The second feature is most prominent in the larger settlements, and concerns the decline of shop densities in central areas after 1851. In cities such as Hull, this change was not specifically one of retail decentralisation, but rather a reorganisation of city centre land use and the growth of larger shops. Smaller settlements did not experience such a change at this period, thus in York and Huddersfield central area shop densities continued to increase between 1851 and 1881.

Table 16.2 *Variations in the mean percentage of food shops within central areas*[1]

Settlement size (population)	1823	1851	1881
>100,000	—	—	24.5
50,000–99,999	27.0	28.7	25.9
<50,000	35.5	29.5	28.0

[1] Central refers to within 200 metres of market place for Leeds, Hull, Halifax, Huddersfield, Oldham, Rochdale, York, Wakefield and Beverley.

The decline in shop densities within central areas was largely due to the suburbanisation of food retailers, especially in the larger towns. In general, therefore, as settlement size increased, the proportion of food shops operating from central sites declined (Table 16.2). Unfortunately, due to data limitations it is not possible from these figures to determine the precise population thresholds at which such structural decentralisation begins. However, earlier work has highlighted those retail food trades which led the move to new suburban sites.[12]

The processes of retail locational change behind these trends are fairly complex and obviously reflect the decisions of a large number of business-men. The scale of such processes, together with a lack of detailed infor-mation, precludes any worthwhile analysis at this city-wide level. To overcome these difficulties some recent, though largely unsuccessful, attempts have been made to focus on individual retail organisations.[13] How-ever, before any firm conclusions and generalities can be made about the decision-making processes of retailers, far more widespread studies need to be undertaken.

A quite different approach can be taken to understanding retail locational trends, which is based less on behavioural studies and orientated more towards an ecological perspective.[14] Thus, the processes of shop change can be considered by measuring variations in shop mortality, the creation of new shops, the upgrading or downgrading of trade types, the location of branch outlets and the amalgamation of shop premises. The interaction of these processes in different parts of the city was responsible for shaping the area's retail character. An examination of such processes moves some way towards developing a more dynamic picture of retail locational change and marks a significant departure from many of the traditional, cross-sectional studies that beset early research on retail patterns.[15]

Table 16.3 shows the results that can be obtained by using this ecological approach on six sample towns. From these data the changing importance of the different mechanisms of shop change can be studied. For example, we can see the changing role of branch shops, both over time and also

Table 16.3 *Processes of shop change in selected towns, 1823–81*

Locations	New	Withdrawn	Amalgamated premises	Branch shops	Up-grading	Down-grading
1823–51 (% of shop in each category)						
Central area	13.8	47.5	90.9	6.5	49.7	29.3
Zone 1	34.4	52.5	9.1	93.5	50.3	70.7
Zone 2	51.8	0.0	0.0	0.0	0.0	0.0
	100.0	100.0	100.0	100.0	100.0	100.0
1851–81 (% of shops in each category)						
Central area	3.7	50.2	85.0	3.8	36.8	22.0
Zone 1	23.9	29.0	13.8	31.9	41.4	36.0
Zone 2	31.8	20.8	1.2	55.0	21.8	42.0
Zone 3	40.6	0.0	0.0	9.3	0.0	0.0
	100.0	100.0	100.0	100.0	100.0	100.0

Zone 1 = built-up area developed between 1798 and 1823; zone 2 = built-up area developed between 1823 and 1851; zone 3 = built-up area developed between 1851 and 1881.
Towns used were Halifax, Huddersfield, Hull, Oldham, Rochdale and York.

in relation to the stages of suburban development. Thus, in the period 1823–51, the inner suburbs (growth zone 1) accounted for 93.5% of all branch shops, whilst between 1851 and 1881 such shops were predominant in the newer suburbs (growth zone 2). This shows one of the ways in which established retailers based in central areas followed the suburbanisation of population.

The scale of shop change is also illustrated in Table 16.3. Thus, the pace of shop closures is shown as being extremely high throughout the period, particularly in central areas. Similarly, other aspects of change concerning shop types are revealed in the figures on upgrading and downgrading processes.[16] By the period 1823–51, the upgrading of shops from lower order food trades to higher order types was significant in both the central area and the inner suburbs, as more food shops were replaced by non-food retailers.

All the processes of change resulted in the creation of a well-developed retail structure in late nineteenth-century British cities. An examination of the intra-urban retail hierarchy, as shown in Figure 16.5, does, however, illustrate some important differences with mid-twentieth-century cities.[17] From this it can be seen that in Hull a diverse range of shopping centres existed within fairly close proximity to one another. For example, in the city there were 38 local/neighbourhood shopping centres, located within a net built-up area of 771 hectares, with the greatest concentration occurring

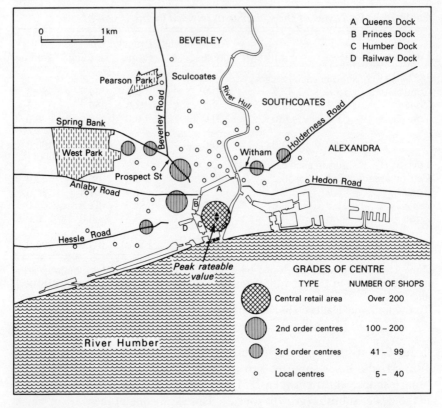

Figure 16.5   The intra-urban shopping hierarchy of nineteenth-century Hull

in predominantly working-class inner suburbs. In addition, more localised needs for basic groceries were provided by over 500 shops located outside recognisable centres. The two 'second order' centres, both located at short distances away from the central retail area, evolved from smaller shopping complexes to cater for a widening, working-class demand after 1870.

The high density of shopping centres in the nineteenth-century city reflected the influence of two quite different factors. The first, and possibly most important, was the low levels of consumer mobility that existed among working-class households. Indeed, transport in urban areas only started to improve in the 1870s, whilst the period of cheap, effective transport for the working classes took place much later after 1880.[18] Consequently, the pattern of shops mirrored fairly closely that of population. The second, and less dominant, factor at work was that particular shopping centres grew up purely to serve the demands of different social groups. Thus, in larger centres the higher income groups often had their own shopping districts, usually in central areas, which contained fashionable stores and shopping arcades.[19]

Retail development and the transformation of central areas

Research on the evolution of commercial land use in central areas has been somewhat neglected in Britain. Reference can be made to early studies by Carter and Rowley, but this type of work was focussed more on identifying central business districts, rather than explaining their evolution.[20] Unfortunately, there are no comparable British studies to match Bowden's detailed analysis of the evolution of commercial land use in large central business districts in the USA.[21] The closest recent work in Britain is Forsyth's research on nineteenth-century Glasgow, which grows from earlier and less rigorous work by Checkland on the same city.[22]

At the start of the nineteenth century most city centres contained a diverse mixture of commercial and industrial activities, in addition to residential areas; and it was not possible to recognise a distinctive pattern of land uses that set these areas apart from other regions of the city. This is not to say that key commercial functions had not concentrated in city centres, but rather that financial institutions and retail activities had not yet gained a monopoly in these areas. As Kellett points out even the great manufacturing cities of Birmingham and Manchester had in the first half of the nineteenth century a wide range of business and financial functions.[23] It would seem that the major exception to this picture was London which, according to Bowden, had already established a recognisable central business district before the nineteenth century.[24]

In most provincial towns and cities the transformation of central areas was a process that only got fully underway after the 1840s and 1850s, and even in London major land use changes occurred during this period. From Forsyth's detailed spatial analysis of functional change in Glasgow between 1800 and 1900, the timing of city centre economic development can be estimated. In the case of Glasgow, Forsyth has shown how definable core functions became concentrated on relatively fewer building blocks, and that such concentrations became more prominent by 1850.[25]

The part that retail functions played in the transformation of city centres was significant, but must also be viewed relative to changes in industry, office developments and the extension of railway networks. Unfortunately, no significant research has yet been undertaken on the impact of industrial land use, and similarly the development of offices has received only scant attention.[26] In contrast, Kellett's research on the coming of the railways illustrates the significant impact that they had on the internal structure of central areas.[27] Apart from increasing accessibility to city centres, the railways had two other significant controls over the emergence of central business districts. The first was to force up land values, indirectly through increasing site accessibility, and directly due to what Kellett terms 'railway land hunger'. To illustrate the scale of the demand Kellett has calculated that railways occupied 5.4% of central area land in London by 1900, and as much as 9.0% in Liverpool. The second control by railway was in restricting the spatial expansion of many central areas, the boundaries of which sometimes coincided with a railway line, as Elrington and Tillott have commented on in the case of Birmingham.[28]

It is against such a background of central area changes that the impact of new retail developments must be assessed. One fact is clear, however, and that is that before the arrival of railways, retail change had already initiated the processes of city centre transformation. The early phases of development were associated with the physical expansion and reorganisation of central markets. The pace and extent of such changes can be highlighted with reference to the increasing number of market improvement acts passed by parliament. A closer inspection of this legislation shows that in the first quarter of the nineteenth century, most of these local acts were associated with general town improvement schemes. These usually involved the widening and re-alignment of the congested streets around the central markets.

By about the 1840s many of the improvement acts referred to specific market schemes, most of which were also indirectly linked with improvements in public health. The impact of these schemes have been described at a local scale for Sheffield, Leeds and Manchester by Blackman, Grady and Scola respectively, whilst more recent work has examined national trends.[29] These developments represented substantial investments in some instances by local authorities, in other cases by joint stock companies. Even in small provincial towns such as Wakefield in Yorkshire, investment for new market facilities was fairly large. In this town a joint stock company brought a private bill before parliament in 1847 to develop a new retail market, with an initial capital outlay of £12,000 for a site of 6,400 square yards.[30] The market developers went to some lengths to stress that the proposed site had the highest rates of mortality in the town, and that these unhealthy conditions would be swept away by the building of a new market. At the other end of the urban hierarchy, in London, similar processes were at work. Thus, in the 1840s Smithfield market became an increasingly popular target of attack by sanitary reformers and in 1850 a Royal Commission recommended the removal of the market from such a central location.[31] It was such improvement schemes that increased both public and private investment in commercial activities in city centres, which directly pushed out many non-core functions through physical redevelopment and also forced up land values, thereby indirectly pushing out lower value functions.

These planned elements initiated important improvements in city centres, which were carried through in the last quarter of the century by the growth of major shopping streets and large stores. The attempts, at first mainly by clothing retailers, to obtain scale economies by increasing the number and range of articles sold, resulted in the demand for larger shop premises. Such processes were evident in all the large urban centres but came particularly early in London where in the 1830s drapers' shops such as Wallis's in Holborn had extended into selling furniture and carpeting.[32]

One early means of achieving increases in retail floorspace was through the amalgamation of adjoining shop premises. In most provincial towns this process became important in central areas after 1850 and remained so until the early years of the twentieth century. From the sample of northern towns shown in Table 16.3, it can be seen that the amalgamation of shop premises remained almost exclusively a central area process during the nineteenth century. The difficulties of assembling these amalgamated sites increased as stores became larger, and the literature on the history of retailing provides a wealth of detail on such processes.[33] Sadly, systematic analysis by historical geographers is lacking, and much opportunity exists for research on the role such processes played in creating central business districts.

The development of larger shops led ultimately to the growth of department stores, a trend that can be best identified in the redevelopment of London's West End. Recent research has highlighted three evolutionary stages that can be recognized in this area. The earliest was the construction of so-called bazaars during the 1830s and 1840s; these were the fashionable equivalents of the market halls found in northern, industrial towns, where retailers could rent a stall. Some of these became the forerunners of department stores, whilst others remained as bazaars until the end of the nineteenth century. A second phase of development, which ran in parallel with the first with regard to timing, was the process of shop amalgamations. In the West End of London there were two types of shops that grew in this way: the long-established firms that increased in size fairly slowly, and those that emerged after 1850, which grew more rapidly. As previously mentioned the ultimate aim of most of the early forerunners of department stores was to obtain an 'island' site or complete street block, by buying up and moving into adjoining buildings. The third phase of growth occurred after 1880 with the construction of purpose-built department stores, a trend that probably reached its peak in the West End with the opening of Selfridges in 1909.[34] These stores laid more stress on vertical development and made far more use of the upper floors as sales areas in response to rising land values and improvements in building construction methods.[35] For example, Lewis's department store in Liverpool had six floors by 1886, and in Manchester the same organisation had plans in 1885 to build a sixteen-storey, 180-foot tower as part of the extensions to the original store. In the end only seven floors were constructed.[36]

Table 16.4 *The changing retail structure of Oxford Street, 1880–1911*

Trades	Number of retail outlets	
	1880	1911
Grocers/tea dealers	13	7
Butchers	3	0
Bakers/confectioners	14	12
Tailors	19	18
Ladies clothing	67	60
Drapers	12	3
Shoes	19	16
Household items	17	17
Booksellers	14	6
Jewellers	18	26
Chemists	9	4
Department stores	3	7
Total	208	176

In London's West End the full extent of new retail developments was to turn it into a fashionable shopping district. Initially, retailers had been attracted to this area through the growth of Knightsbridge and Kensington as high class suburbs in the mid-nineteenth century, but it was the development of large stores that carried through the main transformations. Significantly, as Table 16.4 shows, Oxford Street's retail structure was still undergoing this transformation between 1880 and 1911 as more fashionable stores replaced basic food shops. This table also shows indirectly the increases in shop size, with the declining number of shops being due to the amalgamation of premises as the larger stores expanded.

The processes of change outlined for London also occurred to varying degrees in most large, provincial cities. Consequently, most city centres were by the 1880s and 1890s undergoing a further phase of transition involving the rationalisation of land use in many main shopping streets, which in turn created a major rise in land values. In the case of some cities, such as Birmingham, the local authority was involved in major redevelopments in the city centre during the last quarter of the nineteenth century under the leadership of Joseph Chamberlain. The main part of the scheme was the development of a large new street, Corporation Street, which was to form the focus of a new shopping area for the city. The importance of creating a major new shopping environment was recognised by Chamberlain who declared that 'only a new shopping street ... would permit the city to become the retail shop of the whole of the Midland counties of

England'.[37] Early work by Briggs has gone some way towards highlighting the links between the commercial success of Birmingham's Corporation Street venture and the development of Lewis's new department store on that street in 1885.[38]

Conclusions

This chapter has shown that both structural and distributional changes in British retailing were occurring throughout the nineteenth century. In terms of urban retailing it is clear that British cities of all types were experiencing rapid rates of shop development before 1850, and that the suburbanisation of shops was also a relatively early feature. That such dispersal was taking place before the major developments in transport after 1870 largely reflected high rates of urban population growth and low levels of consumer mobility. By the 1880s retail suburbanisation was an already established feature, and in larger settlements the decentralisation of food shops was in progress.

The latter trend was associated with the development of central area land uses and the creation of central business districts. From the evidence available it seems that the reshaping of city centres passed through a number of stages, during which different factors were at work. In the first part of the century institutional forces of change, related to general improvement schemes, were at work. By 1850 and 1860 railway development, along with the growth of main areas, offices and the redevelopment of market places, became important factors of change. Finally, we can recognise the importance of larger stores in shaping central areas; this occurred both in terms of natural processes of commercial change as well as by local authority involvement.

PART FIVE

Urban morphology and the historicity of townscape

17

Morphogenesis, morphological regions and secular human agency in the historic townscape, as exemplified by Ludlow

M. R. G. CONZEN

Urban communities express the tenor and quality of their past and present life in the external appearance of their habitat. During the course of history the townscape is created and transformed by its 'local urban society'.[1] In historic towns it is the result of secular processes of morphological change, actuated by that society during many centuries in response to successive changes in its social, political, economic and cultural requirements within a wider historical and regional context.

The variety of forms inherited from different historico-cultural periods[2] increases in proportion to the length of local history involved and imparts historical stratification to the townscape.[3] This and any prominence of particular periods endows the townscape with its historicity, a property contributing significantly to the character and quality of the urban environment. Increasing complexity of historical stratification and resulting structure in terms of morphological or townscape regions, and the link between this and the human agency creating and changing the townscape over long periods of time, are fundamental aspects of urban morphology to be discussed in this paper.

The Old Town as an object of morphological study

Usually, historical stratification is greatest in the traditional kernel or Old Town[4] which has normally enjoyed constancy of site from the beginning and has remained the centre of urban life. It is the area of intensive *in situ* accumulation and transformation of forms where historical stratification commands the longest time span, in Britain commonly beginning with the Middle Ages. Here the local urban society and other socio-economic forces connected with its life have been most active in shaping the townscape by sustaining a combination of several distinct but concurrent morphological processes affecting respectively the accumulation, adaptation and persistence, or alternatively replacement, of forms.[5] Here, too, historical stratification and resulting historicity are made more emphatic by the variety of types of localized mixing and period heterogeneity of forms. This gives rise to a whole hierarchy of townscape regions within traditional kernels, even in moderate sized market towns.[6]

For these reasons the discussion will focus on the Old Town and will refer to one representative example for demonstration. It is best to select a historical town of small size but composite kernel in terms of development periods, and which has a history with clear period differences and no absolute decline. Such a choice will give the most coherent picture of development from the Middle Ages to modern times, and will avoid the difficulties with many large towns, where comprehensive modern redevelopment has obliterated former historical stratification.

Ludlow in Shropshire provides an instructive example, strong on basic principles, though weak on some modern morphological processes affecting large historical towns.[7] Its composite medieval town plan and a history of eight and a half centuries with several periods of considerable importance have endowed its Old Town with an historically well-stratified and richly textured townscape.

Ludlow has been an important castle town in the Welsh Borders from the twelfth century and a centre of the medieval wool trade and cloth manufacture from the thirteenth to the sixteenth century. It was the seat of the Council of the Marches of Wales and so virtually the capital of the principality and Border counties during the sixteenth and seventeenth centuries. Thereafter it continued as a fashionable social centre for the surrounding region during the eighteenth and first half of the nineteenth centuries, before it settled down to its present role of the small, but viable service centre of a thriving agricultural area in the Central Welsh Border (present population about 7,700), approximately equidistant (average 37 kilometres or 23 miles) from the nearest English county towns of Shrewsbury, Hereford and Worcester.

Two basic problems of historical urban morphology

Figure 17.1 shows the historic townscape of Ludlow's Old Town in relation to its natural site (Figure 17.1A) and in terms of the three systematic form complexes composing it, namely the town plan with its genetic plan units (17.1B), the building fabric with its historical building types (17.1C), and the generalized land utilization pattern based on existing land use types (17.1D).[8] Plan units and building types contribute directly to the historical stratification of the Old Town. The land utilization pattern does so more indirectly through its individual elements which adhere largely to the traditional plot pattern and its broad land use zones, notably the business core.

The distribution in each of these form complexes produces its own hierarchy of urban morphological or townscape regions (Figure 17.2D).[9]

Together, the maps of Figures 17.1 and 17.2 suggest recurrent regularities in the development of historic townscapes in two respects. First, there is the way in which historical stratification develops under the simultaneous operation of the morphological processes mentioned earlier, imparting a morphogenetically induced regional structure to the townscape, partly by successive medieval town extensions, and more directly through the emergence of varying localized mixtures of forms belonging to different historical periods (period-specific forms). As this is subject to regularities observable in the combined morphological development within the three systematic form complexes, it is a technical aspect best discussed in terms of these.

Secondly, the relation between relative form persistence and period representation among the forms draws attention to secular changes in the application of human agency, on the part of the local urban society, to the creation and transformation of the townscape. These two aspects comprise the basic problems of historical urban morphology discussed below.

The systematic form complexes as a spatial regulating system in townscape development

The three systematic form complexes differ in their specific social utility and, as a result of this, in the degree of form persistence they oppose to morphological change induced by new functional requirements on the part of the local urban society. This has important consequences for the morphological structure of the townscape and for the way spatial historical stratification develops. Town plan and, to a lesser extent, urban building fabric show considerable persistence of forms,[10] usually over many centuries, compared with land utilization; thus reflecting patterns of past land-ownership and fixed capital investment.

The town plan is the most conservative form complex, as its street system, and degree of discipline this imposes as an access pattern on the associated plot pattern, is a fixed commitment of the whole urban community. Thus Ludlow's composite medieval town plan and street system survives to this day as a great common monument of that age (Figure 17.1B). It has remained intact in all its essential features except for minor modifications of plot widths and street lines, and in part of its earlier urban unit where medieval and later encroachments on the original street market interfered with the market space. Today that town plan controls internal access in much the same way as it did when it was first completed. It has therefore exerted a major influence on the topographical organization of Ludlow's urban life for more than 800 years and has determined the higher ranks in the Old Town's hierarchy of morphological regions. Changes to the

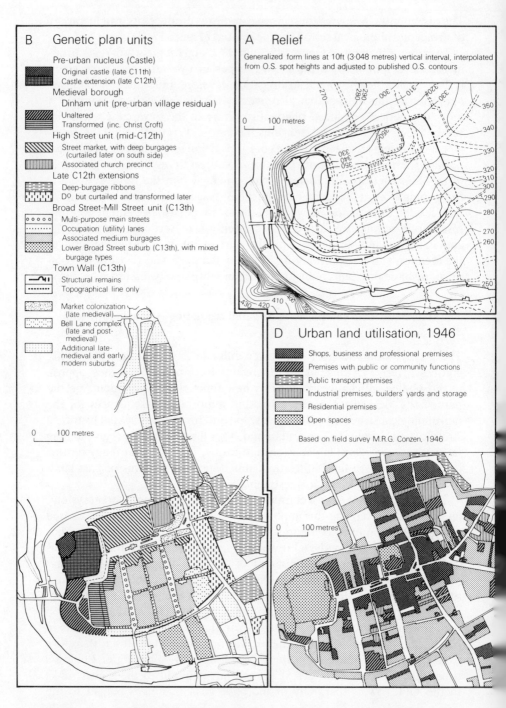

B   Genetic plan units

Pre-urban nucleus (Castle)
Original castle (late C11th)
Castle extension (late C12th)

Medieval borough
Dinham unit (pre-urban village residual)
Unaltered
Transformed (inc. Christ Croft)

High Street unit (mid-C12th)
Street market, with deep burgages
(curtailed later on south side)
Associated church precinct

Late C12th extensions
Deep-burgage ribbons
Do but curtailed and transformed later

Broad Street-Mill Street unit (C13th)
Multi-purpose main streets
Occupation (utility) lanes
Associated medium burgages
Lower Broad Street suburb (C13th), with mixed
burgage types

Town Wall (C13th)
Structural remains
Topographical line only

Market colonization
(late medieval)
Bell Lane complex
(late and post-
medieval)
Additional late-
medieval and early
modern suburbs

0   100 metres

A   Relief

Generalized form lines at 10ft (3·048 metres) vertical interval, interpolated
from O.S. spot heights and adjusted to published O.S. contours

0   100 metres

D   Urban land utilisation, 1946

Shops, business and professional premises
Premises with public or community functions
Public transport premises
Industrial premises, builders' yards and storage
Residential premises
Open spaces

Based on field survey M.R.G. Conzen, 1946

0   100 metres

Figure 17.1   Ludlow: (A) Relief; (B) Genetic plan units; (C) Historic building
types; (D) Urban land utilization

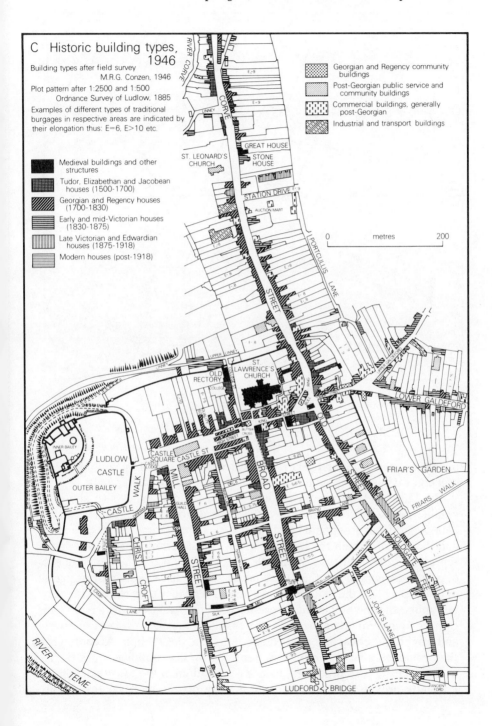

C   Historic building types, 1946

Building types after field survey
                    M.R.G. Conzen, 1946

Plot pattern after 1:2500 and 1:500
        Ordnance Survey of Ludlow, 1885

Examples of different types of traditional
burgages in respective areas are indicated by
their elongation thus: E=6, E>10 etc.

Medieval buildings and other
structures

Tudor, Elizabethan and Jacobean
houses (1500-1700)

Georgian and Regency houses
(1700-1830)

Early and mid-Victorian houses
(1830-1875)

Late Victorian and Edwardian
houses (1875-1918)

Modern houses (post-1918)

Georgian and Regency community
buildings

Post-Georgian public service and
community buildings

Commercial buildings, generally
post-Georgian

Industrial and transport buildings

0   metres   200

RIVER CORVE

GREAT HOUSE

ST. LEONARD'S
CHURCH

STONE
HOUSE

LINNEY

CORVE

STATION DRIVE

AUCTION MART

PORTCULLIS LANE

STREET

UPPER LINNEY

ST.
LAWRENCE'S
CHURCH

OLD
RECTORY

COLLEGE

LOWER GALDEFORD

INNER BAILEY

LUDLOW
CASTLE

OUTER BAILEY

CASTLE
SQUARE

CASTLE ST

CASTLE   WALK

MILL   STREET

BROAD   STREET

FRIAR'S   GARDEN

FRIARS   WALK

HOLDGATE   FEE

CHRIST   CROFT   STREET

LANE

SILK

OLD   STREET

ST. JOHN'S LANE

RIVER   TEME

WATERSIDE

LUDFORD   BRIDGE

ANCIENT
FORD

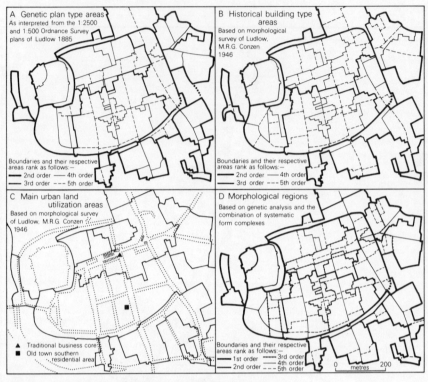

Figure 17.2   Ludlow Old Town: morphological regions

plan have been slight and generally restricted to the traditional plot pattern of medieval burgages, but never to such an extent as to obliterate it.

The building fabric in terms of historical building types also shows a notable persistence though not to the same degree as the medieval town plan. Apart from prominent buildings serving public functions like the castle and the parish church the bulk has always consisted of houses, and these represent a different type of specific social utility, being the commitment of private owners rather than the community. As fixed capital investments in urban property they had of course a clear tendency towards persistence, but unlike the town plan they were exposed to changes of ownership and owners' requirements as well as the changing fortunes of town quarters and neighbourhoods, and the ravages of fire and destruction. Accordingly, they could be adapted, rebuilt or replaced by new building types singly or in groups. These processes, working at random in the townscape, have gradually broken up the architectural unity of the medieval town. The result is the present intricate and irregular pattern of period mixture in the building fabric (Figure 17.1C), showing a great number of distinct juxta-positions and groupings of different period types, varying in period mixture and distribution pattern from one locality to another.

This makes the building fabric not only a major and visually obvious carrier of historical stratification involving all historical periods, but also an important factor in the recognition of the smallest townscape regions, the morphotopes, representing the lowest rank in the hierarchy of morpho-logical regions. Morphotopes are the smallest urban localities obtaining distinctive character among their neighbours from their particular combi-nation of constituent morphological elements. However, the considerable, though not universal, capacity of the building fabric for persistence can be gathered from the dominance of 'traditional', that is pre-1830, rather than 'modern' building types in the Old Town. It is in fact greater than is suggested by Figure 17.1C which is based on period classification of buildings by external appearance only. This hides the fact that a large number of buildings contain structure and residual cores or remnants much older than their façade and corresponding period index on the map, often involving medieval structural remains.

The specific social utility of the pattern of urban land utilization lies in the provision of functionally viable locations for all individual land use units. As this depends on the nature of the internal access pattern, the medieval street system of the Old Town has determined the location of major land use regions within it (Figure 17.1D). The resulting site constancy of these traditional regions applies notably to the business core with its hub in the High Street–King Street–Bull Ring area,[11] notwithstanding the coming of the railway in 1851–2 and the lop-sided development of consider-able new suburbs thereafter. Thus urban land utilization in Ludlow confirms the scheme of traditional townscape regions produced within the other two systematic form complexes.

On the other hand, individual land use units in this small business core have traditionally shown far less site constancy, and since the advent of industrialization have been affected by developments in technology, meth-ods of business organization and retailing techniques. This has eliminated 'historical stratification' of land utilization types in any morphologically meaningful sense or has restricted it to the last 170 years and to indirect expression in the building fabric, for instance surviving examples illustrating the development of banking accommodation, or of types of shop fronts or other retail outlets.

The combination of the systematic form complexes emerges from the preceding discussion, summarized in Figure 17.3, as a spatial regulating system, carrying and conditioning the development of the townscape under the continuous impact of morphological processes and by building up the hierarchy of morphological regions. Study of this aspect reveals recurrent regularities of such general significance as to assume the role of principles of historical urban morphology as follows.

It is an axiom of urban morphology that everywhere in the townscape the systematic form complexes are hierarchically nested in a physical sense, so that the town plan 'contains' or harbours, and through its plot pattern forms the physical frame of, the land utilization pattern and the land use units, each within its own plot, in turn contain the building fabric.[12]

That the development of universal historical stratification increased considerably in volume during the eight centuries or so with which we are concerned in the case of Ludlow is because of the presence of a general regularity. It can be recognized from the previous discussion and Figure 17.3 (column 2) as the principle of differentiation of the systematic form complexes by degree of form persistence.

Figure 17.3 (column 3) presents another recurrent regularity that can be termed the principle of differentiation of the form complexes by range of morphological periods and period emphasis. The town plan emphasizes the earliest possible period which makes it an important constituent of historical stratification. In the totality of its detail the land utilization pattern predictably represents the latest period, while the building fabric commonly commands the widest range of periods, with emphasis if any on particular periods depending on the history of a town. As already mentioned this makes the building fabric an important and visually obvious carrier of historical stratification.

Finally, there is the contribution each of the systematic form complexes makes to the historic townscape's hierarchy of morphogenetic regions (Figure 17.3, column 4). Here, too, a recurrent regularity is apparent in that the complexes range themselves according to the relative importance their main contributions have in that hierarchy. This conforms also to their ranking by relative form persistence which carries the connotation of priority in time. It can be called the principle of morphogenetic priority. Clearly the town plan comes first in that respect and has determined the top and intermediate ranks. The building pattern partakes in the town plan's intermediate ranks to a degree but makes its major contribution in the lowest rank with urban morphotopes. The contribution of the land utilization pattern lies in the intermediate ranks, its business zone being traditional in that it reflects the early location of the business core on the town ridge. However, in its land use detail it has been subject to so many changes in the past that the existing pattern of individual elements appears to be essentially recent and functionally so thoroughly mixed that no significant small-scale grouping is apparent to make any contribution to the lower ranks in the system of townscape regions. Only intensive historical work on the properties in the Old Town can give a clearer picture on this point.

1	2		3	4
Systematic form complex	Degree of form persistence	Morphological periods	Morphological constituents of historical stratification	Contribution to hierarchy of townscape regions
Town plan	Maximal	High medieval 1090–1270	General outlines of street system, plot pattern and building arrangement	High rank (major genetic plan units) intermediate rank (neighbourhoods: street and precinctual units, high medieval suburbs)
		Late medieval 1270–1500 and early post-medieval	Major island and lateral encroachments on street market, ubiquitous changes to street lines by minor lateral encroachments, ubiquitous minor alterations to plot pattern	Intermediate rank (Eastern Dinham transformation, Bell Lane neighbourhood) lowest rank (morphotopes of market encroachments)
		High and late medieval 1090–1500	Few but prominent public buildings and defence structures. Very few houses by external indices, but structural remains inside and at rear of many post-medieval houses	
Building fabric	Considerable though varying with periods	Early modern 1500–1840	Majority of houses in localized period mixtures	Intermediate rank, but principally lowest rank (morphotopes)
		Victorian and Edwardian 1840–1918	Houses in peripheral location or on minor streets. A few commercial buildings in business core	Lowest rank (morphotopes)
		Inter- and post-war, post-1918	Very few buildings within Old Town	
Urban land utilization		Pre-1840	Major land use areas (business core, residential areas, institutional precincts)	Intermediate rank (traditional business core, traditional residential area, recreational area, castle ruins)
	Minimal	Recent (twentieth century)		

Figure 17.3   The systematic form complexes as morphological regulators in the Old Town

Human agency in the creation of the historic townscape and its secular changes

The previous section has been concerned with the morphological mechanism through which the effect of secular morphological processes is assimilated by the townscape. But it does not explain the noticeable secular changes in the topographical mode of townscape transformation, that is the general way in which new forms have been introduced into, or better have obtained their individual emplacement in, the townscape of the Old Town as the result of additional accumulation and/or replacement of forms. In Ludlow as in other historic towns a growing contrast in this respect appears in the morphological effect of different historical periods and is highlighted by a comparison of the first hundred years from the early twelfth to the thirteenth century, comprising the stages of development in the High Middle Ages, with the late stages during the hundred years preceding the Second World War.

It one can hazard a generalization on the basis of existing evidence of medieval English and perhaps other European townscapes, the former period appears to be characterized by predominantly orderly, planned growth with largely standardized urban properties at any rate in the early stages. Such development was conditioned by broad similarities in the limitations of fixed capital outlay for the accommodation of individual economic and family units, and by the traditional building methods and materials of the time.[13] The latter period shows late stages in a secular process of changes in which the unity of aspect and scale of the medieval townscape has given way to a long succession of piecemeal changes causing it to be eroded in several respects. Clearly this is a phenomenon transmitted by the various morphological processes in the course of history. The explanation is to be found in the human agency on the part of the local urban society and any other social forces connected with the development of the townscape.

Two kinds of social motivation and corresponding social action operate simultaneously in the development of the townscape; the corporate or public and the individual or private. Their relative strength in townscape development has been subject to historical change from the Middle Ages to modern times, and this has been reflected in the habitus of the townscape. To test this proposition which suggests a principle of townscape change, the development of the townscape in the traditional centre of Ludlow will be traced from medieval to modern times.

Medieval Ludlow's beginnings (early twelfth century)

There are no explicit records of the origin of this town, though the borough charter of 1461 contains many clauses confirming ancient privileges. However, Ludlow's beginnings are clearly related to the castle as its pre-urban nucleus which in its original smaller form probably dates from between 1086 and 1094.[14] The first mention of the place name Lodelowe in 1138 and of Ludelaw among several *castra et villae* for the same period[15] suggests the presence of a settlement close to the castle, but the ambiguity of meaning of the term *villa* at that time allows no firm conclusion as to the urban nature of the place.[16] A separate, even more enigmatic and probably earlier – but small – agricultural settlement called Dinham lay to the south of the castle.

In the manner of other early castle towns Ludlow may have started as a small open settlement round an informally shaped open space outside and immediately south and east of the original castle gate. It might have been occupied principally by craftsmen living under the same feudal law as the surrounding countryside, dependent on, and working for, the castle, a type of partly or predominantly non-agricultural settlement which in England appears to have no unambiguous traces in the records. On the Continent outside the area of Roman-medieval settlement continuity, such pre- or proto-urban settlements have been known to historians for a long time by various medieval Latin terms. Among these that of *suburbium* (med. Latin 'settlement below or near the fortified place or castle') is in one sense the clearest, and topographically most descriptive one.[17] It is used here for that reason, although not an indigenous term.

Because of its importance for the defence of the Welsh Border Ludlow Castle was enlarged to four and a half times its original size in the late twelfth century,[18] involving the demolition of the presumed craftsmen's *suburbium* together with a considerable part of Dinham. It also meant the reorientation of exit from the castle by an east-facing gate in the new perimeter, leading to the pre-existing track that connected the original castle along the ridge of the town hill with the shallow col at the Bull Ring. Here the track met an important ancient north–south routeway through the Welsh Border following Corve Street to the Bull Ring and continuing southward along Old Street and Holdgate Fee to the ancient 'Lud-ford' across the River Teme (Figure 17.1A).[19] The enlargement of the castle involved either the resiting of the presumed *suburbium* or more likely its substitution by the foundation of a market town on a new site close to the castle. Since Ludlow's historical records are silent on this important matter, the articulated plan of the medieval town as presented on the first large scale Ordnance Survey plans of Ludlow[20] becomes an indispensable historical source of information.

On the O.S. plans the walled part of medieval Ludlow shows a genetically composite layout, which differs in principle from the seven simply structured extramural suburbs by presenting no less than five distinct development units besides its pre-urban nucleus. We shall look at these and the medieval suburbs in chronological order.

The Dinham Unit

This plan unit should be taken first (Figure 17.1B in conjunction with 17.1C), for the characteristically irregular layout of roads in its larger western part about the junction of Dinham and Camp Lane is most likely a remnant of the pattern of lanes in and around the former hamlet of Dinham. If so, it antedates the original town. In its peripheral situation, facing the strongly accented western end of the Teme Gorge, its large and squat plots of detached houses share the rural atmosphere of the adjoining country-side even now, as the enclosing town wall, long since reduced to barely recognizable remains, no longer forms the sharp divide between town and country it did in the Middle Ages.

The smaller eastern part of the Dinham Unit, too small to form a plan unit of its own, consists of Little Dinham, Christ Croft and the urban plot pattern between. It has been inserted into the informal road pattern of the Dinham Unit at a much later date and will be considered in a subsequent subsection on late medieval Ludlow.

The High Street Unit (mid-twelfth century)

The ridgeway between the castle and the ancient routeway crossing the town ridge at the Bull Ring has given rise to the earliest urban plan unit and appears on the O.S. plans transformed into a remarkable street tract comprising Castle Square, Castle Street, High Street with its three companions of Church Street, Harp Lane and Market Street, the Butter Cross, King Street, Pepper Lane with Fish Street, and the triangular part of the Bull Ring (Figures 17.1B and 17.1C). The whole complex, some 300 metres (328 yards) long from west to east and on avarage about 36 metres (39 yards) wide, was originally a large, oblong open space forming the market place or High Street of Ludlow and together with the several burgage series fronting it may be called the High Street Unit (Figure 17.1B). The unit as such must form the earliest part of the medieval town proper since it was not only closely related to the castle gate and the parish church but with its bold design represents a familiar early type of planned market town well known in Britain and the rest of north-western and central Europe. Frequently it is associated with a pre-urban nucleus in the shape of a castle or ecclesiastical establishment.

In Ludlow it may date from the mid-twelfth century, like the castle extension, or later in that century. It is during this period that signs of organized urban life begin to accumulate in documentary records such as references to the township of Ludeleye in 1168–9, to more than thirty people from Ludlow in various connections thereafter, and the appearance after 1172 of seven Ludlow men on the Dublin Roll of Burgesses.[21] At this early stage Ludlow's status as a mesne borough under the Lacys was likely to have been a very modest one, its privileges probably being restricted to the basic ones of free burgage tenure and a market, but no organ of self-government, for Henry II (1154–89) kept tight constitutional control of all towns in his English realm.[22]

Market rights and right of free burgage tenure, the basic privileges protecting the specific function of a town within feudal society, significantly point to the duality of the two kinds of social motivation and action, the corporate and the individual, operative in the development of the townscape. However in the Middle Ages the corporate principle generally took precedence because of the ever present and often acute need for the individual's physical, social and economic security. In medieval corporate society the individual as a rule acted not so much independently but rather as a member and under the effective protection and control of some corporate body or bodies or persons to which he belonged.[23]

In growing towns corporate urban society was reflected in the arrangement of the medieval townscape, with its characteristic concordance of town plan, building fabric and pattern of land and building utilization because of the combination of residence and workplace in the great majority of houses and the occupational and social grouping by streets. Even genetically composite plans were orderly as far as they resulted from corporately orientated and implemented growth by stages, every plan unit being clearly identified by its structure. Such composite plans presented a hierarchy of morphological regions, individual streets and specialized precincts, being sociotopes in a specifically medieval sense. These combined locally so as to form the units of successive urban growth, each with its own street system, and these in turn combining to form the whole town. Ludlow's High Street Unit is the earliest urban component in such a pattern of growth.

The remains of its burgage pattern on the O.S. plans of 1884 show a marked difference between the continuous northern plot series with its very deep and better preserved burgage pattern and the disjointed southern plot series with its remnant sets of stunted and deformed burgages. Taking 2 perches (33 feet or 10 metres) as the reputed frontage of a standard burgage at Ludlow,[24] the elongation, that is the ratio of burgage depth to burgage width or frontage, works out at about 10:1 ($E = 10$) in the western part of the northern burgage series, and about 7.5 in the eastern part. These are therefore very deep, archaic-looking *long burgages*,[25] reminiscent of agricultural selions and are in fact the longest burgages in medieval Ludlow, with depths of up to 115 yards (345 feet or 105 metres). Their general character suggests derivation from manorial agricultural practice, adapted to a standard width of 2 perches to give adequate street frontage for a timber-framed town house of two structural bays.

The later twelfth-century extension

The early success of Ludlow's foundation soon caused the original market town to expand. This posed a new planning problem requiring an extension that would keep the town compact and close to the castle for easy defence and convenience. But the constitutional improvements in town government to provide an organ of competent decision making were not to be expected during Henry II's reign. Therefore expansion was allowed to occur spontaneously along the ancient routeway for a total length of about ½ mile (820 metres), an area more than twice as large as the original borough. It consisted of mostly bilateral ribbon development of traditional long burgages (Figure 17.1B), soon to spread to other radial roads.

From this brief discussion the townscape of twelfth-century Ludlow emerges as one of distinctive period habitus, with the deep burgage as its period index. It took two successive and contrasting forms, caused respectively by the wish of the lord of the manor for a promising income, and by the awkward coincidence of increasing prosperity and constitutional retardation.

The Broad Street–Mill Street Unit, and the town wall (thirteenth century)

This unit (Figure 17.1B) brought a major innovation of medieval town planning to Ludlow. Its technical features are: 1. a rectangular street system for rational accommodation of a maximum number of burgages (ninety-one units); 2. distinction between streets of different function, namely a. wide multi-purpose main streets providing front access to burgages, b. narrow occupation lanes for cross-connection between main streets, or for provision of rear access to burgages; 3. introduction of a standardized type of *medium burgage* 2×12 perches $(E = 6)$; 4. fitting the plan unit to the site so as to: a. make it contiguous with the original town, b. incorporate Broad Street, the recently constructed new main road to the south,[26] c. preserve reasonable access to the town mill from all parts of the town.

Such a sophisticated departure from Ludlow's traditional 'planning' experience prompts questions of provenance of design, the local socio-political situation, the likely local promoter and the time and mode of installation. Most of the features of the new plan unit belonged to the common stock of planning devices of the time, but one distinctive new trait is Raven Lane, first recorded as 'Narrow Lane' *c.* 1270,[27] because it is a rare example of a bilateral occupation lane (original width probably 1 perch, 16.5 feet or 5 metres), intended exclusively for the provision of rear access to burgages; forty-three out of the ninety-one standard burgages in the plan unit enjoyed this advantage. This device was not used elsewhere in the Welsh Border, nor among the other towns with surviving 'clear grid patterns' listed by Beresford for England and Wales.[28] It is an exotic trait pointing to thirteenth-century Gascony under the kings of England as Dukes of Aquitaine, the land of the *bastides* where this feature was developed to perfection. Ste. Foy la Grande, a French foundation of 1255,[29] has only one bilateral rear lane, backing two lines of burgages between two main streets near the market place much as a Ludlow. Monségur, named in 1263 and formally founded in 1265[30] by Henry III's Queen (Eleanor de Provence) on behalf of her son Edward I in the year of the battle of Evesham, was already served efficiently by bilateral back lanes in close connection with the main thoroughfare and the market place. The associated narrow and long street blocks, each containing a single burgage series, result from the use of the Gascon standard burgage, a short burgage of 24×72 pieds (7.9×23.77 metres, $E = 3$).[31] Finally Monpazier, founded 1285 *en pareage* between Edward I and a local French baron,[32] presents the mature 'textbook' plan of a *bastide*, with literally no part of the intramural area left unserved by bilateral back lanes.

Contemporaneity of this development with the dramatic increase of viticulture in, and massive export of, wine from Gascony[33] suggests a link between exporting vintners and the convenience of bilateral back lanes and associated Gascon short burgages with double access. The close commercial ties between Bordeaux and Bristol are relevant to Ludlow as the main commercial route by which Gascon wine reached Bristol and all the towns within the drainage basin of the Severn and its tributaries; similarly, hides, wool and cloth from the central Welsh Border could reach Gascony.[34] The idea of the bilateral back lane could have travelled to Ludlow by the same route. If so, transfer of the idea probably came from the more extensive Monségur and its royal English connection. This suggests a later mid-thirteenth-century date for the incorporation of a 'Narrow Lane' in the design of the Broad Street–Mill Street Unit.

In the meantime considerable changes in their political fortunes since the days of Henry II had caused English towns in the general surge of economic development to become recognized as important sources of income by royalty and other feudal lords. During a period of thirty-eight years, marked by the financial exigencies of Richard I (1189–99) and John (1189–1216), and a progressive caretaker government during Henry III's minority (1216–27), towns were able to purchase chartered privileges and an increasing measure of self-government. Any 'lost' charter of Ludlow, such as is implied by the ancient privileges confirmed in the Charter of 1461, is likely to fall into that period. Only a constitutionally competent corporate body of townsmen could have tackled three major town-planning tasks within one century: the diversion of the main north–south highway through the middle of the existing town soon after the beginning of the thirteenth century,[35] the construction of the Broad Street–Mill Unit in stages and its completion by late mid-century and the town wall and gates by the end of the century.[36]

During the same period records begin to accumulate giving an increasingly tangible picture of the developing urban community and its leading oligarchy of wealthy wool and cloth merchants. By the early thirteenth century Ludlow's fulling mill was recorded and by 1273–8 the town was recorded as one of the fifty-three places in England with merchants licensed to export wool.[37] This included men like Nicolas de Lodelow (died 1278) and particularly his son Lawrence, 'of Ludlow and London', 'most renowned merchant'.[38] Through their wealth, wide experience and foreign investments they had access to special information on urban matters like the plan technicality of Narrow Lane, while involvement in the corporate self-government of Ludlow and in their own property investments gave them a stake in the economic efficiency of the townscape. It is this advanced socio-economic background of the thirteenth-century town that is expressed in the distinctive townscape habitus of the Broad Street–Mill Street layout, a new Ludlow of the medium burgages.

The construction of Broad Street–Lower Broad Street can be assigned to the early years of the thirteenth century, between Ludlow's coming of age as a fully corporate town and the institution of St John's Hospital near Ludford Bridge perhaps at the beginning of the 1220s.[39] The upper two-thirds of the new road, that is Broad Street proper, must have been lined with the new medium burgages from the start for their residual pattern survives quite recognizably on the west side, and only a little less so on the east side. Letters patent for the fortification of the town by walls and gates were issued in 1233,[40] but this must have been prepared and anticipated for some time before that date, for there were topographical indications that such anticipation proceeded in rapport with the evolving design of the Broad Street–Mill Street Unit. One of these is the remarkable strip of sunken gardens parallel to and west of Mill Street at a distance of 72 metres (236 feet). Recently identified as the 'Christ Croft' of earlier documents and as 'my ditch (fossatum) of Ludlow' given to Ludlow Church by Walter de Lacy, lord of the manor, probably in 1229,[41] this feature is comparable in width to the fosse round the inner bailey of the castle. Aligned exactly between the drum tower in the southern town wall it is most plausibly interpreted as an early thirteenth-century essay in town walling orientated on an already mooted, but by no means settled, project for the Broad Street–Mill Street Unit in which Broad Street as yet formed the only definitive line. By the time the final shape of walled Ludlow was decided, the earlier fosse was abandoned in favour of a fortification line that included Dinham and gave the defenders a greater advantage of the terrain. Reservation of land for the defence perimeter must have taken place at the latest by 1233, and from then on development of the Broad Street–Mill Street Unit had to conform to it.

In the meantime Broad Street was rapidly filling up with building development on its medium burgages and the Mill Street half of the new layout had to be finalized. It will have been at this relatively late stage that Narrow Lane was included in the design as a town-planner's trumpcard that must have appealed specially to the oligarchy at the head of Ludlow's corporation. The position of Christ Croft had left ample room for that, so much so as to leave a surplus strip of land on its east side approximately 12 metres (40 feet) wide which was added to the standard medium burgages of the western Mill Street series, giving them a larger elongation (E = 7).

The construction of the town wall was the last major formal undertaking in the shaping of Ludlow's medieval townscape. The five main gates were recorded by *c.* 1270,[42] and the wall may have been completed by the end of the century.

Late medieval Ludlow (1270–1500)

The kinds of transformation wrought on the medieval townscape in this period were many. Free burgage tenure had always been liable to upset the corporately established order among burgage plots to some degree through subdivision and amalgamation, but was kept in check by the custom of longitudinal division, resulting merely in complicated sequences of frontage amounts.[43] But Ludlow's booming economy and increasing concentration of personal wealth in the thirteenth century created a lively property market in the town centre. No sooner had the Broad Street–Mill Street Unit been completed and its burgages been occupied than transverse subdivision began to produce a crop of 'pseudo-burgages' (new tail-end plots cut from the original burgages) along Narrow Lane.[44]

Arguably the most important interference with corporately established order came from private encroachments on public spaces. Of the two kinds found, lateral encroachments on the sides of street spaces are almost ubiquitous in Ludlow though they are not always obvious. Resulting from unconnected individual actions they imparted randomness and irregularity of detail without obscuring the main features of the medieval town plan. On the other hand island encroachments, together with an exceptionally deep lateral encroachment at 'Drapers Row' (south side of King Street), produced a tangible complex of market colonization, virtually a second plan unit within the High Street Unit (Figure 17.1B). These encroachments, documented from *c.* 1270 onwards, originated in open retail stalls (*selda*) in the market street, which in time became shops (*shopa*), and eventually shops with residential accommodation above (*shopa cum solario*).[45] Though contrary to corporate intent, they were condoned for their general convenience and for the extra tax income they brought.

Early modern Ludlow (1500–1830)

The fifteenth century was the last period in which medieval corporate order had largely controlled Ludlow's townscape, though with decreasing effect. By the end of it revolutionary changes affecting European society created a new social and cultural context. Henceforth individual initiative would play a greater part in the development of the townscape of the Old Town. As a result the contribution each new period habitus made to the structure and character of Ludlow's traditional townscape was much smaller than in earlier centuries, though not necessarily less distinct. Changes in the town plan became virtually negligible concerning detail such as isolated amalgamation of contiguous burgages for building development rather than overall change; whereas changes in the building fabric became more prominent, gaining importance through marked architectural period differences and the steadily increasing period mixture as time went on (Figure 17.1C).

In Ludlow the early modern era comprises two periods, that is the time from *c.* 1500 to *c.* 1690 when Ludlow was the seat of the Council of the Marches, and the period from *c.* 1690 to *c.* 1830 when the town was a regional social centre.

The Council of the Marches brought a great influx of higher administrative officials and lawyers, the new professions of the Renaissance period, men of an entirely new socio-political context who owed allegiance not to any local corporate bodies of the old feudal order but as individuals to the new territorial nation state of the Tudor and subsequent periods. They were men with large incomes, considerable social standing and expansive domestic requirements. Their chief impact on the townscape lies in the amalgamation of burgages into blocks large enough for the siting and erection of their new residences or 'fayre houses'.[46] The introduction of these prominent large house types to Ludlow in characteristic random location wherever suitable sites became available symbolizes the unrestrained individual initiative in the development of the townscape.

The second period, comprising the styles of Georgian and Regency architecture, made the largest contribution to Ludlow's townscape. Ludlow, being a fashionable social centre at that time, reflected the settled conditions and the social hierarchy based on large differences in income in its stock of Georgian buildings. Universal adherence to a disciplined and elegant building style was a unifying and generally accepted part of the mores of urban society. It has resulted in the largest contribution of a historically distinctive period habitus to Ludlow's townscape.

Victorian and twentieth-century Ludlow

Situated on the unimportant Welsh Border railway line in a productive agricultural region without any important industrial resources, Ludlow has been by-passed by Victorian industrialization and has shared in its changes and growth symptoms only in terms of a modest, but economically secure country town and central place for the small region around it. During the Victorian period such working-class population as it had was housed partly in the Old Town, largely out of sight in the back yards of medieval burgages during the climax phase of the burgage cycle, or in similarly restricted terrace housing outside it. The bulk of new residential accommodation, however, has been provided outside the traditional town to the north and east, and thus there has been little replacement of houses within the Old Town.

The business centre, although still on its medieval site, likewise has had few replacements of commercial or administrative buildings during the last 150 years, but these replacements during the Victorian and Edwardian periods have been relatively prominent because of their architectural contrast to the traditional building fabric of the Old Town. This has emphasized the randomness of their occurrence and the ethos of an age which had taken *laissez-faire* and unbridled individual initiative as its starting point.

Within this context, Ludlow has a particularly interesting set of bank buildings covering the development of this building type from adapted Georgian houses during the period of early joint stock banks to the late purpose-built mock 'half-timber' bank of 1924, illustrating the change in banking organization and one of its corollaries, the change in the choice of designers from local architects to architects from other regions and London.[47] This last point covers a subject well researched by Whitehand in his work on Northampton and Watford,[48] and illustrates one of the later turns in the long story of the townscape habitus.

Conclusion

The above sketch of Ludlow's townscape development is an attempt to indicate the succession of periods characterized by distinctive kinds of townscape habitus and to trace the latter back to their socio-economic and cultural roots in an urban society changing in the course of time. It appears that the secular change in the townscape habitus of English historic towns reaching back to the High Middle Ages is connected with a corresponding change from medieval corporate to modern industrial society, more particularly with reference to the relative balance between corporate and individual actions in townscape formation. It is suggested – and at present it can be no more than a suggestion – that primacy of corporate action in the High Middle Ages was eroded by stages in subsequent urban history when individual action, with few exceptions, gained primacy in early and mid-Victorian England until the advent of the Public Health Act of 1875, when development began to take a new direction. This is of course an oversimplification, but the difficulties of comprehending this problem in more precise terms appear to lie in social history rather than in urban morphology. In the meantime, it will be an advantage if more morphogenetic investigations of townscapes of at least 750 years' standing can be made with this problem in mind to provide a basis for some form of comparative study.

18

The metrological analysis of early modern planned towns

JÜRGEN LAFRENZ

The foundation of towns in early modern times

In Central Europe the pattern of distribution of towns was more or less completed in the Late Middle Ages, and during early modern times only a few more towns were founded. The forces shaping the towns had changed with regard to their conceptional and material substance. Initially, the concentration of political power was of vital importance, as territorial sovereigns gained administrative power and growing influence on urban development. They not only influenced the growth of specific towns, but also took a keen interest in planning and designing a number of new settlements. In this respect the territorial sovereigns were specifically concerned with towns to house religious refugees (*Exulantenstädte*), with strong mercantile importance. They strictly controlled the planning of new towns that were founded for military or administrative purposes (*Residenzstädte*).[1] The sovereigns' impact on design and planning was likely to be strongest if they engaged in it right from the beginning.

In contrast to the Late Middle Ages, when planning concepts were based on experience, plans in early modern times were designed on the drawing-board. Though there also existed a great variety of theoretical concepts for ideal towns, the majority of new ground-plans followed more simple geometrical patterns, laid out on the basis of exact measuring techniques.

Long-term aims led to generous planning following standardized concepts. But most of the designed projects failed in terms of a sufficient number of potential settlers. A delay in the beginning of settlement quite often caused alterations of the ground-plans, but even more it led to a continual shortage of new citizens.

In the analysis of early modern planned towns emphasis has been placed mostly on a morphographic approach. In particular, theoretical schemes or ideal concepts were analysed. The morphogenetic approach, however, merely reconstructed successive phases of settlement in a very general way, quite often ignoring the topographic development within the towns.

The morphogenetic interpretation of early modern ground-plans

The cartographical sources

With the beginning of the Early Modern period the theoretical and practical foundation for large-scale land surveying was laid. Although there had been rapid progress in technology and organization since the seventeenth century, detailed cadastral maps for the majority of European towns were not surveyed before the early nineteenth century.

While analysing the layout of early modern planned towns, the following gaps in cartographic documentation became apparent, especially for some of the early towns:

1. Often only a few blueprints exist and records on the practical embodiment very rarely survived.
2. Mostly, in older plans, the street network is documented, but not the pattern of the plots.

Because of these deficiencies it is only possible in exceptional cases to follow the development of the ground-plans from their beginning. If sufficient material for the same period does not exist, later plans need to be evaluated.

The morphological analysis

The general method to explain the development of urban layouts is the morphogenetic, ground-plan analysis, by which earlier topographic elements are deduced from the situation of more recent evidence.

The traditional ground-plan analysis assumes that the street network remained remarkably persistent during pre-industrial times. In addition, the plot pattern, if taken into account at all, was considered more or less unchanged. The continuity of streets and plots was taken for granted, just referring to a regular pattern thought to be laid out within a short period of the town's foundation. A detailed morphogenetic analysis reveals evidence of a number of phases of topographic development, documented in elements of inner homogeneity, which are separated from another by irregularities. The homogeneous parts in the ground-plan fit together like a puzzle. In general the shape of the individual plots is not so important as their arrangement in a larger unit.

In uniformly planned towns, the expansion of the layout was carried out in a regular variety of forms, characterized in general by straight lines and corresponding angles. This is why criteria are needed which identify the chronology of such rational ground-plan elements. Furthermore, because of the possibly heterogeneous internal development of speculatively laid out sites it is also important to prove the continuity of individual plots.

The metrological analysis

In order to reconstruct the development process of regular settlement patterns, a quantitative method – that tries to reconstruct the original first survey – could be relevant. This approach involves the use of metrological analysis that was finally elaborated and used by Hannerberg, following some earlier individual attempts.[2] His method is based on the supposition that during the systematic reconstruction of a planning site the different elements of the ground-plan (the blocks and plots) were laid out as multiples of a measuring system. This system of measurement was in turn only applied for a specific period over special areas, during the early development of a town. The reasons for this are twofold: first, due to the alteration or termination of planning (for example, if a general planning programme was not strictly carried out, spontaneous forms of individual units of measurement appeared, which ignored any standardized units); secondly, due to a change of the system of measurement or survey (thus, if a general planning programme was subject to new conditions, the layout could be continued in different units of measurement).

Irregularities in the measuring system are, in general, evidence for a discontinuity in the process of development of a planned site. Even so the original planning concept, even with various breaks, might be proved by a high degree of continuity in the system of the layout.

The metrological analysis consists of three major stages of operation:

1. The measures of the ground-plan elements are determined and compared with their largest unit of division, with the aim of discovering whether one or more systems of measuring were used.
2. If one or more systems of measurement can be proved, then their distribution has to be examined in order that patterns continually used can be deduced.
3. If a number of different homogeneous planning phases can be proved, then the breaks in the town's development should be determined by additional sources.

In contrast to the morphographical interpretation of urban ground-plans, the morphometrical analysis is restricted to those plans with regular patterns and exact measures. Indeed, if the original survey was not carried out accurately, the identification of morphometric systems becomes extremely difficult.

These problems are emphasized in the initial attempts to analyse the ground-plans of the Late Middle Ages within Central Europe. Thus, studies of Lippstadt, Lübeck, some of the towns of Baden and of the Palatinate, all of which are only partly regular, have so far been less than convincing.[3] Significantly, attempts to analyse more regular medieval ground-plans, as for example in Silesia, have been relatively more successful.[4] The aim of the analysis in all these towns, however, was to calculate the size of the planned town and thereby reconstruct the original planning concept. It is only comparatively recently that this morphometric method has been applied to planned, early modern towns as an aid to reconstructing patterns of urban development.[5]

The example of Friedrichstadt

The application of the metrological technique can be demonstrated in the case of Friedrichstadt, a town on the west coast of Schleswig-Holstein. It was founded by the absolutist sovereign Friedrich III, of Schleswig-Holstein-Gottorf, who set his hopes on Dutch refugees to establish an important commercial port at the North Sea to follow his ambitious mercantile aspirations. After a hesitant start in 1621/2, Friedrichstadt reached more than 2,000 inhabitants within a short time, before its development began to stagnate.

Friedrichstadt was selected as an example for the following reasons:
1. The evidence of a hand-drawn outline plan and some copperplates, dating from the first fifty years are a good representation of reality (Figure 18.1).
2. As it is a rational and regular pattern of blocks and plots, the ground-plan can hardly be revealed by traditional techniques of town-plan analysis.
3. The oldest accurate maps are supposed to document a high degree of continuity because of the town's long-term stagnation.

The ground-plan of Friedrichstadt represents a typical Dutch town-plan of the early seventeenth century; similar examples are Gothenburg, Batavia, Mauritzstad and especially Nieuw-Amsterdam. The pattern hardly follows the principles of ideal concepts, but rather the 'down-to-earth spirit' of the Dutch during the early modern period.[6]

The earliest accurate map of the block pattern, after an early ground-plan of 1622 (Figure 18.1), is a military survey produced about 1673, when the Swedes wanted to use the town as a fortress (Figure 18.2).

The scale of the map is measured by:
1 Rhineland rod = 37.67 dm
1 Rhineland foot = 31.39 cm
1 rod   = 12 feet

The first complete town-plan of Friedrichstadt was in an official survey designed as a consequence of war damage in 1851 (Figure 18.3). The scale of this map is measured by

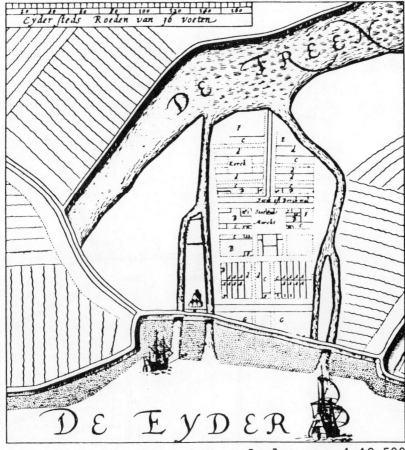

Scale: ca. 1:12.500

Figure 18.1   Friedrichstadt: showing the ground-plan for its foundation in 1622
Source: P. Sax, *Frisia Minor*, 1638

1 Hamburg rod = 46.19 dm
1 Hamburg foot = 28.87 cm
1 rod   = 16 feet

The comparison of both maps shows that the block pattern remained remarkably persistent between 1673 and 1851. Therefore, the metrological analysis of the blocks might be based on the later map without many reservations. The metrological analysis can be intricate, but in the case of Friedrichstadt this method might be simplified by the evaluation of additional sources relating to the early days of the town.

The ideas about how to develop the town progressed step by step. Already

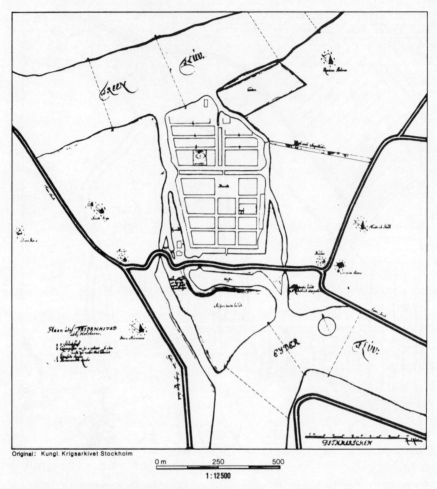

0 m   250   500

1 : 12500

Figure 18.2   Friedrichstadt in 1673

with the first *octroi* to recruit settlers for the town, *normed plots* of different sizes were provided. The surveyor, Reymers, who had engaged in laying out the town in May 1622, wrote that the plan he had followed applied the following normed types of plots:[7]

type A	180 feet long	60 feet broad
type B	144 feet long	24 feet broad
		20 feet broad
type C	72 feet long	18 feet broad
type D	60 feet long	16 feet broad
type E	120 feet long	24 feet broad
		20 feet broad

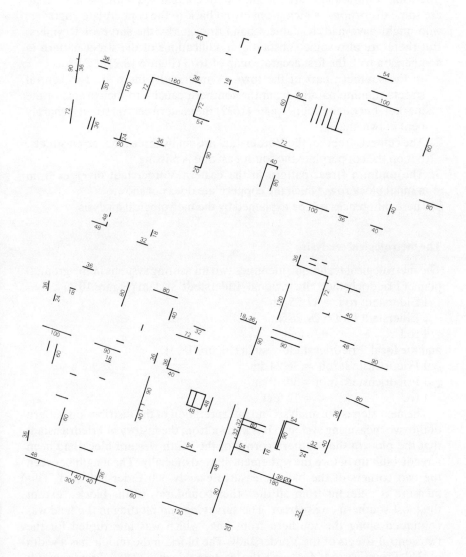

Figure 18.3   Friedrichstadt: distribution of the measuring system of Friedrichstadt feet

Source: J. Jansen, *Survey of Friedrichstadt*, 1851

Reymers also listed the plots of the first thirteen settlers, but so far a corresponding map has not been found, and only a copperplate exists (Figure 18.1). The letters on the map are related to the types of plots, and the figures obviously mark those plots obtained by the first settlers. The codes on the maps are incomplete in comparison with the list. There are some distortions, which probably go back to the copperplate engraver, who might have had available a hand drawing by the surveyor Reymers. But there are also some substantial modifications of the street pattern in comparison with the first accurate map of 1673 (Figure 18.2):

1. In the southern part of the town (Vorderstadt) there are two central streets running parallel from the southern canal into the corners of the market, but on the copperplate (1622) the eastern central street is sharply bent in two angles.
2. The central streets of the Vorderstadt are cut by three inner cross-streets, but on the copperplate the south-east one is missing.
3. The uniform street pattern in the eastern Vorderstadt diverges from a small block row, which the copperplate does not show.

These differences will be explained by the metrological analysis.

The metrological analysis

The metrological technique identifies two measuring systems in the ground-plan of Friedrichstadt: the regional 'Eiderstedt' system (Figure 18.4)

  1 Eiderstedt rod = 47.75 dm
  1 Eiderstedt foot = 29.86 cm
  1 rod   = 16 feet

and the local 'Friedrichstadt' system (Figure 18.3)

  1 Friedrichstadt rod = 36.24 dm
  1 Friedrichstadt foot = 30.20 cm
  1 rod   = 12 feet

The next step is the analysis and interpretation of the distribution pattern of the two measuring systems. It is known from the history of Friedrichstadt that the plots in the southern corner of the south-western block had been already built up before the settlement started officially. The length between the two corners of the block measures exactly 300 Eiderstedt feet. This measure is different from all the other boundaries of the blocks, except the most southern cross-street. The surveying and plotting in the field was continued along the southern front line, which was interrupted for the two central streets of the Vorderstadt. The block in the middle has a width of 240 Friedrichstadt feet and the eastern block is 249.4 Friedrichstadt feet wide.

The second axis of the original survey was the western central street, continued by the single street at the northern part of the town (*Hinterstadt*).

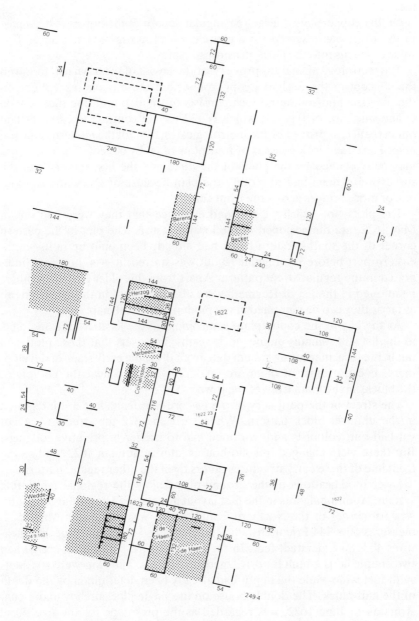

Figure 18.4 Friedrichstadt: distribution of the measuring system of Eiderstadt feet

If we omit the most southern cross-street, the depths of the blocks measure from the south to the north: 360, 216, 216.216.120.132.72 Friedrichstadt feet.

On the copperplate a large rectangular square in the north-western part of the town was reserved for a church, which has never been built. This square also fits into the local measuring system.

The metrological analysis proves that the layout of the town had followed the concept of the unsigned copperplate; but there is one exception: on the plan the mid-southern block consists of the depth of one plot of type C and one plot of type D, which is 132 feet in contrast to 240 feet laid out in reality, as proved by the metrological analysis of the modern cadastral map. Here the block consists of four plots of 60 by 60 feet. The difference may be explained by the plans of the duke and the first settlers, but the surveyor Reymers had to modify the plan because of speculations about one or more bridges across the front canal.

The plots, for which we can find evidence that they were laid out in May 1622, are dimensioned in the local measure. The plot in the eastern corner of the south-western block had already been built up in its south-eastern part before the regular layout was started; it was, however, integrated in the regular street pattern. Apart from this older plot most others mentioned in the list of Reymers were also measured in the local system, as far as they can be identified in the modern cadastral map.

As the key in the copperplate is incomplete, the location of some plots in the list still remains unknown. It seems, however, that those plots laid out in the local measuring system date from the same early stage of development, because most of them are favourably located near the corners of the blocks in the main front of the town.

The street in the periphery of the eastern Vorderstadt is not integrated in the uniform block pattern. When early in 1622 the streets were not yet laid out, colonists and workmen had to shelter in primitive lodgings. But these were changed to solid houses later in autumn 1622, and so the front line of these early structures differs from the other regular pattern.

Later modifications of the ground-plan follow the regional measuring system. Additional plots to the first layout are scarce. The plot in the south-western corner of the Northern Canal, which was laid out in May 1622, measures 60 × 144 Friedrichstadt feet. But it also includes a plot that measures 40 × 80 Eiderstedt feet. In the south-eastern part the sovereign had two double houses built for privileged immigrants. The plots were 40 Eiderstedt feet wide while the depth had already been determined by the depth of the half-block. The double house on the single plot, already under construction in June 1622, was regarded as the prototype for the two ducal double houses. Its foundation-stone was laid in August 1622.

The change of the measuring system can also be verified by the official cutting of a street, dating 1622/3. The primarily deep blocks in the south were divided up according to the settlers' will. Along the western central street the separated blocks measure in the northern block 180 Friedrichstadt feet and in the southern block 150 Eiderstedt feet. The smaller blocks were measured and marked from the northern side. As a consequence of the changed measure the width of the new street does not fit into either of the two systems.

The cutting is called 'New Street' in one part. The reason for this 'New Street' was a general change of the initial idea of the plot pattern, caused by an increase in value of the intra-urban locations during the development of the settlement. The town had originally been planned with an orientation towards the harbour, but soon the development of the market square became a further focus. In addition the tangential canal had its function for shipping. While at the northern front of the middle canal plots now were laid out larger than originally intended, the northern parts of the southern, still undivided, blocks in the Vorderstadt were divided into smaller plots.

The exclusive use of the local measuring system by the surveyor Reymers, who, expecting a rapid growth of the town, laid out the plan in about one month, means that the whole area between the sluice-ways was divided up by streets within a few weeks. The incomplete division of lots at the same time confirms that there was not a sufficient number of settlers, and soon the plot pattern was neglected.

In the case of Friedrichstadt, the metrological analysis is an adequate method for a morphogenetic analysis as two different measuring systems were used alternatively. The local system, however, was only applied for about a month during the fundamental stage of the execution of the plan. But the technique should also be applicable and effective for an analysis of a town which was layed out in one measuring system only.

The ground-plan of Friedrichstadt reflects a specific process of decision-making and development. The high degree of coherence of the block pattern is a reflection of the organization ordered by the sovereign and of his high expectations, but the ground-plan was laid out too generously for the available number of settlers.

In contrast, the high degree of incoherence of the plot pattern is a reflection of the growing influence of the speculating Dutch settlers. Furthermore, it seems that not only the streets or blocks of regular towns have to be examined in respect of their measures, but also the plots.

Comparing measuring systems

In this chapter metrological analysis has been presented as a method which makes it possible to reconstruct the efficiency of intended planning. Past criticism concerning traditional ground-plan analysis has suggested that these approaches have either led to gross generalizations or been limited to individual explanations.[8] Carter has argued that further progress depends on two aims being pursued.[9] First, work is required to quantify the geometrical pattern of the ground-plan. Secondly, analysis needs to separate out the factors determining the ground-plan. Within this latter aim Carter suggests that attention be focussed on the decision-making process during the layout of the plan. His thesis is that uniformity of plan reflects organized central control, so that contrasts in the uniformity of plans are a reflection of the degree of the concentration of power.[10] In practice, however, it is difficult to define plan uniformity, since the layout itself can show a wide variety of forms under the same degree of uniformity. It is perhaps therefore more appropriate to inquire about the rationality of the pattern.

To a certain extent metrological analysis offers an objective method of comparative town-plan analysis and goes some way to satisfying Carter's requirements. Thus, it allows an analysis of the entire ground-plan by means of measurable criteria, behind which may have been factors of political control. It also makes it possible to determine the stringency of a planning programme up to the point where there was a break in the develpment. This stringency might be measured by one or two indices: the relationship between the lengths laid out in an integral measuring system, and the total length on the plan. These perhaps can be subdivided into two indices according to the block margins and the plot boundaries. It should also be stressed that other factors should be considered, since the metric indices may reflect economic and cultural forces as well as political ones, and it is within these areas that further refinements of the technique need to be made.

19

Recent developments in urban morphology

JEREMY WHITEHAND

In 1978 M. P. Conzen detected evidence of renewed research activity in urban morphology after a period of quiescence.[1] Research in the past six years has underlined this resurgence both in Britain[2] and America.[3] In the German-speaking world, the homeland of urban morphology and the scene of its great flowering in the inter-war years, there is less evidence of a resurgence; though there, in comparison with the English-speaking countries, the townscape has remained a more integrated part of urban geographical research in the post-war period.[4] In America, recent research in urban morphology has been concerned largely with architectural styles.[5] There, such studies, in geography at least, have shallow roots historically,[6] though antecedents are arguably to be found among studies emanating from the Berkeley School.[7] In Britain, the revival of urban morphology is based on more developed foundations with particularly important, though at times tenuous, links to work by German-speaking geographers early in this century, if not before.[8] This line of descent is perhaps most evident in the recent town-plan analyses by Slater,[9] but it is a significant strand too in the renewed interest in building form.[10] It is the revival of research in this particular aspect of urban morphology that is the principal concern of this paper.

Intellectual parentage

Recent research on building form by British geographers has a mixed intellectual parentage. An early source of inspiration, now largely forgotten but still exerting influence through later scholars, was the work of Schlüter, especially before the First World War.[11] It was he and, after the First World War, his pupil Geisler[12] who set the standard for urban morphology that was to be maintained up to and even after the Second World War. Less influential in the long term, but noteworthy, was the work on historic architectural styles by Hassinger at about the time of the First World War,[13] and later by his pupil Schaefer.[14] The work of these authors, and of others who were individually less influential, stimulated an unprecedented growth in urban morphological research in the German-speaking countries in the inter-war period. The contributions of historians and architects to this growth were in some ways as important as those of geographers.[15] Within central Europe the legacy of this morphogenetic tradition in modern times is perhaps most evident in the major study of Vienna by Bobek and Lichten-berger.[16]

In modern British urban morphology this central European inheritance has come to have an influence largely through the work of M. R. G. Conzen, who emigrated from Germany to Britain in 1933. His was in some respects a lone voice within British urban geography in the 1950s. In the 1960s and early 1970s, as studies of function almost eclipsed those of form, the intellectual tradition that he represented was particularly at variance with pervasive influences from America that were almost untouched by the German morphogenetic tradition. In retrospect his studies of Whitby, Alnwick and central Newcastle upon Tyne,[17] rich in developmental concepts and meticulous in their reconstructions of townscape change, were naviga-tion lights during a period when the city as a physical entity almost dis-appeared from the agenda of British urban geography. Their significance was twofold. First, they were largely responsible for the morphogenetic component that has enriched the revivified urban morphology of the 1980s. Secondly, in addition to yielding historico-geographical insights, they pro-vided stepping stones towards a theory of townscape management.[18]

But morphogenesis is only one strand in the renewed interest in building form. A second strand emanates principally from British and North Ameri-can urban history, though it has parallels in British historical geography. One of the major pioneering studies in this *genre* was the study by Dyos of a London suburb in the nineteenth century.[19] This type of study fre-quently considers in some detail the individuals and organizations respon-sible for particular urban developments. The study by Beresford of the influence of a single landowner on the development of the east end of Leeds is an example.[20] But perhaps the greatest monuments of all to this type of work are the massive volumes produced under the auspices of the Historic Buildings Committee of the Greater London Council. These document in great detail specific parts of London, not only describing the appearance of individual buildings inside and out but, based on a variety of sources, chronicling their physical changes, the roles of people associated with them, and the events with which they were connected.[21]

A third influence that has contributed to current studies is the application of statistics and model building in morphological analysis. This developed in the late 1960s as a by-product of the rapidly growing interest in statistical applications and mathematics in the economic and social branches of urban geography.[22] Neither the sources of data nor the waning interest in the 1960s in the physical character of cities were conducive to a sustained exploration of statistical methods in urban morphology, such as occurred in many other fields within geography. Nevertheless, the impact of the 'quantitative revolution' has been apparent in at least three respects: increased awareness of the relevance of models derived from land economics;[23] greater circumspection in drawing inferences from the awkward types of data that are all too frequently encountered in studies of urban form; and more attention given to research design.

A fourth, more recent, source of influence stems from the increased interest among social scientists in the 1970s in the workings of capitalism and more particularly the relations between the different types of economic interest involved in the development, use and exchange of property.[24] Instead of the concern being with the reciprocal relations between function and form, which has been a theme underlying much quantitative morphological analysis, attention has been devoted to the financial returns obtained by the various parties with interests in the built environment. For example, instead of thinking of function largely in terms of the use a building performs – for instance as a shop or an office – attention is directed to the role it performs in providing a return for those involved in creating, managing and using buildings.[25] Some owners conceive of buildings primarily as investments, while others view them primarily as shells within which they can undertake their businesses. This has implications for the urban morphologist, as for example over the timing of construction and the design of buildings.

Finally – and here parallels can be drawn with recent geographical research in America – there is a detectable renewal of influence from the arts, not least architectural history.[26] This is in part a reaction against essentially materialistic views of the city, whether in terms of competition between land uses or the interaction of different property interests.

If this set of influences adds up to a pot-pourri and makes recent developments in urban morphology seem highly derivative, it also underlines the extent to which the landscape that is the object of the urban morphologist's attention is the product of relationships scarcely less diverse than those at work in society. This should make us chary of pursuing a single, narrow perspective for too long. The tendency for the present revival of urban morphology to be in some degree eclectic, and at its best integrative, is therefore to be welcomed. It may prove to be a melting-pot out of which there arises a number of new, sometimes of necessity specialized, lines of investigation. For the moment, one of its effects is to draw attention to the artificiality of treating certain explanations of urban development as if they were in competition with one another. For example, landowners and the economic dictates of the market have too often been presented as if they provided alternative explanations.[27] A more realistic perspective is to set individual decision makers into a wider framework of morphogenetics, economics, property interests and artistic considerations, to name only the main influences apparent in the present heightening of geographical interest in the urban landscape.

Research questions

The directions currently being followed by British urban morphology in general, and studies of building form in particular, may be seen as a response to unanswered questions arising from previous work of various persuasions. Two groups of problems may be mentioned here. First, a serious deficiency in previous work was the virtual absence of analytical studies of those who initiated and designed changes to the physical fabric, whether it be the construction of new buildings or the variety of changes to existing buildings. There were individual biographies and histories of particular businesses[28] but seldom were data brought together in a way that made possible more general statements based on large numbers of individuals or firms. A major, largely unanswered, geographical question concerned the extent to which owners, their sources of funds and those they engaged to design and erect their buildings were from the towns and cities in which the buildings were constructed. Could a clear shift be demonstrated from local to non-local control over decision making within the twentieth century and if so what effect did it have on the buildings constructed? It seemed inescapable, for instance, that boardroom decisions taken in the metropolis against a background of national-scale operations would have produced different results from decision making by local individuals with a field of vision ending at the edge of a town's local sphere of influence.

Secondly, these considerations were related to a number of others. These included the linkages between the various individuals, firms and organizations involved in the development process. To what extent had control become more concentrated in major organizations? This question was relevant not only to individual facets of the development process, such as ownership and design, but to the linkages between organizations involved in different aspects of development, such as between funding organizations and owners, between owners and architects, and between architects and builders. What were the implications of these changing relationships for the scale and style of townscape change? These questions raised still others about variations within and between towns and about both fluctuations over time and secular trends. Such questions have stimulated one of the most important lines of investigation in British urban morphology in the 1980s. It is to this that the remainder of this paper is devoted.

Sources

Both ignorance about sources of data and problems in their use have hindered this line of investigation. In order to answer its central questions, not only is information required about buildings – for example, their style, location, data of construction, and how and when they were altered – but about those who initiated, designed and funded them and the changes made to them. To extract this information from sources unique to each building would be a sizable task even for a few buildings. To do it for large areas on this basis would be prohibitive. A far more efficient source, but until recently used scarcely at all for large-scale analyses, is the records compiled in connection with the regulating of new building and changes to existing buildings. Virtually all Western countries have developed some such system. Warner has made considerable use of the building permits that are part of the procedure for regulating constructional work in America.[29] In Great Britain the equivalent records are generally quite detailed, at least from the late nineteenth century onward, although they vary somewhat from one local authority to another. They normally include building plans, and frequently also provide the names and addresses of building owners, architects and others involved in the development process, and correspondence between the local authority and other parties. Although these building applications have been used for research purposes for many years, their full potentialities were not realized until the late 1970s.[30]

Two weaknesses in these records deserve brief mention. First, the source of funds for the constructional work is seldom given. Secondly, the extraction of information is slow since the application forms containing the information about the agents involved are filed with a variety of other, sometimes voluminous, information, including the architect's drawings and, where relevant, the drawings and calculations of consulting engineers, much of which may not be relevant to the research project. Furthermore, speed of access to a file depends on the indexing system used by the local authority. By no means all of them index their records by street location, and without such an index the time taken to locate the application for a particular piece of constructional work may be prohibitive.

The completeness and method of organization of the records of particular local authorities has been an important factor in determining the selection of areas in which research projects have been undertaken. Since the late 1970s seven major studies using these and/or similar records have commenced at the University of Birmingham, involving the records for some twenty towns in various parts of England. A selection of findings from a comparative study of the centres of two somewhat different towns – the county town of Northampton and the suburban town of Watford – serve to illustrate the results that this work is producing.

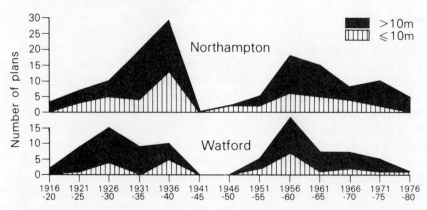

Figure 19.1   Plot frontages of major rebuildings in the central areas of Northampton and Watford, 1916–80

Recent results

The first finding that justifies mention here constitutes a confirmation of previous work as much as a discovery of new facts. It concerns the extent to which changes in the townscape have been constrained by legacies from the past. This is partly a matter of earlier developments constraining later ones. Both Northampton and Watford have predominantly medieval street systems in their central areas and old, if not medieval, plots survive on a large scale. The speed with which medieval plot lineaments have been eroded, however, has varied considerably within the twentieth century. In the period since the early 1950s the proportion of redevelopments that have taken place within plot frontages equal to or less than Conzen's standard burgage width in Alnwick of 10 metres has diminished (Figure 19.1). This has produced a reaction since the mid-1970s, particularly evident in Northampton, in attempts to recreate traditional-scale frontages. This has been done by designing long-fronted buildings so that they give the appearance of consisting of more than one building.[32]

Another important legacy from the past is the local firms, organizations and families that emerged from the nineteenth century to make many of the decisions that changed the townscape in the period between the two world wars. As a major provincial central place well away from the metropolis, Northampton was in 1918 richly endowed with locally based firms and organizations – professional, commercial and cultural. Thus, for example, the small business of a mid-nineteenth-century builder, Richard Cleaver, expanded to become a limited company and one of the major property owners and rebuilders of the town centre in the 1920s and 1930s. Watford, already by the end of the First World War influenced strongly by the proximity of London, also had several examples of continuity of property interests extending well back into the nineteenth century, notably the large holdings of the Fisher family, but these on the whole remained in the hands of private individuals well into the inter-war period, perhaps because of the smaller size of the town. In Watford it was these individuals rather than limited companies or large organizations who were responsible for much of the speculative construction of shopping parades with offices above that occurred in the 1920s.[33]

A second finding is also of especial interest for the light it sheds on previous work. This concerns the degree to which architectural styles that characterize one morphological period continue to be reproduced in the early years of the next. The end of the First World War has come to be regarded as the beginning of a new morphological period.[34] Yet in the centres of both Northampton and Watford Edwardian styles continued to be used in the 1920s (Figure 19.2), largely in the hands of local architects.[35] The change to inter-war styles occurred in Northampton as late as 1927. Significantly, it took a combination of an owner-occupier and a London architect to introduce, in the same building, both modern architecture and Art Deco. Within two years these styles had almost completely ousted Edwardian styles, and Art Deco, together with neo-Georgian, had become the choice of owners and architects, whether external or local. Speculative developers were more conservative, as seems to have been widely the case,[36] but on this occasion they quickly followed the stylistic lead of those building for owner-occupation.

A third finding concerns fluctuations in the incidence of different types of development. Again, an illustration from Northampton is apposite. The small amount of redevelopment in the centre of that town during the First World War and for almost a decade after was largely carried out by a variety of public and private institutions and financial companies, building for their own occupation on the edge of the commercial core. This was mainly a response to changes in organizations whose headquarters were outside the town, such as the YWCA, the Post Office and the Co-operative Wholesale Society. In contrast, the 1930s were dominated by redevelopment for shops. The reasons for these fluctuations were various. In this example the greater resilience of large institutions in the recession following the First World War may well have been a factor, but the existence at the same time of considerable redevelopment for shops in Watford is evidence that other factors were at work.[37]

A further finding concerns two major secular changes.[38] First, there was the large-scale entry of retail chainstores, many of them public companies, into property development in the 1930s (Figure 19.3). Many chainstores already operated nationally and had distinctive house styles reproduced by their own architects' departments or by architects with whom they had

NORTHAMPTON

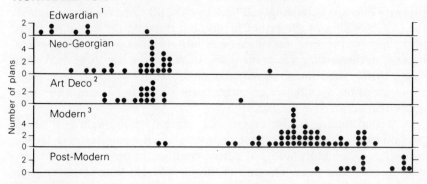

WATFORD

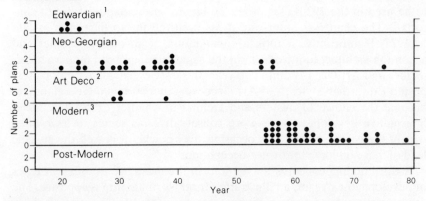

Figure 19.2   Architectural styles of major rebuildings in the central areas of Northampton and Watford, 1916–80

Note: buildings have been categorized according to their predominant style. Only major categories are shown.

1   There is not a sharp division between the neo-classical variant of the Edwardian style and the neo-Georgian style.
2   A number of buildings that exhibited this style weakly are included.
3   Excludes 'People's Architecture'.

standing relationships. It thus became increasingly common for buildings of similar appearance to be erected in town centres over the whole country. The population catchment considered by a particular chainstore to be necessary for it to function profitably therefore became an increasingly important factor underlying the admixture of building styles present in a particular town centre. Secondly, the involvement of property companies and insurance companies in the speculative development and ownership

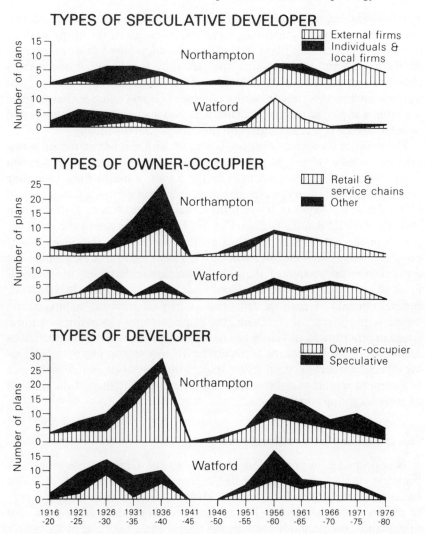

Figure 19.3   Types of development (major rebuildings only) in the central areas of Northampton and Watford, 1916–80

Note: owing to incomplete information there are slight discrepancies in the numbers of plans shown

of property grew slowly but perceptibly in the 1930s and then rapidly from the late 1950s onward. Most of these companies were operating on a national scale. Together with the retail and service chains they largely replaced the local property developers and owners, many of whom in Watford were private individuals even as late as the 1920s (Figure 19.3). By the

1950s in Watford and the 1970s in Northampton these national-scale developers were mainly commissioning architects from outside the towns in which the developments took place, particularly London-based firms in the case of Watford. This, together with the tendency for the retail and service chains to employ their own architects, meant that new buildings designed by local architects were comparatively few. This was a major change from the inter-war period when, particularly in Northampton, local owners and architects left a powerful imprint on the commercial townscape.

These major secular changes are bound up with another matter on which evidence is now coming to light; the effects of the growing concentration of development activity nationally in the hands of major firms operating countrywide.[39] Contrary to expectation, this has not led to the concentration of activity in the hands of fewer firms in the town centres of Northampton and Watford. This reflects the wider geographical spread in the post-war period of the activities of all types of firms involved in the development process.[40] Whereas in the inter-war period a few local firms were responsible for a sizable proportion of the redevelopments undertaken, the national firms of recent decades have seldom undertaken more than two or three redevelopments in each centre. This is true of owners, architects and builders. In the case of architects, the displacement of local firms by those based in other towns and cities has had the effect of dispersing commissions among more firms. Since the 1960s this has been accompanied by an increasing diversity of architectural styles, though this may be more a consequence of the rapid spread of stylistic diversity internationally than of the number of firms accepting commissions.[41]

Past change and future management

It is appropriate in conclusion to return to the German morphogenetic tradition with which this paper began, especially the extension of it that has provided the basis for Conzen's ideas on the construction of a theory of townscape management. Fundamental to these ideas is the view that urban landscapes embody not only the efforts and aspirations of the people occupying them now but also those of their predecessors. It is this, it has been argued, that creates the sense of place and feeling of continuity that enables individuals and groups to take root in an area.[42] It engenders an awareness of the historical dimension of human experience, which stimulates comparison and encourages a less time-bound and more integrated approach to contemporary problems. A major practical implication is that proposals for townscape management adopting this standpoint lay great stress on the way in which new developments fit into, and in a sense are almost an organic outgrowth from, existing townscapes. It is useful to consider in this light recent developments in the two particular town centres that have been discussed here, though the main forces at work in them are undoubtedly of wider significance.

In the centres of both Northampton and Watford up to and including the inter-war period there was a high degree of interdependence between the townscape and the agents of change. Building owners, architects and builders were mostly either resident locally or had a long-term local interest in that they had a branch of their business in the town. The environments in which they took decisions had much in common with those of the residents and users of the services that the town centres provided. Some, at least, of Conzen's ideals of townscape management were met. But by the 1960s in Northampton – somewhat earlier in Watford – many building owners were absentees, frequently located in London and in many cases interested in property primarily as an investment. Architects, instead of being members of the local community, had little knowledge of the towns in which they were commissioned to design buildings and in many cases had never worked there before. Even builders tended to be from outside the town and almost always consulting engineers and specialized contractors were from even farther afield. This change to remote control on a large scale coincided with increased powers of compulsory purchase by local authorities, in many cases effectively acting as the land purchasing agents of speculative developers. It also coincided with the ascendancy, in non-residential building at least, of the modern movement in architecture with its total rejection of historical styles and vernacular forms. The result, in the 1960s in particular, was the introduction of buildings incompatible with existing townscapes in both style and scale. This was a far cry from the view of the townscape that Conzen was promulgating at the time.[43]

Since the 1960s, but having its origins within that period, there has been a reaction against these developments, reminiscent of the reaction against historical architectural styles in the 1920s and against Art Deco and neo-Georgian styles after the Second World War. By the 1970s the reaction against modern architecture and the large-scale redevelopment that accompanied it had gained momentum. In Northampton this was aided by an active local civic society, but more generally it was part of the rising tide of interest in conservation. In new buildings it was manifested in 'post-modern' architecture,[44] which in varying degrees and in different forms was apparent in nearly every building erected in central Northampton after the mid-1970s.

While this is arguably just the latest in an endless series of fashion cycles, each one creating the seeds of its successor, the historical overtones of this particular fashion make it broadly compatible with Conzen's view of townscape management. But it lacks the theoretical basis that Conzen has provided. It particularly lacks a conception of how individual developments from different historical periods fit together – a sense of how some parts of the townscape have a character distinctive from others that relates to their history and that of the community that created them. Since Conzen's contribution to townscape management is concerned primarily with these matters it can provide a theoretical underpinning where it is most needed. The development and harnessing of his ideas for planning purposes certainly merits a place on the agenda for urban morphology in the next decade and is a natural extension of the research described here.

Acknowledgements

Much of the research described here was funded by the Economic and Social Research Council. The author is grateful for the contributions of fellow members of the Urban Morphology Research Group at the University of Birmingham, especially P. J. Aspinall, M. Freeman, P. J. Larkham, T. R. Slater and S. M. Whitehand.

20

Historical geography and conservation planning in British towns

TERRY SLATER and GARETH SHAW

Introduction

There is a long history in Britain of interest in, and the legislative enforcement of, the conservation of historic towns and of buildings in towns. It developed particularly in the late nineteenth century as a reaction against the over-enthusiastic restoration of medieval churches[1] and was manifested in the founding of the Society for the Protection of Ancient Buildings by William Morris, in 1877,[2] and of two Ancient Monuments Acts; the first, in 1882, designed to protect prehistoric monuments, and the second, in 1900, to extend protection to medieval buildings. The development of the current legislative framework has been outlined by a number of authors, notably by Dobby,[3] and Dale,[4] the latter containing a survey of the comparable legislation in four other north European countries.

This legislation progressed through minor provisions in Housing and Planning Acts of the 1920s and 1930s to the important 1947 Town and Country Planning Act. This Act provided for the comprehensive 'listing' of individual historic buildings and their subsequent protection. The next major landmark was the 1967 Civic Amenities Act which initiated the idea of area conservation, particularly important in towns, and these provisions have been successively enhanced and developed through housing and planning legislation enacted in the 1970s.[5] Government legislation has thus gradually shifted in emphasis, with protection of the individual building being extended to areas; it has advanced the official temporal boundary of architectural and historical significance so that it has now reached the 1930s; and it has increased the level of local authority planning control over change in historic areas, and the notion of grant aid for the restoration and maintenance of historic buildings.

The introduction of area-based conservation policies by the 1967 Act provided one source of stimulus for geographical contributions. In theory the potential for overlaps between the geographer's interest in urban topography and urban regionalism during the 1960s offered a possible methodological framework for the study of conservation areas. Thus, urban and historical geographers could call on their skills and expertise in identifying both morphological and functional regions within towns; which in turn would provide a sensible spatial base around which to draw up conservation areas. Sadly, there has been all too little effort by geographers to integrate these different research themes, although morphological studies of the type developed by Conzen have made some significant contributions.

This chapter attempts to examine the role geographers, and historical geographers in particular, have played in the study of urban conservation. Obviously, any attempt to impose strict academic boundaries around such a didactic topic as urban conservation raises many difficulties, since contributions tend to be multi-disciplinary. The intention therefore is not to set out to define and police any boundaries, but rather to explore the contributions historical geography has made, and can make, to the overall research on urban conservation. This is tackled in three ways. First, by reviewing the general context of geographical research. Secondly, by examining the changing nature of conservation studies with reference to one historic town, thereby moving from general statements to specific details. The third approach highlights the conflict between functional change in the central business district of an historic town and the problems of developing conservation areas.

The context of geographical writing

Since 1967 the literature on urban conservation has increased exponentially. However, the great majority of these published papers are of a particular kind: concerned with the practicalities of conservation and with individual case studies of buildings, areas or whole towns. Much of this literature takes the form of illustrated accounts in the journals of the architectural and planning professions: that is, of those groups most concerned with the practicalities of conservation.[6] In contrast, there is a dearth of publication in academic journals within the fields of geography, history, politics and psychology. As a result the practicalities of conservation have largely advanced without benefit of a wider philosophical or theoretical underpinning.[7]

Newcomb's investigation into the conservation-related research of historical geographers in Britain and North America[8] has suggested that they have made only a minor contribution and that, even when the investigation was expanded to encompass other parts of human geography, there seemed to be little consistent interest in the subject of conservation beyond that of the particular case study.

It would be a mistake, however, to suggest that there has been no work

by geographers. International comparisons have been particularly prominent in the past decade, though these studies have been more concerned
with comparing legislation, and the financing of conservation-related
activity, rather than with exploring the differences of attitude and the
reasons for such differences. Kain, for example, has been prominent in
assessing urban conservation measures in France,[9] Lowenthal has made
Anglo-American comparisons,[10] and Burtenshaw *et al.* have compared
conservation and planning in west European towns.[11] Gordon has recently
provided a comparative perspective on the experience of urban conservation in Scotland,[12] which differs in detail from that in England.

A number of geographers and planners have been concerned to explore
the linkages between conservation and other parts of the planning process.
Cherry, for example, has considered conservation in the light of the general
history of planning, and the biographies of planners,[13] who are, of course,
important agents in the implementation of conservation policies. Ashworth
has been concerned to examine conservation within the whole process of
urban renewal and regeneration of central city areas in Western Europe.[14]
He notes, in particular, the conflict of ideals in the expectation that city
centres should be both the preserved symbol of historical values and the
stage for a flourishing commercial function.

Ashworth has also noted the concern in a number of European countries
for the social consequences of conservation activities, most particularly
for its tendency to transform low-status housing to higher status or to commercial use.[15] Eversley has provided papers on this theme[16] and other geographers have investigated these processes of 'gentrification' more generally
in the context of urban development processes[17] – one of which has been
conservation. These socio-political implications of conservation policy have
also been explored in a Canadian context.[18] In Britain, it is perhaps notable
that local planning authorities have been relatively unconcerned with these
issues of social change.

The effects of local amenity societies as pressure groups within the local
political process have been reviewed by Lowe on a national scale[19] and
Jenkins has provided other interesting reflections on conservationists in
the political arena and in their relationship with architects and planners.[20]
The role of amenity societies has been investigated in some detail by Mc-
Namara in the context of office development in central Edinburgh.[21] This
study is notable for its concerted attempt to relate the observed process
to political theories of the state.

Another interesting attempt to explore some wider political implications
of conservation is Newcomb's identification of legislative cycles of conservation-related statutes and activity related to these cycles.[22] There is some
evidence from Britain that this American-based hypothesis has a more

general relevance, but the time-span involved is too short to be certain of such cycles of activity.[23]

Urban morphological studies have made a contribution to the provision of a better theoretical underpinning for urban conservation, which should not come as a surprise given its strong emphasis on understanding the physical fabric of towns. Conzen has seen the key to effective urban management as a thorough understanding of the evolution of the town plan and its built fabric.[24] An early practical application of his ideas is to be found in the survey of Whitby, co-ordinated by Daysh, for the local planning authority.[25] Conzen has subsequently, but briefly, developed some of these ideas.[26] More recently, Whitehand's work on city centres, using local authority data sources to identify the precise chronology of urban fabric changes and the agents responsible for them, provided a basis for understanding the dynamic process at work in conserved townscapes.[27] Larkham has now begun to utilise these sources and methods specifically to investigate the processes of change in urban conservation areas in the West Midlands and to provide an indication of the interaction of many of the agents in these developments, including landowners, architects, local authorities, conservation groups and developers.[28] Buswell, too, has tried to use Conzen's morphological concepts to provide a broader theoretical underpinning to urban conservation practice, using the example of Newcastle upon Tyne, but with less success.[29]

The final theme of consequence in this assessment of geographical contributions is found in the overlap with urban aesthetics and with environmental psychology. Lynch's classic study on *The image of the city*[30] was developed further, a decade later, specifically towards an investigation of people's attitudes towards the historicity of places.[31] However, there have been few large-scale studies of this type, the work of Morris being perhaps the most notable in recent years.[32]

More overtly related to art and architectural aesthetics were the townscape studies of Johns,[33] Cullen[34] and Sharp.[35] These works, with their emphasis on the serial vision of people moving through urban environments, link firmly into the practical literature of the largely architect-trained men who formed the biggest contingent of the planning profession in the 1960s. As a result 'townscape', with its corollaries of façadism and concentration on individual buildings, was a significant concept in the practicalities of conservation in Britain until comparatively recently.

Perhaps the most significant contribution from an historical geographer in this area of overlap with environmental psychology is the work of Lowenthal who has been concerned to provide justification and explanation of the need to conserve historical townscapes in terms of a society's collective psyche.[36] He suggests that conserved townscapes allow the recall of characteristic traits of past ages and provide a sense of continuity between past and present. This allows for a sense of familiarity and identity, for enrichment and escape, as well as being a major educational resource. However, Lowenthal is also careful to specify the opposing pole of disbenefits, and the creative tension between tradition and modernism, the past and future, when these are kept in balance.[37]

In so doing Lowenthal is developing and expanding on Louis's statement that historical townscapes are 'objectivations of the spirit' of the society living and working in them,[38] an idea adopted by Conzen in his conservation-related writing. There can be little doubt that such a philosophy has been slow to develop in Britain and that this contrasts markedly with other parts of Europe. It can perhaps be most clearly appreciated in the reconstruction and restitution of war-damaged historic towns after 1945. In Poland, for example, considerable financial investment and detailed historical research has been devoted to the painstaking reconstruction of historic townscapes destroyed during the Second World War.[39] Much of this destruction was deliberate, with the intent of breaking the spirit of a particular cultural group (in this instance a nation) and the rebuilding, though often in conflict with the underlying political tenets of the government, has been undertaken to renew and enhance that national spirit.

In Britain those historic towns which suffered substantial destruction of their built fabric from war-time bombing, such as Coventry, Exeter, Hull and Plymouth, have chosen to rebuild in the modern idiom rather than to reconstruct the destroyed historical townscape. As a result of extensive redevelopment schemes of this kind even surviving remnants of the historical built fabric have been threatened with destruction. In Hull, the medieval town centre was left to decay as the modern commercial centre was established beyond its bounds.[40] Exeter, in contrast, has seen commercial functions increasingly focussed on the surviving areas of historic buildings which has led to substantial change in their fabric.[41] In Coventry, surviving timber-framed buildings from various places in the city centre have been relocated to provide a streetscape of contiguous historic buildings in retail and craft use within an otherwise overwhelmingly modern townscape.[42]

Conservation in a small town

The changing pattern of conservation in British towns can be illustrated by reference to a detailed case study. Stratford-upon-Avon provides an interesting example of policies in a small town, and that interest is enhanced because of the international cultural significance of the town as the birth and burial place of William Shakespeare. An historic townscape, a subregional commercial centre and a major tourist industry are thereby conflated in a single case study.

Stratford is an important historic town. It is a planned medieval new town, laid out in 1196 for the Bishop of Worcester about a grid of streets on terrace gravels beside the River Avon.[43] It has a large medieval collegiate church, a substantial group of late medieval guild buildings and a variety of early seventeenth-century timber-framed houses. A phase of economic prosperity in the late eighteenth and early nineteenth centuries added estates of attractive brick-built cottages to the fringe of the town but it was largely unaffected by the industrial era[44] (Figure 20.1). In the later twentieth century it has become an important residential centre for high-income households and, as a sub-regional shopping centre, Stratford serves a wide area of south Warwickshire. Since 1974 it has become the administrative centre for this same region.

The tourist industry of the town is varied. It is a seasonal resort for the West Midlands, the fine riverside amenity area providing a major attraction, as do its high-quality shops and services. In addition it is one of the foremost year-round attractions in Britain for visitors from overseas and for coach-based holiday tours. Tourists are primarily day visitors, though the opening of a Hilton hotel in the early 1970s has considerably increased the number of short-stay foreign visitors. The Shakespeare Memorial Theatre provides another focus for visitors, both from the region and overseas.

The problems of preservation, restoration and conservation of historic buildings and townscape in the light of these conflicting functions have long been recognised. During the nineteenth century both concerned individuals and groups activated a variety of schemes to restore and preserve those buildings connected with Shakespeare. The Birthplace was purchased as a national memorial in 1847 and carefully restored, and his New Place estate was purchased in 1862. In 1891 Parliament established the Shakespeare Birthplace Trust and these properties and their contents were vested in the Trust.[45] The 1891 Act provided for the establishment of a Shakespeare Library and for the acquisition of other property and objects of interest. As a result three other buildings are now in the care of the trust. The Shakespeare Memorial Association was founded in 1874 and was largely concerned with the foundation of the theatre, opened in 1879. Between 1890 and 1930 a large number of timber-framed buildings were carefully restored and their later plaster façades removed through private initiatives, beginning with the Guild almshouses in 1892.[46]

In 1920, the Stratford-upon-Avon Preservation Committee was formed in response to proposals to build an aluminium factory in the town.[47] The realisation that the revival of road transport had restored the town's economic advantages at the centre of an important node of the regional road network, meant that some townspeople saw this factory as the shape of things to come and the Preservation Committee was formed to combat similar developments. They commissioned a Planning Report from the

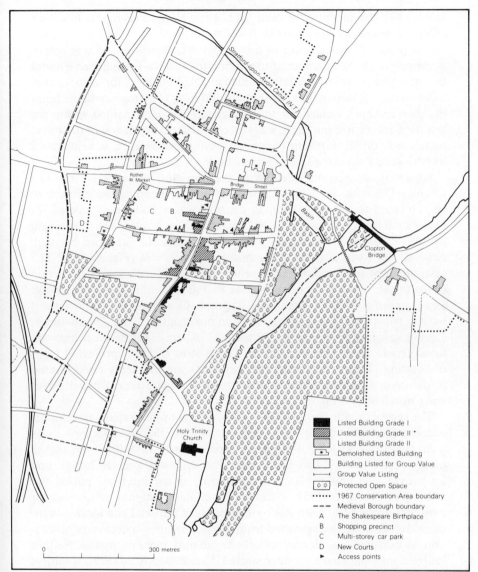

Figure 20.1   Listed buildings and conservation areas in Stratford

eminent planner, Sir Patrick Abercrombie, for presentation to the town council.[48] The tenor of the report is strongly preservationist and buildings-orientated but it is remarkable for its perception of the variety of conflicts involved in the planning of such an historic town. The report has been analysed more fully elsewhere by Slater.[49]

The practical consequence of this report was that Stratford was one of a comparatively few number of towns to implement a Town Scheme under the inter-war planning legislation which enabled the local authority to control a variety of design aspects of new buildings. The preservationist tenor of Abercrombie's report was thereby effectively implemented within the historic town centre but there was substantial areal expansion of the town, particularly on its northern fringe, in the form of housing developments by both the local authority and private builders.

Following the Second World War, the provision in the 1947 Town and Country Planning Act for the 'listing' of historic buildings which were to be subjected to detailed planning controls was quickly implemented. A provisional list was drawn up in 1947 and the list was revised and expanded by 1951.[50] Some 255 buildings were protected in the Stratford borough area, all but forty of them in the historic town centre (Figure 20.1). The assessment of the building fabric relied very much upon visual inspection of the façade and it soon became clear that many timber-framed buildings were concealed behind later brick façades. Consequently, the Stratford list was substantially revised in 1971 and now contains over 380 buildings, a remarkably large number for a town of its size.[51] Of these, twenty are listed Grade I and nineteen Grade II, the most carefully protected types of building. These most important buildings are markedly concentrated in the central spine of the medieval town – High Street, Chapel Street and Church Street (Figure 20.1).

The second major theme of the post-war years was a rapidly developing concern for traffic management policies. No less than seven major roads focus upon the Avon crossing at Stratford, which was still served by the narrow, late medieval Clopton Bridge. Plans for widening the bridge, and for providing a new bridge, were proposed in the inter-war period but not implemented. In 1951, a scheme for a new upstream bridge and for a by-pass around the town was agreed between national and local government. Its route was safeguarded from development[52] – a necessary precaution, as the town's residential suburbs began once more to expand. Neither bridge nor by-pass have yet been started. Consequently Stratford is subject to major traffic delays during the summer months as vehicles have still to funnel across the narrow bridge. However, through traffic is largely excluded from the historic centre because the back lanes which ringed the medieval burgages have been upgraded to deflect vehicles away from the central streets. Sophisticated facilities for parking have had to be developed which differentiate between long and short stay, between tourists and local shoppers, and between coaches visiting the town for a whole day and those bringing visitors only to the Shakespeare buildings for brief visits.

The Stratford Borough Council were quick to take advantage of the provisions of the 1967 Civic Amenities Act and before the end of that year four conservation areas were established, one of which enclosed the whole of the medieval town.[53] A Policy Report followed soon after. It stressed the importance of the preservation of the town's heritage of timbered buildings as an international obligation. The report was quickly followed by the Draft Town Centre Development Map in 1968.[54] It was this document that formed the basis of planning control in subsequent years.

One of its main proposals was to improve the environment in the principal streets of the historic town for both tourist and shopper by pedestrianising those streets and severely restricting vehicle access in others. In conjunction with this policy, under-used land in the centre of street blocks presented an opportunity for providing rear service facilities for the commercial buildings of the street frontages. The report stressed that every care was to be taken 'to ensure that where access is to be gained ... it is achieved without detriment to the street façades'.[55] Such policies are entirely typical of those adopted in other small historic towns in Britain, in the late 1960s, though the precise chronology of events varies from town to town.

The other feature of town-centre development in the 1960s and early 1970s is the provision of enclosed or pedestrian shopping centres with on-site parking provision.[56] Since Stratford had already emerged as an important sub-regional shopping centre by the 1960s, it, no less than other towns, was subject to property development pressures to increase retail floor space through modern purpose-built structures. As a result, one of the central street blocks was comprehensively redeveloped behind the frontage buildings to provide a part-covered shopping precinct in modern style, with rear service facilities and a multi-storey car park.[57] The scheme, again typically, involved the active co-operation of developer and Borough Council, whose compulsory purchase powers were necessary to assemble the land required.

Access to the shopping precinct has not disrupted the principal street façades and the development is not visible from the historic streetscape. An excellent scheme of restoration and repair of timbered cottages in Ely Street accompanied the development. However, disruption of the street frontage on the fourth side, Rother market, is all too evident. It is here that access to the car park and service area has been provided and this provision entailed the demolition of several 'listed' buildings (Figure 20.1). Rear service facilities in the other street blocks have been constructed with comparatively little disruption. It is notable that, nearly twenty years after the initiatives of the conservation area policy for the town centre, no streets have been pedestrianised. This is not typical of historic towns in Britain.

A second element in the conflicting pressures of development and conservation is related to the high-status retail provision of Stratford as a shopping centre. By 1971, the turnover per square foot of floorspace in Stratford was the highest in the region.[58] Consequently all major retail companies were anxious to establish premises in Stratford. Historic buildings are not conducive to modern retail practices and, since the mid-1960s, there has been growing pressure on the local authority to allow total redevelopment behind the preserved street façade of listed buildings. Sometimes, this façade preservation relates only to the building above ground-floor level.[59] Again, this is a common feature of conservation policy in Britain and relates directly to the 'townscape' approach adopted in architectural and planning schools in the 1960s. Where such a policy is widely adopted it leads to the erosion of the built fabric of towns. In Stratford it has affected comparatively few listed buildings. The most recent example has been the construction of a very large store for Marks and Spencer plc behind the preserved façade and roof line of the former Red Horse Hotel on the north side of Bridge Street.[60]

Apart from the retail sector, the greatest conflict between modern building use and traditional building fabric comes from local government and administration. These functions have become increasingly concentrated since 1945 in Britain and consequently require large office buildings. Stratford became the local government centre for the whole of south Warwickshire in 1974 and it is also the location for police headquarters, courts, fire service, district hospital and secondary education. Local authority offices are dispersed amongst several buildings, the largest of which has been recently built at the fringe of the town. In contrast, new police headquarters and courts have been constructed within the historic-town conservation area on the east side of Rother market. Both are set in the midst of extensive plots, so that there is a major dislocation in the street frontage.

Clearly, Stratford-upon-Avon, despite its international historical significance, has not been immune from the general trends and conflicts that have affected all British historic towns in the 1960s and 1970s. Its local planning authority has had to balance guardianship of an important heritage site with a duty to encourage and maintain the economic well-being of the town. Compared with many towns of equivalent size Stratford has fared well. Only about ten of its Grade II listed buildings have been totally demolished, though others survive only as façades. A number of high-quality modern buildings have been added to the townscape, some of them in particularly sensitive sites,[61] though there are inevitably greater numbers of poor buildings. Similarly, there have been some excellent refurbishment schemes for individual historic buildings, some of them undertaken by the local authority and others by private companies,[62] which have enhanced the historic townscape and provided economic uses for old buildings. Finally, it is noteworthy that one of the most contentious of recent developments has enmeshed one of the organisations charged with guardianship – the Shakespeare Birthplace Trust – into conflict both with other such organisations and with the local authority, as they sought to demolish two listed buildings in order to extend and improve the Visitor Centre of the Birthplace. After a Public Enquiry permission was granted and, as a result, the Birthplace, already isolated from its surrounding streetscape by nineteenth-century demolition on either side, has become still more isolated from its historic setting.

Commercial development and conservation planning in Exeter's central business district

The second case study focusses specifically on the relationship between commercial development and the problems of conservation planning. In doing so particular attention will be given to the importance of recognising functional regions within urban centres when establishing conservation areas. The city of Exeter highlights the need for such considerations given the changing nature of its central business district.

Exeter's townscape reflects the influences of a number of historical periods, each of which have contributed distinctive elements to the city's central area. Early Roman beginnings between A.D. 50 and 55 have to a large extent determined the form of the major central routeways and limited the city's ability to introduce full pedestrianisation schemes within the commercial core, since major bus routes must still pass through this area (Figure 20.2). In contrast, the plot sizes and fabric of many buildings owe much to the rapid development that occurred during the medieval period, when Exeter was a key economic centre of the West Country textile trade.[63] Despite the limited impact of later industrialisation on the city, the central area nevertheless contains small, but significant, elements of nineteenth-century buildings. The most important of these are located in Queen Street, which itself was only laid out in the nineteenth century, with George Fowler's Higher Market Hall being particularly impressive (Figure 20.3). Finally, in the more recent past, the most important influence was the destruction of 75 per cent of the central area by a bombing raid in May 1942 (Figure 20.2). This raid, and the subsequent demolition of many of the damaged buildings, meant that the city lost some of its more important historic buildings such as the medieval church of St Lawrence and the Georgian buildings of Bedford Circus. The loss of much of the city's commercial and historic core has subsequently made the surviving historic fabric that much more important.[64]

The immediate post-war redevelopment of the city during the 1950s and early 1960s has only served to underline the significance of the surviving historic buildings. Much of the bombed-out High Street was redesigned

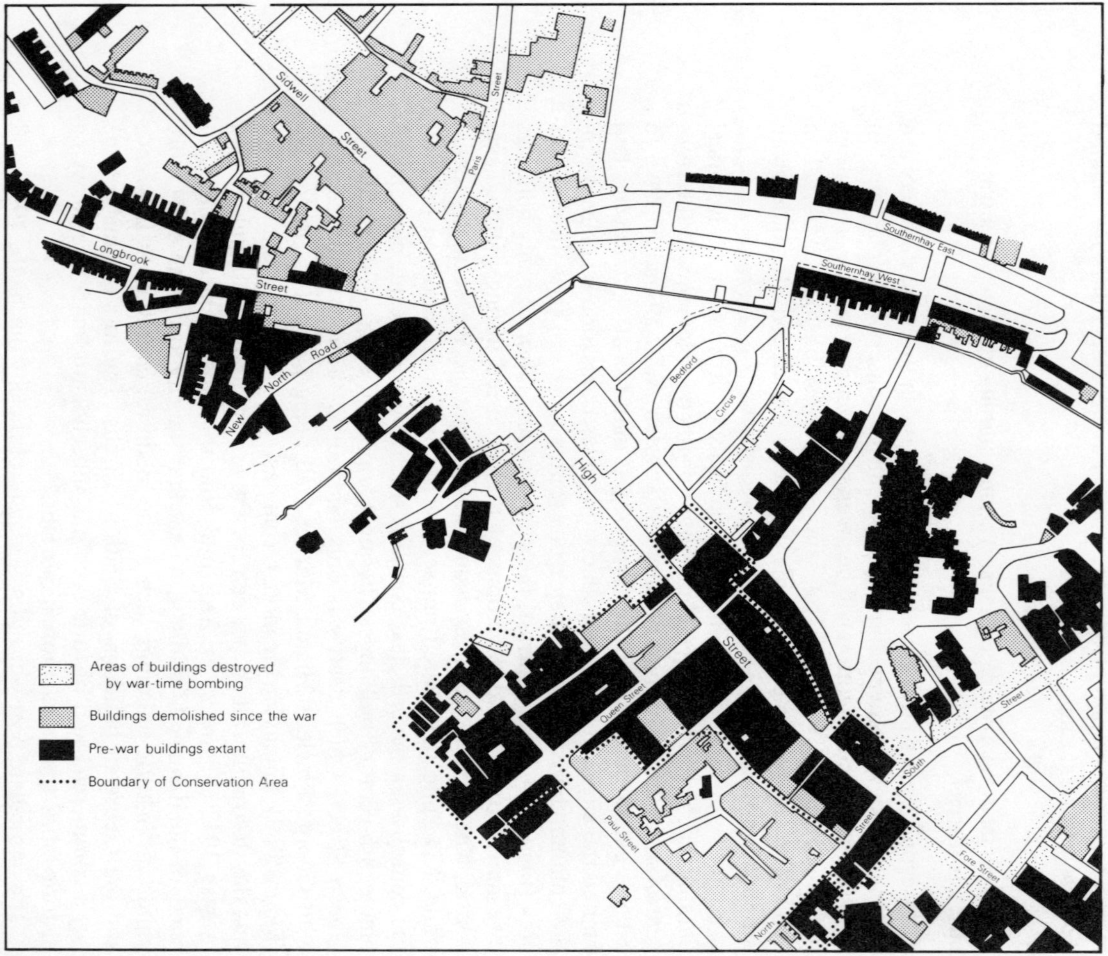

Figure 20.2 Conservation areas and the street pattern of central Exeter

Areas of buildings destroyed
by war-time bombing

Buildings demolished since the war

Pre-war buildings extant

Boundary of Conservation Area

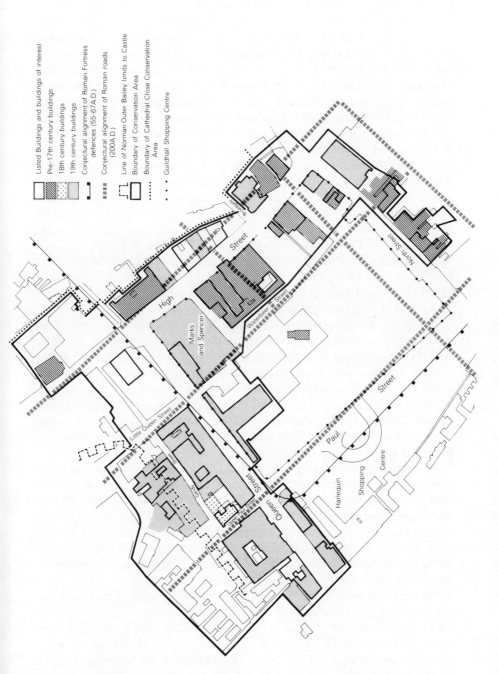

Listed Buildings and buildings of interest

Pre-17th century buildings

18th century buildings

19th century buildings

Conjectural alignment of Roman Fortress defences (55-67A.D.)

Conjectural alignment of Roman roads (200A.D.)

Line of Norman Outer Bailey limits to Castle

Boundary of Conservation Area

Boundary of Cathedral Close Conservation Area

Guildhall Shopping Centre

Figure 20.3 Retail development in part of central Exeter's conservation area

by Thomas Sharp, who was commissioned by the City Council to prepare a rebuilding plan. The monumental and homogeneous style of Sharp's post-war High Street now stands in stark contrast to the intimate and varied nature of historic Exeter, a fact bemoaned by many local commentators.[65] Indeed, it was such schemes, and the mounting criticism of them, that ultimately led to the setting up of conservation areas, and a concern for protecting the older parts of the city. Utilising the powers granted in the Civic Amenities Act of 1967, the Council designated six conservation areas in 1968, one of which was the central conservation area (Figure 20.2). This was later expanded to take in most of the older inner city including the cathedral and its associated buildings. The twin elements of Exeter's conservation policy are first to preserve the city's setting in the surrounding green hills, and secondly to conserve its historic buildings. The former aim is based on the fact that Exeter has an irregular topography and its setting offers views of many attractive skylines, often set against a back-ground of hills. Unfortunately, early post-war high-rise developments such as Debenhams department store at the southern corner of Longbrook Street and Sidwell Street detract from such overall perspectives. To counteract further high-rise buildings the City Council have introduced a general height restriction of 10 metres within the city.

Following the rebuilding of the High Street much of the commercial development prior to 1970 focussed on this area with many of the city's major retailers occupying stores along the southern end of Sidwell Street and its junction with High Street. However, as the success of Exeter's retail and office functions grew, developers went in search of new sites within the city centre and inevitably the conservation area became a prime target. The first redevelopment within the area was by C & A and Austin Reed, whose stores were built with close co-operation with the planning authorities.

In both cases the developments involved the partial demolition of listed buildings, but the retention of important Tudor façades. The C & A store also involved some considerable new building at the corner of Queen Street and High Street (Figure 20.3). However, in both cases the new shop fronts were set back from the face of the building to create an attractive colonade that links the old and new frontages together. More recent developments along the High Street have, on the advice of the City Planning Department, continued the form of the colonnade. More important than these early 1970s buildings was the opening of the Guildhall Shopping Centre in 1976, a substantial part of which was built within the conservation area (Figure 20.3). This centre involved a major increase in the city's net retail floor space by about 180,000 sq. ft, and significantly shifted the balance of shop-ping interests away from the post-war buildings in the upper part of the High Street. Indeed, it is ironical that the conservation area has been an increasing target for retailers due to the commercial success of the Guildhall scheme.

Unfortunately, there is an inherent conflict between the needs of most modern retail firms and many historic buildings. The problem is that retailers usually demand large selling and display areas, with most attention being focussed on ground-level developments. This is typified by the space requirements of most supermarkets, and leads to the problem of functional obsolescence in many central area buildings that are often far too small to meet such needs.[66] Within the conservation area the buildings are generally tall, with narrow frontages and deep plots. Two major difficulties emerge when retailers occupy such premises. First, the upper floors of these buildings are often unused and consequently may be rather neglected. Secondly, the retailer may attempt to increase available ground floor space and shop frontage by amalgamating adjoining buildings. In central Exeter when this process occurs the new shop front very often cuts across two or more architectural styles, partly destroying the variety of the streetscape that gives the conservation area its most important characteristic.

In response to these types of pressures there are three main strategies open to most local authorities. The first and most extreme is to resist all major new developments. In reality this approach is rarely possible, and in Exeter was rejected because of the wider implications on the city's standing as a major sub-regional shopping centre. Alternatively, the demands of new stores can be met by allowing the demolition of existing buildings and replacing them with new, high-quality developments. The third and most popular strategy seeks to meet both the demands of retail organisations and conservationists by the compromise of allowing new stores to develop behind the façades of existing buildings. As was shown in the early part of this chapter this was one approach adopted in Stratford. In Exeter it proved possible to improve on this strategy by retaining the existing buildings and allowing them to serve as the entrances into the new Guildhall Shopping Centre (Figure 20.3). In this case the two main entrances to the Guildhall Centre have been created using historic buildings. The most impressive and significant of which is the use of the former Higher Market, a Grade II listed building. The front of the building along Queen Street has been restored to Charles Fowler's original design, whilst the interior of the old market has been converted into a new shopping arcade, with two floors of shops that form part of the Guildhall Centre. The other major entrance was created off the High Street by using existing streets and retaining the original buildings. Perhaps the major failure of the development was the external design of the new shopping centre behind the historic buildings, as this is of a somewhat inferior quality and uniform in style. This therefore presents a rather poor image in the area around St Pancras Church off Waterbeer Street (Figure 20.3).

Table 20.1 *Local policies operating in Exeter's conservation areas*

1. *Positive policies*
    1.1 Establishment of design guides for streets, open spaces and buildings.
    1.2 Special attention to replacement of doors and windows.
    1.3 Priority for grant aid given to roof repairs of listed buildings.
    1.4 Grant aid for environmental improvement schemes in conservation areas.

2. *Negative policies*
    2.1 Restriction on building height (max. 10 m).
    2.2 Restriction on building demolition unless there are compelling economic, social or aesthetic reasons.
    2.3 Provision to vary development control policies in special cases.

Source: Exeter Local Plan, 1982

The opportunities for retaining original buildings or frontages, however, are sometimes limited, a fact quickly thrust upon Exeter City Council when Marks and Spencer wanted to develop one of the most sensitive sites in the conservation area during the late 1970s. The site concerned is on the corner of Higher Street and Queen Street, and as such provides an important link between the nineteenth-century character of Queen Street and the older buildings along the High Street (Figure 20.3). Any thoughts of retaining one of the existing buildings or even its façade were rapidly dispelled when the developers persuaded the local authority that only complete redevelopment was feasible. The final solution involved the demolition of one building, but the retention of a more important stucco building dating from 1837 (listed as Grade II).

The 1968 and 1971 Planning Acts have led to the initiation of new planning frameworks by introducing both Structure and Local Plans, which in places such as Exeter have added further conservation policies (Table 20.1). Despite these new policies, planning mechanisms and the longer-term aims of conservation planning, commercial arguments very often seem to hold sway. One major reason for this is that the survival of many listed buildings depends largely on private capital in spite of the widespread availability of grants. Such grants are available to listed buildings under the 1953 Historic Buildings and Ancient Monuments Act, together with more recent legislation culminating in the Local Government Planning and Land Act of 1980. The problem is that whilst residential properties can obtain grants of up to 50 per cent towards the costs of repairs and maintenance, commercial properties receive much lower aid, putting emphasis on private funds. In Exeter the restoration of historic buildings and associated environmental improvements is further aided by money from the city's conservation fund set up in 1978. Unfortunately, within the central area such locally raised money is merely covering the diminishing funds from central government, particularly in the area of environmental improvements.

In many cases, helpful though these financial aids are, the survival of most historic buildings that are not owned by some public authority is still closely linked to them having a commercial function. Thus, in Exeter, as elsewhere, the buildings most often at risk are those left unoccupied and therefore very often unmaintained. These usually account for between 2–3 per cent of all Exeter's listed buildings. The existence of such vacant properties raises two important questions for the City Council. First, whether the local authority should take positive steps to find new uses for such listed buildings, and secondly, whether normal planning control practices should be varied in order to assist in the maintenance of these properties. Such considerations have forced the local authority to relax their policy on restricting office development in residential areas, since this has been one way of supporting listed buildings.

A further problem identified by the city's 'Master Plan for Conservation' (1977), is where multiple occupancy of historic buildings occurs. Under these conditions historic properties are very often not kept in good order, as the owner does not occupy part or all of the building. Such conditions are particularly noticeable on the periphery of the inner city conservation area, with a number of buildings in disrepair. Related to these difficulties is the fact that many owners, in an attempt to save money, are carrying out repairs with inferior and unsuitable materials.

In the case of Exeter, as with other historic towns, much of the problem depends on more money being made available, a perception from private developers that historic builders have a viable future and a positive system of conservation planning. These factors are in turn conditioned by the changing functions of central retail areas, and the spatial characteristics of central business districts. Such processes put the emphasis clearly on area-based policies and calls for an understanding of the functional structure of different sub-areas within the city centre. These areas need to be distinguished in terms of their historicity, the potential for the redevelopment of historic buildings, as well as their historic commercial role. In addition, central areas need to have positive management strategies similar to those adopted in Covent Garden and proposed for Oxford Street, rather than a mere collection of restrictive planning policies.

Conclusion

The two case studies highlighted in this chapter have stressed the great importance and impact that commercial change has on historic townscapes, and that much of the pressure on listed buildings has recently been generated by large retail developers. It is equally clear that in the present economic climate the survival of many historic buildings in city centres depends on them having a viable commercial future. All these factors point toward the increasing need for co-operation between local authorities and property developers. Within this context there may be a role for urban historical geographers to become more involved in the strategies towards conservation planning.

In 1979 Newcombe saw urban conservation as being a combination of expressed civic pride, the ethnic rediscovery of a group's past and a good business investment; and felt that the geographer should be in a position to contribute to all three.[67] More specifically the historical geographers' reminders of past functions of urban regions is a useful contribution to the planning of conservation areas. Very often in this context the historical geographers' role has been in studies of local landscape history or more particularly inventory work and resource assessment.[68] Thus, in Exeter the geography department is involved in constructing a computer-based geographic information base of historic buildings to aid the planning department's work.[69]

Obviously, such tasks are a necessary and valuable part of conservation planning, although urban historical geographers can offer much more particularly through their knowledge of the structure of city centres. Conservation planners, for example, need to be made far more aware of the changing geography of central business districts. Indeed, within this context important distinctions can be made between the structure and treatment of historic British cities compared with their West German counterparts. In Britain the emphasis has been very much on the planned centralisation of commercial facilities, thereby increasing development pressures on many historic city centres. Furthermore, British urban geographers have never effectively distinguished between the historic core of the central business district and the rest of the commercial area. In Germany, the emphasis has been first on the recognition of a distinct historical core (*Altstadt*), which is part of the geographical and planning literature, and, more significantly, treated very differently in the development of commercial functions.[70] Perhaps it is for such reasons that historic German cities have fared better than those in Britain with regard to conservation planning. Such observations serve only to highlight the importance of area-based policies and also strengthen the potential role of urban historical geographers in the interdisciplinary approach to conservation planning.

Acknowledgements

The authors are grateful for the assistance and bibliographical help of Peter Larkham.

PART SIX
Conclusions

21

Future developments in Anglo-German studies of urban historical geography

DIETRICH DENECKE and GARETH SHAW

Commonality and divergence

It is evident from many of the contributions in this book that there is some degree of common interest between British and German geographers in the field of urban historical geography. This commonality embraces a wide range of themes, but essentially tends to centralise around three rather broad concerns. The first is an interest in maintaining some viable link between traditional geographic fieldwork and historical research based on written sources. As was discussed in the introduction, this fieldwork element provided an important basis for the two seminars, since the idea was to focus on the approach of field evidence, physical analysis and interpretation as a basis for comparative observation and conclusion. In reality such interests were, and still are, far stronger in Germany where there exists considerably more research on the landscape, which in an urban context owed much to the initial stimulus of Bobek, Dörries and their followers.[1] As Lichtenberger explains, such an approach is understandable given the fact that the careers of many geographers in German-speaking countries involved a shift from traditional geomorphology to work on urban geography.[2] This resulted in a transfer of reasoning and research method from the study of landforms to historical landscape analysis, which focussed on the search for genetic regularities. In turn such borrowing of ideas led to well-developed standards of field techniques, a preoccupation with micro-scale studies and the predominance of original field-based data. This type of genetic urban geography also has strong links with aspects of landscape history (or townscape history) within German-speaking countries, often combining to produce regional historical geographies. As a consequence the historical development of townscape, often in its local or regional setting, still provides an important theme, despite its relative demise during the 1970s. Moreover, its significance is re-emphasised by the fact that it often serves as a backcloth for studies of social change, giving rise to research on social topography and the use of landscape indicators in social geography.[3]

A second area of common concern is in research on urban morphology, which in some ways follows on from the interests in urban fieldwork and the genetic approach to urban geography. Within Britain the techniques of analysis have moved somewhat away from the sole dependence on field observations toward the use of archival data sources, which contrasts somewhat with the steady refinement of more traditional approaches developed in Germany. These variations are the result of very different evolutionary pathways. Thus, in Britain the study of urban morphology has been marked by a period of initial vigour in the 1950s, mainly due to the studies of M. R. G. Conzen, to one of relative decline (in terms of the numbers of active research workers) during the 1960s. In Germany, as Conzen points out, the urban landscape tradition has proceeded without any major interruptions up to the 1970s.[4] Indeed, it is the fairly strong element of continuity that gives German historical geography its distinctive character. This continuity is partly due to a lack of theoretical and ideological experiments or new directions. The academic tradition of empirical work based on sources and documents is still successful and plays an important role in academic training. In addition to this, new emphasis supports morphological and physical studies in urban research through the rapid development of urban archaeology, through the European projects of town atlases, and with applied research for urban preservation.

The third common theme reflected by this volume concerns the preoccupation with empirical approaches to urban historical geography. In this context, the term 'empirical geography' embraces a wide range of interests and epistemologies, as illustrated by the previous chapters. Furthermore, many of the commonalities and links exposed by both the seminars and published papers may be seen to be initially framed around similar research experiences, the use of data sources and the methods of data collection. The debate over differing ideological approaches between German and British historical geographers still remains to be addressed.

Whilst it is important to dwell on common interests and approaches, it would be misleading to ignore the many evident differences that exist between British and German historical geography. The two review chapters cover these variations in some detail, although it is worthwhile making a further examination of these since they provide the base from which future collaborative Anglo-German studies must develop.

One of the most apparent differences between the two countries is the pace and nature of change in methods and approaches. In Britain emphasis is very much on a rapidly changing discipline, marked by major shifts in philosophical and methodological frameworks. As an early example, Baker, Butlin, Phillips and Prince highlighted the rapidity of developments in the late 1960s and concluded that 'it is, paradoxically, the future that matters most in historical geography'.[5] This is a sentiment that underlines the nature of change in British historical geography, which is very often achieved through a series of innovations and breaks with more traditional approaches. The image of change is to be found in a number of recent reviews; for example, to Butlin 'there were two faces of historical geography, in the early 1970s, representing continuity and change', although it was the latter which was always stressed.[6] For others innovations were too limited and too slow, despite 'so many bugle calls' to rally the forces of change,[7] and historical geographers were urged to examine new explanatory structures.[8] By comparison, progress in German historical geography is of a more gradual and incremental nature. However, this is not to imply that research in Germany does not take any notice of new theories, ideologies or paradigms in urban studies. On the contrary, British and American publications are followed and used intensively to the near total neglect of studies in other languages. The difference is that new and progressive approaches are more gradually and selectively integrated, and developed more steadily on the solid base of empirical, source-oriented scientific work.

These evolutionary differences can be illustrated at a general level by comparing two past reviews of the discipline in Germany and Britain by Jäger and Baker.[9] Jäger's paper emphasised the continuity of the subject in German-speaking countries, stressing the importance of methodology and in particular the tradition of retrogressive methods and morphogenetic analysis dating back to the 1930s and 1940s respectively.[10] In contrast, Baker focussed on the 'new' historical geography in Britain that was developing during the 1970s. Once again the emphasis lay on change when he stressed the need for new research strategies 'which are authentically related to the new paradigms of both history and geography'.[11] Significantly, almost fifteen years later the same differences are revealed by the two review chapters in this book, and perhaps if anything the divergence between the practice of historical geography in the two countries is that much greater.

The reasons for such different rates of change, and in turn types of approach, lie in the relationship between historical geography and other disciplines, together with variations in the structure of the academic systems.[12] In addition, within the group of historical geographers in Britain as well as in Germany, it is also a question of different individuals, their activities and ideological backgrounds. The stimulus of various influences has been explored by Buttimer, who highlighted two significant forces: 'choreographic awareness', and the relationship to socio-economic reference systems.[13] The former encompasses the academic's 'lived experience' which underlies his/her approach; whilst this in turn is prescribed by the prevailing environment. This hermeneutical view of development is perhaps relatively more important in German-speaking countries, given the nature of change and the longevity of influence of key individuals, such as Bobek. In Germany, work is based more on a steady progress within a traditional framework, but nevertheless open to new ideas, though not running to the imagination of 'a new beginning'. In Britain, the situation is rather more complex and diffuse, partly because of the larger number of academics researching within the subject area. Indeed, the attempts to develop some of Buttimer's ideas within British historical geography have yielded only a limited success, and the authors thought it 'inappropriate to talk of schools of historical geography based on one or two individuals'.[14]

In Britain since the 1960s there has been an increasingly strong influence of social science within urban historical geography. To some extent it began with the work on the social structure of nineteenth-century cities and the ensuing borrowing of analytical techniques.[15] However, by the 1970s the links and influence were more far reaching as historical geographers became interested in utilising a wide range of models.[16] Indeed, some writers charged historical geographers with the 'task of extending back into the past, models constructed to fit present situations'.[17] Today the influence of social science theory provides a new and even stronger attraction for many historical geographers through the utilisation of the ideas of such research workers as Giddens and Habermas.[18]

The influences in German historical geography come from more tradition-al disciplines, in particular from archaeology, history and urban history. These subjects provide a very different framework for progress in historical research, and the role of social science is by comparison much less influential even via contemporary urban geography.[19] This may be partially illustrated by the German interdisciplinary working group 'Arbeitskreis für gentische Siedlungsforschung in Mitteleuropa' and the major new journal of settle-ment history (*Siedlungsforschung*) which commenced publication in 1983, and provided a joint forum for archaeologists, historians and geographers.

Within German urban historical geography perhaps the greatest influence is exerted by urban historians, especially since the foundation of the Insti-tute of Comparative Urban History (Institut für vergleichende Städteges-chichte) at Münster in 1969. This provides a major focus for research in urban history and to some extent urban historical geography since it com-mands large research resources and organises multidisciplinary conferences on the history of towns. Furthermore, the influence of urban history is all the more significant in Germany given the small number of historical geographers.

Future developments: cooperation and comparison

There is no Anglo-German school of urban historical geography, but rather, as this book shows, a small group of individuals interested in exchanging ideas and learning more about developments in each other's countries. In this sense it is extremely difficult to predict what course future developments will take, or indeed firmly to outline a research agenda for such an eclectic group of urban historical geographers.

From our previous meetings and discussions it does seem clear, however, that progress depends on initiating some comparative studies and methods of comparative investigation. This in turn will depend on other conditions being satisfied. The first of these has already been mentioned in the introduction, and concerns the understanding of different terminology. It is essential that some progress is made in drawing up a set of comparative terms used in urban historical geography. The importance of understanding the use of different terminology may be illustrated by a simple example, the use of the term *Altstadt* by German urban geographers. This is used to denote the historic core of a city, but it is also a concept in urban development, a distinctive spatial unit for research in historical geography, as well as a framework for urban conservation planning. There is no equivalent term in Britain, where historical geographers are content to talk of the central area of the central business district in a far more general context.[20]

An appraisal of comparative data sources in the two countries is another area requiring some attention. In Britain census data, particularly that available at a household level after 1841, has dominated much of the work on nineteenth-century cities; although more recently other sources have been explored more systematically.[21] This situation contrasts with Germany in a number of ways, but primarily because of a lack of any comprehensively available census data, especially at a small area scale. Research beyond a local or regional level, often within the same administrative area or political state (*Länder*), is frustrated because of the absence of any comparable statistics. It is this political fragmentation and the constantly changing historico-political map of Germany that limits the availability of official sources. Perhaps one of the most widely used data sources for work on nineteenth-century German cities are commercial directories (*Adressbücher*), which are available throughout the country and generally were not constrained by political boundaries. Unfortunately, no modern comprehensive guide exists to these publications; and furthermore little assessment has been made of the availability and reliability of such sources for the study of urban historical geography in Germany. Given that research is partly conditioned by the availability of source materials, then clearly progress in comparative Anglo-German studies may be limited initially to those areas utilising the most accessible data. Finally, a comparative approach needs to find out and to focus on comparable processes and implications of urban development. To develop comparative urban studies in history necessitates the creation of general indices which allow comparison, initially neglecting local and historical individualities. This aim might be reached within a theoretical or ideological framework, but it also has to be encountered on a more empirical basis.

Such considerations suggest that it is most important to formulate any research agenda for comparative studies in terms of meaningful projects set against the background of recent progress in the two countries. Differences in the academic climates and data sources set the obvious general limits. However, other constraints are introduced by the number of historical geographers interested in such work and the availability of financial resources. Given these limitations it would seem that scope already exists for comparative research in urban morphology, functional change in nineteenth-century cities (given the comparability of directory sources) and the social geography of early modern towns (see for example the chapters by Baigent (9) and Erdmann (11)). Progress on the examination of comparative socio-geographical processes operating in nineteenth-century cities is another possibility due to the recent interest in this period by German historical geographers, although this is one area that is progressively dominated by urban historians in Germany.[22]

An important question for the future of urban historical geography in both Britian and Germany is the type of relationship the subject has with urban history and other social sciences. In Germany there is a strong tendency towards interdisciplinary cooperation, pushed forward especially by historical geographers, which no doubt has an integrating impact on research questions and approaches. Geographical aspects are often taken up in a variety of ways by historians, and geographers have to try to cope with this rapid progress. On the other hand, urban studies by historians as well as geographers quite often tend more towards social analysis than geographical studies of the urban settlement and its structure. However, contrary to this, the emphasis on social topographic studies in Germany was a successful attempt to integrate social aspects into traditional topographic reconstruction and analysis. Another aspect of the future of urban historical geography is the question of orientation towards the rapidly developing contemporary urban geography. In Germany, historical geography is losing contact with contemporary fields of research, leaning more towards urban or social historians. Similarly, contemporary urban geography is neglecting its historical dimensions. Such a tendency may only be changed by an integration of more recent periods, for which much better sources exist, with urban historical geography. For example, recent focus on the impact of industrialisation and planning history in the late nineteenth and twentieth centuries has gone some way towards strengthening the link with contemporary urban geography.

A final condition for future developments in Anglo-German historical geography is the availability of a common forum for joint meetings. The previous two seminars have provided just such an occasion, and it is hoped that these will become more firmly established and held on a regular basis in the future. This would certainly broaden the interchange of information about recent progress and projects on urban historical geography in English- and German-speaking countries. International meetings on urban historical geography would also complement the long-established (since 1957) 'Permanent European Conference for the Study of the Rural Landscape'. However, besides information and discussion of new approaches and results, cooperation should proceed to joint research projects, prepared and steered by joint meetings. This cooperative research and work would concentrate on fields which need knowledge and input from both sides, thus opening up a new type of international contribution in historical geography. There might also be a quite pragmatic aim of Anglo-German cooperation and that is to provide the English-speaking world with selected reviews of major studies and source material (data and cartographic sources) on Central Europe; whilst at the same time introducing the greater variety of methods used in Britain to research in Germany.

Notes

1 Introduction

1 The activities of the first meeting (19–26 Sept. 1982) are reported in G. Shaw and B. Graham, 'Historical geography on the move', *Area*, 15, 2 (1983), pp. 135–6; D. Denecke, 'Historische Stadtgeographie. Bericht über das deutsch–englische Symposium vom 19–26 Sept. 1982', *Siedlungsforschung*, 1 (1983), pp. 245–8; C. Erdmann, 'Anglo-German Symposium on urban historical geography', *Journal of Historical Geography*, 9, 1 (1983), pp. 65–7. Reports on the second meeting (11–18 Sept. 1983): G. Shaw and D. Denecke, 'Historical geography moves on', *Area*, 16, 1 (1984), pp. 129–30. T. Slater, 'Second Anglo-German seminar on urban historical geography', *Journal of Historical Geography*, 10, 1 (1984), pp. 77–8. H. Heineberg, 'Historische Stadtgeographie. Bericht über das "Second Anglo-German Seminar on Urban Historical Geography" vom 11–18 Sept. 1983', *Siedlungsforschung*, 2 (1984), pp. 259–62.
2 See in this context the review by D. Denecke, in *Planning History Bulletin*, 6, 1 (1984), pp. 11–12, of H. Carter, *An introduction to urban historical geography* (London, 1983).
3 R. Geipel, 'The Landscape Indicators School in German geography', in D. Ley and M. S. Samuels (eds.), *Humanistic geography: prospects and problems* (London, 1978), chap. 10, pp. 155–72.
4 A. Lees, 'Historical perspectives on cities in modern Germany', *Journal of Urban History*, 5, 4 (1979), pp. 411–46. J. Reulecke and G. Muck, 'Urban history research in Germany: its development and present condition', *Urban History Yearbook* (Leicester, 1981), pp. 39–54.
5 H. B. Clarke and A. Simms, 'Towards a comparative history of urban origins', in H. B. Clarke and A. Simms (eds.), *The comparative history of urban origins in non-Roman Europe*, British Arch. Reports, International Series 255 (Oxford, 1985), pp. 669–714, here p. 669.
6 H. Prince, 'Historical geography in 1980', in E. H. Brown (ed.), *Geography yesterday and tomorrow* (Oxford, 1986), chap. 10, pp. 229–50.
7 M. R. G. Conzen, 'A note on the historic towns atlas', *Journal of Historical Geography*, 2 (1976), pp. 361–2.
8 T. Tanioka and V. Annenkov, 'Historical changes in spatial organisation',

324

I.G.U. Bulletin, 30 (1979), pp. 129–34.

9 A brief observation about international cooperation is contained in A. Baker, 'Historical geography in Czechoslovakia', *Area*, 18, 2 (1986), pp. 223–8.

10 M. Bloch, 'Toward a comparative history of European societies', in F. C. Lane and J. C. Riemersman (eds.), *Enterprise and secular change* (Illinois, 1953).

11 W. H. Sewell, 'Marc Bloch and the logic of comparative history', *History and Theory*, 6 (1967), pp. 208–18.

12 Bloch, 'Toward a comparative history'.

13 H. Uhlig and C. Lienau, 'Rural settlements', in *Basic material for the terminology of the agricultural landscape*, vol. 2 (Giessen, 1972), p. 6.

14 A few comparative literature reviews exist with perhaps the most comprehensive in urban historical geography being M. P. Conzen, 'Historical geography: changing spatial structure and social patterns of western cities', *Progress in Human Geography*, 7, 1 (1983), pp. 88–107. See also P. Abrams and E. A. Wrigley (eds.), *Towns in societies: essays in economic history and historical sociology* (Cambridge, 1978), for a consolidated bibliography of urban history. For Germany see the following selection of bibliographies or literature reviews: E. Keyser, *Bibliographie zur Stadtgeschichte Deutschlands* (Köln/Wien, 1969); W. Ehbrecht, 'Neue Veröffentlichungen zur vergleichenden Städtgeschichte, 1975–1978', *Blätter f. deutsche Landesgeschichte*, 110 (1980), pp. 393–454. From 1982 onwards see the current interdisciplinary and European bibliography by D. Denecke and K. Fehn, 'Bibliographie zur europäischen Siedlungsforschung, Archäologie – Geschichte – Geographie', *Siedlungsforschung*, 1 (1983), ch. 4, pp. 261–94, *Siedlungsforschung*, 2 (1984), pp. 295–343, and following volumes. There are also special bibliographies on specific topics, such as H. Grabowski, *Bibliographie zur Stadtsanierung, internationale Auswahl* (Paderborn, 1980). For many towns there are also quite recent local bibliographies; for Austria see W. Rausch (ed.), *Bibliographie zur Geschichte der Städte Österreichs* (Linz, 1984).

15 H. Jankuhn, W. Schlesinger and H. Steuer (eds.), 'Vor- und Frühformen der europäischen Stadt im Mittelalter', *Abhandlungen der Akademie der Wissenschaften in Göttingen*, phil.-hist. Kl., 3, 83/4 (Göttingen, 1973/4); G. P. Fehring (ed.), 'Seehandelszentren des nördlichen Europa. Der Strukturwandel vom 12. zum 13. Jahrhundert', *Lübecker Schriften zur Archäologie und Kulturgeschichte*, 7 (Lübeck, 1983); H. Jankuhn, K. Schietzel and H. Reichstein (eds.), *Archäologische und naturwissenschaftliche Untersuchungen an ländlichen und frühstädtischen Siedlungen im deutschen Küstengebiet vom 5. Jahrhundert vor Chr. bis zum 11 Jahrhundert nach Chr.*, vol. 2: *Handelsplätze des frühen und hohen Mittelalters* (Weinheim, 1984); Clarke and Simms, *Urban origins*.

16 D. Denecke, 'Der geographische Stadtbegriff und die räumlich-funktionale Betrachtungsweise bei Siedlungstypen mit zentraler Bedeutung in Anwendung auf historische Siedlungsepochen', in Jankuhn, Schlesinger and Steuer, 'Vor- und Frühformen der europäischen Stadt im Mittelalter', pp. 33–55.

17 E. Lichtenberger, *Die Wiener Altstadt. Von der mittelalterlichen Burgstadt zur City* (Wien, 1977); see also for this general topic: P. Kriedte, 'Die Stadt im Prozeß der europäischen Proto-Industrialisierung', *Die alte Stadt*, 9 (1982), pp. 19–51.

18 H. Blotevogel, 'Zentrale Orte und Raumbeziehungen in Westfalen vor der Industrialisierung (1780–1850)', *Veröffentlichungen d. Provinzialinstituts f. Westfälische Landes und Völksforschung d. Landschaftsverbandes Westfalen-Lippe*, 1st series, 19, (Münster, 1975). In addition, a small part of this work has been published in English by H. Blotevogel, M. Hommel and P. Schöller, 'The urban system of the Federal Republic of Germany', *Acta Geographica Lovaniensia*, 22 (1982), pp. 164–206.
19 M. P. Conzen, 'Analytical approaches to the urban landscape', in K. W. Butzer (ed.), *Dimensions in human geography: essays on some familiar and neglected schemes* (Chicago, 1978), pp. 128–65.
20 In Britain see, for example, R. Kain (ed.), 'Planning for conservation, an international perspective', *Studies in History, Planning and the Environment*, 3 (London, 1980); as for Germany, see the general overview by D. Denecke, 'Historische Geographie und räumliche Planung', *Mitt. d. Geogr. Gesellschaft in Hamburg*, 75 (Hamburg, 1985), pp. 3–55.

2 Research in British urban historical geography

1 H. Carter, *An introduction to urban historical geography* (London, 1983).
2 R. A. Butlin (ed.), *The development of the Irish town* (London, 1977); B. J. Graham, *Medieval Irish settlement: a review*, Historical Geography Research Series 3 (Norwich, 1980); I. H. Adams, *The making of urban Scotland* (London, 1978); G. Gordon and B. Dicks (eds.), *Scottish urban history* (Aberdeen, 1983); G. Gordon (ed.), *Perspectives of the Scottish city* (Aberdeen, 1985); H. Carter, *The growth of the Welsh city system* (Cardiff, 1969); R. A. Griffiths (ed.), *Boroughs of medieval Wales* (Cardiff, 1978).
3 J. W. R. Whitehand and J. Patten (eds.), 'Change in the town', *Trans. IBG*, NS, 2 (1977), pp. 257–416; R. J. Dennis (compiler), 'The Victorian city', *Trans. IBG*, NS, 4 (1979), pp. 125–319; J. H. Johnson and C. G. Pooley (eds.), *The structure of nineteenth-century cities* (London, 1982), derives from an SSRC seminar on 'The internal structure of nineteenth-century British cities'; publications based on SSRC/ESRC research projects include R. Lawton and C. G. Pooley, 'The social geography of Merseyside in the nineteenth century', final report to SSRC (Liverpool, 1976); H. Carter and S. Wheatley, *Merthyr Tydfil in 1851: a study of the spatial structure of a Welsh industrial town* (Cardiff, 1982); C. G. Pooley and S. Irish, *The development of corporation housing in Liverpool 1869–1945* (Lancaster, 1984).
4 A. Briggs, *Victorian cities* (London, 1963); H. J. Dyos, *Victorian suburb: a study of the growth of Camberwell* (Leicester, 1961); H. J. Dyos (ed.), *Urban History Newsletter* (Leicester, 1963–76, nos. i–xxii); H. J. Dyos (ed.), *Urban History Yearbook* (Leicester, 1974–9); D. Reeder (ed.), *Urban History Yearbook* (Leicester, 1980–); on the history of common people, see the journals *Oral History* and *History Workshop Journal* and the History Workshop series, published by Routledge and Kegan Paul, London, edited by R. Samuel.
5 M. R. G. Conzen, 'The use of town plans in the study of urban history', and H. Carter, 'Phases of town growth in Wales', in H. J. Dyos (ed.), *The study of urban history* (London, 1968), pp. 113–30 and 231–52.

6 G. Bryant (compiler), *Register of research in urban history 1984*, Urban History Group (Leicester, 1984).
7 K. A. Whyte (ed.), *Register of research in historical geography 1984*, Historical Geography Research Series 14 (Norwich, 1984).
8 Until 1972 the Historical Geography Research Group was entitled the Agrarian Landscape Research Group. The changing pattern of research in historical geography is discussed in A. R. H. Baker, 'Historical geography', *Prog. Hum. Geogr.*, 3 (1977), pp. 465–74: H. Prince, 'Trends in historical geography 1975–81', *Area*, 14 (1982), pp. 235–9.
9 For example, P. Clark and P. Slack, *English towns in transition 1500–1700* (Oxford, 1976); C. Phythian-Adams, *Desolation of a city: Coventry and the urban crisis of the late middle ages* (Cambridge, 1978); P. Clark (ed.), *The transformation of English towns 1600–1800* (London, 1984); D. Keene, 'A new study of London before the Great Fire', *Urban History Yearbook* (Leicester, 1984), pp. 11–21; M. J. Power, 'John Stow and his London', *Journ. Hist. Geogr.*, 11 (1985), pp. 1–20.
10 The classic case study was M. R. G. Conzen, 'Alnwick, Northumberland: a study in town-plan analysis', *Trans. IBG*, 27 (1960); for a more recent review, see J. W. R. Whitehand (ed.), 'The urban landscape: historical development and management', *Institute of British Geographers Special Publication*, No. 13 (London, 1981).
11 H. C. Darby (ed.), *A new historical geography of England* (Cambridge, 1973).
12 R. J. P. Kain and H. C. Prince, *The tithe surveys of England and Wales* (Cambridge, 1985). Compare J. A. Yelling, *Common field and enclosure in England 1450–1850* (London, 1977), with the same author's 'The selection of sites for slum clearance in London, 1875–88', *Journ. Hist. Geogr.*, 7 (1981), pp. 155–65, and 'LCC slum clearance policies, 1889–1907', *Trans. IBG*, NS, 7 (1982), pp. 292–303.
13 M. W. Beresford, 'Review of Whitehand and Patten (eds.), "Change in the town"', *Journ. Hist. Geogr.*, 5 (1979), pp. 346–8; M. J. Daunton, 'Review of Dennis (compiler), "The Victorian city"', *Journ. Hist. Geogr.*, 6 (1980), pp. 332–3.
14 H. J. Dyos and M. Wolff (eds.), *The Victorian city: images and realities*, 2 vols. (London, 1973); D. Fraser and A. Sutcliffe (eds.), *The pursuit of urban history* (London, 1983).
15 D. Fraser and A. Sutcliffe, 'Introduction', in Fraser and Sutcliffe, *The pursuit of urban history*, p. xxv.
16 For a detailed survey and bibliography, see R. J. Dennis, *English industrial cities of the nineteenth century: a social geography* (Cambridge, 1984), esp. chaps. 1 and 7.
17 E. A. Wrigley (ed.), *Nineteenth-century society: essays in the use of quantitative methods for the study of social data* (Cambridge, 1972); R. Lawton (ed.), *The census and social structure: an interpretative guide to nineteenth-century censuses for England and Wales* (London, 1978).
18 M. Shaw, 'Reconciling social and physical space: Wolverhampton 1871', *Trans. IBG*, NS, 4 (1979), pp. 192–213; J. T. Jackson, 'Housing areas in mid-Victorian Wigan and St Helens', *Trans. IBG*, NS, 6 (1981), pp. 413–32.

19 G. Sjoberg, *The preindustrial city* (New York, 1960); R. J. Johnston, *Urban residential patterns* (London, 1971); D. Timms, *The urban mosaic: towards a theory of residential differentiation* (Cambridge, 1971).

20 D. Ward, 'Victorian cities: how modern?', *Journ. Hist. Geogr.*, 1 (1975), pp. 135–51. For the subsequent debate, see D. Cannadine, 'Victorian cities: how different?', *Social History*, 2 (1977), pp. 457–82; D. Cannadine, 'Residential differentiation in nineteenth-century towns: from shapes on the ground to shapes in society', in Johnson and Pooley, *The structure of nineteenth-century cities*, pp. 235–51; C. G. Pooley, 'Residential differentiation in Victorian cities: a reassessment', *Trans. IBG*, NS, 9 (1984), pp. 131–44.

21 Dennis, *English industrial cities*, esp. pp. 235–45; Pooley, 'Residential differentiation'.

22 Daunton, 'Review of Dennis'.

23 D. Ward, 'Environs and neighbours in the "Two Nations": residential differentiation in mid-nineteenth century Leeds', *Journ. Hist. Geogr.*, 6 (1980), pp. 133–62; D. Ward, 'The place of Victorian cities in developmental approaches to urbanization', in J. Patten (ed.), *The expanding city: essays in honour of Professor Jean Gottmann* (London, 1983), pp. 355–79; D. Ward, 'The progressives and the urban question: British and American responses to the inner city slums 1880–1920', *Trans. IBG*, NS, 9 (1984), pp. 299–314; Pooley, 'Residential differentiation'.

24 J. E. Vance, 'Land assignment in the precapitalist, capitalist and postcapitalist city', *Economic Geography*, 47 (1971), pp. 101–20; J. E. Vance, *This scene of man: the role and structure of the city in the geography of western civilization* (New York, 1977); J. Langton, 'Residential patterns in pre-industrial cities: some case studies from seventeenth-century Britain', *Trans. IBG*, 65 (1975), pp. 1–27; J. Langton, 'Late medieval Gloucester: some data from a rental of 1455', *Trans. IBG*, NS, 2 (1977), pp. 259–77. For a critique of Sjoberg, see P. Burke, 'Some reflections on the pre-industrial city', *Urban History Yearbook* (Leicester, 1975), pp. 13–21.

25 R. J. Dennis, 'Distance and social interaction in a Victorian city', *Journ. Hist. Geogr.*, 3 (1977), pp. 237–50.

26 R. M. Pritchard, *Housing and the spatial structure of the city* (Cambridge, 1976); R. J. Dennis, 'Intercensal mobility in a Victorian city', *Trans. IBG*, NS, 2 (1977), pp. 349–63; C. G. Pooley, 'Residential mobility in the Victorian city', *Trans. IBG*, NS, 4 (1979), pp. 258–77. Overviews include Dennis, *English industrial cities*, chap. 8, and R. Lawton, 'Mobility in nineteenth-century British cities', *Geogr. Journ.*, 145 (1979), pp. 206–24. More critical comments are offered by M. Anderson, 'Indicators of population change and stability in nineteenth-century cities: some sceptical comments', in Johnson and Pooley, *The structure of nineteenth-century cities*, pp. 283–98.

27 A. M. Warnes, 'Early separation of homes from workplaces and the urban structure of Chorley, 1780–1850', *Trans. Hist. Soc. Lancs and Cheshire*, 122 (1970), pp. 105–35; H. McLeod, *Class and religion in the late Victorian city* (London, 1974); H. McLeod, 'White-collar values and the role of religion', in G. Crossick (ed.), *The lower middle class in Britain 1870–1914* (London, 1977), pp. 61–88; W. Bramwell, 'Pubs and localised communities in mid-

Victorian Birmingham', *Queen Mary College (University of London) Dept of Geography Occasional Paper*, 22 (1984); R. Dennis and S. Daniels, ' "Community" and the social geography of Victorian cities', *Urban History Yearbook* (Leicester, 1981), pp. 7–23; Dennis, *English industrial cities*, pp. 132–40, 280–5.

28 For example, see some of the contributions to A. R. H. Baker and M. Billinge (eds.), *Period and place: research methods in historical geography* (Cambridge, 1982), and A. R. H. Baker and D. Gregory (eds.), *Explorations in historical geography: interpretative essays* (Cambridge, 1984). See also G. Kearns, 'Making space for Marx', *Journ. Hist. Geogr.*, 10 (1984), pp. 411–17; D. Harvey, *Consciousness and the urban experience* (Oxford, 1985), and *The urbanization of capital* (Oxford, 1985).

29 R. Dennis, 'Why study segregation? More thoughts on Victorian cities', *Area*, 12 (1980), pp. 313–17; R. Harris, 'Residential segregation and class formation in the capitalist city: a review and directions for research', *Progr. Hum. Geogr.*, 8 (1984), pp. 26–49.

30 A. Pred, 'Place as historically contingent process: structuration and the time-geography of becoming places', *Annals Assn. Am. Geogr.*, 74 (1984), p. 282.

31 F. Gray, 'Non-explanation in urban geography', *Area*, 7 (1975), pp. 228–35.

32 R. E. Pahl, *Whose city?*, 2nd edn (Harmondsworth, 1975); K. Bassett and J. Short, *Housing and residential structure: alternative approaches* (London, 1980).

33 Dyos, *Victorian suburb*; D. Cannadine and D. Reeder (eds.), *Exploring the urban past: essays in urban history by H. J. Dyos* (Cambridge, 1982).

34 D. Cannadine, *Lords and landlords: the aristocracy and the towns, 1774–1967* (Leicester, 1980); D. Cannadine (ed.), *Patricians, power and politics in nineteenth-century towns* (Leicester, 1982); C. W. Chalklin, *The provincial towns of Georgian England: a study of the building process 1740–1820* (London, 1974); F. M. L. Thompson, *Hampstead, building a borough, 1650–1964* (London, 1974); F. M. L. Thompson (ed.), *The rise of suburbia* (Leicester, 1982); D. J. Olsen, *The growth of Victorian London* (London, 1976); D. J. Olsen, *Town planning in London: the eighteenth and nineteenth centuries*, 2nd edn (New Haven, 1982); M. J. Daunton, *Coal metropolis: Cardiff 1870–1914* (Leicester, 1977); M. J. Daunton, *House and home in the Victorian city: working-class housing 1850–1914* (London, 1983).

35 D. Ward, 'The pre-urban cadaster and the urban pattern of Leeds', *Annals Assn. Am. Geogr.*, 52 (1962), pp. 150–66; M. J. Mortimore, 'Landownership and urban growth in Bradford and environs in the West Riding conurbation, 1850–1950', *Trans. IBG*, 46 (1969), pp. 105–19; J. Springett, 'Landowners and urban development: the Ramsden estate and nineteenth-century Huddersfield', *Journ. Hist. Geogr.*, 8 (1982), pp. 129–44.

36 Compare Lawton and Pooley, 'Merseyside', and C. G. Pooley, 'The residential segregation of migrant communities in mid-Victorian Liverpool', *Trans. IBG*, NS, 2 (1977), pp. 364–82, with C. G. Pooley, 'Housing for the poorest poor: slum clearance and rehousing in Liverpool, 1890–1918', *Journ. Hist. Geogr.*, 11 (1985), pp. 70–88; also compare Dennis, *English industrial cities*, chaps. 7–9, with R. J. Dennis, 'Victorian values and housing policy: London then and now', *Bloomsbury Geographer*, 13 (1985), pp. 71–4, and R. J. Dennis, 'The geography of Victorian values: private housing in London, 1860–1914',

paper presented to the Historical Geography Research Group, IBG Annual Conference, Reading, January 1986.

37 Among a series of papers by J. W. R. Whitehand, see especially: 'Building cycles and the spatial pattern of urban growth', *Trans. IBG*, 56 (1972), pp. 39–55; 'Building activity and intensity of development at the urban fringe: the case of a London suburb in the nineteenth century', *Journ. Hist. Geogr.*, 1 (1975), pp. 211–24; 'Fluctuations in the land-use composition of urban development during the industrial era', *Erdkunde*, 35 (1981), pp. 129–40; 'Commercial townscapes in the making', *Journ. Hist. Geogr.*, 10 (1984), pp. 174–200; and J. W. R. Whitehand and S. M. Whitehand, 'The physical fabric of town centres: the agents of change', *Trans. IBG*, NS, 9 (1984), pp. 231–47.

38 G. Gordon, 'The shaping of urban morphology', *Urban History Yearbook* (Leicester, 1984), pp. 1–10.

39 E. Hobsbawm, 'From social history to the history of society', *Daedalus*, 100 (1971), p. 34, quoted in D. Cannadine, 'Urban history in the United Kingdom: the "Dyos phenomenon" and after', in Cannadine and Reeder, *Exploring the urban past*, pp. 203–21.

40 Cannadine, in Cannadine and Reeder, *Exploring the urban past*, p. 208.

41 Dennis, *English industrial cities*, chap. 1.

42 P. Abrams, 'Introduction' and 'Towns and economic growth: some theories and problems', in P. Abrams and E. A. Wrigley (eds.), *Towns in societies: essays in economic history and historical sociology* (Cambridge, 1978), pp. 1–7, 9–33.

43 R. E. Pahl, 'Concepts in contexts: pursuing the urban of "urban" sociology', in Fraser and Sutcliffe, *The pursuit of urban history*, pp. 371–82.

44 M. Castells, 'Is there an urban sociology?', in C. G. Pickvance (ed.), *Urban sociology: critical essays* (London, 1976), pp. 33–59; P. Saunders, *Social theory and the urban question* (London, 1981).

45 Carter, *Urban historical geography*, pp. xiii–xv.

46 A. Sutcliffe, 'In search of the urban variable: Britain in the later nineteenth century', in Fraser and Sutcliffe, *The pursuit of urban history*, pp. 234–63.

47 R. Lee, 'The economic basis of social problems in the city', in D. T. Herbert and D. M. Smith (eds.), *Social problems and the city* (Oxford, 1979), pp. 47–62.

48 K. Marx and F. Engels, *Manifesto of the Communist Party*, originally 1848 (Moscow, 1973).

49 Saunders, *Social theory*, p. 257.

50 B. I. Coleman (ed.), *The idea of the city in nineteenth-century Britain* (London, 1973); A. Lees, *Cities perceived: urban society in European and American thought, 1820–1940* (Manchester, 1985).

51 B. Disraeli, *Sybil* (London, 1945); E. Gaskell, *North and south* (London, 1854–5).

52 D. Harvey, *Social justice and the city* (London, 1973); D. Harvey, *The limits to capital* (Oxford, 1982); J. Foster, *Class struggle and the industrial revolution* (London, 1974); G. Stedman Jones, *Outcast London: a study in the relationship between classes in Victorian society* (Oxford, 1971).

53 M. Dear and A. J. Scott (eds.), *Urbanization and urban planning in capitalist society* (London, 1981); J. Doherty, 'Urbanization, capital accumulation and

class struggle in Scotland, 1750–1914', in G. Whittington and I. D. Whyte (eds.), *An historical geography of Scotland* (London, 1983), pp. 239–67; Baker and Gregory, *Explorations in historical geography*; F. Driver, 'Power, space and the body: a critical assessment of Foucault's *Discipline and Punish*', *Environment and Planning D: Society and Space*, 3 (1985), pp. 425–46.

54 M. Billinge, 'Reconstructing societies in the past: the collective biography of local communities', in Baker and Billinge, *Period and place*, pp. 19–32; M. Billinge, 'Hegemony, class and power in late Georgian and early Victorian England: towards a cultural geography', in Baker and Gregory, *Explorations in historical geography*, pp. 28–67.

55 For example, research by recent Cambridge postgraduates: C. Philo (on the social construction of mental illness), F. Driver (on juvenile and poor law institutions) and M. Heffernan (on literacy and formal education). See also A. D. King (ed.), *Buildings and society: essays on the social development of the built environment* (London, 1980).

56 D. Cosgrove, *Social formation and symbolic landscape* (London, 1984).

57 R. Woods and J. Woodward (eds.), *Urban disease and mortality in nineteenth-century England* (London, 1984); G. Kearns, *Urban epidemics and historical geography: cholera in London, 1848–9*, Historical Geography Research Series 15 (Norwich, 1985).

58 J. J. Tobias, *Crime and industrial society in the nineteenth century* (London, 1967); D. Jones, *Crime, protest, community and police in nineteenth-century Britain* (London, 1982); D. T. Herbert, *The geography of urban crime* (London, 1982).

59 C. Booth, *Life and labour of the people of London*, 17 vols. (London, 1902); A. Fried and R. Elman (eds.), *Charles Booth's London* (London, 1969); H. W. Pfautz (ed.), *Charles Booth on the city: physical pattern and social structure* (Chicago, 1967).

60 D. R. Green, 'From artisans to paupers: the manufacture of poverty in mid-nineteenth century London', unpublished PhD thesis (Cambridge, 1985).

61 P. G. Hall, *The industries of London since 1861* (London, 1962); E. J. Connell and M. Ward, 'Industrial development, 1780–1914', in D. Fraser (ed.), *A history of modern Leeds* (Manchester, 1980), pp. 142–76.

62 R. Scola, 'Food markets and shops in Manchester, 1770–1870', *Journ. Hist. Geogr.*, 1 (1975), pp. 153–68; G. Shaw and M. T. Wild, 'Retail patterns in the Victorian city', *Trans. IBG*, NS, 4 (1979), pp. 278–91; R. Jones, 'Consumers' cooperation in Victorian Edinburgh: the evolution of a location pattern', *Trans. IBG*, NS, 4 (1979), pp. 292–305; P. J. Atkins, 'London's intra-urban milk supply, circa 1790–1914', *Trans. IBG*, NS, 2 (1977), pp. 383–99; G. Shaw, 'The role of retailing in the urban economy', in Johnson and Pooley, *The structure of nineteenth-century cities*, pp. 171–94; G. Shaw, 'Changes in consumer demand and food supply in nineteenth-century British cities', *Journ. Hist. Geogr.*, 11 (1985), pp. 280–96; D. R. Green, 'Street trading in London: a case study of casual labour, 1830–60', in Johnson and Pooley, *The structure of nineteenth-century cities*, pp. 129–51.

63 B. J. L. Berry, 'Cities as systems within systems of cities', *Papers & Proceedings Reg. Sci. Assn.*, 13 (1967), pp. 147–63.

64 Overviews of pre-census population change and urban growth include J. Langton, 'Industry and towns 1500–1730', and R. M. Smith, 'Population and its geography in England 1500–1730', both in R. A. Dodgshon and R. A. Butlin (eds.), *An historical geography of England and Wales* (London, 1978), pp. 173–98 and 199–237. J. Sheail, 'The distribution of taxable population and wealth in England during the early sixteenth century', *Trans. IBG*, 55 (1972), pp. 111–26, and H. C. Darby, R. E. Glasscock, J. Sheail and G. R. Versey, 'The changing geographical distribution of wealth in England 1086–1334–1525', *Journ. Hist. Geogr.*, 5 (1979), pp. 247–62, illustrate the use of sources and contain much incidental information on urban populations. Geographical case studies of particular places include R. Finlay, *Population and metropolis: the demography of London 1580–1650* (Cambridge, 1981); T. R. Slater, 'The urban hierarchy in medieval Staffordshire', *Journ. Hist. Geogr.*, 11 (1985), pp. 115–37.

65 J. Patten, *English towns 1500–1700* (Folkestone, 1978); A. R. Bridbury, *Economic growth: England in the later middle ages*, 2nd edn (London, 1975); S. H. Rigby, 'Urban decline in the later middle ages', *Urban History Yearbook* (Leicester, 1979), pp. 46–59; S. Reynolds, 'Decline and decay in late medieval towns', *Urban History Yearbook* (Leicester, 1980), pp. 76–8; A. R. Bridbury, 'English provincial towns in the later middle ages', *Economic History Review*, 2nd series, 34 (1981), pp. 1–24; R. Hilton, 'Towns in societies – medieval England', *Urban History Yearbook* (Leicester, 1982), pp. 7–13; S. H. Rigby, 'Urban decline in the later middle ages: the reliability of the non-statistical evidence', *Urban History Yearbook* (Leicester, 1984), pp. 45–60; R. Tittler, 'Late medieval urban prosperity', *Economic History Review*, 2nd series, 37 (1984), pp. 551–4.

66 B. E. Coates, 'The origin and distribution of markets and fairs in medieval Derbyshire', *Derbyshire Archaeological Journal*, 85 (1965), pp. 92–111; T. Unwin, 'Rural marketing in medieval Nottinghamshire', *Journ. Hist. Geogr.*, 7 (1981), pp. 231–51; Slater, '*The urban hierarchy*'.

67 B. T. Robson, *Urban growth: an approach* (London, 1973).

68 B. T. Preston, 'Rich town, poor town: the distribution of rate-borne spending levels in the Edwardian city system', *Trans. IBG*, NS, 10 (1985), pp. 77–94; S. V. Ward, 'Approaches to public intervention in shaping the urban environment 1919–1939', unpublished PhD thesis (Birmingham, 1983); R. J. Bennett, *The geography of public finance* (London, 1980); E. P. Hennock. 'Central/local government relations in England: an outline 1800–1950', *Urban History Yearbook* (Leicester, 1982), pp. 38–49.

69 Carter, *Urban historical geography*, chap. 6.

70 Dyos and Wolff, *The Victorian city*, esp. N. Taylor, 'The awful sublimity of the Victorian city', pp. 431–47.

71 Olsen, *Victorian London*; D. J. Olsen, 'The city as a work of art', in Fraser and Sutcliffe, *The pursuit of urban history*, pp. 264–85.

72 C. Dellheim, *The face of the past: the preservation of the medieval inheritance in Victorian England* (Cambridge, 1982), p. 133.

73 S. J. Daniels, 'Moral order and the industrial environment in the woollen textile districts of West Yorkshire 1780–1880', unpublished PhD thesis (London, 1980); S. J. Daniels, 'Landscaping for a manufacturer: Humphry Repton's commission for Benjamin Gott at Armley in 1809–10', *Journ. Hist. Geogr.*, 7 (1981), pp. 379–96.

74 Cosgrove, *Social formation*.
75 D. Cosgrove, 'The myth and stones of Venice: an historical geography of a symbolic landscape', *Journ. Hist. Geogr.*, 8 (1982), pp. 145–69.
76 Harvey, *Consciousness*.
77 R. Williams, *The country and the city* (London, 1973), is mostly about the country but discusses the swelling city from p. 142 onwards. In an urban context, novels by Charles Dickens, Elizabeth Gaskell, George Gissing, Arthur Morrison, H. G. Wells and Arnold Bennett provide contemporary insights into the geography of social change in the city. See D. C. D. Pocock, 'The novelist's image of the North', *Trans. IBG*, NS, 4 (1979), pp. 62–76; B. J. Hudson, 'The geographical imagination of Arnold Bennett', *Trans. IBG*, NS, 7 (1982), pp. 365–79.
78 J. Barrell, 'Review of D. C. D. Pocock (ed.) "Humanistic geography and literature"', *Journ. Hist. Geogr.*, 9 (1983), pp. 95–7.
79 J. A. Burgess and J. Gold (eds.), *Geography, the media and popular culture* (London, 1985).
80 R. Banham, 'Machine aesthetic', *Architectural Review*, 117 (1955), pp. 225–8; A. Sutcliffe, 'The metropolis in the cinema' in A. Sutcliffe (ed.), *Metropolis 1890–1940* (London, 1984), pp. 147–71; J. Gold, 'From "Metropolis" to "The City": film visions of the future city, 1919–39', in Burgess and Gold, *Geography*, pp. 123–43.
81 J. Burnett (ed.), *Useful toil* (London, 1974); J. Burnett (ed.), *Destiny obscure* (London, 1983); R. Lawton and C. G. Pooley, 'David Brindley's Liverpool: an aspect of urban society in the 1880s', *Trans. Hist. Soc. Lancs and Cheshire*, 125 (1975), pp. 149–68; P. Thompson, 'Voices from within', in Dyos and Wolff, *The Victorian city*, pp. 59–80; J. White, *Rothschild buildings: life in an East End tenement block 1887–1920* (London, 1980).
82 A. R. H. Baker and D. Gregory, 'Some *terrae incognitae* in historical geography: an exploratory discussion', in Baker and Gregory, *Explorations in historical geography*, pp. 187–8. A similar view was expressed in C. O. Sauer, 'Foreword to historical geography', *Annals Assn. Am. Geogr.*, 31 (1941), pp. 1–24.
83 D. Lowenthal and M. Binney (eds.), *Our past before us: why do we save it?* (London, 1981); D. Lowenthal, *The past is a foreign country* (Cambridge, 1985), esp. pp. 384–412.
84 R. Kain (ed.), *Planning for conservation* (London, 1981); R. Kain, 'Europe's model and exemplar still? The French approach to urban conservation', *Town Planning Review*, 52 (1982), pp. 403–22; H. Clout, 'Bordeaux: urban renovation, conservation and rehabilitation', *Planning Outlook*, 27 (1984), pp. 84–92; T. R. Slater, 'Preservation, conservation and planning in historic towns', *Geogr. Journ.*, 150 (1984), pp. 322–34.
85 Slater, 'Preservation, conservation and planning', p. 333.
86 E. Roberts, *A woman's place: an oral history of working-class women, 1890–1940* (Oxford, 1984); M. Prior (ed.), *English women 1500–1800* (London, 1984); Women and Geography Study Group of the IBG, *Geography and gender: an introduction to feminist geography* (London, 1984).
87 M. Ebury and B. Preston, 'Domestic service in late Victorian and Edwardian England, 1871–1914', *Univ. of Reading Dept of Geography Geographical Papers*, 42 (1976).

88 M. L. Davies (ed.), *Life as we have known it* (London, 1931); M. S. Pember Reeves, *Round about a pound a week* (London, 1914); R. Roberts, *The classic slum* (Manchester, 1971); A. L. Jasper, *A Hoxton childhood* (London, 1969).

89 J. Langton, 'The industrial revolution and the regional geography of England', *Trans. IBG*, NS, 9 (1984), pp. 145–67.

3 Research in German urban historical geography

1 For early reviews on urban geography, which might stand as references for the period of traditional urban geography before 1960, see W. Geisler, 'Beiträge zur Stadtgeographie', *Zeitschr. d. Gesellschaft f. Erdkunde Berlin*, 55 (1920), pp. 274–96; B. Carlberg, 'Stadtgeographie', *Geographischer Anzeiger*, 27 (1926), pp. 148–53; H. Bobek, 'Grundfragen der Stadtgeographie', *Geographischer Anzeiger*, 28 (1927), pp. 213–24; H. Dörries, 'Der gegenwärtige Stand der Stadtgeographie', *Petermanns Geogr. Mitteilungen*, Ergänzungsheft, 209 (1930), pp. 310–25; H. Dörries, 'Siedlungs- und Bevölkerungsgeographie (1908–1938)', *Geographisches Jahrbuch*, 55 (1940); P. Schöller, 'Aufgaben und Probleme der Stadtgeographie', *Erdkunde*, 7 (1953), pp. 161–84. For early reviews of urban history, see E. Keyser, 'Neue Forschungen zur Geschichte der deutschen Städte', *Blätter f. deutsche Landesgeschichte*, 83 (1937), pp. 46–53.

2 H. Bobek, 'Innsbruck. Eine Gebirgsstadt, ihr Lebensraum und ihre Erscheinung', *Forschungen zur deutschen Landes- u. Volkskunde*, 25, 3 (1928); H. Dörries, *Die Städte im oberen Leinetal, Göttingen, Northeim und Einbeck* (Göttingen, 1925). An interesting recent example along the line of this tradition to study and describe 'townscapes' is the work by historian F. Escher, 'Berlin und sein Umland, Zur Genese der Berliner Stadtlandschaft bis zum Beginn des 20. Jahrhunderts', *Einzelveröffentlichungen der Historischen Kommission zu Berlin*, 47 (Berlin, 1985). Escher succeeds in improving the traditional landscape approach by integrating modern analytic historic and geographic views.

3 For reviews reflecting the new analytical approach, see P. Schöller, 'Tendenzen der stadtgeographischen Forschung in der Bundesrepublik Deutschland', *Erdkunde*, 27 (1973), pp. 26–34; E. Lichtenberger, 'Perspektiven der Stadtgeographie', in *42. Deutscher Geographentag Göttingen 1979. Tagungsberichte u. wissenschaftl. Abhandlungen* (Wiesbaden, 1980), pp. 103–28. For the influences of parallels between American and European urban geography, see, for example, B. Hofmeister, 'Stadtgeographie', *Das Geographische Seminar* (Braunschweig, 1980); E. Lichtenberger, 'Stadtgeographie – Begriffe, Konzepte, Modelle, Prozesse', *Teubner Studienbücher Geographie* (Stuttgart, 1986). For links between urban history and urban historical geography in America and Europe (Sweden) see D. R. Goldfield, 'The studies of cities. On urban history research in the United States and Sweden', in T. Hall (ed.), *Städer i utveckling, Festschr. I. Hammarström* (Stockholm, 1984), pp. 199–205. The influences in Germany have not yet been analysed; they became important for urban historians during the middle of the 1970s, but did not affect historical geographers very much.

4 For the first recent brief reviews specifically on urban historical geography in

Germany, see B. von der Dollen, 'Forschungsschwerpunkte und Zukunftsaufgaben der historischen Geographie: Städtische Siedlungen', *Erdkunde*, 36 (1982), pp. 96–102; D. Denecke, 'Historisch-geographische Stadtforschung. Problemstellungen, Betrachtungsweisen, Perspektiven', in *44. Deutscher Geographentag Münster 1983. Tagungsberichte u. wissenschaftl. Abhandlungen* (Wiesbaden, 1984), pp. 136–44. See also I. Boy, 'Die Stadt als Problem interdisziplinärer Forschung', *Die alte Stadt*, 3 (1976), pp. 173–80.

5 For a short history of the institute see H.-K. Junk, 'Das Institut für vergleichende Städtegeschichte zu Münster', *Siedlungsforschung*, 3 (1985), pp. 235–56. The institute was founded in 1969 under the organizing committee 'Kuratorium für vergleichende Städtegeschichte'. It was the initiative of urban historians under the chair of Professor Heinz Stoob. Later a few historical geographers joined the committee and then participated in actual research work. A number of long-term research projects were initiated by this institute, especially the project sponsored by the German Research Foundation (DFG), under the title 'Vergleichende geschichtliche Städteforschung' (Sonderforschungsbereich 164). One of the numerous (more than 20) sub-projects is the German towns atlas (Deutscher Städteatlas in Verbindung mit dem Westfälischen Städteatlas). Publications/series: *Deutscher Städteatlas*, 1 (1973), 2 (1979), 3 (1984); *Westfälischer Städteatlas*, 1 (1975), 2 (1981). Series: *Städteforschung*: A, Darstellungen (1984 = 20 vols.); B, Handbücher; C, Quellen und Regesten. All publications and activities of the Sonderforschungsbereich 164 are listed in a small brochure: *Forschungsprojekte und Gesamtbibliographie* (Münster, 1984).

6 For a special bibliography on urban geography in Germany, see H. H. Blotevogel, H. J. Buchholz and M. Hommel, 'Bibliographie zur Stadtgeographie. Deutschsprachige Literatur 1952–1970', *Bochumer Geographische Arbeiten*, 14 (Paderborn, 1973). For bibliographies on urban history, see B. Schroeder and H. Stoob, 'Bibliographie zur deutschen historischen Städteforschung', *Städteforschung*, B 1, 1st edn (Köln/Wien, 1986); various authors, 'Neue Veröffentlichungen zur vergleichenden Städtegeschichte', *Blätter f. deutsche Landesgeschichte* (currently, since vol. 90, 1953); a substantial current record on recent publications on urban history is held in the Institut für vergleichende Städtegeschichte, Münster. The new current bibliography, 'Bibliographie zur europäischen Siedlungsforschung, Archäologie – Geschichte – Geographie', in *Siedlungsforschung*, 1 (1983ff), compiled by D. Denecke, has a section (IV) on 'Regionale Stadtforschung', covering Central Europe and – giving only selected titles – also other European countries. It is an interdisciplinary bibliography under the theme of urban historical geography as settlement geography. For a recent comprehensive bibliography for Austria, see W. Rausch (ed.), *Bibliographie zur Geschichte der Städte Österreichs* (Linz, 1984). See also the special bibliography on urban renewal and conservation by H. Grabowski, *Bibliographie zur Stadtsanierung, internationale Auswahl* (Paderborn, 1980). An important journal on urban history and urban conservation is: *Die alte Stadt – Zeitschrift für Stadtgeschichte, Stadtsoziologie und Denkmalpflege*, published since 1974. For papers on urban history see the continuing series *Städteforschung* (Köln/Wien, 1976) and the chronological closed series edited by W. Rausch, *Beiträge zur Geschichte der Städte Mitteleuropas*, vols. 1–8 (Linz, 1977–84). An

important series of handbooks containing historical data on German towns arranged by Länder and alphabetically by towns is E. Keyser (ed.), *Deutsches Städtebuch Handbuch städtischer, Geschichte*, vols. 1–4 (Stuttgart, 1939–74).

7 A general study on the town on the basis of a marxist theory may be mentioned: H. Lefebvre, *Die Stadt im marxistischen Denken* (Ravensburg, 1975).

8 In Germany there is the Institut für vergleichende Städtegeschichte in Münster and the special research project 'Vergleichende geschichtliche Städteforschung' as a Sonderforschungsbereich (164) of the Deutsche Forschungsgemeinschaft (DFG), following comparative studies. In Japan the journal *Comparative Urban History* was launched, focussed on comparative European (especially German) and Japanese approaches. Also for the early period of urban origins in Europe the comparative method of research was stressed: H. B. Clarke and A. Simms, 'Towards a comparative history of urban origins', in H. B. Clarke and A. Simms (eds.), *The comparative history of urban origins in non-Roman Europe*, British Arch. Reports, International Series 255 (Oxford, 1985), pp. 669–714. Unfortunately there is not yet a basic theory of the historic-geographical comparative approach and not even a general discussion.

9 D. Denecke, 'Der geographische Stadtbegriff und die räumlich-funktionale Betrachtungsweise bei Siedlungstypen mit zentraler Bedeutung in Anwendung auf historische Siedlungsepochen', in H. Jankuhn, W. Schlesinger and H. Steuer (eds.), 'Vor- und Frühformen der europäischen Stadt im Mittelalter', *Abhandlungen der Akademie der Wissenschaften in Göttingen*, phil.-hist. Kl., 3, 83 (Göttingen, 1973), pp. 33–55; A. Heit, 'Die mittelalterlichen Städte als begriffliches und definitorisches Problem', *Die alte Stadt*, 4 (1978), pp. 350–408; D. Denecke, 'Stadtkern und Stadtkernforschung. Ein Beitrag zur Terminologie und Fragestellung', in H. Jäger (ed.), 'Stadtkernforschung', *Städteforschung*, A 27 (Köln, 1988), pp. 11–21.

10 H. Stoob, 'Kartographische Möglichkeiten zur Darstellung der Stadtentstehung in Mitteleuropa, besonders zwischen 1450 und 1800', *Historische Raumforschung*, 1 (Bremen, 1956), pp. 21–76; C. Haase, 'Stadtbegriff und Stadtentstehungsschichten in Westfalen. Uberlegungen zu einer Karte der Stadtentstehungsschichten', *Westfälische Forschungen*, 11 (1958), pp. 16–32; C. Haase, *Die Entstehung der westfälischen Städte* (Münster, 1960); E. Ennen, 'The different types of formation of European towns', in S. L. Thrupp (ed.), *Early medieval society* (New York, 1967), pp. 174–82. Picking up the model of phases of urban origins and developing morphogenetic and functional urban typologies: A. Scheuerbrandt, 'Südwestdeutsche Stadttypen und Städtegruppen bis zum frühen 19. Jahrhundert. Ein Beitrag zur Kulturlandschaftsgeschichte und zur kulturräumlichen Gliederung des nördlichen Baden-Württemberg und seiner Nachbargebiete', *Heidelberger Geographische Arbeiten*, 32 (Heidelberg, 1972); in contrary to this regional approach (regionalism and urban landscapes), see the traditional local morphogenetic interpretation of street patterns and urban forms: E. Keyser, 'Städtegründungen und Städtebau in Nordwestdeutschland im Mittelalter', *Forschungen zur deutschen Landeskunde*, 111 (Remagen, 1958).

11 An interesting aspect in a regional sense was followed by W. Schlesinger, 'Über mitteleuropäische Städtelandschaften der Frühzeit', *Blätter f. deutsche Landes-*

geschichte, 93 (1957), pp. 15–42.

12 H. Jankuhn, W. Schlesinger and H. Steuer (eds.), 'Vor- und Frühformen der europäischen Stadt im Mittelalter', *Abhandlungen der Akademie der Wissenschaften in Göttingen*, phil.-hist. Kl., 3, 83/4 (Göttingen, 1973/4). For a recent summary report on the long-term research project in Haithabu and Schleswig, see H. Jankuhn, K. Schietzel and H. Reichstein (eds.), *Archäologische und naturwissenschaftliche Untersuchungen an ländlichen und frühstädtischen Siedlungen im deutschen Küstengebiet vom 5. Jahrhundert vor Chr. bis zum 11. Jahrhundert nach Chr.*, vol. 2: *Handelsplätze des frühen und hohen Mittelalters* (Weinheim, 1984); see also contributions on Germany in Clarke and Simms, *Urban origins*, see especially the recent research report by H. Steuer, 'Zum Stand der archäologisch-historischen Stadtforschung in Europa, Bericht über ein Kolloquium 1982 in Münster', *Zeitschr. f. Archäologie des Mittelalters*, 12 (1984), pp. 35–72.

13 See the special volume edited by Jäger, 'Stadtkernforschung'.

14 H. Planitz, *Die alte Stadt im Mittelalter* (Köln/Graz, 1954), pp. 186ff; D. Denecke, 'Die Ortswüstung Oldendorp bei Einbeck und die "Alten Dörfer" im Leinebergland', *Einbecker Jahrbuch*, 29 (1970), p. 31 and Fig. 5.

15 M. Mitterauer, 'Markt und Stadt im Mittelalter. Beiträge zur historischen Zentralitätsforschung', *Monographien zur Geschichte des Mittelalters*, 21 (Stuttgart, 1980).

16 See the contributions by Hans Stephan and Heiko Steuer in this volume.

17 H. Louis, 'Die geographische Gliederung von Gross-Berlin', in H. Louis and W. Panzer (eds.), *Länderkundliche Forschung, Festschrift N. Krebs* (Stuttgart, 1936), pp. 146–71. For the development from the German tradition of a morphogenetic approach towards a cyclical approach, see J. Whitehand, 'Urban morphology', in M. Pacione (ed.), *Historical geography: progress and prospect* (London, 1987), pp. 250–76.

18 One example of a morphogenetic study is I. Möller, 'Die Entwicklung eines Hamburger Gebietes von der Agrar- zur Grosstadtlandschaft, mit einem Beitrag zur Methode der städtischen Aufrissanalyse', *Hamburger Geographische Studien*, 10 (Hamburg, 1959). This also considered architectural, social and functional aspects.

19 R. Hartog, 'Stadterweiterungen im 19. Jahrhundert', *Schriftenreihe d. Vereins z. Pflege Kommunalwissenschaftl. Aufgaben*, 6 (Stuttgart, 1962); E. Maschke and J. Sydow (eds.), 'Stadterweiterung und Vorstadt', *Veröffentlichungen d. Kommission f. geschichtliche Landeskunde in Baden-Württemberg*, B 51 (Stuttgart, 1969); T. Rönnebeck, 'Stadterweiterung und Verkehr im 19. Jahrhundert', *Schriftenreihe der Institute f. Städtebau d. Techn. Hochschulen u. Universitäten*, 5 (Stuttgart, 1971); F. Baltzarek, A. Hoffmann and H. Stekl, 'Wirtschaft und Gesellschaft der Wiener Stadterweiterung', *Die Wiener Ringstrasse*, 5 (Wiesbaden, 1975); H. Kneile, 'Stadterweiterungen und Stadtplanungen im 19. Jahrhundert. Auswirkungen des ökonomischen und sozialen Strukturwandels auf die Stadtphysiognomie im Grossherzogtum Baden', *Veröffentlichungen aus dem Archiv der Stadt Freiburg*, 15 (Freiburg, 1978); H. Matzerath, 'Städtewachstum und Eingemeindungen im 19. Jahrhundert', in J. Reulecke (ed.), *Die deutsche Stadt im Industriezeitalter* (Wuppertal, 1978), pp. 67–89; H. Meynen, 'Die Wohn-

bauten im nordwestlichen Vorortsektor Kölns mit Ehrenfeld als Mittelpunkt. Bauliche Entwicklung seit 1845, Wechselbeziehungen von Baubild und Sozial-struktur', *Forschungen zur deutschen Landeskunde*, 210 (Trier, 1978); H. J. Selig, 'Münchener Stadterweiterungen von 1860–1910. Stadtgestalt und Stadt-baukunst', Diss. phil. (München, 1978); C. Engeli, 'Stadterweiterungen in Deutschland im 19. Jahrhundert', in W. Rausch (ed.), *Die Städte Mitteleuropas im 19. Jahrhundert, Beiträge zur Geschichte der Städte Mitteleuropas*, 7 (Linz, 1983); W. R. Krabbe, 'Die Eingemeindungen und Stadterweiterungen Münsters im 19. und 20. Jahrhundert. Bevölkerungsdruck, städtischer Flächenbedarf und Zwang zum staatlich-kommunalen Verwaltungshandeln', *Quellen und Forschun-gen zur Geschichte der Stadt Münster*, NF, 11 (Münster, 1984), pp. 127–53; I. Thienel-Saage, 'Städtewachstum in der Gründerzeit, Beispiel Berlin', *Fra-genkreise* (Paderborn, 1984). This series of studies will reflect different views of various disciplines, but also a development in approach.

20 K. Blaschke, 'Altstadt – Neustadt – Vorstadt. Zur Typologie genetischer Stadt-geschichtsforschung', *Vierteljahrschrift f. Sozial- und Wirtschaftsgeschichte*, 57 (1970), pp. 350–62; K. Czock, 'Vorstädte: Zu ihrer Entstehung, Wirtschaft und Sozialentwicklung in der älteren deutschen Stadtgeschichte', *Sitzungsberichte der sächsischen Akademie d. Wissenschaften zu Leipzig*, phil.-hist. Kl., 121, 1 (Berlin, 1979).

21 Maschke and Sydow, 'Stadterweiterung und Vorstadt'; H. Raisch, 'Stadterwei-terung und Vorstadt in historisch-geographischer Sicht, dargelegt am Beispiel einiger Kleinstädte', in *ibid.*; B. von der Dollen, 'Vorortbildung und Residenz-funktion. Eine Studie zu den vorindustriellen Stadt – Umland – Beziehungen, dargestellt am Beispiel Bonn – Poppelsdorf', *Veröffentlichungen des Stadtarchivs Bonn*, 20 (Bonn, 1978); B. von der Dollen, 'Die Koblenzer Neustadt. Planung und Ausführung einer Stadterweiterung des 18. Jahrhunderts', *Städteforschung*, A 6 (Köln/Wien, 1979); B. von der Dollen, 'Vorortbildung. Zur Überformung ländlicher Siedlungen durch die Stadt vor der Industrialisierung', *Die alte Stadt*, 7 (1980), pp. 3–28.

22 B. Hofmeister, 'Die Angerdörfer des Raumes von West-Berlin. Beispiele für die grossstädtische Überformung ehemaliger Dorfkerne', *Berichte zur deutschen Landeskunde*, 26 (1960), pp. 1–23; K. Ganser, 'Dörfliche Strukturen am Stadt-rand, eine sozialwissenschaftliche Analyse des alten Stadtteils Perlach' (Mün-chen, 1968); S. Häsler, 'Alte Dorfkerne in Stuttgart. Sozial-geographische Untersuchungen am Beispiel von Möhringen, Plieningen und Weilimdorf', *Berichte zur deutschen Landeskunde*, 53 (1979), pp. 285–306; E. Blaschke, S. Claasen and J. Maier, 'Alte Dorfkerne und neue Stadtrandsiedlungen. Aubing und Lochkausen/Langwied an der westlichen Stadtgrenze Münchens', *Arbeits-materialien zur Raumordnung u. Raumplanung*, 4 (Bayreuth, 1980).

23 A. Papageorgiou, *Stadtkerne im Konflikt. Die historischen Stadtkerne und ihre Rolle im künftigen räumlichen Gefüge* (Berlin, 1970).

24 E. W. Hübschmann, 'Die Zeil. Sozialgeographische Studie über eine Strasse', *Frankfurter Geographische Hefte*, 30 (Frankfurt, 1952); K. D. Wiek, 'Kurfür-stendamm und Champs-Elysées. Geographischer Vergleich zweier Weltstrassen – Gebiete', *Abhandlungen d. Geographischen Instituts d. Freien Universität Ber-lin*, 11 (Berlin, 1967); E. Lichtenberger, 'Wirtschaftsfunktion und Sozialstruktur

der Wiener Ringstrasse', *Die Wiener Ringstrasse*, 6 (Wien, 1970).

25 B. von der Dollen, 'Stadtrandphänomene in historisch-geographischer Sicht', *Siedlungsforschung*, 1 (1983), pp. 15–38; in the same volume there are a number of case studies on the same topic.

26 F. R. Klaube, *Der Friedrichsplatz in Kassel* (Kassel, 1980); H. U. Stockmann, 'Der Aegidienplatz. Entwicklung und Veränderung eines Platzes am Rande der Innenstadt von Hannover', *Hannoversche Geschichtsblätter*, NF, 35 (1981), pp. 159–80.

27 H. Meynen, 'Die Kölner Grünanlagen. Die städtebauliche und gartenarchitektonische Entwicklung des Stadtgrüns und des Grünsystems Fritz Schumachers', *Beiträge zu den Bau- und Kunstdenkmälern im Rheinland*, 25 (Düsseldorf, 1979); R. Schediwy and F. Baltzarek, *Grün in der Grossstadt. Geschichte und Zukunft europäischer Parkanlagen unter besonderer Berücksichtigung Wiens* (Wien, 1982); F. Falter, 'Die Grünflächen der Stadt Basel. Humangeographische Studie zur Dynamik urbaner Grünräume im 19. und 20. Jahrhundert, mit besonderer Berücksichtigung der Kleingärten', *Basler Beiträge zur Geographie*, 28 (Basel, 1984).

28 A. Buff, *Bauordnung im Wandel historisch-politische, soziologische und technische Aspekte* (München, 1971).

29 L. Zimmermann, 'Forstschutz und Bauordnungen zur Blütezeit des hessischen Fachwerbaus', *Zeitschr. f. hessische Geschichte und Landeskunde*, 65 (1954), pp. 91–105; E. Gloede, 'Einfluss der Baupolizei auf die bauliche Entwicklung Hamburgs', Diss. (Braunschweig, 1955); K. Haubner, 'Die Stadt Göttingen im Eisenbahn- und Industriezeitalter', *Schriften d. Wirtschaftswissenschaftlichen Gesellschaft z. Studium Niedersachsens*, A 1, 75 (Hildesheim, 1964); O. Birkner, 'Die Bedeutung der Bauordnung im Städtebau des 19. Jahrhunderts', *Die alte Stadt*, 1 (1976), pp. 26–37.

30 M. Neumann, 'Stadtplanung und Wohnhausbau in Oldenburg 1850–1914', *Oldenburger Studien*, 22 (Oldenburg, 1982); G. Fehl and J. Rodriguez-Lores, 'Aufstieg und Fall der Zonenplanung – städtebauliches Instrumentarium und stadträumliche Ordnungsvorstellungen zwischen 1870 und 1905', *Stadtbauwelt*, 73 (1982), pp. 45–52; G. Fehl and J. Rodriguez-Lores, 'Die Gartenstadtbebauung. Ein Blick auf die Reform von Bebauungsplan und Bebauungsweise in deutschen Vorstadtsiedlungen zwischen 1910 und 1918', *Stadtbauwelt*, 77 (1983), pp. 72–81; G. Fehl and J. Rodriguez-Lores (eds.), 'Stadterweiterungen 1800–1875. Von den Anfängen des modernen Städtebaus in Deutschland', *Stadt – Planung – Geschichte*, 2 (Hamburg, 1983); G. Fehl, 'Die europäische Stadt. Beiträge zur Stadtbaugeschichte und Stadtgestaltung', *Städtebauliches Institut der Universität Stuttgart*, 41 (1984); J. Rodriguez-Lores and G. Fehl (eds.), 'Städtebaureform 1865–1900. Von Licht, Luft und Ordnung in der Stadt der Gründerzeit', *Stadt – Planung – Geschichte*, 5, 1 and 2 (Hamburg, 1985). For the very recent history of urban planning, see G. Albers and A. Papageorgiou-Venetas, *Stadtplanung. Entwicklungslinien 1945–1980*, 2 vols. (Tübingen, 1984).

31 L. O. Larsson, *Die Neugestaltung der Reichshauptstadt: Albert Speers Generalbebauungsplan für Berlin* (Stockholm, 1978); U. Peltz-Dreckmann, 'Nationalsozialistischer Siedlungsbau. Versuch einer Analyse der die Siedlungspolitik bestimmenden Faktoren am Beispiel des Nationalsozialismus', *Minerva –*

Fachserie: Geisteswissenschaften, (München, 1978); K. Arndt, 'Tradition und Unvergleichbarkeit. Zu Aspekten der Stadtplanung im nationalsozialistischen Deutschland', in Rausch, *Die Städte Mitteleuropas*, pp. 149–66; E. Forndran, 'Die Stadt- und Industriegründun Wolfsburg und Salzgitter. Entscheidungsprozesse im nationalsozialistischen Herrschaftssystem', *Campus Forschung*, 402 (Frankfurt, 1984); M. Frank (ed.), 'Faschistische Architekturen. Planen und Bauen in Europa 1930–1945', *Stadt – Planung – Geschichte*, 3 (Hamburg, 1984); T. Harlander and G. Fehl (eds.), 'Hitlers sozialer Wohnungsbau 1940–1945. Wohnungspolitik, Baugestaltung und Siedlungsplanung', *Stadt – Planung – Geschichte*, 6 (Hamburg, 1986); J. Lafrenz, 'Planung und Neugestaltung von Hamburg 1933–1945', in H. Heineberg (ed.), *Innerstädtische Differenzierung und Prozesse im 19. und 20. Jahrhundert. Geographische und historische Aspekte. Städteforschung*, A 25 (Köln, 1987), pp. 385–437.

32 F. Werner, *Städtebau Berlin-Ost* (Berlin, 1969); F. Werner, *Stadtplanung Berlin. Theorien und Realität*, vol. 1: *1900–1960*, (Berlin, 1976); P. Schöller, 'Paradigma Berlin. Lehren aus einer Anomalie. Fragen und Thesen zur Stadtgeographie', *Geographische Rundschau*, 26 (1974), pp. 425–34; H. Heineberg, 'Zentren in West- und Ost- Berlin. Untersuchungen zum Problem der Erfassung und Bewertung grossstädtischer funktionaler Zentrenausstattungen in beiden Wirtschafts- und Gesellschaftssystemen Deutschlands', *Bochumer Geographische Arbeiten*, Sonderheft 9 (Paderborn, 1977); D. Schubert, 'Stadtplanung als Ideologie. Eine theoriegeschichtliche, ideologiekritische Untersuchung der Stadt, des Städtebaus und Wohnungsbaus in Deutschland von ca. 1850 bis heute', sozialwiss. Diss., Freie Universität (Berlin, 1981).

33 A. Bernatzky, *Von der mittelalterlichen Stadtbefestigung zu den Wallgrünflächen von heute* (Berlin, 1960); P. Grobe, *Die Entfestigung Münchens* (München, 1970); W. Vogl, 'Die ehemaligen Festungsanlagen von Ingolstadt. Heutige Nutzung und Auswirkungen auf die Stadtentwicklung', *Nürnberger wirtschafts- und sozialgeographische Arbeiten*, 28 (Nürnberg, 1978); B. von der Dollen, 'Residenzstadt und Entfestigung an Beispielen aus dem Rheinland', in H. W. Herrmann *et al.* (eds.), *Beiträge zur Geschichte der Garnisons- und Festungsstadt, Veröffentlichungen d. Kommission f. Saarländische Landesgeschichte und Volksforschung*, 13 (Saarbrücken, 1983).

34 D. Most and J. Schlier, *Wohnungsbau in Kassel während der Weimarer Republik* (Kassel, 1983); J. F. Geist and K. Cürvers, *Das Berliner Miethaus 1862–1945* (München, 1984).

35 R. Dauber, 'Die Anfänge der Wohnungspolitik und Bautätigkeit des gemeinnützigen Wohnungsbaus im Rheinland', *Die alte Stadt*, 7 (1980), pp. 133–54; W. R. Krabbe, 'Die Anfänge des sozialen Wohnungsbaus vor dem ersten Weltkrieg. Kommunalpolitische Bemühungen um eine Lösung des Wohnungsproblems', *Vierteljahrschrift f. Sozial- u. Wirtschaftsgeschichte*, 71 (1984), pp. 30–58; H. J. Teuteberg and C. Wischermann (eds.), 'Wohnungsnot und soziale Frage im 19. Jahrhundert. Beiträge zur Sozialgeschichte der Urbanisierung (1850–1914)', *Studien zur Geschichte des Alltags*, 5 (Münster, 1985); Harlander and Fehl, 'Hitlers sozialer Wohnungsbau 1940–1945'.

36 C. Wischermann, 'Wohnen in Hamburg vor dem ersten Weltkrieg', *Studien zur Geschichte des Alltags*, 2 (Münster, 1984); H. J. Teuteberg and C. Wischer-

mann, 'Gebaute Umwelt und Wohnalltag im 19. Jahrhundert. Bilder, Daten, Dokumente', *Studien zur Geschichte des Alltags*, 3 (Münster, 1984); H. J. Teuteberg (ed.), 'Homo habitans. Zur Sozialgeschichte des Wohnens seit der Neuzeit', *Studien zur Geschichte des Alltags*, 4 (Münster, 1984); see also the theme volume *Siedlungsforschung*, 5 (1987).

37 G. Bayerl, 'Materialien zur Geschichte der Umweltproblematik', *Technologie und Politik*, 16 (1980), pp. 180–222; J. Sydow (ed.), *Städtische Versorgung und Entsorgung im Wandel der Geschichte* (Sigmaringen, 1981); M.-E. Hübner, 'Umweltprobleme als Alltagserfahrungen in der frühneuzeitlichen Stadt? Überlegungen anhand des Beispiels der Stadt Hamburg', *Die alte Stadt*, 11 (1984), pp. 112–38. On the history and patterns of epidemics in German medieval towns, see E. Woehlkens, *Pest und Ruhr im 16. und 17. Jahrhundert. Grundlagen einer statistisch-topographischen Beschreibung der grossen Seuchen, insbesondere in der Stadt Uelzen* (Uelzen, 1954); N. Bulst, 'Vier Jahrhunderte Pest in niedersächsischen Städten. Vom schwarzen Tod (1349–1351) bis in die erste Hälfte des 18. Jahrhunderts', in C. Meckseper (ed.), *Stadt im Wandel*, vol. 4 (Stuttgart, 1985), pp. 251–70.

38 R. Klöpper, 'Entstehung, Lage und Verteilung der zentralen Siedlungen in Niedersachsen', *Forschungen zur deutschen Landeskunde*, 71, (Godesberg, 1952); K. D. Vogt, 'Uelzen. Seine Stadtumlandbeziehungen in historisch-geographischer Betrachtung', *Göttinger Geographische Abhandlungen*, 47 (Göttingen, 1968).

39 H. Ammann, 'Vom Lebensraum der mittelalterlichen Stadt. Eine Untersuchung an schwäbischen Beispielen', *Berichte z. deutschen Landeskunde*, 31 (1963), pp. 284–316; K. Fehn, *Die zentralörtlichen Funktionen früher Zentren in Altbayern. Raumbindende Umlandbeziehungen im Bayerisch-Österreichischen Altsiedelland von der Spätlatenezeit bis zum Ende des Hochmittelalters* (Wiesbaden, 1970); D. Fliedner, 'Zum Problem der wirtschaftlichen Beziehungen zwischen Stadt und Umland im Mittelalter, dargestellt am Beispiel des Raumes um Bremen links der Weser', *Braunschweiger Geographische Studien*, 3 (1971), pp. 101–18; D. Fliedner, 'Wirtschaftliche und soziale Stadtumlandbeziehungen im hohen Mittelalter', *Veröffentlichungen d. Akademie f. Raumforschung u. Landesplanung, Forschungs- und Sitzungsberichte*, 88 (Hannover, 1974), pp. 123–37. Also see the general and methodological study by Denecke, 'Der geographische Stadtbegriff'.

40 H. H. Blotevogel, 'Zentrale Orte und Raumbeziehungen in Westfalen vor der Industrialisierung (1780–1850)', *Veröffentlichungen d. Provinzialinstituts f. Westfälische Landes- und Völksforschung d. Landschaftsverbandes Westfalen-Lippe*, 1st series, 19 (Münster, 1975); G. Wölfing, 'Die Beziehungen der Kleinstädte des oberen Werratals zu ihrer ländlichen Umgebung vom 15. bis zur Mitte des 16. Jahrhunderts', in W. Mägdefrau (ed.), *Europäische Stadtgeschichte in Mittelalter und früher Neuzeit* (Weimar, 1979), pp. 259–385; K. Grieve, 'Zentrale Orte im Herzogtum Schleswig um 1800. Ein Grundriss wirtschaftsräumlicher Verflechtungsmuster vor der Industrialisierung', *Zeitschrift d. Gesellschaft f. Schleswig-Holsteinische Geschichte*, 106 (1981), pp. 89–115; N. Toporowsky, 'Zentrale Orte und zentralörtliche Beziehungen in der Nordeifel und ihrem Bördenvorland vom Ende des 18. Jahrhunderts bis zur Gegenwart', *Kölner*

Geographische Arbeiten, 40 (Köln, 1982).

41 P. Schöller (ed.), *Zentralitätsforschung, Wege der Forschung*, 301 (Darmstadt, 1972); and 'Stadt-Land-Beziehungen und Zentralität als Problem der historischen Raumforschung', *Veröffentlichungen d. Akademie f. Raumforschung u. Landesplanung, Forschungs- und Sitzungsberichte*, 88 (Hannover, 1974); G. Kaufmann, 'Stadt-Land-Beziehungen', *Verhandlungen d. 19. deutschen Volkskundekongresses 1973* (Göttingen, 1975); E. Maschke and W. Sydow, 'Stadt und Umland', *Veröffentlichungen d. Kommission f. geschichtliche Landeskunde in Baden-Württemberg*, 82 (Stuttgart, 1974); E. Meynen (ed.), 'Zentralität als Problem der mittelalterlichen Stadtgeschichtsforschung', *Städteforschung*, A 8 (Köln/Wien, 1979); N. Bulst, J. Hook and F. Irsigler (eds.), *Bevölkerung, Wirtschaft und Gesellschaft. Stadt-Land-Beziehungen in Deutschland und Frankreich, 14. bis 19. Jahrhundert* (Trier, 1983). The final volume of collected papers contains a selected bibliography on historical urban centrality: N. Bulst and J. Hoock, 'Auswahlbibliographie zum Problem der Stadt-Land-Beziehungen in Deutschland und Frankreich', covering the period 1970–83 (pp. 321–30).

42 See, for example, Klöpper, 'Entstehung, Lage und Verteilung', or the models in Denecke, 'Der geographische Stadtbegriff', Figs. 1 and 2.

43 Blotevogel, 'Zentrale Orte und Raumbeziehungen', pp. 177–96.

44 M. Mitterauer, 'Das Problem der zentralen Orte als sozial- und wirtschaftshistorische Forschungsaufgabe', *Vierteljahrschrift f. Sozial- und Wirtschaftsgeschichte*, 58 (1971), pp. 433–67; M. Mitterauer, 'Markt und Stadt im Mittelalter. Beiträge zur historischen Zentralitätsforschung', *Monographien zur Geschichte des Mittelalters*, 21 (Stuttgart, 1980).

45 Ammann, 'Vom Lebensraum der mittelalterlichen Stadt'.

46 D. Denecke, 'Beziehungen zwischen Stadt und Land in Nordwestdeutschland während des späten Mittelalters und der frühen Neuzeit. Historische Geographie städtischer Zentralität', in Meckseper, *Stadt im Wandel*, vol. 3, pp. 191–218; also see K. Fritz, 'Probleme der Stadt-Land-Beziehungen, im Bereich der wendischen Hansestädte nach 1370', *Hansische Geschichtsblätter*, 85 (1967), pp. 38–58.

47 T. Penners, 'Fragen der Zuwanderung in den Hansestädten des späten Mittelalters', *Hansische Geschichtsblätter*, 83 (1965), pp. 12–45; H. Vasarhelyi, 'Einwanderung nach Nördlingen, Esslingen und Schwäbisch-Hall zwischen 1450 und 1550', in Maschke and Sydow, *Veröffentlichungen d. Kommission f. geschichtliche Landeskunde* (1974), pp. 129–65; also see Blotevogel, 'Zentrale Orte und Raumbeziehungen', pp. 159–76, or Denecke, 'Beziehungen zwischen Stadt und Land'.

48 Blotevogel, 'Zentrale Orte und Raumbeziehungen', pp. 104–45; H. H. Blotevogel, 'Standorte und Einzugsbereiche von Universitäten und Gymnasien in Westfalen im 18. and 19. Jahrhundert', *Städteforschung*, A 15 (Köln/Wien, 1978), pp. 49–98; G. Wiegelmann, 'Kulturelle Stadt-Land-Beziehungen in der Neuzeit', *Beiträge zur Volkskultur in Nordwestdeutschland*, 9 (Münster, 1978); Denecke, 'Beziehungen zwischen stadt und Land', pp. 198–201.

49 R. Busch, 'Hannover, Wolfenbüttel und Celle. Stadtgründungen und Stadterweiterungen in drei welfischen Residenzen vom 16. bis zum 18. Jahrhundert', *Quellen und Darstellungen zur Geschichte Niedersachsens*, 75 (Hildesheim,

1969); K. W. Ohnesorge, 'Wolfenbüttel. Geographie einer ehemaligen Residenzstadt', *Braunschweiger Geographische Studien*, 5 (Braunschweig, 1974).

50 E. Mulzer, 'Der Wiederaufbau der Altstadt von Nürnberg 1945–1970', *Mitteilungen d. Fränkischen Geographischen Gesellschaft*, 19 (1972), pp. 1–225; N. Gutschow *et al.*, *Dokumentation Wiederaufbau der Stadt Münster 1945–1961* (Münster, 1982); J. Paczkowski, 'Der Wiederaufbau der Stadt Würzburg nach 1945', *Mainfränkische Studien*, 30 (Würzburg, 1982).

51 There is an interesting case study by B. von der Dollen, 'Massnahmen der Sanierung und Verschönerung der Altstadt Koblenz in der frühen Neuzeit', *Landeskundliche Vierteljahresblätter*, 24 (1978), pp. 3–15; for a case study for the period between the wars see H. Schulz, *Altstadtsanierung in Kassel – Stadtumbau und erhaltende Stadterneuerung vor dem zweiten Weltkrieg* (Kassel, 1983).

52 W. Sauerländer, 'Erweiterung des Denkmalbegriffs', *Deutsche Kunst und Denkmalpflege*, 33 (1975), pp. 117–30; F. Mielke, *Die Zukunft der Vergangenheit. Grundsätze, Probleme und Möglichkeiten der Denkmalpflege* (Stuttgart, 1975); H. Beseler, 'Denkmalpflege. Auftrag, Realität, Perspektiven', *Denkmalschutz*, 7 (1983), pp. 33–50.

53 E. Spiegel, 'Der Wert und Unwert des Alten für die Bewohner historischer Städte. Bedeutung und Bedeutungsverlust kollektiver Erinnerungen für die Erhaltung alter Wohnquartiere', *Die alte Stadt*, 1 (1974), pp. 285–306; G. Albers, 'Über den Rang des Historischen im Städtebau', *Die alte Stadt*, 11 (1984), pp. 214–26; C. Meckseper and H. Siebenmorgen (eds.), *Die alte Stadt: Denkmal oder Lebensraum? Die Sicht der mittelalterlichen Stadtarchitektur im 19. and 20. Jahrhundert* (Göttingen, 1985).

54 N. Schmidt-Relenberg and G. Feldhusen, *Sanierung und Sozialplan* (München, 1973); J. Blenk, 'Stadtsanierung. Sozial- und wirtschaftswissenschaftliche vorbereitende Untersuchungen nach dem Städtebauförderungsgesetz. Ablauf, Umfang, Inhalt, regionaler Bezug', *Geographische Rundschau*, 26 (1974), pp. 93–9; B. Schäfers, 'Soziale Strukturen und Prozesse bei der Sanierung von Innenstadtbezirken', *Die alte Stadt*, 1 (1974), pp. 283–98; G. Feldhusen, 'Soziologische Aspekte der vorbereitenden Untersuchungen im Städtebauförderungsgesetz', in O. Kiessler and H. Korte, *Soziale Stadtplanung* (Düsseldorf, 1975), pp. 89–118.

55 To give a few selected examples: H.-D. v. Frieling and J. Strassel, 'Sozialstrukturelle Situationsanalyse im Sanierungsgebiet Göttingen Neustadt – Ostseite und Überlegungen zu den Grundlagen des Sozialplanes', *Göttingen. Planung und Aufbau*, 15 a, b, c (Göttingen, 1973); I. Thienel-Saage, 'Grossstadtsanierung: Beispiel Berlin – Neukölln. Fachwissenschaftliche Analyse und didaktische Planung', *Gegenwartskunde*, 24 (1975), pp. 355–94; W. F. Killisch, 'Erhaltende Erneuerung eines historischen Stadtkerns. Zur Praxis der Sanierungsplanung in der Lübecker Alstadt', *Berichte z. deutschen Landeskunde*, 54 (1980), pp. 165–210; F. Spengelin and H. Wunderlich (eds.), 'Stadtbild und Gestaltung, Modellvorhaben Hameln', *Schriftenreihe Stadtentwicklung d. Bundesministers f. Raumordnung, Bauwesen u. Städtebau* (Bonn, 1983); in the journal *Die alte Stadt* a series of local examples of urban conservation were discussed under different aspects (7 (1980), and following issues).

56 A substantial case study developed from scientific urban geography elaborating a broad material applicable for planning is the one by J. Lafrenz, 'Die Stellung

der Innenstadt im Flächennutzungsgefüge des Agglomerationsraumes Lübeck. Grundlagenforschung zur erhaltenden Stadterneuerung', *Hamburger Geographische Studien*, 33 (Hamburg, 1977); B. von der Dollen, 'City planning, conservation and urban historical geography in Germany', *Planning History Bulletin*, 5 (1983), pp. 39–43.
57 D. Denecke, 'Applied historical geography and geographies of the past, historico-geographical change and regional processes in history', in A. R. H. Baker and M. Billinge (eds.), *Period and place: research methods in historical geography* (Cambridge, 1982), pp. 133–4; A. Klaar, *Baualterpläne Österreichischer Städte, 1:2000*, 9 parts (Wien, 1968ff); V. Mayr, 'Baualtersplan zur Stadtsanierung, Amberg', in Bayerisches Landesamt f. Denkmalpflege (ed.), *Baualterspläne zur Stadtsanierung in Bayern*, 1 (München, 1972).
58 D. Uthoff, 'Das historische Stadtbild als Wirtschaftsfaktor. Eine Fallstudie am Beispiel der Stadt Gosler', *Denkmalpflege 1975* (Hannover, 1976), pp. 73–80.
59 Denecke, 'Applied historical geography'; D. Denecke, 'Historische Geographie und räumliche Planung', *Mitteilungen d. Geographischen Gesellschaft in Hamburg*, 75 (1985), pp. 3–55.

4 The town in the Norman colonisations of the British Isles

1 G. W. S. Barrow, *The Anglo-Norman era in Scottish history* (Oxford, 1980), p. 5.
2 R. Hilton, 'Towns in English feudal society', *Journal of the Fernand Braudel Centre for the Study of Economies, Historical Systems and Civilisations*, 111 (1979), pp. 3–20.
3 G. Duby, *The early growth of the European economy* (London, 1974), p. 187.
4 R. Hilton, 'Towns in societies – medieval England', *Urban History Yearbook* (Leicester, 1982), p. 7.
5 M. M. Postan, *Medieval economy and society* (London, 1972), p. 212.
6 Hilton, 'Towns in English feudal society', p. 10.
7 M. W. Beresford, *New towns of the Middle Ages. Town plantation in England, Wales and Gascony* (London, 1967), p. 233.
8 Duby, *European economy*, p. 210.
9 Hilton, 'Towns in English feudal society', p. 10.
10 L. Musset, 'Peuplement en bourgage et bourgs ruraux en Normandie', *Cahiers de Civilisation Médiévale*, 9 (1966), pp. 177–208.
11 R. Hilton, 'Small town society in England before the Black Death', *Past and Present*, 105 (Nov. 1984), pp. 53–78; 'Lords, burgesses and hucksters', *Past and Present*, 97 (1982), pp. 3–15; 'The small town and urbanisation – Evesham in the Middle Ages', *Midland History*, 7 (1982), pp. 1–8.
12 R. A. Dodgshon, 'The early Middle Ages, 1066–1350', in R. A. Dodgshon and R. A. Butlin (eds.), *An historical geography of England and Wales* (London, 1978), p. 81.
13 Barrow, *The Anglo-Norman era in Scottish history*, p. 132.
14 R. Frame, *Colonial Ireland, 1169–1369* (Dublin, 1981), p. 70.
15 R. Frame, 'Power and society in the Lordship of Ireland, 1272–1377', *Past and Present*, 76 (1977), pp. 3–33.

16 B. J. Graham, 'The evolution of urbanisation in medieval Ireland', *Journal of Historical Geography*, 5 (1979), pp. 111–26.

17 For example, see C. Doherty, 'Some aspects of hagiography as a source for Irish economic history', *Peritia* (1982), pp. 300–28; 'Exchange and trade in early medieval Ireland', *Journal of the Royal Society of Antiquaries of Ireland*, 110 (1980), pp. 67–89.

18 B. J. Graham, *Anglo-Norman settlement in Ireland*, Irish Settlement Studies 1 (Athlone, 1985), pp. 4–8.

19 B. J. Graham, 'The towns of medieval Ireland', in R. A. Butlin (ed.), *The development of the Irish town* (London, 1977), pp. 28–60; J. F. Lydon, *The Lordship of Ireland in the Middle Ages* (Dublin, 1972).

20 R. R. Davies, 'Lordship or colony?', in J. Lydon (ed.), *The English in medieval Ireland* (Dublin, 1984), pp. 142–60.

21 See discussion in H. B. Clarke and A. Simms, 'Towards a comparative history of urban origins', in H. B. Clarke and A. Simms (eds.), *The comparative history of urban origins in non-Roman Europe*, British Arch. Reports, International Series 255 (Oxford, 1985), pp. 669–714.

22 S. Reynolds, *An introduction to the history of English medieval towns* (Oxford, 1977), p. 97.

23 S. Reynolds, 'Medieval urban history and the history of political thought', *Urban History Yearbook* (Leicester, 1982), pp. 14–23.

24 R. Hodges, *Dark Age economics: the origin of towns and trade, A.D. 600–1000* (London, 1982), p. 23.

25 Reynolds, *Medieval towns*, p. ix. J. Bradley, 'Planned Anglo-Norman towns in Ireland', in Clarke and Simms, *Urban origins*, pp. 441–68.

26 For example, H. Schledermann, 'The idea of the town; typology, definitions and approaches to the study of the medieval town in Northern Europe', *World Archaeology*, 2 (1970–1), pp. 115–27.

27 Frame, *Colonial Ireland*, p. 84.

28 Hodges, *Dark Age economics*, p. 23.

29 A settlement is considered a borough if it fulfils one of a *kriterienbundel*; see Beresford, *New towns*; C. M. Heighway (ed.), *The erosion of history: archaeology and planning in towns* (London, 1972); M. W. Beresford and H. P. R. Finberg, *English medieval boroughs: a handlist* (New Jersey, 1973).

30 Reynolds, *Medieval towns*, p. 44.

31 M. W. Barley (ed.), *European towns: their archaeology and early history* (London, 1977).

32 P. F. Wallace, 'The archaeology of Viking Dublin', in Clarke and Simms, *Urban origins*, pp. 103–46; 'The archaeology of Anglo-Norman Dublin', *ibid.*, pp. 379–412.

33 Extant medieval Irish urban charters are contained in G. MacNiocaill, *Na buirgeisi*, 2 vols.; (Dublin, 1964); for Wales, see I. Soulsby, *The towns of medieval Wales* (Chichester, 1983).

34 Beresford and Finsberg, *Handlist*.

35 Soulsby, *Towns of medieval Wales*, pp. 62–272.

36 G. S. Pryde, *The burghs of Scotland; a critical list* (Oxford, 1965).

37 B. J. Graham, 'The documentation of medieval Irish boroughs', *Bulletin of*

the Group for the Study of Irish Historic Settlement, 4 (1977), pp. 9–20; 5 (1978), pp. 41–5.

38 G. Martin, 'Plantation borough in medieval Ireland, with a handlist of boroughs to *circa* 1500', in D. Harkness and M. O'Dowd (eds.), *The town in Ireland*, Historical Studies 13 (Belfast, 1981), pp. 23–54.

39 See, for example, D. H. Hill, 'Continuity from Roman to medieval Britain', in Barley, *European towns*, pp. 293–302.

40 Reynolds, *Medieval towns*, p. 42.

41 D. A. Binchy, 'Secular institutions', in M. Dillon (ed.), *Early Irish society* (Dublin, 1954), p. 55.

42 E. A. Lewis, *The medieval boroughs of Snowdonia* (London, 1912), p. 5.

43 T. Jones Hughes, 'The origin and growth of towns in Ireland', *University Review*, 11 (1957–62), pp. 8–15.

44 W. Mackay Mackenzie, *The Scottish burghs* (Edinburgh, 1959), p. 6.

45 A. Small, 'Dark Age Scotland', in G. Whittington and I. D. Whyte (eds.), *An historical geography of Scotland* (London, 1983), p. 42.

46 N. P. Brooks, 'Urban archaeology in Scotland', in Barley, *European towns*, pp. 18–33.

47 A. M. Duncan, *Scotland; the making of a kingdom* (Edinburgh, 1975), pp. 467–70.

48 I. H. Adams, *The making of urban Scotland* (London, 1978), p. 4.

49 R. A. Griffiths (ed.), *Boroughs of medieval Wales* (Cardiff, 1978), p. 12.

50 W. Davies, *Wales in the early Middle Ages* (Leicester, 1982), pp. 57–8.

51 H. Carter, *The towns of Wales* (2nd edn, Cardiff, 1966), p. 7.

52 T. Jones Pierce, 'A Caernarvonshire manorial borough: studies in the medieval history of Pwllheli', in J. Beverley Smith (ed.), *Medieval Welsh society: selected essays by T. Jones Pierce* (Cardiff, 1972), pp. 127–93.

53 Soulsby, *Towns of medieval Wales*, p. 19.

54 E. G. Bowen, *The settlements of the Celtic saints in Wales* (Cardiff, 1954), p. 160.

55 The most succinct discussion of possibilities is in R. A. Butlin, 'Urban and proto-urban settlements in pre-Norman Ireland', in Butlin, *Irish town*, pp. 11–27.

56 C. Doherty, 'The monastic town in early medieval Ireland', in Clarke and Simms, *Urban origins*, pp. 45–76.

57 See Clarke and Simms, 'Towards a comparative history of urban origins'.

58 H. B. Clarke, 'The topographical development of early medieval Dublin', *Journal of the Royal Society of Antiquaries of Ireland*, 107 (1977), p. 47.

59 A. Simms, 'Medieval Dublin; a topographical analysis', *Irish Geography*, 12 (1979), pp. 25–41.

60 P. F. Wallace, 'The origins of Dublin', in B. G. Scott (ed.), *Studies on early Ireland: essays in honour of M. V. Duignan* (Dublin, 1981), pp. 129–43.

61 L. de Paor, 'The Viking towns of Ireland', in B. Almquist and D. Greene (eds.), *Proceedings of the 7th Viking Congress, Dublin 1973* (Dublin, 1976), pp. 29–37.

62 Hodges, *Dark Age economics*, p. 195.

63 De Paor, 'The Viking towns of Ireland', p. 34.

64 K. Nicholls, *Gaelic and Gaelicised Ireland in the Middle Ages* (Dublin, 1972), p. 122.

65 Butlin, 'Urban and proto-urban settlements in pre-Norman Ireland', pp. 20–5.
66 See, for example, C. Platt, *The English medieval town* (London, 1976).
67 Beresford and Finsberg, *Handlist*, p. 39.
68 Dodgshon, 'The early Middle Ages, 1066–1350', p. 108.
69 J. L. Bolton, *The medieval English economy, 1150–1500* (London, 1980), p. 56.
70 Hilton, 'Towns in English feudal society', p. 8.
71 Beresford and Finsberg, *Handlist*, p. 36.
72 T. R. Slater, 'Urban genesis and medieval town plans in Warwickshire' in T. R. Slater and P. J. Jarvis (eds.), *Field and forest* (Norwich, 1982), pp. 173–202.
73 Reynolds, 'Medieval towns', p. 53.
74 T. Unwin, 'Rural marketing in medieval Nottinghamshire', *Journal of Historical Geography*, 7 (1981), pp. 231–251; T. R. Slater, 'The urban hierarchy in medieval Staffordshire', *Journal of Historical Geography*, 11 (1985), pp. 115–137.
75 Beresford and Finsberg, *Handlist*, p. 43.
76 Beresford, *New towns*, pp. 263–4.
77 J. C. Russell, *British medieval population* (Albuquerque, 1948), p. 351. He later revised the Irish figure to 650,000, 'Late thirteenth-century Ireland as a region', *Demography*, 3 (1966), pp. 500–12. T. H. Hollingsworth, *Historical demography* (Cambridge, 1969), p. 268, places it between 400,000 and 800,000.
78 Soulsby, *Towns of medieval Wales*, pp. 20–3.
79 R. Fox, 'Urban development, 1100–1700', in Whittington and Whyte, *An historical geography of Scotland*, p. 85.
80 *Calendar of documents relating to Ireland, 1302–1307*, no. 653.
81 *Ibid.*, no. 617.
82 Hollingsworth, *Historical demography*, p. 269.
83 Graham, 'The towns of medieval Ireland', pp. 46–7.
84 Griffith, *Boroughs of medieval Wales*, p. 5.
85 A. J. Otway-Ruthven, 'The character of Norman settlement in Ireland', *Historical Studies*, 5 (1965), pp. 75–84.
86 Soulsby, *Towns of medieval Wales*, p. 16.
87 Beresford, *New towns*, p. 183.
88 L. Butler, 'Planned Anglo-Norman towns in Wales', in Clarke and Simms, *Urban origins*, pp. 469–504.
89 D. Walker, 'The Norman settlement in Wales', *Proceedings of the Battle Conference on Anglo-Norman Studies* (now *Anglo-Norman Studies*), 1 (1978), pp. 131–43.
90 Adams, *The making of urban Scotland*, p. 25.
91 *Ibid*, p. 36.
92 Graham, 'The evolution of urbanisation in medieval Ireland', p. 116.
93 See, for example, S. Reynolds, *Kingdoms and communities in Western Europe, 900–1300* (Oxford, 1984).

5 Urban archaeological research in Germany: a regional review of medieval topographic development

1 For Haithabu see H. Jankuhn, *Haithabu. Ein Handelsplatz der Wikingerzeit* (6th edn, Neumünster, 1986); H. Jankuhn, *Archäologische und naturwissen-*

schaftliche Untersuchungen an ländlichen und frühstädtischen Siedlungen im deutschen Küstengebiet vom 5. Jahrhundert vor Chr. bis zum Jahrhundert nach Chr., vol. 2: *Handelsplätze des frühen und hohen Mittelalters (Weinheim, 1984)*, with full bibliography; K. Schietzel (ed.), *Berichte über die Ausgrabungen in Haithabu*, 1 (1969ff). For Lübeck see *Lübecker Schriften zur Archäologie und Kulturgeschichte*, 1 (Lübeck, 1978ff), a short review is given in vol. 4 (1980), pp 9–15; in vol. 7 (1983) there are a number of reports about other seaports: G. P. Fehring (ed.), 'Seehandelszentren des nördlichen Europa. Der Strukturwandel vom 12. zum 13. Jahrhundert. Beiträge des Ostseekolloquiums Lübeck 1981'; 'Archäologie in Lübeck', *Hefte zur Kunst und Kulturgeschichte der Hansestadt Lübeck*, 3 (Lübeck, 1980); G. P. Fehring and K. Hammel, 'Die Topographie der Stadt Lübeck bis zum 14. Jahrhundert', in C. Meckseper (ed.), *Stadt im Wandel*, vol. 3 (Stuttgart, 1985), pp. 167–90.

2 For Frankfurt see U. Fischer, 'Altstadtgrabungen in Frankfurt am Main', *Ausgrabungen in Deutschland 1950–1975*, vol. 2 (Mainz, 1975), pp. 426ff; U. Fischer, 'Ausgrabungen in der Altstadt Frankfurt am Main. Vorgeschichte bis Hochmittelalter', *Bildheftchen des Frankfurter Museums für Vor- und Frühgeschichte*, 2 (Frankfurt, 1976).

3 For a bibliography of Rhenish and South German towns see articles in M. W. Barley (ed.), *European towns: their archaeology and early history* (London, 1977); H. B. Clarke and A. Simms (eds.), *The comparative history of urban origins in non-Roman Europe*, British Arch. Reports, International Series 255 (Oxford, 1985); H. Jankuhn, W. Schlesinger and H. Steuer (eds.), 'Vor- und Frühformen der europäischen Stadt im Mittelalter', *Abhandlungen der Akademie der Wissenschaften in Göttingen*, phil.-hist. Kl., 3, 83/4 (Göttingen, 1973/4); H. Jäger (ed.), 'Stadtkernforschung', *Städteforschung*, A 27 (Köln, 1987).

4 H.-G. Stephan, 'Archäologische Stadtforschung in Niedersachsen, Ostwestfalen, Hamburg und Bremen', in Meckseper, *Stadt im Wandel*, vol. 3, pp. 29–79.

5 F. Oswald, L. Schäfer and H. R. Sennhauser, 'Vorromanische Kirchenbauten. Katalog der Denkmäler bis zum Ausgang der Ottonen', *Veröffentlichungen des Zentralinstituts für Kunstgeschichte in München*, 3 (München, 1966–71). The spatial and functional aspects are excluded in the mentioned catalogue as well as in most art historical studies; for this see the publications mentioned in nn. 1–4.

6 See *ibid.*, and O. Doppelfeld and W. Weyres, 'Die Ausgrabungen im Dom zu Köln', *Kölner Forschungen*, 1 (Köln, 1980); H. Steuer, 'Spiegel des täglichen Lebens. Archäologische Funde des Mittelalters aus Köln', *Ausstellung Kölnisches Stadtmuseum* (Köln, 1982); see also the critical review by G. Binding, 'Die Domgrabung Köln', *Zeitschrift für Archäologie des Mittelalters*, 11 (1983), pp. 201–4, with bibliography.

7 For Frankfurt see n. 2; for Goslar see n. 4, and U. Hoelscher, 'Die Kaiserpfalz Goslar', *Die Deutschen Kaiserpfalzen*, 1 (1927). For imperial palaces generally, see Max-Planck-Institut für Geschichte (ed.), *Deutsche Königspfalzen*, vols. 1–3 (Göttingen, 1968–81).

8 Pioneers in town archaeology have been H. Jankuhn (Haithabu), W. Neuge-

bauer (Lübeck), R. Schindler (Hamburg), H. Plath (Hannover), E. W. Huth (Frankfurt an der Oder), E. Nickel (Magdeburg), H. Küas (Leipzig), H. W. Mechelk (Dresden) and W. Stamm (Frankfurt am Main). Generally, see the studies mentioned in nn. 3 and 4, and G. P. Fehring, 'Der Beitrag der Archäologie zum "Leben in der Stadt des späten Mittelalters"', in H. Appelt (ed.), 'Das Leben in der Stadt des Spätmittelalters', *Veröffentlichungen des Instituts für mittelalterliche Realienkunde Österreichs*, 2 (Wien, 1977), pp. 9–35; H.-G. Stephan, 'Stand und Aufgaben der Archäologie des Mittelalters und der Neuzeit in Nordwestdeutschland', in G. Wiegelmann (ed.), 'Geschichte der Alltagskultur', *Beiträge zur Volkskultur in Nordwestdeutschland*, 21 (Münster, 1980), pp. 23–51.

9 See n. 1.

10 See n. 4, and H. Rötting *et al.*, 'Braunschweig', in Meckseper, *Stadt im Wandel*, vol. 1, pp. 56–76; H. Rötting (ed.), 'Stadtarchäologie in Braunschweig. Ein fachübergreifender Arbeitsbericht zu den Grabungen 1976–1984', *Forschungen der Denkmalpflege in Niedersachsen*, 3 (Hameln, 1985).

11 See the articles in regional journals and periodicals for archaeology, history and history of arts.

12 See n. 1, and H. Lüdtke, 'Die Entdeckung einer mittelalterlichen Kirche unter dem Marktplatz von Schleswig', *Archäologisches Korrespondenzblatt*, 14 (1984), pp. 111–17.

13 See *ibid.*

14 I. Gabriel, 'Burg, Siedlung und Gräberfeld im frühmittelalterlichen Starigard' (Oldenburg in Holstein), *Archäologisches Korrespondenzblatt*, 5 (1975), pp. 225–30.

15 H. Hinz, 'Archäologische Beobachtungen in der Altstadt von Kiel', *Offa*, 29 (1972), pp. 172–221.

16 See n. 4, with bibliography. For Hannover, H. Plath, 'Die Anfänge der Stadt Hannover', *Hannoversche Geschichtsblätter*, NF, 15 (1961), pp. 169–216, and for Hamburg, R. Schindler, *Ausgrabungen in Alt-Hamburg. Neue Ergebnisse zur Frühgeschichte der Hansestadt* (Hamburg, 1958), are still the most comprehensive studies.

17 See nn. 4 and 10. Generally, W. A. van Es *et al.*, *Het bodemarchiev bedreigt. Archeologie en planologie in de binnensteden* (Amersfoort, 1983); C. Heighway, *The erosion of history. Archaeology and planning in towns. A study of historic towns affected by modern development in England, Wales and Scotland* (London, 1972).

18 See the articles by W. Hübener, particularly 'Archäologische Untersuchungen in Bardowick 1979–1982', *Hamburger Beiträge zur Archäologie*, 10 (Hamburg, 1983), and 'Zu den Anfängen von Bardowick', *Neue Ausgrabungen und Forschungen in Niedersachsen*, 17 (1986), pp. 201–18, with bibliography.

19 C. H. Seebach, 'Die Königspfalz Werla. Die baugeschichtlichen Untersuchungen', *Göttinger Schriften zur Vor- und Frühgeschichte*, 8 (Hildesheim, 1967); see also the article in *Deutsche Königspfalzen* (see n. 7).

20 P. Grim, *Tilleda. Eine Königspfalz am Kyffhäuser* (Magdeburg, 1968); P. Grimm, 'Zur Marktsiedlung Tilleda des 12./13. Jahrhunderts', *Ausgrabungen und Funde*, 25 (1980), pp. 273–86.

21 H. G. Griep, 'Ausgrabungen und Bodenfunde im Stadtgebiet Goslar', *Harz-zeitschrift*, 9 (1957), pp. 53–80; 35 (1983), pp. 1–54; and see n. 4.

22 See n. 4, with bibliography; unfortunately major publications are lacking.

23 See n. 4, with bibliography; also S. Schütte (ed.), *5 Jahre Stadtarchäologie. Das neue Bild des alten Göttingen* (Göttingen, 1984); H.-G. Stephan, 'Gedanken und Befunde zur Problematik der archäologischen Datierung von hochmittelalterlichen Stadtgründungen am Beispiel von Göttingen. Ein dendrochronologisches Datum zur Frühgeschichte von Göttingen', *Göttinger Jahrbuch*, 32 (1984), pp. 41–55.

24 A comprehensive study on town archaeology is still missing, but see U. Lobbedey, 'Mittelalterliche Archäologie als Quelle zur westfälischen Landesgeschichte', *Westfalen*, 51 (1973), pp. 33–46. Find-reports are in *Neujahrsgruss des Westfälischen Museums für Archäologie Münster*, 1ff (1981ff), and in the periodical *Ausgrabungen und Funde in Westfalen-Lippe*, 1ff (1984ff).

25 U. Lobbedey, in Barley, *European towns*.

26 For Paderborn see U. Lobbedey, in Jäger, 'Stadtkernforschung'.

27 Lobbedey, 'Mittelalterliche Archäologie', p. 45.

28 A catalogue about town archaeology in Minden was published by the Westfälisches Museumsamt in 1986.

29 See Lobbedey, 'Mittelalterliche Archäologie', pp. 37–9; and *Neujahrsgruss*, (1983), pp. 39–41 (1985), p. 60.

30 G. Isenberg, 'Soest', *Ausgrabungen und Funde in Westfalen-Lippe*, 1 (1984), pp. 203–7. Full reports on Soest are missing.

31 Lobbedey, 'Mittelalterliche Archäologie', p. 39.

32 W. Leidinger, 'Die Vor- und Frühgeschichte des Raumes Werl', *Soester Zeitschrift* (1969), pp. 5ff; Lobbedey, 'Mittelalterliche Archäologie'.

33 See n. 4, and H.-G. Stephan, 'Archäologische Beiträge zur Frühgeschichte der Stadt Höxter', *Münstersche Beiträge zur Vor- und Frühgeschichte*, 7 (Münster, 1973); H.-G. Stephan, 'Archäologische Stadtkernforschung in Höxter', *Kreis Höxter. Jahrbuch* (1981), pp. 135–51.

34 Publications on these activities are naturally mostly lacking but see the short reports in *Neujahrsgruss* since 1981, and in *Ausgrabungen und Funde in Westfalen-Lippe* since 1984.

35 The unpublished investigations in Billerbeck and Coesfeld were done by Wulf Holtmann and Peter Ilisch, both from Münster, who informed me about their results.

36 For this see the periodicals *Bonner Jahrbücher, Mainzer Jahrbuch, Trierer Jahrbuch* and catalogues, e.g., *Die Römer im Rheinland*.

37 Oswald, Schäfter and Sennhauser, 'Vorromanische Kirchenbauten'. G. P. Fehring, 'Missions- und Kirchenwesen in archäologischer Sicht', in H. Jankuhn and R. Wenskus, 'Geschichtswissenschaft und Archäologie', *Vorträge und Forschungen*, 22 (1979), pp. 547–91; G. P. Fehrung, 'Kirche und Burg in der Archäologie des Rheinlandes', *Kunst und Altertum am Rhein. Führer des Rheinischen Landesmuseums in Bonn*, 8 (Bonn, 1962).

38 The interpretation of 'Reihengräberfelder' and churches as indicators for settlement processes in the early Middle Ages was worked out by K. Böhner for the land in Trier and subsequently widely applied. With regard to early urban

development see K. Böhner, 'Germany (Rhineland)', in Barley, *European towns*, pp. 186–202. Although this method seems to be important and stimulating in some regards, it cannot compensate for archaeological investigations within the settlements themselves.

39 For Köln see Doppelfeld and Weyres, 'Die Ausgrabungen in Dom zu Köln'; Steuer, 'Spiegel des täglichen Lebens'; W. Lung, 'Zur Topographie der frühmittelalterlichen Kölner Altstadt', *Kölner Jahrbuch*, 2 (1956), pp. 54–70. For Duisburg see n. 40. For Aachen, Xanten, Neuss and Bonn see H. Borger, 'Die Entstehung der mittelalterlichen Stadt und der Alltag der Menschen im Mittelalter', in *Rhein und Maas*, 2 (Köln, 1973), pp. 129–42; H. Borger, 'Bemerkungen zu den Wachstumsstufen einiger mittelalterlicher Städte im Rheinland', in Landschaft und Geschichte, *Festschrift für Franz Petri zum 65. Geburtstag,* (Bonn, 1970), pp. 52–89, with bibliography. See also Fehring, 'Kirche und Burg'; Böhner, 'Germany (Rhineland)', in Barley, *European towns*; W. Janssen, in Clarke and Simms, *Urban origins*; and Oswald, Schäfer and Sennhauser, 'Vorromanische Kirchenbauten'. For Worms see M. Grünewald, 'Worms im Mittelalter', in C. Grimm (ed.), *Glück und Glas. Zur Kulturgeschichte des Spessartglases* (Würzburg, 1984), pp. 48–56.

40 For Duisburg see G. and E. Bindin, 'Archäologisch-Historische Untersuchungen zur Frühgeschichte Duisburgs', *Duisburger Forschungen*, 12 (Duisburg, 1969); G. Krause and J. Milz, *Duisburg im Mittelalter. 1100. Jahre Duisburg 883–1983*, Begleitschrift zur Ausstellung (Duisburg, 1983).

41 These excavations have been performed by the conservation staff of the municipal office occupied by prehistorians and art historians. See n. 2, and O. Stamm, 'Spätrömische und mittelalterliche Keramik der Altstadt Frankfurt am Main', *Schriften des Frankfurter Museums für Vor- und Frühgeschichte*, 1 (Frankfurt, 1962). W. Sage, 'Das Bürgerhaus in Frankfurt am Main', *Das Deutsche Bürgerhaus*, 2 (Frankfurt, 1959).

42 Some of the medieval finds from the town will be worked up in a Ph.D thesis. Early modern archaeological sources have only been recorded to a minor degree; see A. Junker, 'Frankfurt um 1600. Alltagsleben in der Stadt', *Kleine Schriften des Historischen Museums*, 7 (Frankfurt, 1980).

43 For Fulda see H. Hahn, 'Die Ausgrabungen am Fuldaer Domplatz 1953', in *Sankt Bonifatius, Gedenkausgabe zum 1200. Todestag* (Fulda, 1954), pp. 641–86; J. Vonderau, *Die Gründung des Klosters Fulda und seine Bauten bis zum Tode Sturms* (Fulda, 1944). For comments on recent unpublished excavations I thank H. Kirchhoff (Fulda) and J. Kulick (Wiesbaden).

44 For Lorsch see W. Selzer, *Das karolingische Reichskloster Lorsch* (Frankfurt, 1955). For Gelnhausen see F. Arens, 'Die staufischen Königspfalzen', in *Die Zeit der Staufer. Geschichte Kunst Kultur*, Katalog der Ausstellung Stuttgart 1977, vol. 3 (Stuttgart, 1977), pp. 129–42. For Hersfeld see a short paragraph in R. Gensen, 'Althessens Frühzeit: Frühgeschichtliche Fundstätten und Funde in Nordhessen', *Führer zur Hessischen Vor- und Frühgeschichte*, 1 (Frankfurt, 1979). For Büraburg and Holzheim see N. Wand, 'Die Büraburg bei Fritzlar. Burg – "Oppidum" – Bischofssitz in karolingischer Zeit', *Kasseler Beiträge zur Vor- und Frühgeschichte*, 4 (Kassel, 1974); J. H. Schotten, N. Wand and U. Weiss, 'Ausgrabungen in jüngerkaiserzeitlichen und früh- bis spätmittelalterli-

chen Siedlungsbereichen der Wüstung Holzheim bei Fritzlar, Schwalm-Eder-Kreis', *Fundberichte aus Hessen*, 17/18 (1980), pp. 213ff. For Geismar and Fritzlar see Gensen, 'Althessens Frühzeit'; and for the early period generally see H. Roth and E. Wamers (eds.), *Hessen im Frühmittelalter. Archäologie und Kunst*, Ausstellungskatalog (Frankfurt, 1984).

45 See n. 474, esp. Gensen, 'Althessens Frühzeit'; Roth and Wamers, *Hessen im Frühmittelalter;* and Schotten, Wand and Weiss, 'Ausgrabungen in jüngerkaiserzeitlichen', with bibliography.

46 For this see the publications of the 'Marburger Arbeitsgruppe für Bauforschung und Dokumentation', edited by the Stadtplanungsamt Marburg, and articles in *Jahrbuch für Hausforschung*, 32 (1981). Members of this working group have also been active in other Hessian towns.

47 See I. Scholkmann, 'Sindelfingen/Obere Vorstadt. Eine Siedlung des hohen und späten Mittelalters', *Forschungen der Archäologie des Mittelalters in Baden-Württemberg*, 3 (Stuttgart, 1978).

48 See G. Biegel (ed.), 'Ausgrabungen auf dem Augustinerplatz', *Museum für Ur- und Frühgeschichte. Die Kleine Ausstellung*, 1 (Stuttgart, 1983).

49 See H. Schäfter, in Jäger and Stoob, 'Stadtkernforschung'.

50 For this see the periodical *Forschungen und Berichte der Archäologie des Mittelalters in Baden-Württemberg*, 1 (1972), 8 (1983). D. Lutz, 'Die Archäologie des Mittelalters in Baden-Württemberg, Entwicklung und Aufgaben. Mit einer Bibliographie 1945–1975', *Forschungen und Berichte der Archäologie des Mittelalters in Baden-Württemberg*, 4 (1977), pp. 247–307; U. Lobbedey, 'Untersuchungen mittelalterlicher Keramik aus Süd-Westdeutschland', *Arbeiten zur Frühmittelalterforschung*, 3 (Münster, 1968). Some, but very restricted, activities have been carried out in places like Esslingen, Heilbronn, Heidelberg, Pforzheim, Ulm and Breisach. In Tübingen a volunteer group for town archaeology was recently set up. For Konstanz see J. Oexle, 'Stadtkernarchäologie in Konstanz', in *Der Keltenfürst von Hochdorf. Methoden und Ergebnisse der Landesarchäologie*, Ausstellung in Stuttgart, 1985 (Stuttgart, 1985), pp. 450–62; J. Oexle, 'Scherben sind Geschichte. Das Projekt Konstanz des Landesdenkmalamtes Baden-Württemberg stellt sich vor', *Alte und neue Funde zur Konstanzer Stadtarchäologie*', Ein Begleitheft zur Ausstellung im Rosgartenmuseum 1984 (Stuttgart, 1984).

51 See H. Dannheimer, 'Keramik des Mittalalters aus Bayern. Ein Katalog', *Jahresberichte der Bayerischen Bodendenkmalpflege* (München, 1973); W. Endres, 'Zum Stand der Keramikforschung in Süddeutschland vom 12./13. Jahrhundert an. – Mit einer Bibliographie', *Zeitschrift für Archäologie des Mittelalters*, 10 (1982).

52 See *Das Archäologische Jahr in Bayern* (1982), pp. 149–50.

53 The whole of the material is unpublished except for some recent finds, see R. Kahsnitz and R. Brandl, *Aus dem Wirtshaus zum Wilden Mann. Funde aus dem mittelalterlichen Nürnberg*, Eine Ausstellung des Germanischen Nationalmuseums (Nürnberg, 1984).

54 See the articles and find-reports in *Bayerisches Jahrbuch für Denkmalpflege*, the short reviews in *Das Archäologische Jahr in Bayern*, and W. Sage, in Jäger, 'Stadtkernforschung'.

55 See H. T. Fischer and S. Rieckhoff-Pauli, *Von den Römern zu den Bajuwaren.* *Stadtarchäologie in Regensburg* (Regensburg, 1982); W. Endres and V. Loers, *Spätmittelalterliche Keramik aus Regensburg. Neufunde in Prebrunn* (Regensburg, 1981). For comments on unpublished finds I have to thank W. Endres and U. Fischer (Regensburg).

56 It is to be hoped that the Roman period, the Middle Ages and early modern period will in future be documented equally well. See H. Bakker, in *Das Archäologische Jahr in Bayern* (1980), pp. 168–9; (1982), pp. 160–2; (1983), pp. 150–6.

57 See *Ausgrabungen in Deutschland*, vol. 2 (1975); B. U. Abels, W. Sage and C. Züchner, *Oberfranken in vor- und frühgeschichtlicher Zeit* (Bamberg, 1986).

58 W. Endres, 'Straubinger Keramik um 1600', *Jahresbericht des Historischen Vereins für Straubing und Umgebung*, 83 (1981), p. 86.

59 See the short articles in *Das Archäologische Jahr in Bayern.*

60 See the reviews of P. Grimm, 'Zum Stand der archäologischen Erforschung der Stadtentwicklung in der Deutschen Demokratischen Republik', in *Visby Symposion* (Stockholm, 1963, 1965); J. Herrmann, 'Archäologische Forschungen zur frühen Stadtentwicklung', *Ausgrabungen und Funde*, 21 (1976), pp. 168–77; J. Herrmann, 'Research into the early history of the town in the territory of the German Democratic Republic', in Barley, *European towns*, pp. 243–59.

61 For Quedlinburg see H. Wäscher, *Der Burgberg in Quedlinburg* (Quedlinburg, 1959).

62 For this and other Saxon towns see J. Herrmann and P. Donat (eds.), *Corpus archäologischer Quellen zur Frühgeschichte auf dem Gebiet der DDR (7. bis 12. Jahrhundert)*, vol. 1 (Berlin, 1973), vol. 2 (Berlin, 1979), pp. 323–8.

63 For these towns see my critical review: H. Steuer, 'Bestandsaufnahme der archäologischen Forschungsergebnisse zur Stadt des Mittelalters und ihren Ursprüngen', *Siedlungsforschung*, 4 (1986), pp. 225–37, and Janssen, in Clarke and Simms, *Urban origins.*

64 See n. 20, and P. Grimm, 'Archäologische Beiträge zur Lage ottonischer Marktsiedlungen in den Bezirken Halle und Magdeburg', *Jahresschrift für Mitteldeutsche Vorgeschichte*, 41/2 (1958), pp. 519–42.

65 Until now there have been only short reports published about the Brandenburg excavations: see K. Grebe, 'Die Ergebnisse der Grabung Brandenburg', in *Berichte über den II. Internationalen Kongress für slawische Archäologie*, vol. 3 (Berlin, 1973), pp. 269–78, and numerous find-reports in *Ausgrabungen und Funde.*

66 For urban development during the twelfth and following centuries in Germany see R. Hoffman, 'Die Stadtkernforschungen in Potsdam in den Jahren 1958–1960', *Ausgrabungen und Funde*, 6 (1961), pp. 143–53; G. Mangelsdorf, 'Mittelalterliche Siedlungsaufschlüsse des 14. Jahrhunderts aus der Neustadt Brandenburg', *Ausgrabungen und Funde*, 26 (1981), pp. 109–13; H. Küas, *Das alte Leipzig in archäologischer Sicht* (Berlin, 1976); E. W. Huth, *Die Entstehung und Entwicklung der Stadt Frankfurt (Oder) und ihr Kulturbild vom 13. bis zum frühen 17. Jahrhundert auf Grund archäologischer Befunde* (Berlin, 1975); H. Mechelk, *Zur Frühgeschichte der Stadt Dresden und zur Herausbildung einer spätmittelalterlichen Keramikproduktion im sächsischen Elbegebiet aufgrund archäologischer Befunde* (Berlin, 1981); E. Müller-Mertens, 'Untersuchungen

zur Geschichte der brandenburgischen Städte im Mittelalter', *Wissenschaftliche Zeitschrift*, Berlin GDR 5 (1955/6), pp. 191–222, 271–307; 6 (1956/7), pp. 1–28; C. and F. Plate, 'Untersuchungen auf der Stadtwüstung Freyenstein, Kr. Wittstock, Bezirk Potsdam', *Ausgrabungen und Funde*, 27 (1982), pp. 89–94; W. Schich, 'Stadtwerdung im Raum zwischen Elbe und Oder im Übergang von der slawischen zur deutschen Periode', in W. Fritze (ed.), *Germania Slavica I, Berliner Historische Studien*, 1 (Berlin, 1980), pp. 191–238.

67 A. von Müller, 'Zur Entwicklung der Stadt Spandau im frühen und hohen Mittelalter', in W. Fritze and K. Zernack (eds.), *Grundfragen der geschichtlichen Beziehungen zwischen Deutschen, Polaben und Polen* (Berlin, 1976), pp. 86–117, with bibliography.

68 K. Riehm, 'Das Salzsiedergebiet Halla und das Karolingische Kastell am Giebichenstein', *Jahresschrift für Mitteldeutsche Vorgeschichte*, 58 (1974), pp. 295–320.

69 H. Strecher and U. Lappe, 'Stadtkernforschung in Erfurt', *Ausgrabungen und Funde*, 24 (1979), pp. 246–53.

70 Good examples for this are Dresden, Leipzig, Frankfurt an der Oder, Chemnitz and other less important towns. H. J. Vogt, 'Archäologische Stadtkernforschung in Sachsen', in K. H. Kerrmann (ed.), *Siedlung, Burg und Stadt*, Festschrift für Paul Grimm (Berlin, 1969), pp. 248–57.

6 Recent developments in early medieval urban history and archaeology in England

1 H. Clarke, *The archaeology of medieval England* (London, 1984). p. 172.

2 C. Stephenson, *Borough and town: a study of urban origins in England* (Cambridge, 1933); J. Tait, *The medieval English borough* (Manchester, 1936).

3 S. Reynolds, *An introduction to the history of English medieval towns* (Oxford, 1977), pp. ix–x.

4 M. Biddle, 'Towns', in D. M. Wilson (ed.), *The archaeology of Anglo-Saxon England* (London, 1976), p. 100.

5 M. Todd, 'The small towns of Roman Britain', *Britannia*, 1 (1970), pp. 114–30; W. Rodwell and T. Rowley, *The 'small towns' of Roman Britain*, British Archaeological Reports, 15 (1975); P. Salway, *Roman Britain* (Oxford, 1981), pp. 593–7.

6 P. A. Barker, 'Excavations on the site of the Baths Basilica at Wroxeter; an interim report', *Britannia*, 6 (1975), pp. 106–17.

7 T. Tatton-Brown, 'The towns of Kent', in J. Haslam (ed.), *Anglo-Saxon towns in southern England* (Chichester, 1984), p. 5; C. Heighway, 'Anglo-Saxon Gloucester to A.D. 1000', in M. L. Faull (ed.), *Studies in late Anglo-Saxon settlement* (Oxford, 1984), pp. 35–9.

8 M. Biddle, 'The development of the Anglo-Saxon town', *Settimane di Studio del Centro Italiano di studi sull'alto medioevo*, 21 (Spoleto, 1974), pp. 205–12.

9 W. Rodwell, 'Churches in the landscape: aspects of topography and planning', in Faull, *Studies in late Anglo-Saxon settlement*, pp. 3–12.

10 J. Campbell, 'Bede's words for places', in P. H. Sawyer (ed.), *Places, names and graves* (Leeds, 1979), pp. 34–53; M. Hunter, 'Germanic and Roman an-

tiquity and the sense of the past in Anglo-Saxon England', *Anglo-Saxon England*, 3 (1974), pp. 35–7.

11 H. Pirenne, *Medieval cities* (New York, 1956), especially pp. 39–53; see also F. L. Ganshof, *Étude sur le développement des villes entre Loire et Rhin au moyen age* (Paris and Brussels, 1943).

12 P. Holdsworth, 'Saxon Southampton; a new review', *Medieval Archaeology*, 20 (1976), pp. 26–61; P. Holdsworth, *Excavations at Melbourne Street, Southampton, 1971–76*, Council for British Archaeology Research Report, no. 33 (London, 1980); K. Wade, *Origins of Ipswich* (Ipswich, 1981); A. Vince, 'The Aldwych: mid-Saxon London discovered?', *Current Archaeology*, no. 93 (1984), pp. 310–12; M. Biddle, D. Hudson and C. Heighway, *The future of London's past* (Worcester, 1973); A. Carter, 'The Anglo-Saxon origins of Norwich: the problems and approaches', *Anglo-Saxon England*, 7 (1978), pp. 175–204; Biddle, 'Towns', pp. 112–16.

13 D. Pelteret, 'Slave raiding and slave trading in early England', *Anglo-Saxon England*, 9 (1981), pp. 99–114.

14 D. Hill, 'The Burghal Hidage: the establishment of a text', *Medieval Archaeology*, 13 (1967), pp. 84–92; N. Brooks, 'England in the ninth century: the crucible of defeat', *Transactions of the Royal Historical Society*, 5th ser., 29 (1979), pp. 1–20; R. H. C. Davis, 'Alfred and Guthrum's frontier', *English Historical Review*, 97 (1982), pp. 803–10.

15 P. V. Addyman and M. Biddle, 'Medieval Cambridge: recent finds and excavations', *Proceedings of the Cambridge Antiquarian Society*, 58 (1965), pp. 74–137; Carter, 'Anglo-Saxon origins of Norwich'.

16 H. C. Darby, *Domesday England* (Cambridge, 1977), pp. 364–8.

17 N. Brooks, *The early history of the Church of Canterbury* (Leicester, 1984), p. 27.

18 M. O. H. Carver, 'Three Saxo-Norman tenements in Durham City', *Medieval Archaeology*, 23 (1979), pp. 1—80: D. Perring, *Early medieval occupation at Flaxengate, Lincoln*, Lincoln Archaeological Trust (1981); R. A. Hall (ed.), *Viking Age York and the north*, Council for British Archaeology Research Report, no. 27 (London, 1978).

19 H. K. Kenward *et al.*, 'The environment of Anglo-Scandinavian York', in Hall, *Viking Age York*.

20 H. R. Loyn, *Anglo-Saxon England and the Norman Conquest* (London, 1962), pp. 93–4.

21 M. Biddle and D. Hill, 'Late Saxon planned towns', *Antiquaries Journal*, 51 (1971), pp. 70–85.

22 R. Hodges, *Dark Age economics: the origins of towns and trade, A.D. 600–1000* (London, 1982), p. 198.

23 P. H. Sawyer, 'Kings and merchants', in P. H. Sawyer and I. N. Wood (eds.), *Early medieval kingship* (Leeds, 1977), pp. 139–58.

24 J. Campbell, 'Observations on English government from the tenth to the twelfth century', *Transactions of the Royal Historical Society*, 5th ser., 25 (1975), pp. 39–54.

25 Holdsworth, 'Saxon Southampton', p. 60.

26 D. M. Metcalf, 'Monetary affairs in Mercia in the time of Aethelbald', in A. Dornier (ed.), *Mercian studies* (Leicester, 1977), pp. 87–106.

27 N. P. Brooks, 'The unidentified forts of the Burghal Hidage', *Medieval Archaeology*, 8 (1964), pp. 74–90.

28 B. Durham, 'Archaeological investigations in St. Aldates, Oxford', *Oxoniensia*, 42 (1977), pp. 176–83; Brooks, *Early history of the Church of Canterbury*, pp. 27–36; H. B. Clarke and C. C. Dyer, 'Anglo-Saxon and early Norman Worcester: the documentary evidence', *Transactions of the Worcestershire Archaeological Society*, 3rd ser., 2 (1968–9), pp. 28–9; Heighway, 'Anglo-Saxon Gloucester', pp. 39–40.

29 J. H. Williams, 'A review of some aspects of late Saxon urban origins and development', in Faull, *Studies in late Anglo-Saxon settlement*, pp. 30–2.

30 G. Duby, *The early growth of the European economy* (London, 1974); R. Fossier, *L'Enfance de L'Europe* (Paris, 1982).

31 T. Rowley (ed.), *The origins of open-field agriculture* (London, 1981), pp. 34–8, 98–102.

32 P. Wade-Martins, *Village sites in Launditch Hundred*, East Anglian Archaeology, no. 10 (1980), pp. 24–86.

33 P. H. Sawyer, 'The wealth of England in the eleventh century', *Transactions of the Royal Historical Society*, 5th ser., 15 (1965), pp. 145–64.

34 J. G. Hurst, 'The pottery', in Wilson, *Archaeology of Anglo-Saxon England*, pp. 283–348; C. Mahaney *et al.*, *Excavations in Stamford, Lincolnshire 1963–1969*, Society for Medieval Archaeology, Monograph no. 9 (London, 1982), pp. 9–10; F. A. Pritchard, 'Late Saxon textiles from the City of London', *Medieval Archaeology*, 28 (1984), pp. 46–76.

35 R. H. Hilton, 'Small town society in England before the Black Death', *Past and Present*, 105 (1984), pp. 53–78.

36 The role of the royal tun is emphasized in Haslam, *Anglo-Saxon towns in southern England*, pp. 87–147.

37 J. Haslam, 'A middle Saxon iron smelting site at Ramsbury, Wiltshire', *Medieval Archaeology*, 24 (1980), pp. 1–68.

38 P. H. Sawyer, 'The royal *tun* in pre-conquest England', in P. Wormald *et al.* (eds.), *Ideal and reality in Frankish and Anglo-Saxon society* (Oxford, 1983), pp. 273–99.

39 R. H. Hilton, 'The small town and urbanisation: Evesham in the middle ages', *Midland History*, 7 (1982), pp. 1–8.

7 Urban archaeology in Germany and the study of topographic, functional and social structures

1 General studies on the history and archaeology of early medieval towns in Europe:
   a. The problem of definition: M. Weber, 'Die Stadt. Begriff und Kategorien', in M. Weber, *Wirtschaft und Gesellschaft. Grundriss der verstehenden Soziologie* (5th edn, Tübingen, 1972), pp. 727–41; now printed in C. Haase (ed.), 'Die Stadt des Mittelalters – Begriff, Entstehung und Ausbreitung', *Wege der Forschung*, vol. 243 (Darmstadt, 1969), pp. 34–59; H. Callies, 'Der Stadtbegriff bei Max Weber', in H. Jankuhn, W. Schlesinger and H. Steuer (eds.), 'Vor- und Frühformen der europäischen Stadt im Mittelalter', *Abhandlungen*

der Akademie der Wissenschaften in Göttingen, phil.-hist., Kl., 3, 83 (2nd edn, Göttingen, 1975), pp. 56–60; Edith Ennen, *Die europäische Stadt des Mittelalters* (3rd edn, Göttingen, 1979), pp. 13–16; H. Stoob, 'Die hochmittelalterliche Städtebildung im Okzident', in H. Stoob (ed.), *Die Stadt. Gestalt und Wandel bis zum industriellen Zeitalter* (Köln/Wien, 1979), pp. 131–78; F. Kolb, *Die Stadt im Altertum* (München, 1984), pp. 11–17.

b. Towns as central places: D. Denecke, 'Der geographische Stadtbegriff und die räumlich-funktionale Betrachtungsweise bei Siedlungstypen mit zentraler Bedeutung in Anwendung auf historische Siedlungsepochen', in Jankuhn, Schlesinger and Steuer, 'Vor- und Frühformen der europäischen Stadt im Mittelalter', pp. 33–55.

c. Fortified or not fortified 'suburbia': W. Schlesinger, 'Der Markt als Frühform der deutschen Stadt', in Jankuhn, Schlesinger and Steuer, in 'Vor- und Frühformen der europäischen Stadt im Mittelalter', pp. 262–93; *idem*, 'Zur Frühgeschichte des norddeutschen Städtewesens', *Lüneburger Blätter*, 17 (1966), pp. 5–22; *idem*, 'Stadt und Vorstadt', in E. Maschke and J. Sydow (eds.), 'Stadterweiterung und Vorstadt', *Veröffentlichungen der Kommission f. geschichtliche Landeskunde in Baden-Württemberg*, B 51 (Stuttgart, 1969), pp. 1–20; *idem*, 'Vorstufen des Städtewesens im Ottonischen Sachsen', in W. Besch, K. Fehn, D. Höroldt *et al.* (eds.), *Die Stadt in der europäischen Geschichte*, Festschrift f. Edith Ennen (Bonn, 1972), pp. 234–58; H. Brachmann, 'Zu einigen Aspekten der Produktivkräfte-Entwicklung im frühen Mittelalter am Beispiel und auf der Grundlage der Forschungen zu den sächsischen Bistumssitzen des 9. Jahrunderts', in F. Horst and B. Krüger (eds.), *Produktivkräfte und Produktionsverhältnisse in ur- und frühgeschichtlicher Zeit* (Berlin, 1985), pp. 339–54.

d. Prototowns and early towns: Jankuhn, Schlesinger and Steuer, 'Vor- und Frühformen der europäischen Stadt im Mittelalter'; T. Mayer (ed.), 'Studien zu den Anfängen des europäischen Städtewesens', *Vorträge und Forschungen*, 4 (4th edn, Konstanz/Lindau, 1975); M. W. Barley (ed.), *European towns: their archaeology and early history* (London, 1977); H. B. Clarke and A. Simms (eds.), *The comparative history of urban origins in non-Roman Europe*, British Arch. Reports, International Series 225 (Oxford, 1985); L. Klappauf and K. Wilhelmi, 'Stadtkernarchäologie in Niedersachsen', *Berichte zur Denkmalpflege in Niedersachsen*, 3, 1 (1983), pp. 28–34. H.-G. Stephan, 'Archäologische Stadtforschung in Niedersachsen, Ostwestfalen, Hamburg und Bremen', in C. Meckseper (ed.), *Stadt im Wandel*, vol. 3 (Stuttgart, 1983), pp. 29–75.

e. High medieval urban development: E. Herzog, *Die ottonische Stadt* (Berlin, 1964); C. Meckseper, *Kleine Kunstgeschichte der deutschen Stadt im Mittelalter* (Darmstadt, 1982), pp. 32–59, 97–8; B. Schwineköper, *Königtum und Städte bis zum Ende des Investiturstreites* (Sigmaringen, 1977); T. Hall, *Mittelalterliche Stadtgrundrisse. Versuch einer Übersicht der Entwicklung in Deutschland und Frankreich* (Stockholm, 1978).

f. Review on recent research: H. Steuer, 'Zum Stand der archäologisch-historischen Stadtforschung in Europa – Bericht über ein Kolloquium 1982 in Münster', *Zeitschrift für Archäologie des Mittelalters*, 12 (1984), pp. 35–72.

2 G. P. Fehring, 'Der Beitrag der Archäologie zum "Leben in der Stadt des späten Mittelalters"', in H. Appelt (ed.), 'Das Leben in der Stadt des Spätmittelalters', *Veröffentlichungen des Instituts für mittelalterliche Realienkunde Österreichs*, 2 (Wien, 1977), pp. 9–35; J. G. N. Renaud (ed.), Symposium 'De middeleeuwse stad en de kwaliteit van het bestaan', *Rotterdam Papers*, 4 (Rotterdam, 1982); *Aus dem Alltag der mittelalterlichen Stadt*, Handbuch zur Sonderausstellung im Bremer Landesmuseum für Kunst und Kulturgeschichte (Bremen, 1982); H. Steuer, 'Zur Erforschung des Alltagslebens im mittelalterlichen Köln', in H. Kier and U. Krings (eds.), 'Köln. Die Romanischen Kirchen', *Stadtspuren*, vol. 1 (Köln, 1984), pp. 79–109; H. Kühnel (ed.), *Alltag im Spätmittelalter*, 2nd edn (Graz, 1985); 'Zur Lebensweise in der Stadt um 1200 – Ergebnisse der Mittelalter-Archäologie', *Zeitschrift für Archäologie des Mittelalters Beiheft*, 4 (Bonn/Köln, 1986).

3 Cf. the wooden houses in Haithabu, ninth and tenth centuries, and the stone houses in Zürich, thirteenth century: K. Schietzel, 'Die Baubefunde in Haithabu', in H. Jankuhn, K. Schietzel and H. Reichstein (eds.), *Archäologische und naturwissenschaftliche Untersuchungen an ländlichen und frühstädtischen Siedlungen im deutschen Küstengebiet vom 5. Jahrhundert vor Chr. bis zum 11. Jahrhundert nach Chr.*, vol. 2: *Handelsplätze des frühen und hohen Mittelalters* (Weinheim, 1984), pp. 135–58; J. Schneider *et al.*, 'Der Münsterhof in Zürich. Bericht über die Stadtkernforschungen 1977/78', *Schweizer Beiträge zur Kulturgeschichte und Archäologie des Mittelalters*, 9 (1982), pp. 75–120.

4 H. Rötting, 'Stadtarchäologie in Braunschweig. Ein fachübergreifender Arbeitsbericht zu den Grabungen 1976–1984', *Forschungen der Denkmalpflege in Niedersachsen*, 3 (Hameln, 1985), pp. 100–8.

5 B. Herrmann, 'Parasitologische Untersuchung mittelalterlicher Kloaken', in B. Herrmann (ed.), *Mensch und Umwelt im Mittelalter* (Stuttgart, 1986), pp. 160–9; E. Hess and C. Breer, 'Bakteriologische Untersuchung des Inhaltes der Fäkaliengrube 4', in Schneider *et al.*, 'Der Münsterhof in Zürich', p. 282.

6 Meckseper, *Stadt im Wandel*, vol. 1, pp. 206–10, 218–23, 677.

7 Stoob, 'Die hochmittelalterliche Städtebildung im Okzident', p. 142.

8 Steuer, 'Zum Stand der archäologisch-historischen Stadtforschung in Europa', according to H. Stoob.

9 *Deutscher Städteatlas*, ed. Institut für vergleichende Städtegeschichte, Münster (Dortmund, 1973ff.).

10 W. A. van Es and W. J. H. Verwers, s.v. 'Dorestad', in *Reallexikon der germanischen Altertumskunde*, vol. 6 (Berlin, 1985), pp. 65–76.

11 K. Schietzel, 'Stand der siedlungsarchäologischen Forschung in Haithabu – Ergebnisse und Probleme', *Berichte über die Ausgrabungen in Haithabu*, 16 (1981), pp. 45, 82.

12 V. Vogel, 'Die archäologischen Ausgrabungen im Stadtkern von Schleswig', *Ausgrabungen in Deutschland, Monographien des Römisch-Germanischen Zentralmuseums*, 1, 3 (Mainz, 1975), pp. 72–86; *idem*, 'Archäologische Stadtkernforschung in Schleswig 1969–1982', *Ausgrabungen in Schleswig – Berichte und Studien*, 1 (Neumünster, 1983), pp. 9–54.

13 K. Böhner, 'Bonn im frühen Mittelalter', *Bonner Jahrbücher*, 178 (1978), pp. 395–426; E. Nickel, 'Magdeburg in karolingisch-ottonischer Zeit', *Zeitschrift*

für Archäologie, 7 (1973), pp. 102–42.

14 E. Nickel, *Der Alte Markt in Magdeburg* (Berlin, 1964).

15 Stephan, 'Archäologische Stadtforschung', 'Verden', p. 34; H. Hinz, 'Archäologische Beobachtungen in der Altstadt von Kiel', *Offa*, 29 (1972), pp. 172–221.

16 H. Härke, 'Die Grabungen des Jahres 1976 auf dem Münsterplatz in Neuss', *Bonner Jahrbücher*, 180 (1980), pp. 493–571, especially 552–65.

17 Rötting, *Stadtarchäologie in Braunschweig*, pp. 113–19, 235.

18 W. Erdmann, 'Fronerei und Fleischmarkt: Archäologische Befunde eines Platzes im Marktviertel des mittelalterlichen Lübeck (Vorbericht I)' *Lübecker Schriften zur Archäologie und Kulturgeschichte*, 3 (1980), pp. 107–59, Fig. 50; J. Herrmann and P. Donat (eds.), 'Corpus archäologischer Quellen zur Frühgeschichte auf dem Gebiet der DDR (7. bis 12. Jahrhundert)', vol. 1 (Berlin, 1973), No. 27/78: Magdeburg, p. 250.

19 B. Schwineköper, 'Zu den topographischen Grundlagen der Freiburger Stadtgründung', in W. Müller (ed.), *Freiburg im Mittelalter* (Bühl/Baden, 1970), pp. 7–23; H. Keller, 'Die Zähringer und die Entwicklung Freiburgs zur Stadt', in K. Schmid (ed.), *Die Zähringer. Eine Tradition und ihre Erforschung*, Veröff. zur Zähringer-Ausstellung, vol. 1 (Sigmaringen, 1986), pp. 17–29; H. Keller, 'Über den Charakter Freiburgs in der Frühzeit der Stadt', in H. Maurer and H. Patze (eds.), *Festschrift für B. Schwineköper* (Sigmaringen, 1982), pp. 249–82; H. Schadek and K. Schmid (eds.), *Die Zähringer, Anstoss und Wirkung*, Veröff. zur Zähringer-Ausstellung, vol. 2 (Sigmaringen, 1986), pp. 224–32.

20 P. Hofer, B. Gassner, J. Mathez and B. Furrer, 'Der Kellerplan der Berner Altstadt. Aufnahme eines Stadtplans auf Kellerniveau', *Schriften der Historisch-Antiquarischen Kommission der Stadt Bern*, 4 (1982); R. Koch, 'Die Keller im Bereich der Pfalz Wimpfen', *Forschungen und Berichte der Archäologie des Mittelalters in Baden-Württemberg*, 8 (1983), pp. 383–96; H. Schäfer, 'Burg, Schloss und Stadt Marbach am Neckar', *Denkmalpflege in Baden-Württemberg*, 9 (1980), pp. 59–69; L. Schmidt, 'Kulturdenkmale in der Freiburger Altstadt', *Denkmalpflege in Baden-Württemberg*, 12 (1983), pp. 169–78; J. E. Schneider, 'Zürichs Weg zur Stadt', in *Nobile Turegum multarum copia rerum. Drei Aufsätze zum mittelalterlichen Zürich* (Zürich, 1982), pp. 3–20; A. Fuhs, 'Ein Beitrag zur Methodik der Kellerforschung. Studien zur Topographie Gelnhausens', *Hessisches Jahrbuch für Landesgeschichte*, 7 (1957), pp. 165.

21 K. Günther, 'Die Stadtwüstung Landsberg bei Wolfshagen', *Zeitschrift des Vereins für hessische Geschichte und Landeskunde*, 77/8 (1966/7), pp. 71–124; H. Stoob, 'Blankenrode', in *Führer zu vor- und frühgeschichtlichen Denkmälern*, 20 (Mainz, 1971), pp. 261–7; B. U. Hucker, 'Die untergegangene Bergstadt Blankenrode im Diemel-Eder-Kupfererzrevier. Beobachtungen zum Problem abgegangener Bergstädte', *Der Anschnitt*, 37 (1985) pp. 103–10; U. Lobbedey, 'Eine Grabung in der Stadtwüstung Blankenrode', *Westfalen*, 61 (1983), pp. 20–4; D. Lutz, 'Die Archäologie des Mittelalters in der Denkmalpflege, dargestellt an einigen Beispielen aus dem Regierungsbezirk Karlsruhe', *Denkmalpflege in Baden-Württemberg*, 4 (1975), pp. 67–77, 69: Rockesberg; D. Lutz, 'Die Archäologie des Mittelalters', *Archäologische Ausgrabungen in Baden-Württemberg 1984* (Stuttgart, 1985), pp. 187–99, 192: Rockesberg; C. and F. Plate, 'Untersuchungen auf der Stadtwüstung Freyenstein, Kr. Wittstock, Bezirk Pots-

dam', *Ausgrabungen und Funde*, 27 (1982), pp. 89–94; H. Amman and R. Metz, 'Die Bergstadt Prinzbach im Schwarzwald', *Alemannisches Jahrbuch* (1956), pp. 282–313.

22　N. Wand, 'Die Büraburg bei Fritzlar. Burg – "Oppidum" – Bischofssitz in karolingischer Zeit', *Kasseler Beiträge zur Vor- und Frühgeschichte*, 4 (1974); R. Gensen, 'Christenburg, Burgwald und Amöneburger Becken in der merowingisch-karolingischen Zeit', *Althessen im Frankenreich, Nationes*, 2 (Sigmaringen, 1975), pp. 121–72.

23　U. Lobbedey, 'Northern Germany', in Barley, *European towns*, pp. 127–57; W. Janssen, 'The origins of the non-Roman town in Germany', in Clarke and Simms, *Urban origins*, pp. 217–35.

24　The example of Köln: A. Steuer, 'Köln in Mittelalter und Neuzeit – Geschichte und Stadtbild', *Führer zu vor- und frühgeschichtlichen Denkmälern*, 37/1: Köln (Mainz, 1980), pp. 219–32.

25　H. Steuer, 'Historisch-archäologische Stadtforschung im römischen und mittelalterlichen Köln', in H. Jäger (ed.), 'Stadtkernforschung', *Städteforschung*, A 27 (Köln, 1988), pp. 61–102; *Deutscher Städteatlas*, vol. 2, 6, Blatt Köln, Veröffentlichung des Instituts für vergleichende Städtegeschichte (Münster, 1979).

26　P. Grimm, *Tilleda. Eine Königspfalz am Kyffhäuser*, vol. 1: *Die Hauptburg* (Berlin, 1968); *idem*, 'Beiträge zu Handel und Handwerk in der Vorburg der Pfalz Tilleda', *Zeitschrift für Archäologie*, 6 (1972), pp. 104–47; *idem*, 'Die untere Vorburg der Pfalz Tilleda', *Zeitschrift für Archäologie*, 10 (1976), pp. 261–306.

27　Koch, 'Die Keller im Bereich der Pfalz Wimpfen'; M. Remmele, 'Die Entwicklung der mittelalterlichen Stadtbefestigung von Wimpfen am Berg', *Forschungen und Berichte der Archäologie des Mittelalters in Baden-Württemberg*, 8 (1983), pp. 423–42.

28　W. A. van Es and W. J. H. Verwers, *Excavations at Dorestadt I. The Harbour: Hoogstraat*, vol. 1 (Amersfoort, 1980); *idem*, *Reallexikon der germanischen Altertumskunde*, p. 71.

29　Schietzel, 'Stand der siedlungsarchäologischen Forschung in Haithabu', pp. 94–7.

30　Vogel, 'Die archäologischen Ausgrabungen', pp. 23–5; *idem*, 'Die Anfänge des Schleswiger Hafens', *Ausgrabungen in Schleswig, 7. Bericht, Beiträge zur Schleswiger Stadtgeschichte*, 22 (1977), pp. 21–8.

31　The Roman wooden quay: S. Neu, 'Die Ausgrabungen zwischen Dom und Rhein', *Ausgrabungen im Rheinland 1981/82* (Bonn/Köln, 1983), pp. 251–9; the medieval waterfront: city prospect by Anton Woensam (1531) and by Arnold Mercator (1570/1). The oldest painting by the 'Meister der Kleinen Passion' from *ca.* 1411: *Das Martyrium der Heiligen Ursula vor der Stadt Köln*, cf. H. Berger and F. G. Zehnder, *Köln, Die Stadt als Kunstwerk. Stadtansichten vom 15. bis 20. Jahrhundert* (Köln, 1982), p. 66.

32　J. Oexle, 'Felix mater Constantia?', *Archäologie in Deutschland*, 4 (1985), pp. 20–3; *idem*, 'Die Grabungen im Salmansweilerhof zu Konstanz', in *Archäologische Ausgrabungen in Baden-Württemberg 1985* (Stuttgart, 1986), pp. 228–35; *idem*, 'Stadtkernarchäologie in Konstanz', in *Der Keltenfürst von Hochdorf. Methoden und Ergebnisse der Landesarchäologie* (Stuttgart, 1985), pp. 450–4.

33　W. Erdmann, 'Hochmittelalterliche Baugrundgewinnung in Lübeck und das

Problem der Lokalisierung beider Gründungssiedlungen: Erste Befunde aus den Gebieten Grosse Petersgrube und An der Untertrave', *Lübecker Schriften zur Archäologie und Kulturgeschichte*, 6 (Bonn, 1982), pp. 7–31.

34 R. Schindler, *Ausgrabungen in Alt-Hamburg. Neue Ergebnisse zur Frühgeschichte der Hansestadt* (Hamburg, 1958), p. 146; Stephan, 'Archäologische Stadtforschung', p. 30.

35 Rötting, *Stadtarchäologie in Braunschweig*, p. 25.

36 Steuer, 'Historisch-archäologische Stadtforschung im römischen und mittelalterlichen Köln'.

37 H. Plath, 'Die Anfänge der Stadt Hannover', *Hannoversche Geschichtsblätter*, NF, 15 (1961), pp. 169–216, especially p. 15.

38 G. Krause, 'Archäologische Zeugnisse zum mittelalterlichen Duisburg', in *Duisburg im Mittelalter: 1100 Jahre Duisburg 883–1983*, Begleitschrift zur Ausstellung (Duisburg, 1983), pp. 23–77.

39 K. Grewe, 'Zur Wasserversorgung und Abwasserentsorgung in der Stadt um 1200', in 'Zur Lebensweise in der Stadt um 1200'.

40 Stephen, 'Archäologische Stadtforschung'; Schindler, *Ausgrabungen in Alt-Hamburg*, p. 16.

41 S. Schütte, 'Das Haus eines mittelalterlichen Knochenschnitzers an der Johannisstrasse in Göttingen', *Göttinger Jahrbuch*, 26 (1978), pp. 55–62.

42 Köln: W. Herborn, 'Sozialtopographie des Kölner Kirchspiels St. Kolumba im ausgehenden 13. Jahrhundert', in H. Kellenbenz (ed.), *Zwei Jahrtausende Kölner Wirtschaft*, vol. 1 (Köln, 1975), pp. 205–15; *Führer zu vor- und frühgeschichtlichen Denkmälern*, vol. 37/1 (Mainz, 1980), p. 224; Lübeck: R. Hammel, 'Sozial- und wirtschaftsgeschichtliche Untersuchungen zum Grundeigentum in Lübeck im 14. Jahrhundert. Ein Zwischenbericht', *Lübecker Schriften zur Archäologie und Kulturgeschichte*, 4 (Lübeck, 1980), pp. 31–65, figs. 3–6; Hannover: Annemarie Büscher, W. Gläseker, L. Klappauf and M. H. Schormann, 'Die Ausgrabung 1982 am Bohlendamm zu Hannover. Vorbericht und stadtgeschichtliche Zusammenhänge', *Nachrichten aus Niedersachsens Urgeschichte*, 53 (1984), pp. 133–82; Göttingen: H. Steenweg, 'Berufstopographie Göttingens um 1459', *Historisch-archäologische Stadtführungen in Göttingen. Materialien*, 2 (Göttingen, 1985), p. 13.

43 J. Oexle, 'Würfel- und Paternosterhersteller im Mittelalter', in *Der Keltenfürst von Hochdorf. Methoden und Ergebnisse der Landesarchäologie* (Stuttgart, 1985), pp. 455–62.

44 H. Steuer, 'Ein Handwerkerviertel am Rheinufer in Köln', *Ausgrabungen im Rheinland 1981/82* (Köln/Bonn, 1983), pp. 286–7; *idem*, 'Spiegel des täglichen Lebens. Archäologische Funde des Mittelalters aus Köln' (Köln, 1982), pp. 29–30.

45 Gabriele Isenberg, 'Mittelalterliche Salzgewinnung in Soest. Ein Vorbericht über die Ausgrabungen auf dem Kohlbrink 1981–1982', *Soester Zeitschrift*, 95 (1983), pp. 25–33; *idem*, in *Neujahrsgruss 1983-Jahresbericht für 1982-Westfälisches Museum für Archäologie, Amt für Bodendenkmalpflege* (Münster, 1983), pp. 41–4; G. Billig, 'Vorbericht über die Stadtkerngrabung im Domhof von Halle (Saale)', *Ausgrabungen und Funde*, 6 (1963), pp. 52–9; L. Süss, *Die frühmittelalterliche Saline von Bad Nauheim* (Frankfurt a.M., 1978).

46 B. Beckmann, 'Der Scheroenhügel in der Siegburger Aulgasse', *Rheinische Aus-grabungen*, 16 (Bonn, 1975); W. Herborn, 'Die wirtschaftliche und soziale Bedeutung und die politische Stellung der Siegburger Töpfer', *Rheinisches Jahrbuch für Volkskunde*, 24 (1982), pp. 127–62.

47 S. Schütte, 'Zu Architektur und Funktion des mittelalterlichen Bürgerhauses in Nordwestdeutschland unter besonderer Berücksichtigung von Beispielen aus Göttingen', in Herrmann, *Mensch und Umwelt*, pp. 180–93.

48 Basel: P. Lavicka and D. Rippmann, 'Hochmittelalterliche Bürgerhäuser in Basel', *Archäologie der Schweiz*, 8 (1985), pp. 109–16; Zürich: J. E. Schneider and Th. M. Kohler, 'Mittelalterliche Fensterformen an Zürcher Bürgerhäusern. Ein Beitrag zur Monumenten-archäologie in der Zürcher Altstadt', *Zeitschrift für Schweizer Archäologie und Kunstgeschichte*, 40 (1983), pp. 157–80; J. Schweizer, 'Der städtische Hausbau im südwest-deutsch-schweizerischen Raum', in 'Zur Lebensweise in der Stadt um 1200'; Freiburg: P. Schmidt-Thomé, 'Archäologie in der Altstadt von Freiburg im Breisgau', *Archäologische Ausgra-bungen in Baden-Württemberg 1985* (Stuttgart, 1986), pp. 239–45; I. Beyer, 'Turmhaus (Salzstrasse 20) in Freiburg i. Br.', in Schadek and Schmidt, *Die Zähringer, Anstoss und Wirkung*, pp. 231–2; Regensburg: R. Strobel, 'Wehr-turm, Wohnturm, Patrizierturm in Regensburg', in *Festschrift K. Oettinger* (Erlangen, 1967), pp. 93–116; Meckseper, *Kleine Kunstgeschichte*, pp. 125–8.

49 A. Wiedenau, 'Romanischer Wohnbau im Rheinland', *Veröff. der Abteilung Architektur des Kunsthistorischen Instituts der Universität Köln*, 16 (Köln, 1979); *idem*, 'Form, Funktion und Bedeutung romanischer Wohnhäuser in Köln und im Rheinland', *Wallraf-Richartz-Jahrbuch*, 41 (1980), pp. 7–24; *idem*, 'Katalog der romanischen Wohnbauten in westdeutschen Städten und Siedlungen', *Das deutsche Bürgerhaus*, 34 (Tübingen, 1984).

50 W. Erdmann, 'Entwicklungstendenzen des Lübecker Hausbaus 1100 bis um 1340 – Eine Ideenskizze', *Lübecker Schriften zur Archäologie und Kulturge-schichte*, 7 (Bonn, 1983), pp. 19–38; G. P. Fehring, 'Fachwerkhaus und Stein-werk als Elemente der frühen Lübecker Bürgerhausarchitektur, ihre Wurzeln und Ausstrahlung', *Offa*, 37 (1980), pp. 267–81; *idem*, 'Früher Hausbau in den hochmittelalterlichen Städten Norddeutschlands', *Die Heimat*, 91 (1984), pp. 392–401; *idem*, 'Städtischer Hausbau in Norddeutschland von 1150 bis 1250', in 'Zur Lebensweise in der Stadt um 1200'.

51 U. Klein, 'Datierte Fachwerkbauten des 13. Jahrunderts', *Zeitschrift für Archäo-logie des Mittelalters*, 13 (1985), pp. 145–56.

52 Slavic towns: W. Hensel, 'The origins of Western and Eastern European Slav towns', in Barley, *European towns*, pp. 374–90; L. Leciejewicz, 'Zur Entwick-lung von Frühstädten an der südlichen Ostseeküste', *Zeitschrift für Archäologie*, 3 (1969), pp. 182–210; *idem*, 'Polish archaeology and the medieval history of Polish towns', in Clarke and Simms, *Urban origins*, pp. 335–51; J. Herrmann, 'Archäologische Forschungen zur frühen Stadtentwicklung', *Ausgrabungen und Funde*, 21 (1976), pp. 168–77; urban colonisation in east Germany and Poland of the thirteenth century: the essays by H. Quirin, W. Schich and W. Kuhn in Clarke and Sims, *Urban origins*; J. Herrmann, 'Research into the early history of the town in the territory of the German Democratic Republic', in Barley, *European towns*, pp. 243–59; H. Küas, *Das alte Leipzig in archäologischer Sicht*

(Berlin, 1976); H. W. Mcchelk, *Stadtkernforschung in Dresden* (Berlin, 1970); E. W. Huth, *Die Entstehung und Entwicklung der Stadt Frankfurt/Oder und ihr Kulturbild vom 13. bis zum frühen 17. Jahrhundert aufgrund archäologischer Befunde* (Berlin, 1975).

53 H. Stoob, 'The historic town atlas: problems and working methods', in Clarke and Sims, *Urban origins*, pp. 583–615; the stages of growth 'Wachstumsphasen': Herzog, *Die ottonische Stadt*; B. Schwineköper, 'Die Problematik von Begriffen wie Stauferstädte, Zähringerstädte und ähnliche Bezeichnungen', in E. Maschke and J. Sydow (eds.), 'Südwestdeutsche Städte im Zeitalter der Staufer', *Stadt in der Geschichte*, 6 (1980), pp. 95–172; H. Borger, 'Bemerkungen zu den "Wachstumsstufen" einiger mittelalterlicher Städte im Rheinland', in *Festschrift F. Petri* (Bonn, 1970), pp. 52–89.

54 W. Janssen, 'The origins of the non-Roman town in Germany', pp. 217–35.

55 Schleswig: Vogel, 'Die archäologischen Ausgrabungen'; *idem, Ausgrabungen in Schleswig*; Lübeck: G. Fehring, 'Zur archäologischen Erforschung topographischer, wirtschaftlicher und sozialer Strukturen der Hansestadt Lübeck', *Berichte zur deutschen Landeskunde*, 54 (1980), pp. 133–63; *idem*, 'Lübeck, Archäologie einer Grossstadt des Mittelalters', *Lübeck 1226. Reichsfreiheit und frühe Stadt* (Lübeck, 1976), pp. 267–98.

56 Reports: H. Steuer, 'Berichte über die "Arbeitsgemeinschaft Mittelalter" bei den deutschen Verbänden für Altertumsforschung', *Zeitschrift für Archäologie des Mittelalters*, 5 (1977), pp. 251–3.

57 C. Meckseper and E. Schraut (eds.), *Mentalität und Alltag im Spätmittelalter* (Göttingen, 1985).

8 English medieval town planning

1 S. Reynolds, *An introduction to the history of English medieval towns* (Oxford, 1977), provides a recent survey.

2 M. R. G. Conzen, 'The use of town plans in the study of urban history', in H. J. Dyos (ed.), *The study of urban history* (London, 1968), pp. 113–30.

3 M. W. Beresford, *New towns of the Middle Ages* (London, 1967).

4 K. Rodwell (ed.), *Historic towns in Oxfordshire* (Oxford, 1974); M. R. Eddy and M. R. Petchey (eds.), *Historic towns in Essex* (Chelmsford, 1983), are two examples amongst many.

5 I. Soulsby, *The towns of medieval Wales* (Chichester, 1983).

6 J. Haslam (ed.), *Anglo-Saxon towns in southern England* (Chichester, 1984).

7 C. Platt, *The English medieval town* (London, 1976).

8 I. H. Adams, *The making of urban Scotland* (London, 1978).

9 H. Carter, *The towns of Wales* (2nd edn, Cardiff, 1966).

10 M. Aston and C. J. Bond, *The landscape of towns* (London, 1976).

11 J. W. R. Whitehand and K. Alauddin, 'The town plans of Scotland: some preliminary considerations', *Scottish Geographical Magazine*, 85 (1969), pp. 109–21.

12 T. R. Slater, 'Urban genesis and medieval town plans in Warwickshire and Worcestershire', in T. R. Slater and P. J. Jarvis (eds.), *Field and forest: an historical geography of Warwickshire and Worcestershire* (Norwich, 1981), ch. 10.

13 M. R. G. Conzen, 'Alnwick, Northumberland: a study in town-plan analysis', *Institute of British Geographers Publication*, 27 (1960).

14 M. R. G. Conzen, 'The plan analysis of an English city centre', in K. Norborg (ed.), *Proceedings of the IGU Symposium in urban geography, Lund 1960* (Lund, 1962), pp. 383–414.

15 J. W. R. Whitehand (ed.), 'The urban landscape: historical development and management', *Institute of British Geographers Special Publication*, 13 (London, 1981).

16 N. P. Brooks and G. Whittington, 'Planning and growth in the medieval Scottish burgh: the example of St. Andrews', *Transactions, Institute of British Geographers*, NS 2 (1977), pp. 278–95.

17 C. J. Bond, 'The topography of Pershore', in C. J. Bond and A. M. Hunt, 'Recent archaeological work in Pershore', *Vale of Evesham Historical Society Research Papers*, 6 (1977), pp. 18–26.

18 See the comments of Whitehand, 'The urban landscape'.

19 M. Biddle, D. Hudson and C. Heighway, *The future of London's past* (Worcester, 1973); C. N. L. Brooke, *London 800–1216: the shaping of a city* (London, 1975).

20 Royal Commission on Historical Monuments, England, *City of York*, 6 vols. (London, 1962–81); R. Hall, *The excavations at York, the Viking dig* (London, 1984).

21 Sir J. W. F. Hill, *Medieval Lincoln* (Cambridge, 1948); C. Colyer, *Lincoln, the archaeology of an historic city* (Lincoln, 1975).

22 M. Biddle, *Winchester in the early Middle Ages* (Oxford, 1976).

23 T. Tatton-Brown, 'Canterbury's urban topography: some recent work', in Haslam, *Anglo-Saxon towns in southern England*, pp. 1–36.

24 C. Platt, *Medieval Southampton, the port and trading community A.D. 1000–1600* (London, 1976).

25 M. D. Lobel (ed.), *Historic towns*, vol. 1 (London, 1969), vol. 2 (London, 1975).

26 See, for example, H. J. Fleure, 'Some types of cities in temperate Europe', *Geographical Review*, 10 (1920), pp. 357–74; R. E. Dickinson, *The West European city* (London, 1951); T. F. Tout, 'Medieval town planning', *Bulletin John Rylands Library*, 4 (1917).

27 W. H. S. Hope, 'The ancient topography of Ludlow', *Archaeologia*, 61 (1909), pp. 383–9.

28 E. A. Lewis, *The medieval boroughs of Snowdonia* (London, 1912).

29 E. Critall (ed.), 'Salisbury', in *Victoria County History of Wiltshire*, 6 (London, 1962); W. M. Homan, 'The founding of New Winchelsea', *Sussex Archaeological Collections*, 88 (1949), pp. 22–41.

30 Beresford, *New towns*.

31 L. Butler, 'The evolution of towns: planned towns after 1066', in M. W. Barley (ed.), *The plans and topography of medieval towns in England and Wales* (CBA Research Report No. 14, 1976), pp. 32–480.

32 M. W. Barley, 'Town defences in England and Wales after 1066', in *ibid.*, pp. 57–70.

33 D. J. Keene, 'Suburban growth', in *ibid.*, pp. 71–82.

34 Conzen, 'The use of town plans'.
35 T. R. Slater, 'The analysis of burgage patterns in medieval towns', *Area*, 13 (1981), pp. 211–16.
36 W. Urry, *Canterbury under the Angevin Kings* (London, 1967).
37 M. Biddle and D. J. Keene, 'Winchester in the eleventh and twelfth centuries', in Biddle, *Winchester in the early Middle Ages*, pp. 241–448.
38 Copies of the survey, carried out by extramural classes under the direction of Robert Bearman, are available in the Shakespeare Birthplace Trust Record Office.
39 M. E. Speight and D. J. Lloyd, *Ludlow houses and their residents* (Ludlow Research Papers No. 1, 1978); D. Lloyd, *Broad Street, its houses and residents through eight centuries* (Ludlow Research Papers No. 3, 1979).
40 T. R. Slater, 'The analysis of burgages in medieval towns: three case studies from the West Midlands', *West Midlands Archaeology*, 23 (1981), pp. 53–66.
41 Slater, 'The analysis of burgage patterns'.
42 P. D. Wood, 'The topography of East Grinstead borough', *Sussex Archaeological Collections*, 106 (1968), pp. 49–62.
43 Slater, 'The analysis of burgages'.
44 T. R. Slater, 'Medieval new town and port: a plan analysis of Hedon, East Yorkshire', *Yorkshire Archaeological Journal*, 57 (1985).
45 M. W. Beresford, *History on the ground* (London, 1957), pp. 125–50.
46 C. Hayfield and T. R. Slater, *The medieval town of Hedon: excavations 1975–6* (Hull, 1985).
47 M. Hollings (ed.), 'The red book of Worcester', *Worcester Historical Society*, 3 (1934–9); see also E. M. Carus-Wilson, 'The first half-century of the borough of Stratford-upon-Avon', *Economic History Review* (Series 2), 18 (1965), pp. 46–63.
48 A. Ballard, *British borough charters, 1042–1216* (Cambridge, 1913); A. Ballard and J. Tait, *British borough charters, 1216–1307* (Cambridge, 1923).
49 See Rodwell, *Historic towns in Oxfordshire*.
50 Conzen, 'Alnwick, Northumberland', pp. 31–3.
51 A. E. Nash, 'Perch and acre sizes in medieval Sussex', *Sussex Archaeological Collections*, 116 (1978), pp. 57–67.
52 Homan, 'The founding of New Winchelsea'.
53 Beresford, *New towns*, pp. 14–28.
54 T. R. Slater and C. Wilson, *Archaeology and development in Stratford-upon-Avon* (Birmingham, 1977); Slater, 'The analysis of burgages'.
55 Conzen, 'The use of town plans'.
56 Slater, 'The analysis of burgage patterns'.
57 See for example the frequency graphs of Shipston-upon-Stour and Pershore in Slater, 'The analysis of burgages'.
58 For the definition of primary boundaries see Slater, 'The analysis of burgage patterns'.
59 Lloyd, *Broad Street*.
60 T. R. Slater, 'The urban hierarchy in medieval Staffordshire', *Journal of Historical Geography*, 11 (1985).
61 C. C. Taylor, 'The origins of Lichfield', *Transactions of South Staffordshire*

Archaeological and Historical Society, 10 (1969), pp. 43–52.

62 H. Thorpe, 'Lichfield, a study of its growth and function', *Staffordshire Historical Collections for 1950–51* (1954), pp. 139–211; Taylor, 'The origins of Lichfield'; J. Gould, *Lichfield: archaeology and development* (Birmingham, 1976); S. Bassett, 'Medieval Lichfield: a topographical review', *Transactions of South Staffordshire Archaeological and Historical Society*, 22 (1980–1), pp. 93–121.

63 Bassett's comprehensive paper (*ibid.*) pays little regard to the established principles of town plan analysis within the borough area and confuses ideal and reality in its interpretation.

64 R. Gradmann, *Die Städtischen Siedlungen des Königreichs Württemburg*, Forschungen zur deutschen Landes-und Volkeskunde, 21 (Stuttgart, 1914); see also W. Geisler, *Die deutsche Stadt: ein Beitrag zur Morphologie der Kulturlandschaft*, Forschungen zur deutschen Landes- und Volkeskunde, 22 (Stuttgart, 1924).

65 The ferry was partly superseded by a new stone causeway constructed in 1310 by Bishop Walter Langton. However, the causeway was only some 7 feet wide and thus suitable only for packhorses and travellers on foot; see Thorpe, 'Medieval Lichfield', p. 188.

66 A comprehensive burgage analysis of Lichfield has been undertaken but has not been published.

67 See Bassett, 'Medieval Lichfield', plate VIII, which illustrates the fossilised boundary ditch.

68 As, for example, in Bassett, 'Medieval Lichfield'.

9 Economy and society in eighteenth-century English towns: Bristol in the 1770s

1 J. H. C. Patten, 'Urban occupations in pre-industrial England', *Transactions of the Institute of British Geographers*, NS, 2 (1970), pp. 269–313; J. H. C. Patten (ed.), *Pre-industrial England: Geographica essays* (Folkestone, 1979).

2 P. Clark and P. Slack (eds.), *Crisis and order in English towns 1500–1700* (London, 1972); P. Clark and P. Slack (eds.), *English towns in transition 1500–1700* (London, 1976).

3 P. Corfield, *The impact of English towns 1700–1851* (Oxford, 1982); J. Walvin, *English urban life 1776–1851* (London, 1984).

4 M. D. George, *London life in the eighteenth century* (Harmondsworth, 1966); N. Rogers, 'Aristocratic clientage, trade and independency: popular politics in pre-radical Westminster', *Past and Present*, 61 (1973), pp. 70–106; N. Rogers, 'Money, land and lineage: the big bourgeoisie of Hanoverian London', *Social History*, 4 (1979), pp. 437–54; G. Rudé, *Hanoverian London 1714–1808* (London, 1971); L. D. Schwarz, 'Occupations and incomes in late eighteenth-century East London', *East London Papers*, 14 (1972), pp. 87–100; L. D. Schwarz, 'Income distribution and social structure in London in the late eighteenth century', *Economic History Review*, 2nd series, 32 (1979), pp. 250–9; E. Jones, 'London in the early nineteenth century: an ecological approach', *London Journal*, 6 (1980), pp. 123–34.

5 R. S. Neale, *Bath 1680–1850: a social history* (London, 1981); S. McIntyre, 'Towns as health and pleasure resorts: Bath and Weymouth 1700–1815', DPhil

thesis, University of Oxford, 1983; S. McIntyre, 'Bath: the rise of a resort town, 1600–1800', in P. Clark (ed.), *Country towns in pre-industrial England* (Leicester, 1981), pp. 197–249; R. G. Wilson, *Gentlemen merchants: the merchant community in Leeds 1700–1830* (Manchester, 1971); J. Money, *Experience and identity: Birmingham and the West Midlands, 1760–1800* (Manchester, 1977).

6 J. Langton and P. Laxton, 'Parish registers and urban structure: the example of late-eighteenth-century Liverpool', *Urban History Yearbook* (Leicester, 1978), pp. 74–84.

7 G. Sjoberg, *The preindustrial city* (New York, 1960): J. E. Vance, 'Land assignment in the precapitalist, capitalist and postcapitalist city', *Economic Geography*, 47 (1971), pp. 101–20.

8 B. Little, *The city and county of Bristol: a study in Atlantic civilisation* (London, 1954), p. 327.

9 Although registers have been used, see, e.g., Langton and Laxton, 'Parish registers'.

10 F. Tönnies, *Gemeinschaft und Gesellschaft* (1887; Leipzig, 1935).

11 See review in G. Shaw, 'British directories as sources in historical geography', *Historical Geography Research Series*, 8 (Norwich, 1982); M. Katz, 'Occupational classification in history', *Journal of Interdisciplinary History*, 3 (1972–3), pp. 63–88.

12 J. Sketchley, *Bristol directory* (Bristol, 1775).

13 M. Drake, 'The mid-Victorian voter', *Journal of Interdisciplinary History*, 1 (1971–2), pp. 473–90. R. J. Morris, 'Property titles and the use of British urban Poll Books for social analysis', *Urban History Yearbook* (Leicester, 1983), pp. 29–38. W. A. Speck, *Tory and Whig: the struggle in the constituencies 1701–1715* (London, 1970); G. Rudé, 'The Middlesex electors of 1768–1769', *English Historical Review*, 75 (1960), pp. 601–17; G. Rudé, *Wilkes and liberty: a social study of 1763–1774* (Oxford, 1962).

14 for Bristol P. Slack, 'The local incidence of epidemic disease: the case for Bristol 1540–1650', in P. Slack *et al.*, *The plague reconsidered: a new look at its origins and effects in sixteenth- and seventeenth-century England*, Local Population Studies Supplement (Stafford, 1977), pp. 49–62.

15 Sketchley, *Bristol directory*; W. Pine, *Bristol Poll Book* (Bristol, 1775). Returns for Poor Rate, Pitching and Paving Rate, Watching Rate, Sewer Rate, Lamping and Scavenging Rate and city Bridge Tax and for national Window and Land Taxes, in Bristol Record Office.

16 Personal Database System 101 used on an ICL 2988 computer.

17 Corfield, *The impact of English towns*, p. 45.

18 Anon., *A general discription of trades. Digested in alphabetical order* (London, 1747); R. Campbell, *The London tradesman* (London, 1747).

19 J.-P. Gutton, *La Société et les pauvres: l'example de la généralité de Lyons 1534–1789* (Paris, 1971).

20 P. Corfield, 'The social and economic history of Norwich 1650–1850: a study in urban growth', PhD thesis, University of London, 1976, p. 212.

21 See above note 10.

22 Though of course *rates* of growth in population and production were often extremely high in rural industrial areas.

10 Social status and place of residence in preindustrial German towns: recent studies in social topography

1 The general discussion of social stratification and the great number of local studies on the social structure of towns and cities in historic periods will not be discussed here as most of them do not refer to any spatial dimension of urban social hierarchies or social topography. For a general discussion of social stratification see: K. M. Bolte, D. Kappe and F. Neidhardt, 'Soziale Schichtung. Struktur und Wandel der Gesellschaft', *Beiträge zur Sozialkunde*, B 4 (Opladen, 1966); R. Dahrendorf, 'Die gegenwärtige Lage der Theorie der sozialen Schichtung', in R. Dahrendorf, *Pfade aus Utopia* (München, 1967), pp. 336–52; B. Seidel and S. Jenker (eds.), *Klassenbildung und Sozialschichtung* (Darmstadt, 1968); E. Wiehn, *Theorien der sozialen Schichtung. Eine kritische Diskussion* (München, 1968). For a general discussion of social status, see R. Mayntz, 'Begriff und empirische Erfassung des sozialen Status in der heutigen Soziologie', *Kölner Zeitschrift für Soziologie und Sozialpsychologie*, 10 (1958), pp. 58–73.

For references on local studies on social stratification see D. Denecke, 'Sozialtopographie und sozialräumliche Gliederung der spätmittelalterlichen Stadt. Problemstellungen, Methoden und Betrachtungsweisen der historischen Wirtschafts- und Sozialgeographie', in J. Fleckenstein and K. Stackmann (eds.), 'Über Bürger, Stadt und städtische Literatur im Spätmittelalter', *Abhandlungen d. Akademie der Wissenschaften in Göttingen*, phil.-hist. Kl., 3, 121 (Göttingen, 1980), pp. 161–202.

2 See especially the studies by P. Guyer, 'Die soziale Schichtung der Bürgerschaft Zürichs vom Ausgange des Mittelalters bis 1798', *Schweizerische Zeitschr. f. Geschichte*, 2 (1952), pp. 569–98; E. K. Scheuch and H. Daheim, 'Sozialprestige und soziale Schichtung', *Kölner Zeitschr. f. Soziologie und Sozialpsychologie*, 5 (Köln, 1961), pp. 65, 103; K. Bosl, 'Kasten Stände, Klassen im mittelalterlichen Deutschland. Zur Problematik soziologischer Begriffe und ihrer Anwendung auf die mittelalterliche Gesellschaft', *Zeitschr. f. Bayerische Landesgeschichte*, 32 (1969), pp. 422ff; E. Maschke and J. Sydow (eds.), 'Gesellschaftliche Unterschichten in den südwestdeutschen Städten', *Veröff. d. Kommission f. Geschichtl. Landeskunde in Baden-Württ.*, B 41 (1967), pp. 1–79; E. Maschke and J. Sydow, 'Städtische Mittelschichten', *Veröff. d. Kommission f. geschichtl. Landeskunde in Baden-Württ.*, B 69 (1972); E. Maschke, 'Die Schichtung der mittelalterlichen Stadtbevölkerung Deutschlands als Problem der Forschung', in Methodologie de l'histoire et des sciences humaines, *Mélanges en l'Honneur de Ferdinand Braudel* (Toulouse, 1974), pp. 367–79; A. von Brandt, 'Die gesellschaftliche Struktur des spätmittelalterlichen Lübeck', in 'Untersuchungen zur gesellschaftlichen Struktur der mittelalterlichen Städte in Europa', *Vorträge und Forschungen*, 11 (Konstanz/Stuttgart, 1966), pp. 215–39; M. Mitterauer, J. Morrissey, W. Schindle, K. Weber and R. Wilfing, 'Soziale Schichtung im Mittelalter', *Beiträge zur historischen Sozialkunde*, 6 (1976), pp. 63–80; M. Mitterauer, 'Probleme der Stratifikation in mittelalterlichen Gesellschaftssystemen', in J. Kocka (ed.), 'Theorien in der Praxis des Historikers', *Geschichtliche Grundbegriffe*, vol. 3 (Göttingen, 1977), pp. 13–43; C. G. Andrae, 'Ett social historiens dilemma. Några försök att definera sociala grupper och klasser i svensk historia',

Historisk tidskrift, 98, NF 41 (1978), pp. 1–9; J. Söderberg, 'Metodes alt analy-
sera social rörlighet', *Historisk tidskrift*, 98, NF 41 (1978), pp. 283–304; H.
Wunder, 'Probleme der Stratifikation in mittelalterlichen Gesellschaftssystemen', *Geschichtliche Grundbegriffe*, 4 (1978), pp. 542–50; J. Ellermeyer, 'Schichtung und Sozialstruktur in spätmittelalterlichen Städten. Zur Verwendbarkeit
sozialwissenschaftlicher Kategorien in historischer Forschung', *Geschichtliche
Grundbegriffe*, 6 (1980), pp. 125–49; A. Czacharowski, 'Forschungen über die
sozialen Schichten in den Städten des deutschen Ordenslandes im 13. u. 14.
Jh.', in B. Diestelkamp (ed.), 'Beiträge zum spätmittelalterlichen Städtewesen',
Städteforschung, A 12 (Köln/Wien, 1982), pp. 119–29.
3 General studies: D. W. G. Timms, *The urban mosaic: towards a theory of residential differentiation* (Cambridge, 1971). Examples of case studies for the twentieth
century: H. Fischer, 'Viertelsbildung und sozial bestimmte Stadteinheiten untersucht am Beispiel der inneren Stadtbezirke der Grosstadt Stuttgart', *Ber. z.
dt. Landeskunde*, 30 (1963), pp. 101–20; P. Braun, 'Die sozialräumliche Gliede-
rung Hamburgs', *Weltwirtschaftliche Studien*, 10 (Göttingen, 1968); B. Backé,
'Die sozialräumliche Gliederung in Florisdorf', Dissertationen der Universität
Wien 9 (Wien, 1968); H. Förster, 'Die funktionale und sozialgeographische
Gliederung der Mainzer Innenstadt', *Bonner Geogr. Arbeiten*, 4 (Bonn, 1968);
A. Mayr, 'Ahlen in Westfalen. Siedlung und Bevölkerung einer industriellen
Mittelstadt mit besonderer Berücksichtigung der innerstädtischen Gliederung',
Quellen und Forschungen zur Geschichte der Stadt Ahlen, 2 (Ahlen, 1968);
O. Weise, 'Sozialgeographische Gliederung und innerstädtische Verflechtungen
in Wuppertal', *Geowissenschaftl. Diss.* (Bochum, 1971). Studies on the eigh-
teenth and nineteenth centuries: I. E. Momsen, 'Die Bevölkerung der Stadt
Husum von 1769 bis 1860. Versuch einer historischen Sozialgeographie', *Schriften des Geogr. Inst. der Universität Kiel*, 31 (Kiel, 1964); E. Lichtenberger,
'Die sozialökologische Gliederung Wiens. Aspekte eines Stufenmodells', *Österreich in Geschichte und Literatur*, 17 (1973), pp. 25–49; E. Lichtenberger, 'Das
sozialökologische Modell einer barocken Residenz um die Mitte des 18. Jahrhunderts', in W. Rausch (ed.), *Städtische Kultur in der Barockzeit* (Linz, 1982),
pp. 235–62; E. Lichtenberger, 'Historische Stadtforschung und Kartographie.
Die sozialräumliche und funktionale Gliederung von Wien um 1770', in E. Arn-
berger (ed.), *Kartographie der Gegenwart in Österreich* (Wien, 1984), pp. 170–
92; H. J. Schwippe, 'Sozialökologie der Stadt Berlin 1875–1910. Ein Beitrag
zur räumlich-sozialen Segregation', in *Westfalen – Nordwestdeutschland – Nord-
seesektor* (Münster, 1981), pp. 315–51; C. Erdmann, 'Wirtschafts- und sozialräumliche Gliederung einer frühindustriellen Stadt. Aachen im Jahre 1812',
Geographische Zeitschr., 71 (1983), pp. 166–83; C. Erdmann, 'Aachen im Jahre
1812. Wirtschafts- und sozialräumliche Differenzierung einer frühindustriellen
Stadt', *Erdkundliches Wissen*, 78 (Stuttgart, 1986). Comparable British studies:
G. Gordon, 'The status areas of early to mid-Victorian Edinburgh', *Transactions
of the Institute of British Geographers*, NS, 4 (1979), pp. 168–91; C. G. Pooley,
'The residential segregation of migrant communities in mid-Victorian Liverpool', *Transactions of the Institute of British Geographers*, NS, 2 (1977), pp. 364–
82. Studies on the medieval period: D. Meckseper, 'Stadtplan und Sozialstruktur
in der deutschen Stadt des Mittelalters', *Stadtbauwelt*, 33 (1972), pp. 52–7; J.

Roth, 'Die Steuerlisten von 1363/64 und 1374/75 als Quellen zur Sozialstruktur der Stadt Trier im Spätmittelalter', *Kurtrierisches Jahrbuch*, 16 (1976), pp. 24–37; T. Roslanowski, 'Comparative sociotopography: on the example of early medieval towns in Central Europe', *Acta Poloniae Historica*, 34 (1976), pp. 7–27; F. de Capitani, 'Untersuchungen zum Tellbuch der Stadt Bern von 1389', *Berner Zeitschrift f. Geschichte u. Heimatkunde*, 39 (1977), pp. 73–100; W. Schich, 'Würzburg im Mittelalter. Studien zum Verhältnis von Topographie und Bevölkerungsstruktur', *Städteforschung*, A 3 (Köln/Wien, 1977); E. Piper, 'Der Stadtplan als Grundriss der Gesellschaft. Topographie und Sozialstruktur in Augsburg und Florenz um 1500', *Campus Forschung*, 305 (Frankfurt, 1982).

4 The special term 'Sozialtopographie' shows up already in 1929 in a German dissertation but did not come into use before the 1970s.

5 W. H. Riehl, 'Augsburger Studien, II: Der Stadtplan als Grundriss der Gesellschaft', in W. H. Riehl, *Culturstudien aus drei Jahrhunderten* (1859), pp. 270–84.

6 K. F. Leonhardt, 'Karte der Berufsverteilung in Hannover nach dem Stande von 1435', 1:2500, *Karten zur Entwicklungsgeschichte der Stadt Hannover* (Hannover, 1933).

7 For general and comparative studies see: H.-Ch. Rublack, 'Probleme der Sozialtopographie der Stadt im Mittelalter und in der frühen Neuzeit', in W. Ehrbrecht (ed.), 'Voraussetzungen und Methoden geschichtlicher Stadteforschung', *Städteforschung*, A 7 (Köln/Wien, 1979) pp. 177–93; D. Denecke, 'Die historische Dimension der Sozialtopographie am Beispiel südniedersächsischer Städte', *Berichte z. dt. Landeskunde*, 54 (1980), pp. 211–52; D. Denecke, 'Die sozio-ökonomische Gliederung südniedersächsischer Städte im 18 und 19 Jahrhundert-Historische-geographische Stadtpläne und ihre Analyse', *Neidersächsisches Jahrbuch*, 52 (1980) pp. 25–38; Denecke, 'Sozialtopographie und sozialräumliche Gliederung'. For local case studies see: W. Meibeyer, 'Bevölkerungs- und sozialgeographische Differenzierung der Stadt', *Braunschweiger Jahrbuch*, 47 (1966), pp. 125–57; H. Klein, 'Beiträge zur geographischen Entwicklung des Lingener Raumes im 19. und 20. Jh., Kap. IV: Gesellschaft und städtischer Raum – Sozialtopographie der Stadt Lingen im 19. Jahrhundert', in W. Ehrbrecht (ed.), *Lingen 975–1975* (Lingen, 1975), pp. 160–98, esp. pp. 180–94; W. Herborn, 'Sozialtopographie des Kölner Kirchspiels St. Kolumba im Ausgehenden 13. Jahrhundert', in H. Keltenbenz (ed.), *Zwei Jahrtausende Kölner Wirtschaft*, vol. 1 (Köln, 1975), pp. 205–15; A. Czacharowski, 'Sociotopography of medieval and late medieval towns in the North European zone as exemplified by Torun', *Acta Poloniae Historica*, 34 (1976), pp. 121–30; J. Wojtowicz, 'Quelques problèmes de la sociotopographie de da ville Européenne à l'époque des lumières. Aperçu de la problématique', *Acta Poloniae Historica*, 34 (1976), pp. 243–54; E. Lichtenberger, *Die Wiener Altstadt. Von der mittelalterlichen Bürgerstadt zur City*, 2 vols. (Wien, 1977); Th. Schuler, 'Wohnlage und Sozialstruktur in Bielefeld im Jahr 1718', in F. Irsigler (ed.), 'Quantitative Methoden in der Wirtschafts- und Sozialgeschichte', *Historisch-Sozialwissenschaftl. Forschungen*, 4 (1978), pp. 50–69; B. Sachse, 'Soziale Differenzierung und regionale Verteilung der Bevölkerung Göttingens im 18. Jahrhundert', *Veröff. d. Inst. f. Historische Landesforschung d. Universität Göttingen*, 11 (Hildesheim, 1978); K. Lorenzen-Schmidt, 'Die Vermögens- und Berufsstruktur Lübecks im Jahre 1762.

Materialien zur Sozialtopographie', *Zeitschrift d. Vereins f. Lübeckische Geschichte*, 62 (1982), pp. 155–94; H. Rüthing, 'Bemerkungen zur Sozialstruktur und Sozialtopographie Höxters am Ausgang des Mittelalters', in B. Diestelkamp (ed.), 'Beiträge zum spätmittelalterlichen Städtewesen', *Städtesforschung*, A 12 (Köln/Wien, 1982), pp. 130–43; T. Jasinski, 'Z zagadnien topografii spolecznej sredniowiesznego Torunia', part 1: 'Stare Miasto' (Zu Fragen der Sozialtopographie des mittelalterlichen Thorn, Teil 1, Die Altstadt), *Zapiski Historyczne*, 48 (1983), pp. 5–47; M. Siekmann, 'Die Struktur der Stadt Münster am Ausgang des 18. Jahrhunderts. Ein Beitrag zur geographisch-topologischen Stadtforschung', *Siedlung und Landschaft in Westfalen*, 18 (Münster, 1986); M. Siekmann and K.-H. Kirchoff, 'Sozialtopographie in der Stadt Münster 1770 und 1890 mit Ausblicken auf 1971', in H. Heineberg (ed.), *Innerstädtische Differenzierung und Prozesse im 19. und 20. Jahrhundert. Geographische und historische Aspekte, Städteforschung*, A 25 (Köln, 1987), pp. 159–94. Similar studies in Britain: J. Langton, 'Residential patterns in pre-industrial cities: some case studies from seventeenth-century Britain', *Transactions of the Institute of British Geographers*, 65 (1975), pp. 1–27; J. Langton, 'Late medieval Gloucester: some data from a rental of 1455', *Transactions of the Institute of British Geographers*, NS, 2 (1977), pp. 259–77.

8 G. Sjoberg, *The preindustrial city* (New York, 1960).

9 Langton, 'Residential patterns'.

10 As a case study on a nineteenth-century town see: E. Walser, 'Wohnraum und Familienstruktur am Ende des 19. Jahrhunderts. Die Wohnungszählung von 1896 in der Stadt Bern als sozialgeschichtliche Quelle', *Berner Zeitschr. f. Geschichte und Heimatkunde*, 41 (1979), pp. 113–31.

11 A very interesting contribution to this question by Lichtenberger on medieval Vienna should be mentioned here: *Die Wiener Altstadt*.

12 See Meibeyer, 'Bevölkerungs- und sozialgeographische Differenzierung der Stadt', map 1, density of population in 1758 (Brunswick), indicated in dots, and fig. 1, density of street row; for another good example, giving households per house and size of household (*Personenziffer*) in Göttingen in 1763, see Sachse, 'Soziale Differenzierung', map 3.

13 See, for example: H. Rosenau, 'Zum Sozialproblem in der Architekturtheorie des 15. bis. 19. Jahrhunderts', in Kunstgeschichtliches seminar d. Universität Münster (ed.), *Festschrift f. Martin Wackernagel* (Köln, 1958), pp. 185–93; I. Möller, 'Die Entwicklung eines Hamburger Gebietes von der Agrar- zur Grosstadtlandschaft, mit einem Beitrag zur Methode der städtischen Aufrissanalyse', *Hamburger Geographische Studien*, 10 (Hamburg, 1959); H. Meynen, 'Die Wohnbauten im nordwestlichen Vorortsektor Kölns mit Ehrenfeld als Mittelpunkt. Bauliche Entwicklung seit 1845, Wechselbeziehungen von Baubild und Sozialstruktur', *Rheinisches Archiv*, 104 (Bonn, 1978), also published in *Forschungen z. dt. Landeskunde*, 210 (Trier, 1978); see also: R. J. Johnston, 'Towards an analytical study of the townscape: the residential building fabric', *Geografiska Annaler*, B 51 (1969), pp. 20–32.

14 See following examples: Göttingen 1763, standard of house classification, in Sachse, 'Soziale Differenzierung', map 2; presented in a circled diagram, see Denecke, 'Die historische Dimension', fig. 2; Einbeck, 1868, building tax rates,

in Denecke, 'Sozialtopographie und sozialräumliche Gliederung', fig. 8.

15 As an example: St Kolumba (Köln), 1286, property value, in Herborn, 'Sozialtopographie des Kölner Kirchspiels St. Kolumba', figs. 1 and 2, pp. 207 and 209.

16 See the act of 1667 for rebuilding the city of London (in C. C. Knowles and P. H. Pitt, *The history of building regulation in London 1189–1972* (London, 1972), pp. 31–2.

17 Distribution of houses with brewing rights in Seesen, in Denecke, 'Die historische Dimension', fig. 15.

18 Street names of medieval and early modern German towns are compiled and discussed by; E. Volckmann, *Alte Gewerbe und Gewerbegassen* (Würzburg, 1921); E. Volckmann, *Die deutsche Stadt im Spiegel alter Gassennamen* (Würzburg, 1926); A. Hoffmann, 'Die typischen Strassennamen im Mittelalter', Phil. Diss. (Königsberg, 1913). For many German towns there are local studies on the history of street names.

19 Riehl, 'Augsburger Studien', pp. 279–80, and more often up to recent historical studies. For a number of examples, see J. Cramer, 'Zur Frage der Gewerbegassen in der Stadt am Ausgang des Mittelalters', *Die alte Stadt*, 11 (1984), pp. 81–111, here pp. 86–9. Obvious clusters also show up in the map for Hannover in 1435, especially for butchers, bakers and coppersmiths (see no. 7). As for special quarters, see, for example, M. J. Wise, 'On the evolution of the jewellery and gem quarters in Birmingham', *Transactions of the Institute of British Geographers* (1949), pp. 58–72.

20 Recent studies opposing the common suggestion of a segregation of occupations and trades in specific streets of trade: Denecke, 'Sozialtopographie und sozialräumliche Gliederung', p. 177–183; G. Dahlbäck, 'Fannes det skomakare på skomakargaten? Om den näringsgeografiska strukturen i 1460 – talets Stockholm', *St. Eriks årsbok* (1983), pp. 29–52; Cramer, 'Zur Frage der Gewerbegassen', pp. 89ff. The general opposition by Cramer is too much generalized and exaggerated. It is also not always proved by his own examples.

21 K. Brethauer, 'Töpfer und Pfeifenbrenner in Münden. Die Schriftquellen', *Neue Ausgrabungen und Forschungen in Niedersachsen*, 16 (1983), pp. 387–99.

22 U. Dirlmeier, 'Umweltprobleme in deutschen Städten des Spätmittelalters', *Technikgeschichte*, 48 (1981), pp. 177–205; of special interest in the context of pollution, lower-class houses, distributions of special crafts and social topography in general might be the comparisons with distribution patterns of the Black Death and other epidemics. As examples, see the studies by: E. Woehlkens, *Pest und Ruhr im 16. und 17. Jahrhundert. Grundlagen einer statistisch-topographischen Beschreibung der grossen Seuchen, insbesondere in der Stadt Uelzen* (Uelzen, 1954); H. van der Haegen and R. de Vos, 'De cholera-epidemie te Leuwen in 1849', *Driemaandelijks Tijdschrift van het Gemeentekrediet van België*, 133 (1980), pp. 197–210.

23 See the special and fundamental study by J. Cramer, 'Gerberhaus und Gerberviertel in der mittelalterlichen Stadt', *Studien zur Bauforschung*, 12 (Bonn, 1981).

24 Cramer, 'Zur Frage der Gewerbegassen', figs. 13 and 14: Landshut 1600.

25 See, for example, traffic-oriented trades in Göttingen 1763, in Sachse, 'Soziale Differenzierung', map 6; see also cartwrights in Strassburg 1450 and 1475, in

Cramer, 'Zur Frage der Gewerbegassen', fig. 5. This observation was also stated by Langton, 'Residential patterns', for a number of medieval British towns.

26 There are a number of examples, such as: R. Hammel, 'Vermögensverhältnisse und Absatzmöglichkeiten der Bäcker in hansischen Seestädten am Beispiel Lübecks. Ein Beitrag zur hansischen Gewerbegeschichte des späten 14. Jahrhunderts', *Hansische Geschichtsblätter*, 99 (1981), pp. 33–60; St Kolumba (Köln) 1286; Herborn, 'Sozialtopographie des Kölner Kirchspiels St. Kolumba', fig. 3; Erfurt 1511: Denecke, 'Sozialtopographie und sozialräumliche Gliederung', fig. 3; Göttingen 1550, 1763, 1864: Denecke, 'Die historische Dimension', figs. 9, 11, 12; Göttingen 1763: Sachse, 'Soziale Differenzierung', map 10; Goslar 1803: Denecke, 'Die sozio-ökonomische Gliederung', fig. 1.

27 See the following examples: Hannover 1435: Leonhardt, 'Karte der Berufsverteilung in Hannover'; Göttingen 1458: Denecke, 'Die historische Dimension', fig. 10; München 1600: Cramer, 'Zur Frage der Gewerbegassen', fig. 12.

28 Hammel, 'Vermögensverhältnisse und Absatzmöglichkeiten der Bäcker', p. 36.

29 See especially for Göttingen 1763, Sachse, 'Soziale Differenzierung', maps 12–14. For Münster 1770 and 1890, see Siekmann, 'Die Struktur der Stadt Münster'.

30 G. Nagel, *Das mittelalterliche Kaufhaus und seine Stellung in der Stadt* (Berlin, 1971).

31 As one example see Lichtenberger, *Die Wiener Altstadt*; for medieval Göttingen also see D. Neitzert, 'Göttingens Wirtschaft, besonders im 15. Jahrhundert', in D. Denecke and H.-M. Kühn (eds.), *Göttingen – Geschichte einer Universitätsstadt* (Göttingen, 1987), fig. 5.

32 Denecke, 'Die sozio-ökonomische Gliederung', fig. 1: occupations and trade in Goslar. 1803.

33 J. Hagel, 'Die Verteilung der Weingärtner in Stuttgart 1794', *Tübinger Geographische Studien*, 90 (1985), pp. 217–24. This study is based on an early printed directory giving all the households and occupations for the complete town of Stuttgart for the year 1794. With this directory also goes a map, specifically designed together with the directory. An ideal, but exceptional, source: C. F. Roth, *Alphabetisches Verzeichnis der Besitzer derjenigen Gebäude, welche in dem am Ende 1794, über die Herzogl. Wirtembergische Residenzstadt Stuyttgart, verfertigten Grundris vorkommen, und in demselben nach Nummern angezeigt sind* (Stuttgart, 1795).

34 See Denecke, 'Die historische Dimension', fig. 14. For this kind of study secondary sources might be used, histories of houses and their owners (*Häuserbücher*), acribic compilations of any historical data available, generally from the seventeenth century onwards. There are published *Häuserbücher* for the towns of Biberach an der Riss, Freiburg in Breisgau, Hersbruck, Landshut, München and Strassburg (see Cramer, 'Zur Frage der Gewerbegassen') and also for Seesen and Gandersheim.

35 K. J. Uthmann, 'Sozialstruktur und Vermögensbildung in Hildesheim im 15. und 16. Jahrhundert', *Schriften der wirtschaftswissenschaftlichen Gesellschaft z. Studium Niedersachsens e.V.*, NF, 65 (1957). Denecke, 'Sozialtopographie und sozialräumliche Gliederung', pp. 194–201; Hammel, 'Vermögensverhältnisse und Absatzmöglichkeiten'; especially from the research project on medieval Lübeck basic results might be expected.

36 Hildesheim 1401–1572: Denecke, 'Sozialtopographie und sozialräumliche Glie- derung', fig. 11; Höxter 1501: Rüthing, 'Bemerkungen zur Sozialstruktur', fig. 2; Göttingen 1763: Sachse, 'Soziale Differenzierung', maps 18–20, and also Denecke, 'Die historische Dimension', fig. 4.

37 There are many interesting examples of reconstructed or rebuilt towns after fire in Germany. The hitherto results of research, however, are hidden in numer- ous local histories. No comprehensive and comparative work has yet been done.

38 Cramer, 'Zur Frage der Gewerbegassen', fig. 16.

39 D. Denecke, 'Aspekte sozialgeographischer Interpretationen innerstädtischer Mobilität im 19. und 20. Jahrhundert. Allgemeiner Forschungsstand und For- schungsbeispiele', in Heineberg, 'Innerstädtische Differenzierung'; see also R. Dennis, 'Distance and social interaction in a Victorian city', *Journal of Historical Geography*, 3 (1977), pp. 237–50.

40 See the results of the interdisciplinary research project (Historians and archaeol- ogists) on medieval Lübeck: A. Falk and R. Hammel, 'Zur Konzeption eines archäologisch-historischen Forschungsprojekts in Lübeck', *Zeitschr. d. Vereins f. Lübeckische Geschichte u. Altertumskunde*, 59 (1979), pp. 223–6; see also Hammel, 'Vermögensverhältnisse und Absatzmöglichkeiten'; for an archaeo- logical approach to early medieval towns, see also L. Leciejewicz, 'Early medie- val socio-topographical transformations in West Slavonic urban settlements in the light of archaeology', *Acta Poloniae Historica*, 34 (1976), pp. 29–56.

41 Czacharowski, 'Sociotopography of medieval and late medieval towns'; Wajtow- icz, 'Quelques problèmes'; Roslanowski, 'Comparative sociotopography'.

42 See the maps on social topography integrated in the *Scandinavian Atlas of His- toric Towns*, No. 4: Uppsala (Odense, 1963); see also Dahlbäck, 'Fannes det skomakare påskomargaten?'; C. G. Andrae, 'Att veta sin plats, människorna, husen och den sociala miljön i Uppsala mot 1800-talets slut', in T. Hall (ed.), *Städer i utveckling*, Festschrift for I. Hammarström, (Stockholm, 1984), pp. 97– 114.

43 See the contribution by Claudia Erdmann in this volume.

11 The economic and social spatial structure of an early industrial town: Aachen

1 E. Ennen, 'Wirtschaftsleben und Sozialstruktur Bonns im Zeitalter der französis- chen Revolution und des Kaiserreiches', *Annalen d. hist. Vereins für d. Nieder- rhein*, 166 (1964), pp. 129–51.

2 Stadtarchiv Aachen, 'Einwohnerliste der Stadt Aachen. 2 Bde. 1812'.

3 H. Carter and S. Wheatley, 'Residential segregation in nineteenth-century cities', *Area*, 12 (1980), pp. 57–62. K. A. Cowlard, 'The identification of social areas and their place in the nineteenth century urban development', *Transactions of the Inst. of Brit. Geographers*, 4 (1979), pp. 239–57. R. Harris, 'Residential segregation and class formation in the capitalist city: a review and directions for research', *Progress in Human Geography*, 8 (1984), pp. 26–49. M. Shaw, 'Reconciling social and physical space: Wolverhampton 1871', *Transactions of the Inst. of Brit. Geographers*, NS, 4 (1979), pp. 192–213.

4 J. H. Johnson and C. G. Pooley, 'The internal structure of the nineteenth- century British city – an overview', in J. H. Johnson and C. G. Pooley (eds.),

The structure of nineteenth-century cities (London, 1982), pp. 3–35. J. Langton and P. Laxton, 'Parish registers and urban structure, the example of late eighteenth-century Liverpool', *Urban History Yearbook* (Leicester, 1978), pp. 74–84.

5 G. Sjoberg, *The preindustrial city* (New York, 1960).

6 M. S. X. de Golbery, *Considérations sur le départment de la Roer suivies de la notice d'Aix-la-Chapelle et de Borcette* (Aix-la-Chapelle, 1811), p. 367.

7 M. Schultheis-Friebe, 'Die französische Wirtschaftspolitik im Roer-Departement 1792–1814', Diss. (Bonn, 1967), pp. 128. Golbery, *Considérations*, p. 368.

8 Golbery, *Considérations*.

9 Sjoberg, *The preindustrial city*, p. 326.

10 J. Strauch, 'Die Aachener Tuchindustrie während der französischen Herrschaft 1794–1814', Diss (Münster, 1927).

11 W. Fischer, 'Aachener Werkbauten des 18. und 19. Jahrhunderts', Diss. Ing. (Aachen, 1946).

12 J. Koch, 'Geschichte der Aachener Nähnadelzunft und Nähnadelindustrie bis zur Aufhebung der Zinfte in der französischen Zeit (1798)', *Zeitschrift d. Aachener Geschichtsvereins*, 41 (1920), pp. 16–122.

13 H. Kisch, 'Das Erbe des Mittelalters, ein Hemmnis wirtschaftlicher Entwicklung: Aachens Tuchgewerbe vor 1790', *Rheinische Vierteljahresblätter*, 30 (1965), pp. 253–308.

14 Koch, 'Geschichte der Aachener Nähnadelzunft', p. 41.

15 W. Franken, 'Die Entwicklung des Gewerbes in den Städten Mönchengladbach und Rheydt im 19. Jahrhundert', *Schriften zur rheinisch-westfälischen Wirtschaftsgeschichte*, 19, NF (1969).

16 F.-W. Henning, *Die Industrialisierung in Deutschland. 1800 bis 1914. Wirtschafts- u. Sozialgeschichte*, vol. 2 (Paderborn, 1973), and Schultheis-Friebe, 'Die französische Wirtschaftspolitik', p. 24.

17 Fischer, 'Aachener Werkbauten', p. 61.

18 K. M. Bolte, 'Typen sozialer Schichtung in der Bundesrepublik Deutschland', *Hamburger Jahrbuch für Wirtschafts- u. Sozialpolitik*, 8 (Tübingen, 1963), pp. 150–68. D. Kappe and F. Neidhardt, *Soziale Ungleichheit. Struktur und Wandel der Gesellschaft*, Beiträge zur Sozialkunde, B 3, Aufl. (Opladen, 1974). H. Jecht, 'Studien zur gesellschaftlichen Struktur der mittelalterlichen Städte', *Vierteljahresschrift f. Sozial- u. Wirtschaftsgeschichte* (1926), pp. 48–85. E. Lichtenberger, 'Von der mittelalterlichen Bürgerstadt zur City. Sozialstatistische Querschnittsanalysen am Wiener Beispiel', in H. Helcmanovszki (ed.), *Beiträge zur Bevölkerungs- u. Sozialgeschichte Österreichs* (München, 1973), pp. 297–331.

19 E. Meynen, 'Die produktionsgewerblichen Standorte Kölns und seines engeren Umlandes. Entwicklung und Wandel', in *Der Wirtschaftsraum. Beiträge zur Methode und Anwendung eines geographischen Forschungsansatzes. Festschrift für E. Otremba zu seinem 60. Geburtstag*, Geographische Zeitschrift, Beihefte, Erdkundliches H. Wissen., 41, (Wiesbaden, 1975), p. 171. J. Klersch, *Von der Reichsstadt zur Gross-stadt. Stadtbild und Wirtschaft in Köln 1797-1860* (Köln, 1875).

20 Stadtarchiv Aachen, 'Les Membres du Bureau de Bienfaisance de la Commune

d'Aix-la-Chapelle. Collecte faite par les collecteurs pour les premiers nécessaires à l'établissement de l'attelier de charité. Aix-la-Chapelle 1830'.

21 W. Abel, *Massenarmut und Hungerkrisen im vorindustriellen Deutschland* (Göttingen, 1972). W. Fischer, *Wirtschaft und Gesellschaft im Zeitalter der Industrialisierung* (Göttingen, 1972).

22 F. Blendinger, 'Versuch einer Bestimmung der Mittelschicht in der Reichsstadt Augsburg vom Ende des 14. bis zum Anfang des 18. Jahrhunderts', in E. Maschke and J. Sydow (eds.), *'Städtische Mittelschichten', Veröff. d. Kommission f. geschichtl. Landeskunde in Baden-Württemberg*, B 69 (1972), pp. 33–78.

23 W. Köllmann, *Sozialgeschichte der Stadt Barmen im 19. Jahrhundert* (Tübingen, 1960). W. Fischer, *Der Staat und die Anfänge der Industrialisierung in Baden 1800–1850*, vol. 1: *Die staatliche Gewerbepolitik* (Berlin, 1962).

24 R. Stewig, *Die Stadt in Industrie- und Entwicklungsländern* (Paderborn, 1983).

25 Bolte, 'Typen sozialer Schichtung', p. 152.

26 C. Erdmann, 'Zuwanderung in die frühindustrielle Stadt Aachen (Ende 18./Anfang 19. Jh.)', in F. Ahnert and R. Zschocke (eds.), *Festschrift für Felix Monheim zum 65. Geburtstag. Aachener Geogr. Arbeiten*, vol. 14 (1981), pp. 399–423. See also: D. Denecke, 'Beziehungen zwischen Stadt und Land in Nordwestdeutschland während des späten Mittelalters und der frühen Neuzeit. Historische Geographie städtischer Zentralität', in C. Meckseper (ed.), *Stadt im Wandel*, vol. 3 (Stuttgart, 1985), pp. 191–218.

27 P. Wheatley, 'What the greatness of a city is said to be. Reflections on Sjoberg's "Preindustrial City"', *Pacific Viewpoint*, 6 (1963), pp. 163–88. P. Burke, 'Some reflections on the preindustrial city', *Urban History Yearbook* (Leicester, 1975), pp. 13–21. D. T. Herbert and C. J. Thomas, *Urban geography. A first approach* (Chichester, 1982). H. Carter, *An introduction to urban historical geography* (London, 1983).

28 C. Haase (ed.), 'Die Stadt des Mittelalters – Begriff, Entstehung und Ausbreitung', *Wege der Forschung*, vol. 243 (Darmstadt, 1969). F. Braudel, 'Pre-modern towns', in P. Clark (ed.), *The early modern town* (London, 1976), pp. 53–90.

29 E. Ennen, 'Das Städtewesen Nordwestdeutschlands von der fränkischen bis zur salischen Zeit', *Das erste Jahrtausend* (Düsseldorf, 1964); repr. in Haase, *Die Stadt des Mittelalters*, pp. 139–95. D. Denecke, *Göttingen. Materialien zur historischen Stadtgeographie und zur Stadtplanung* (Göttingen, 1979). E. Lichtenberger, 'Die europaische Stadt – Wesen, Modelle, Probleme', *Berichte zur Raumforschung und Raumplanung*, 16 (1972), pp. 3–25.

30 Kisch, 'Das Erbe des Mittelalters', p. 268.

31 J. E. Vance, *The scene of man: the role and structure of the city in the geography of western civilization* (New York, 1977), p. 210. J. Langton, 'Residential patterns in pre-industrial cities: some case studies from seventeenth-century Britain', *Transactions of the Inst. of Brit. Geographers*, 65 (1975), p. 22.

32 D. Ward, 'The industrial revolution and the emergence of Boston's Central Business District', *Economic Geography*, 42 (1966), p. 158. N. J. Johnston, 'The caste and class of the urban form of historic Philadelphia', in S. F. Fava (ed.), *Urbanism in world perspective: a reader* (New York, 1968), p. 248.

33 J. Swauger, 'Pittsburgh's residential pattern in 1815', *Annals of the Ass. of American Geographers*, 68 (1978), p. 275.

34 J. P. Radford, 'Testing the model of the preindustrial city: the case of antebellum Charleston, South Carolina', *Transactions of the Inst. of Brit. Geographers*, NS, 4 (1979), p. 400.

35 E. Lichtenberger, *Die Wiener Altstadt Von der mittelalterlichen Bürgerstadt zur City (Wien, 1977)*. J. H. Bater, *St. Petersburg: industrialization and change* (London, 1976). B. von der Dollen, 'Stadtrandphänomene in historisch-geographischer Sicht', *Siedlungsforschung*, 1 (Bonn, 1983), pp. 15–37.

36 E. Sabelberg, *Regionale Stadttypen in Italien*, Erdkundiches Wissen, H. 66 (Wiesbaden, 1984), p. 61.

37 R. Kistemaker and R. van Gelder, *Amsterdam. The golden age 1275–1797* (New York, 1983), pp. 69–70.

38 P. Kriedtke, 'Die Stadt im Prozess der europäischen Proto-Industrialisierung', *Die alte Stadt*, 9 (1982), pp. 19–51. R. Braun, 'Protoindustrialization and demographic changes in the canton of Zürich', in C. Tilly (ed.), *Historical studies of changing fertility* (Princeton, 1978), pp. 289–334.

12 The social geography of nineteenth-century British cities: a review

1 For a comprehensive review see R. A. Kent, *A history of British empirical sociology* (Aldershot, 1981).

2 A. F. Wells, *The local social survey in Great Britain* (London, 1935).

3 Influential post-war work includes W. Watson, 'The sociological aspects of geography', in G. Taylor (ed.), *Geography in the twentieth century* (New York, 1953), pp. 403–99; E. Jones, *A social geography of Belfast* (Oxford, 1960); R. E. Pahl, 'Trends in social geography', in R. J. Chorley and P. Haggett (eds.), *Frontiers in geographical teaching* (London, 1965); R. E. Pahl 'Sociological models in geography', in R. J. Chorley and P. Haggett (eds.), *Models in geography* (London, 1967); A. Buttimer, 'Social space in interdisciplinary perspective', *Geographical Review*, 59 (1969), pp. 417–26.

4 On 'genres de vie' see P. Vidal de la Blache, *Principles of human geography* (English translation; London, 1926); on 'social space' see M. Sorre, *Les Fondements de la géographie humaine*, 3 vols. (Paris, 1943–52), and *Rencontres de la géographie et sociologie* (Paris, 1957). The concept of social space was first advanced by E. Durkheim, *De la division du travail social* (Paris, 1893). For a review and appraisal of the significance of this concept see Buttimer, 'Social space'.

5 For reviews of the scope of modern social geography see E. Jones, *Readings in social geography* (Oxford, 1975), pp. 1–14; E. Jones and J. Eyles, *An introduction to social geography* (Oxford, 1977); D. Ley, *A social geography of the city* (New York, 1983); P. Jackson and S. Smith, *Exploring social geography* (London, 1984).

6 For most recent developments see P. Jackson, 'Social geography culture and capital', *Progress in Human Geography*, 8 (1984), pp. 105–12.

7 See for instance D. Fraser and A. Sutcliffe (eds.), *The pursuit of urban history* (London, 1983), pp. xxv, 212; M. J. Daunton, *House and home in the Victorian city: working-class housing 1850–1914* (London, 1983), p. 4.

8 See listings of research in progress in various issues of the *Urban History Year-*

book (Leicester), also, T. Wild (ed.), *Register of research in historical geography* (Norwich, 1980); H. S. A. Fox (ed.), *Register of research in historical geography* (Belfast, 1976).

9 D. Gregory, *Regional transformation and industrial revolution* (London, 1982).

10 D. Harvey, *Social justice and the city* (London, 1973); D. Harvey, 'Class structure in capitalist society and the theory of residential differentiation', in R. Peel *et al.* (eds.), *Processes in physical and human geography* (London, 1975), pp. 354–72.

11 For example R. J. Dennis and S. Daniels, '"Community" and the social geography of Victorian cities', *Urban History Yearbook* (Leicester, 1981), pp. 7–23; R. Lawton and C. G. Pooley, 'David Brindley's Liverpool: an aspect of urban society in the 1880s', *Transactions of the Historical Society of Lancashire and Cheshire*, 125 (1975), pp. 149–68; W. Bramwell, 'Pubs and localised communities in mid-Victorian Birmingham', *Queen Mary College (University of London) Dept of Geography Occasional Paper*, 22 (1984). See also W. Kirk, 'Problems of geography', *Geography*, 48 (1963), pp. 357–71, for an early statement on the 'Behavioural Environment'.

12 A. Charlesworth (ed.), *An atlas of rural protest in Britain 1549–1900* (London, 1982); Gregory, *Regional transformation*.

13 D. Ward, 'Social structure and social geography in large cities of the U.S. urban-industrial heartland', *Historical Geography Research Series*, 12 (Norwich, 1983), pp. 1–31; D. Ward, 'The place of Victorian cities in developmental approaches to urbanisation', in J. Patten (ed.), *The expanding city: essays in honour of Professor Jean Gottmann* (London, 1983), pp. 355–79.

14 Clearly exemplified by C. R. Lewis, 'A stage in the development of the industrial town: a case study of Cardiff, 1845–75', *Transactions of the Institute of British Geographers*, NS, 4 (1979), pp. 129–52; H. Carter and S. Wheatley, *Merthyr Tydfil in 1851: a study of the spatial structure of a Welsh industrial town* (Cardiff, 1982).

15 For example, R. M. Pritchard, *Housing and the spatial structure of the city* (Cambridge, 1976); R. J. Dennis, 'Intercensal mobility in a Victorian city', *Transactions of the Institute of British Geographers*, NS, 2 (1977), pp. 349–63; C. G. Pooley, 'Residential mobility in the Victorian city', *Transactions of the Institute of British Geographers*, NS, 4 (1979), pp. 258–77; J. T. Jackson, 'Housing areas in mid-Victorian Wigan and St Helens', *Transactions of the Institute of British Geographers*, NS, 6 (1981), pp. 413–32.

16 H. Carter and S. Wheatley, 'Residential segregation in Victorian cities', *Area*, 12 (1980), pp. 57–62; R. J. Dennis, 'Why study segregation?', *Area*, 12 (1980), pp. 313–17; C. G. Pooley, 'Residential differentiation in Victorian cities: a reassessment', *Transactions of the Institute of British Geographers*, NS, 9 (1984), pp. 131–44. R. J. Dennis *English industrial cities of the nineteenth century: a social geography* (Cambridge, 1984), pp. 200–49.

17 A succinct discussion of these issues will be found in H. Carter, *An introduction to urban historical geography* (London, 1983), pp. 171–204.

18 See the discussion in D. Cannadine, 'Victorian cities: how different?', *Social History*, 2 (1977), pp. 457–82; D. Ward, 'Victorian cities: how modern?', *Journal of Historical Geography*, 1 (1975), pp. 135–51; J. H. Johnson and C. G. Pooley (eds.), *The structure of nineteenth-century cities* (London, 1982), Part IV.

19 Carter and Wheatley, 'Residential segregation'; Jackson, 'Housing areas', pp. 429–30; C. G. Pooley, 'Residential differentiation in the nineteenth-century city', in B. C. Burnham and J. Kingsbury (eds.), *Space, hierarchy and society* (BAR International Series, 59, Oxford, 1979); Pooley, 'Residential differentiation', pp. 131–5.

20 A. M. Warnes, 'Residential patterns in an emerging industrial town', in B. D. Clark and M. B. Gleave (eds.), *Social patterns in cities* (IBG Special Publication 5, London, 1973), pp. 169–89.

21 B. R. Bristow, 'Residential differentiation in mid-nineteenth century Preston', unpublished PhD thesis, University of Lancaster, 1982. See also M. Anderson, *Family structure in nineteenth-century Lancashire* (Cambridge, 1971).

22 Grid squares have been successfully used in a number of studies of medium-sized towns, for example: M. Shaw, 'The ecology of social change: Wolverhampton 1851–71', *Transactions of the Institute of British Geographers*, NS, 2 (1977), pp. 332–48; Carter and Wheatley, *Merthyr Tydfil*; R. A. Tansey, 'Residential patterns in the nineteenth-century city: Kingston upon Hull 1851', unpublished PhD thesis, University of Hull, 1973.

23 R. Lawton and C. G. Pooley, 'The social geography of Merseyside in the nineteenth century' (SSRC final report, HR 1672, Liverpool, 1976).

24 Ward, 'Victorian Cities: How Modern?'; D. Ward, 'Environs and neighbours in the "Two Nations": residential differentiation in mid-nineteenth century Leeds', *Journal of Historical Geography*, 6 (1980), pp. 133–62.

25 Pooley, 'Residential differentiation', pp. 134–5.

26 H. Carter and C. R. Lewis, 'Processes and patterns in nineteenth-century cities', Unit 15 of Open University D301 *Aspects of Historical Geography* (Milton Keynes, 1983) pp. 43–95.

27 Notable exceptions include M. J. Daunton, *Coal metropolis: Cardiff 1870–1914* (Leicester, 1977); D. Cannadine, *Lords and landlords: the aristocracy and the towns 1774–1967* (Leicester, 1980).

28 For a review of the scope of this work see R. Lawton, 'Mobility in nineteenth-century British cities', *Geographical Journal*, 145 (1979), pp. 206–24; R. Lawton and C. G. Pooley, 'Problems and potentialities for the study of internal population mobility in nineteenth-century England', *Canadian Studies in Population*, 5 (1978, Special Issue, 1980), pp. 69–84.

29 See the comments of M. Anderson, 'Indicators of population change and stability in nineteenth-century cities: some sceptical comments', in J. H. Johnson and C. G. Pooley (eds.), *The structure of nineteenth-century cities* (London, 1982), pp. 283–98.

30 Dennis, 'Intercensal mobility', p. 353.

31 Pooley, 'Residential mobility', pp. 260–1.

32 C. Booth, *Life and labour of the people of London*, vol. 1 (London, 1889), p. 26; L. H. Lees, 'Patterns of lower-class life: Irish slum communities in nineteenth-century London', in S. Thernstom and R. Sennett (eds.), *Nineteenth-century cities: essays in the new urban history* (New Haven, 1969), pp. 359–85; Anderson, *Family structure*, pp. 41–2.

33 Pritchard, *Housing*, pp. 49–67; Dennis 'Intercensal mobility'; Pooley, 'Residential mobility'.

34 For instance J. Burnett (ed.), *Useful toil* (London, 1974); R. Roberts, *The classic slum* (Manchester, 1971); M. S. Pember Reeves, *Round about a pound a week* (London, 1914); E. Roberts, 'Working wives and their families', in T. Barker and M. Drake (eds.), *Population and society in Britain 1850–1980* (London, 1982), pp. 140–71.

35 Lawton and Pooley, 'David Brindley's Liverpool', pp. 153–6.

36 But see Pritchard, *Housing*; Jackson, 'Housing areas'; C. G. Pooley, 'Choice and constraint in the nineteenth-century city: a basis for residential differentiation', in Johnson and Pooley, *The structure of nineteenth-century cities*, pp. 199–233.

37 For instance H. J. Dyos, 'The slums of Victorian London', *Victorian Studies*, 11 (1967), pp. 5–40; S. D. Chapman, *The history of working-class housing* (Newton Abbot, 1971); A. S. Wohl, *'The external slum': housing and social policy in Victorian London* (London, 1977); S. M. Gaskell, 'Housing and the lower middle class, 1870–1914', in G. Crossick (ed.), *The lower middle class in Britain 1870–1914* (London, 1977), pp. 159–83; Cannadine, *Lords and landlords*; Daunton, *House and home*; D. Englander, *Landlord and tenant in urban Britain 1838–1918* (London, 1983).

38 R. J. Springett, 'Landowners and urban development: the Ramsden estate and nineteenth-century Huddersfield', *Journal of Historical Geography*, 8 (1982), pp. 129–44; P. J. Aspinall, 'The internal structure of the housebuilding industry in nineteenth-century cities', in Johnson and Pooley, *The structure of nineteenth-century cities*, pp. 75–106; J. W. R. Whitehand, 'Building activity and intensity of development at the urban fringe: the case of a London suburb in the nineteenth century', *Journal of Historical Geography*, 1 (1975), pp. 211–24.

39 I. C. Taylor, 'The court and cellar dwelling: the eighteenth-century origin of the Liverpool slum', *Transactions of the Historic Society of Lancashire and Cheshire*, 112 (1970), pp. 67–90; C. A. Forster, *Court housing in Kingston-upon-Hull* (Hull, 1972).

40 The classic work on building cycles and their effects is: J. P. Lewis, *Building cycles and Britain's growth* (Manchester, 1965). See also A. Offer, *Property and politics 1870–1914: land ownership, law, ideology and urban development in England* (Cambridge, 1981).

41 M. Shaw, 'Reconciling social and physical space: Wolverhampton 1871', *Transactions of the Institute of British Geographers*, NS, 4 (1979), pp. 192–213; H. Carter and S. Wheatley, 'Fixation lines and fringe belts, land uses and social areas: nineteenth-century change in the small town', *Transactions of the Institute of British Geographers*, NS, 4 (1979), pp. 214–38.

42 J. T. Jackson, 'Nineteenth-century housing in Wigan and St Helens', *Transactions of the Lancashire and Cheshire Historic Society*, 129 (1980), pp. 125–44; Jackson, 'Housing areas'.

43 J. E. Vance, 'Housing the worker: the employment linkage as a force in urban structure', *Economic Geography*, 42 (1966), pp. 294–325; J. E. Vance, 'Housing the worker: determinative and contingent ties in nineteenth-century Birmingham', *Economic Geography*, 43 (1967), pp. 95–127. See also A. M. Warnes, 'Early separation of homes from workplaces and the urban structure of Chorley,

1780–1850', *Transactions of the Lancashire and Cheshire Historic Society*, 122 (1970), pp. 105–35.

44 Ward, 'Environs and neighbours'.

45 G. Stedman Jones, *Outcast London: a study in the relationship between classes in Victorian society* (Oxford, 1971); J. Foster, *Class struggle and the industrial revolution* (London, 1974); R. Q. Gray, *The labour aristocracy in Victorian Edinburgh* (Oxford, 1976); G. Crossick, *An artisan elite in Victorian society* (London, 1978); P. Joyce, *Work, politics and society* (London, 1980).

46 Lawton and Pooley, 'Social geography of Merseyside', pp. 56–64.

47 Stedman Jones, *Outcast London*, pp. 52–66.

48 D. R. Green, 'Street trading in London: a case study of casual labour 1830–60', in Johnson and Pooley, *The structure of nineteenth-century cities*, pp. 129–51.

49 For instance D. Fraser, *Urban politics in Victorian England* (Leicester, 1976); D. Fraser, *Power and authority in the Victorian city* (Oxford, 1979); A. Sutcliffe, *Towards the planned city: Germany, Britain, the United States and France, 1870–1914* (Oxford, 1981); P. J. Waller, *Democracy and sectarianism: a political and social history of Liverpool 1868–1939* (Liverpool, 1981).

50 For example I. C. Taylor, 'The insanitary housing question and tenements dwellings in nineteenth-century Liverpool', in A. Sutcliffe (ed.), *Multi-storey living. The British working-class experience* (London, 1974), pp. 41–87; R. Woods, 'Mortality and sanitary conditions in the "Best Governed City in the World" – Birmingham 1870–1910', *Journal of Historical Geography*, 4 (1978), pp. 35–56; G. E. Cherry, 'The town planning movement and the late-Victorian city', *Transactions of the Institute of British Geographers*, NS, 4 (1979), pp. 306–19; J. A. Yelling, 'The selection of sites for slum clearance in London 1875–88', *Journal of Historical Geography*, 7 (1981), pp. 155–65; essays in R. Woods and J. Woodward (eds.), *Urban disease and mortality in nineteenth-century England* (London, 1984).

51 I. C. Taylor, 'Black spot on the Mersey: environment and society in eighteenth- and nineteenth-century Liverpool', unpublished PhD thesis, University of Liverpool, 1976; M. E. Pooley and C. G. Pooley, 'Health, society and environment in nineteenth-century Manchester', in Woods and Woodward, *Urban disease*, pp. 148–75; R. I. Woods, 'Mortality and sanitary conditions in late-nineteenth century Birmingham', in Woods and Woodward, *Urban disease*, pp. 176–202.

52 Research in progress, G. Kearns, Department of Geography, University of Liverpool.

53 For instance Sutcliffe, *Multi-storey living*; S. Merrett, *State housing in Britain* (London, 1979); J. Melling (ed.), *Housing, social policy and the state* (London, 1980); M. Swenarton, *Homes fit for heroes* (London, 1981); M. J. Daunton (ed.), *Councillors and tenants: local authority housing in English cities 1919–39* (Leicester, 1984).

54 C. G. Pooley and S. Irish, *The development of corporation housing in Liverpool 1869–1945* (University of Lancaster, Centre for NW Regional Studies, Resource Paper 3, 1984); C. G. Pooley, 'Housing for the poorest poor: slum clearance and rehousing in Liverpool 1890–1918', *Journal of Historical Geography*, 11 (1985).

55 Dennis, 'Why study segregation?'.

56 Daunton, *House and home*, p. 4.
57 For instance Anderson, 'Indicators of population change'; D. Cannadine, 'Residential differentiation in nineteenth-century towns: from shapes on the ground to shapes in society', in Johnson and Pooley, *The structure of nineteenth-century cities*, pp. 235–52; Pooley, 'Residential differentiation'.
58 R. J. Dennis, 'Distance and social interaction in a Victorian city', *Journal of Historical Geography*, 3 (1977), pp. 237–50; Dennis and Daniels, '"Community"'; R. J. Dennis, 'Stability and change in urban communities: a geographical perspective', in Johnson and Pooley, *The structure of nineteenth-century cities*, pp. 253–82.
59 For instance C. G. Pooley, 'The residential segregation of migrant communities in mid-Victorian Liverpool', *Transactions of the Institute of British Geographers*, NS, 2 (1977), pp. 304–82; L. H. Lees, *Exiles of Erin* (Manchester, 1979); J. Papworth, 'The Irish in Liverpool 1835–71: segregation and dispersal', unpublished PhD thesis, University of Liverpool, 1981.
60 See Bramwell, 'Pubs and localised communities'; Dennis, *English industrial cities*.
61 These ideas are developed in Pooley, 'Residential differentiation', pp. 135–141. See also R. Harris, 'Residential segregation and class formation in the capitalist city', *Progress in Human Geography*, 8 (1984), pp. 26–49.
62 For instance P. Laxton, 'Liverpool in 1801: a manuscript return for the first national census of population', *Transactions of the Historic Society of Lancashire and Cheshire*, 130 (1981), pp. 73–113; Pooley and Irish, *The development of corporation housing*.
63 See for instance the two issues of *Transactions of the Institute of British Geographers*, 'Change in the Town', NS, 2 (1977), and 'The Victorian City', NS, 4 (1979).
64 The work of historical geographers was notably absent from a recent compilation of research in urban history: Fraser and Sutcliffe, *The pursuit of urban history*.

13 Patrician urban landlords: research on patronal relations in nineteenth-century 'estate towns' in the British Isles

The following abbreviations are used in the notes:
CW. MS: Devonshire Papers, Chatsworth
CW. (Currey) MS: Papers deposited by Currey & Co. at Chatsworth
L.E.O. MS: Devonshire Papers, Lismore Estate Office
N.L.I.: National Library of Ireland
P.R.O.N.I.: Public Record Office of Northern Ireland
  1 J. R. Kellett, *Railways and Victorian cities* (London, 1979), pp. 127, 151, 176, 209, 246; M. J. Mortimore, 'Landownership and urban growth in Bradford and its environs in the West Riding conurbation', *Transactions of the Institute of British Geographers*, 46 (1969), pp. 109–19; D. J. Olsen, *Town planning in London: the eighteenth and nineteenth centuries* (New Haven, 1964), pp. 27–96; D. Spring, 'English landowners and nineteenth century industrialism', in J. T. Ward and R. G. Wilson (eds.), *Land and industry: the landed estate and the industrial revolution* (Newton Abbot, 1971), pp. 39–40, 42–3; J. Springett, 'Landowners and urban development: the Ramsden estate and

nineteenth-century Huddersfield', *Journal of Historical Geography*, 8 (1982), pp. 129–44; D. Ward, 'The pre-urban cadaster and the urban pattern of Leeds', *Annals of the Association of American Geographers*, 52 (1962), pp. 151–66.

2 D. Cannadine, *Lords and landlords: the aristocracy and the towns 1774–1967* (Leicester, 1980); D. Cannadine (ed.), *Patricians, power and politics in nineteenth-century towns* (Leicester, 1982); J. Davies, *Cardiff and the Marquesses of Bute* (Cardiff, 1981).

3 D. Cannadine, 'From "feudal" lords to figureheads: urban landownership and aristocratic influence in nineteenth-century towns', *Urban History Yearbook* (Leicester, 1978), pp. 23–35.

4 F. H. A. Aalen, *Man and the landscape in Ireland* (London, 1978), pp. 279–84; N. T. Burke, 'An early modern Dublin suburb: the estate of Francis Augnier, Earl of Longford', *Irish Geography*, 6, 4 (1972), pp. 365–85; G. Camblin, *The town in Ulster* (Belfast, 1951), pp. 75–94; L. M. Cullen, *Irish towns and villages* (Dublin, 1979); A. Horner, 'Land transactions and the making of carton demesne', *Kildare Archaeological Society Journal*, 15, 4 (1974–5), pp. 387–96; T. J. Hughes, 'Village and town in mid nineteenth century Ireland', *Irish Geography*, 14 (1981), pp. 99–106; A. R. Orme, *Ireland* (London, 1970), pp. 132–44.

5 J. Bardon, *Belfast. An illustrated history* (Belfast, 1982), pp. 71–6; M. E. Daly, *Dublin. The deposed capital. A social and economic history 1860–1914* (Cork, 1984), pp. 152–202; M. E. Daly, 'Late nineteenth and early twentieth century Dublin', in D. Harkness and M. O'Dowd (eds.), *The town in Ireland*, Historical Studies 13 (Belfast, 1981), pp. 239–40; W. A. Maguire, *Living like a Lord. The Second Marquis of Donegall 1769–1844* (Belfast, 1984), pp. 75–97; W. A. Maguire, 'Lord Donegall and the sale of Belfast: a case history from the encumbered estates court', *English Historical Review*, 29 (1976) pp. 570–84; W. A. Maguire, 'Lords and landlords – the Donegall family', in J. C. Beckett *et al.*, *Belfast. The making of the city 1800–1914* (Belfast, 1983), pp. 27–40.

6 P.R.O.N.I. T.3158/1799, H. Bowman to J. Heaton, 4 Feb. 1800.

7 CW. (Currey) MS L/5/4, T. Knowlton to J. Heaton, 20 Oct. 1808; Sir T. Osborne to T. Knowlton, 10 Nov. 1808; T. Knowlton to J. Heaton, 5 Dec. 1808; L/9/18, Deed of Conveyance, Osborne Premises Dungarvan, 1809.

8 D. Cannadine, 'The landowner as millionaire: the finances of the Dukes of Devonshire, c. 1800–c. 1926', *Agricultural History Review*, 25 (1977), pp. 77–97; S. Pollard, 'Barrow-in-Furness and the Seventh Duke of Devonshire', *Economic History Review*, 2nd series, 8 (1955), pp. 213–21; S. Pollard, 'Town planning in the nineteenth century: the beginnings of modern Barrow-in-Furness', *Transactions of the Lancashire and Cheshire Antiquarian Society*, 63 (1952–3), pp. 87–116.

9 Cannadine, *Lords and landlords*, pp. 229–390.

10 R. G. Heape, *Buxton under the Dukes of Devonshire* (London, 1948).

11 Cannadine, *Patricians*, pp. 11–13.

12 The literature on population change in nineteenth-century Ireland is extensive. For a recent survey, see D. B. Grigg, *Population growth and agrarian change. An historical perspective* (Cambridge, 1980), pp. 115–40.

13 L. M. Cullen, *An economic history of Ireland since 1660* (London, 1972),

pp. 123–5, 144–8, 156–64; E. R. R. Green, 'Industrial decline in the nineteenth century', in L. M. Cullen (ed.), *The formation of the Irish economy* (Cork, 1969), pp. 89–100; J. M. Goldstrom, 'The industrialisation of the north-east', in Cullen, *The formation of the Irish economy*, pp. 101–12.

14 J. C. Beckett, *A short history of Ireland* (London, 1977), pp. 130–66; S. Clarke and J. S. Donnelly (eds.), *Irish peasants, violence and political unrest 1780–1914* (Manchester, 1983); W. H. Crawford, 'Ulster as a mirror of the two societies', in T. M. Devine and D. Dickson (eds.), *Ireland and Scotland 1600–1850* (Edinburgh, 1983), pp. 60–9; F. S. L. Lyons, *Culture and anarchy in Ireland 1890–1939* (Oxford, 1979), pp. 134–80; W. E. Vaughan, 'Landlord and tenant relations in Ireland between the famine and the Land War, 1850–78', in L. M. Cullen and T. C. Smout (eds.), *Comparative aspects of Scottish and Irish economic and social history 1600–1900* (Edinburgh, 1977), pp. 216–26.

15 Aalen, *Man and the landscape*, pp. 285–9; Cullen, *An economic history*, pp. 121–2, 140–2, 147–8, 164–5; T. W. Freeman, 'Irish towns in the eighteenth and nineteenth centuries', in R. A. Butlin (ed.), *The development of the Irish town* (London, 1977), pp. 121–35; J. Lee, *The modernisation of Irish society 1848–1918* (Dublin, 1979), pp. 97–9.

16 Grigg, *Population growth*, p. 116.

17 *Ibid.*, pp. 127–9.

18 H. C. Darby (ed.), *A new historical geography of England after 1600* (Cambridge, 1976), pp. 91, 166, 296, 374–5.

19 Cannadine, *Lords and landlords*, 406–8.

20 J. Pearson, *Stags and serpents* (London, 1983), pp. 91–2.

21 J. Davies, 'Aristocratic town-makers and the coal metropolis: the marquesses of Bute and the growth of Cardiff, 1776 to 1947', in Cannadine, *Patricians*, pp. 25–6.

22 L.E.O. MS C/1/2, W. S. Currey to B. Currey, 6 Apr. 1830.

23 CW. (Currey) MS L/9/7 1659–1831, Bundle: Youghal 1804–7; T. Knowlton to J. Heaton, 6 Oct. 1807; 7 Oct. 1807.

24 P.R.O.N.I. T.3158/1700, T. Garde to J. Heaton, 8 Jan. 1792.

25 CW. (Currey) MS L/9/7, Bundle: letters from the Duke of Devonshire's Irish Steward, 1784, 1785, 1786; W. Connor to Baron Hotham, 4 Sept. 1786.

26 CW. (Currey) MS L/83/2, J. Heaton to 6th Duke, 24 Aug. 1813.

27 P.R.O.N.I. T.3158/1692, Sir R. Musgrave to Lord Frederick Cavendish, 14 Dec. 1790; T.3158/1694, Sir R. Musgrave to J. Heaton, 22 Dec. 1790.

28 P.R.O.N.I. T.3158/1710, Memo. by J. Heaton, 11 July 1792.

29 CW. (Currey) MS L/83/2, J. Heaton to 6th Duke, 26 Aug. 1812; J. Heaton to 6th Duke, 24 Aug. 1813.

30 CW (Currey) MS L/9/7, Bundle: correspondence relating to Bandon, 1766–1831; Lord Shannon to Lord Frederick Cavendish, 29 Sept. 1767. L.E.O. MS C/1/19, correspondence of Col. W. S. Currey relating to Bandon, 1811–27.

31 Pearson, *Stags and serpents*, p. 145.

32 CW. (Currey) MS L/9/7 1659–1831, Bundle: Youghal 1804–7; T. Knowlton to J. Heaton, 29 Sept. 1807. L.E.O. MS C/1/11, copy correspondence concerning the Borough of Youghal, Co. Cork, 1809–21. I. d'Alton, *Protestant society and politics in Cork, 1812–1844* (Cork, 1980), pp. 103–6.

33 B. M. Walker (ed.), *Parliamentary election results in Ireland, 1801–1922* (Dublin, 1978), pp. 214–15.

34 L.E.O. MS C/1/20, Bandon election correspondence 1830–1. D'Alton. *Protestant society*, pp. 101–3.

35 CW. (Currey) MS L/83/4 29 1837, 6th Duke to Lord Duncannon, no date.

36 CW. (Currey) MS L/83/4 30 1839, F. E. Currey to B. Currey, 25 May 1839; L/83/4 33 1839–44, W. S. Currey to 6th Duke, 29 May 1839.

37 CW. (Currey) MS L/83/4 29 1837, 6th Duke to B. Currey, 30 June 1837.

38 N.L.I., Lismore Papers, MS 6929, estate accounts, 1818–89.

39 CW. (Currey) MS L/83/4 (27) 1829, P. Fogarty to B. Currey, 27 Oct. 1840, CW. MS, Paxton Group: 103, J. Paxton to S. Paxton, 24 Oct. 1840.

40 Derived from N.L.I., Lismore Papers, MS 6929, estate accounts, 1818–89.

41 Cannadine, 'The landowner as millionaire', p. 82.

42 CW. MS, Paxton Group: 232, 6th Duke to B. Currey, 18 July 1844.

43 CW. MS, Paxton Group: 231, Memo. by J. Paxton, no date [1844].

44 CW. MS, Paxton Group: 233, B. Currey to 6th Duke, 20 July 1844; 251, B. Currey to 6th Duke, 24 Aug. 1844.

45 CW. MS, Paxton Group: 100.42, J. Paxton to 7th Duke, 12 Feb. 1858; 100.43, J. Paxton to 7th Duke, 6 Mar. 1858.

46 N.L.I., Lismore Papers, MS 7188, Letter Book, W. Currey, 1855–8: F. E. Currey to W. Currey, 19 Feb. 1858, 7 Apr. 1858, 13 Apr. 1858, 1 May 1858, 31 July 1858, 10 Aug. 1858.

47 CW. MS, 6th Duke correspondence, 2nd series: 4.52, Duke of Bedford to 7th Duke, 15 May 1858; 4.54, Duke of Bedford to 7th Duke, 21 May 1858; 4.55, Duke of Bedford to 7th Duke, 22 May 1858.

48 N.L.I., Lismore Papers, MS 7190, Letter Book, W. Currey, 1858–63: F. E. Currey to 7th Duke, 30 Oct. 1858.

49 L.E.O. MS C/1/4, Co. Waterford election correspondence, 1807: 1819: 1825: 6th Duke to Roman Catholic freeholders of Co. Waterford, 9 Sept. 1825.

50 L.E.O. MS C/1/17, general political correspondence, 1829: W. S. Currey to B. Currey, 20 June 1829; B. Currey to W. S. Currey, 7 July 1829; J. Abercrombie to B. Currey, 29 July 1829. L.E.O. MS C/1/8, Co. Waterford election correspondence, Aug. 1829–Jan. 1830: instructions to Col. Currey, post 7 Oct. 1829.

51 L.E.O. MS C/1/16, Youghal election correspondence, 1832: B. Jackson to W. S. Currey, 12 Dec. 1832, 15 Dec. 1832: L.E.O. C/1/17, Youghal election correspondence, 1834/5: G. Roche to W. S. Currey, 1 Jan. 1835, 3 Jan. 1835.

52 N.L.I., Lismore Papers, MS 7191, Letter Book, Dungarvan, 1850–70: F. E. Currey to J. J. Byrne, 8 Oct. 1859.

53 L.E.O. MS C/2/23, Youghal Copy Letter Book, 1860–80: F. E. Currey to J. J. Byrne, 5 Sept. 1860. N.L.I., Lismore Papers, MS 7190, Letter Book, W. Currey, 1858–63: F. E. Currey to 7th Duke, 18 Feb. 1862.

54 N.L.I., Lismore Papers, MS 7190, Letter Book, W. Currey, 1858–63: F. E. Currey to 7th Duke, 22 Dec. 1859.

55 N.L.I., Lismore Papers, MS 7190, Letter Book, W. Currey, 1858–63: F. W. Currey to 7th Duke, 14 Oct. 1861.

56 See, for example, L.E.O. MS C/1/85, D-K, agents' correspondence, 1870–9:

7th Duke to F. E. Currey, 2 June 1980, 22 June 1870, 5 Mar. 1872, 17 June 1873, 6 Jan. 1878; C/1/85, M-R agents' correspondence, 1880–9: 7th Duke to F. E. Currey, 4 May 1881.

57 L.E.O. MS C/1/85, D-K, agents' correspondence, 1870–9: J. R. Berwick to F. E. Currey, 31 Dec. 1873; 7th Duke to F. E. Currey, 1 Feb. 1875.

58 L.E.O. MS C/1/85, D-K, agents' correspondence, 1870–9: J. Berwick to F. E. Currey, 31 Feb. 1879.

59 N.L.I., Lismore Papers, MS 7190, Letter Book, W. Currey, 1858–63: F. E. Currey to W. Currey, 26 Mar. 1861, 6 Nov. 1861, 15 Jan. 1863. L.E.O. MS C/2/2, Letter Book, 1880–90: F. E. Currey to C. P. Cotton, 19 June 1884.

60 N.L.I., Lismore Papers, MS 7189, Letter Book, 1856–69: F. E. Currey to J. Hollway, 8 Dec. 1856, 5 Feb. 1857, 11 Feb. 1857; F. E. Currey to R. Griffith, 7 Feb. 1863.

61 L.E.O. MS C/1/85, M-R, agents' correspondence, 1880–9: J. Berwick to F. E. Currey, 1 Jan. 1883, 9 June 1885. L.E.O. MS C/2/21, Letter Book, 1883–98: F. E. Currey to J. Berwick, 18 Feb. 1884.

62 L.E.O. MS C/1/85, M-R, agents' correspondence, 1880–9: J. Berwick to R. Power, 21 Dec. 1886.

63 Derived from N.L.I., Lismore Papers, MS 6929, estate accounts, 1818–89.

64 L.E.O. MS C/2/21, Letter Book, 1883–98: F. E. Currey to J. Berwick, 23 Apr. 1883; R. Power to D. Craig, 9 Jan. 1889.

65 Monies were channelled through the Irish agents in their capacity as directors of the various railway companies and thus appear in the cash books (N.L.I., Lismore Papers, MSS 7100–14) but not in the annual accounts (N.L.I., Lismore Papers, MSS 6945–57).

66 Cannadine, *Lords and landlords*, p. 294.

67 Cannadine, 'The landowner as millionaire', p. 87; Cannadine, *Lords and landlords*, pp. 294–5.

68 Cannadine, *Lords and landlords*, p. 291.

69 *Ibid.*, pp. 285–7.

70 *Ibid.*, pp. 305–20.

71 *Ibid.*, pp. 245–51.

72 Cannadine, 'The landowner as millionaire', pp. 87–91.

73 D. J. O'Donoghue, *History of Bandon* (Cork, 1970), p. 20.

74 Cannadine, *Lords and landlords*, p. 329.

75 *Ibid.*, pp. 337–42.

76 Davies, 'Aristocratic town-makers', pp. 25–44, 48–55.

77 *Ibid.*, p. 35.

78 *Ibid.*, pp. 33–5.

79 *Ibid.*, pp. 48–55.

80 R. Trainor, 'Peers on an industrial frontier: the earls of Dartmouth and of Dudley in the Black Country, c. 1810 to 1914', in Cannadine, *Patricians*; D. Cannadine, 'The Calthorpe family and Birmingham, 1810–1910: a "conservative interest" examined', *Historical Journal*, 18 (1975), pp. 725–60; Cannadine, *Lords and landlords*, pp. 128–228; J. Liddle, 'Estate management and land reform politics: the Hesketh and Scarisbrick families and the making of Southport, 1842 to 1914', in Cannadine, *Patricians*.

81 Trainor, 'Peers on an industrial frontier', pp. 82–9.
82 *Ibid.*, p. 99.
83 *Ibid.*, pp. 103–13.
84 Cannadine, 'The Calthorpe family', pp. 730–6.
85 *Ibid.*, pp. 749–60.
86 CW. (Currey) MS L/83/4 32 (1839–43), F. E. Currey to 6th Duke, 25 Sept. 1843; F. E. Currey to B. Currey, 29 Sept. 1843. N.L.I., Lismore Papers, MS 7191, Letter Book, Dungarvan, 1848–86: F. E. Currey to T. Foley, 30 Mar. 1857.
87 CW. (Currey) MS L/83/4 (27) 1829, W. S. Currey to B. Currey, 27 June 1829.
88 CW. (Currey) MS L/83/4 32 (1839–43), F. E. Currey to 6th Duke, 23 Sept. 1843.
89 N.L.I., Lismore Papers, MS 7191, Letter Book, Dungarvan, 1850–70: F. E. Currey to F. J. Howard, 3 Apr. 1857.
90 N.L.I., Lismore Papers, MS 7188, Letter Book, W. Currey, 1855–8: F. E. Currey to W. Currey, 4 Apr. 1857.
91 P.R.O.N.I. T.3158/1809, T. Garde to J. Heaton, 21 Sept. 1800; /1820, T. Garde to J. Heaton, 17 July 1801; /1821, copy of Commissioner's adjudication in respect of Lismore, 22 July 1801; /1822, copy of same in respect of Tallow, 22 July 1801.
92 Walker, *Parliamentary election results*, pp. 400–1.
93 *Ibid.*, pp. 278, 324.
94 Cannadine, *Patricians*, p. 4.
95 D'Alton, *Protestant society*, pp. 103–6.
96 CW. (Currey) MS L/5/4, T. Knowlton to J. Heaton, 20 Oct. 1808; L/83/2, J. Heaton to 6th Duke, 24 Aug. 1813.
97 Trainor, 'Peers on an industrial frontier', pp. 116–18; Liddle, 'Estate management', pp. 163–6; R. Roberts, 'Leasehold estates and municipal enterprise: landowners, local government and the development of Bournemouth, c. 1850 to 1914', in Cannadine, *Patricians*, p. 211; Cannadine, *Lords and landlords*, p. 421.
98 N.L.I., Lismore Papers, MS 7183, Letter Book, 1844, 1849–51: F. E. Currey to B. Currey, 31 Dec. 1842.
99 L.E.O. MS C/2/1, copy Letter Book, 1869–80: F. E. Currey to Clerk Lismore Town Commissioners, 18 July 1876.
100 L.E.O. MS C/2/2, Copy Letter Book, 1880–1980: R. Power to M. Healy, 7 Nov. 1885.
101 CW. MS, 7th Duke's diaries, vol. 13, 1858–60: entry for 13 May 1859.
102 L.E.O. MS A/2/40–3, Draft Ledgers, 1919–35.

14 The development of urban centrality in England and Wales

1 A. Pred, *City systems in advanced economies* (London, 1977).
2 H. Loyn, 'Towns in late Anglo-Saxon England', in P. Clemoes and K. Hughes (eds.), *England before the Conquest* (Cambridge, 1971), pp. 115–28.
3 B. Cunliffe, 'The origins of urbanization in Britain', in B. Cunliffe and T. Rowley

(eds.), *Oppida: the beginning of urbanization on Barbarian Europe*, British Archaeology Reports, Supplementary Series, No. 11 (Oxford, 1976).

4 J. Wacher, *The towns of Roman Britain* (London, 1974), p. 18.

5 *Ibid.*, p. 18.

6 *Ibid.*, pp. 79–87.

7 I. Hodder, 'The human geography of Roman Britain', in R. A. Dodgshon and R. A. Butlin (eds.), *An historical geography of England and Wales* (London, 1978), pp. 36–40.

8 H. C. Darby, 'Domesday England', in H. C. Darby (ed.), *A new historical geography of England before 1600* (Cambridge, 1976), p. 71.

9 S. Reynolds, *An introduction to the history of English medieval towns* (Oxford, 1977), p. 34.

10 *Ibid.*, p. 36.

11 D. Hill, *An atlas of Anglo-Saxon England* (Oxford, 1981), p. 126.

12 W. K. D. Davies, 'Centrality and the central place hierarchy', *Urban Studies*, 4 (1967), p. 61.

13 Hill, *An Atlas of Anglo-Saxon England*, p. 126.

14 *Ibid.*, p. 133.

15 A. Everitt, 'The Banburys of England', in H. J. Dyos (ed.), *Urban History Yearbook* (Leicester, 1974), pp. 28–38.

16 Darby, 'Domesday England', p. 67.

17 H. Williams (ed.), *De Excidio Britaniae*, Cymmrodorion Record Series, No. 3 (London, 1899–1901).

18 G. C. Boon, *Roman Silchester* (London, 1954, revised 1974).

19 J. R. Russell, *British medieval population* (Albuquerque, 1948).

20 R. A. Donkin, 'Changes in the early middle ages', in Darby, *A new historical geography of England*, p. 132.

21 F. V. Emery, 'England circa 1600', in Darby, *A new historical geography of England*, p. 298.

22 M. W. Beresford, *New towns of the Middle Ages. Town plantation in England, Wales and Gascony* (London, 1967).

23 T. James, *Carmarthen. An archaeological and topographical survey* (Carmarthen, 1980).

24 Donkin, 'Changes in the early middle ages', p. 127.

25 J. Patten, *English towns 1500–1700* (Folkestone, 1978).

26 *Ibid.*, p. 274.

27 H. Carter, *The towns of Wales* (Cardiff, 1965).

28 A. R. H. Baker, 'Changes in the later middle ages,' in Darby, *A new historical geography of England*, p. 241.

29 P. Clark and P. Slack, *English towns in transition 1500–1700* (Oxford, 1976), p. 13.

30 *Ibid.*, p. 159.

31 H. C. Darby, 'The age of the improver 1600–1800', in Darby, *A new historical geography of England*, pp. 381–2.

32 A. F. Weber, *The growth of cities in the nineteenth century. A study in statistics* (Ithaca, N.Y., 1967; originally published New York, 1899).

33 B. T. Robson, *Urban growth: an approach* (London, 1973).

34 Pred, *City systems*, p. 70.

35 Robson, *Urban growth*, pp. 131–85.

36 C. M. Law, 'The growth of urban populations in England and Wales, 1801–1911', *Trans. Inst. Brit. Geogrs.*, 41 (1967), pp. 125–44.

37 W. K. D. Davies, 'Towards an integrated study of central places', in H. Carter and W. K. D. Davies (eds.), *Urban essays: studies in the geography of Wales* (London, 1970), pp. 202–13.

38 Robson, *Urban growth*, p. 30.

39 C. H. Madden, 'On some indications of stability in the growth of cities in the United States', *Econ. Devel. and Cultural Change*, 4 (3) (1956), pp. 236–52.

40 G. W. Zipf, *National unity and disunity* (Bloomington, Ill., 1941).

41 Robson, *Urban growth*, p. 126.

42 G. Rozman, *Urban networks in Russia, 1750–1800, and premodern periodization* (Princeton, N.J., 1976).

43 J. de Vries, 'Patterns of urbanization in pre-industrial Europe, 1500–1800', in H. Schmal (ed.), *Patterns of European urbanization* (London, 1981).

44 R. J. Johnston, *City and society. An outline for urban geography* (London, 1980).

15 The persistence and dynamics of office functions in West German cities since the late nineteenth century

1 P. W. Daniels, *Office location: an urban and regional study* (London, 1975); P. W. Daniels, *Spatial patterns of office growth and location* (Chichester, 1979); P. W. Daniels, *Service industries: growth and location* (Cambridge, 1982); J. B. Goddard, 'Office communications and office location: a review of current research', *Regional Studies*, 5 (1971), pp. 263–80; J. B. Goddard, *Office location in urban and regional development* (London, 1975).

2 H. von Frieling, 'City-Forschungs-"defizite" und Thesen zu den ökonomischen und politischen Bedingungen der Citybildung, am Beispiel von Göttingen', *Erdkunde*, 34 (1980), pp. 16–22; H. Heineberg and G. Heinritz, 'Konzepte und Defizite der empirischen Bürostandortforschung in der Geographie', *Beiträge zur empirischen Bürostandortforschung, Münchener Geographische*, 50 (Regensburg, 1983),pp. 9–28.

3 H. Demmler-Mosetter, 'Die Maximilianstrasse. Entwicklung, Gestalt und Funktionswandel eines zentralen Raumes der Stadt Augsburg', *Augsburger Sozialgeographische*, 2 (Augsburg, 1978); J. C. Tesdorpf, 'Ein Beitrag zur Innenstadtentwicklung dargestellt am Beispiel der Scheffelstrasse in Singen/Hohentwiel', *Freiburger geographische Mitteilungen*, 1 (1975), pp. 1–38; H.-G. Wagner (ed.), 'Städtische Strassen als Wirtschaftsräume. Dokumentation zum Funktionswandel Würzburger Geschäftsstrassen', *Würzburger Universitätsschriften zur Regionalforschung*, 2 (Würzburg, 1980).

4 I. D. Wolcke, 'Die Entwicklung der Bochumer Innenstadt', *Schriften des Geographischen Instituts der Universität Kiel*, 1 (Kiel, 1968). See also: H. Heineberg, 'Zentren in West- und Ost-Berlin, Untersuchungen zum Problem der Erfassung und Bewertung grossstädtischer funktionaler zentrenausstathung in beiden Wirtschafts- und Gesellschaftssystemen Deutschlands', *Bochumer Geographische*

Arbeiten, Sonderreihe (Paderborn, 1977); E. Lichtenberger, *Die Wiener Altstadt. Von der mittelalterlichen Bürgenstadt zur City* (Wien, 1977).

5 G. Gad, 'Büros im Stadtzentrum von Nürnberg', *Erlanger Geographische Arbeiten*, 23 (Erlangen, 1968).

6 P. Dach, 'Struktur und Entwicklung von peripheren Zentren des tertiären Sektors, dargestellt am Beispiel Düsseldorf', *Düsseldorfer Geographische Schriften*, 13 (Düsseldorf, 1980); J. Hartwieg, 'Der Suburbanisierungsprozess unter den kleinen Bürofirmen und freien Berufen im Verdichtungsraum München', *Beiträge zur empirischen Bürostandortforschung, Münchener Geographische*, 50 (Regensburg, 1983), pp. 101–56.

7 H. Heineberg, 'Innerstädtische Standortentwicklung ausgewählter quartärer Dienstleistungsgruppen seit dem 19. Jahrhundert anhand der Städte Münster und Dortmund', in H. Heineberg (ed.), *Innerstädtische Differenzierung und Prozesse im 19. und 20. Jahrhundert. Geographische und historische Aspekte, Städteforschung*, A 25 (Köln, 1987), pp. 263–306; H. Heineberg and N. de Lange, 'Die Cityentwicklung in Münster und Dortmund seit der Vorkriegszeit – unter besonderer Berücksichtigung des Standortverhaltens quartärer Dienstleistungsgruppen', in P. Weber and F. Schreiber (eds.), *Westfalen und angrenzende Regionen. Festschrift zum 44. Deutschen Geographentag in Münster, Münstersche Geographische Arbeiten*, 15 (Paderborn, 1983), pp. 221–85; N. de Lange, 'Standortverhalten ausgewählter Bürogruppen in Innenstadtgebieten westdeutscher Metropolen', in *Beiträge zur empirischen Bürostandortforschung, Münchener Geographische*, 50 (Regensburg, 1983), pp. 61–100; N. de Lange, 'Standortverhalten des Finanzwesens in den Regionalzentren Düsseldorf und Hannover seit dem 19. Jahrhundert', in Heineberg, *Innerstädtische Differenzierung*.

8 The project is part of the so-called 'Sonderforschungsbereich 164: Vergleichende geschichtliche Städteforschung' (Special Research Field 164: Comparative Historical City Research), which was sponsored by the Deutsche Forschungsgemeinschaft (Seminar Association for the Advancement of Scientific Research) until the end of 1986. The Sonderforschungsbereich 164 is located at Münster.

9 H. Schmidt, *Citybildung und Bevölkerungsdichte in Grossstädten* (München, 1909).

10 Gad, 'Büros im Stadtzentrum von Nürnberg', p. 170.

11 M. Pohl, 'Einführung in die Deutsche Bankengeschichte. Die Entwicklung des gesamten deutsche Kreditwereng', *Taschenbücher für Geld, Bank und Bürse*, 79 (Frankfurt, 1976), p. 51.

12 H. H. Blotevogel and M. Hommel, 'Struktur und Entwicklung des Städtesystems', *Geographische Rundschau*, 32 (1980), pp. 155–64.

13 *Ibid.*; N. de Lange, 'Städtetypisierung in Nordrhein-Westfalen im raum-zeitlichen Vergleich 1961 und 1970 mit Hilfe multivariater Methoden – eine empirische Städtesystemanalyse', *Münstersche Geographische Arbeiten*, 8 (Paderborn, 1980).

14 H. Louis, 'Die geographische Gliederung von Grossberlin', *Länderkundliche Forschung, Festschrift für Norbert Krebs* (Stuttgart, 1936), pp. 146–71.

15 De Lange, 'Standortverhalten ausgewählter Bürogruppen'.

16 Heineberg, 'Innerstädtische Standortentwicklung'.

17 Heineberg and de Lange, 'Die Cityentwicklung in Münster und Dortmund'.
18 P. Cowan *et al.*, *The office: a facet of urban growth* (London, 1969); G. Gad, 'Die Dynamik der Bürostandorte: Drei Phasen der Forschung', *Beiträge zur empirischen Bürostandforschung, Münchener Geographische,* 50 (Regensburg, 1983), pp. 29–59; J. B Goddard, 'Office development and urban and regional development in Britain', in Daniels, *Spatial patterns,* pp. 29–60; G. Pritchard, 'A model of professional office location', *Geografiska Annaler,* 57B (1975), pp. 100–8; G. Törnqvist, *Contact systems and regional development,* Series B, vol. 35 (Lund, 1970).

16 Recent research on the commerical structure of nineteenth-century British cities

1 R. Dennis, *English industrial cities of the nineteenth century: a social geography* (Cambridge, 1984), chap. 1; J. H. Johnson and C. G. Pooley (eds.), *The structure of nineteenth-century cities* (London, 1982), chap. 1.
2 C. H. Lee, 'The service sector, regional specialization, and economic growth in the Victorian economy', *Journal of Historical Geography,* 10 (1984), pp. 139–55.
3 P. G. Hall, *The industries of London since 1861* (London, 1962); J. E. Martin, 'The industrial geography of Greater London', in R. Clayton (ed.), *The geography of Greater London* (London, 1964), pp. 111–42.
4 W. Forsyth, 'Urban economic morphology in nineteenth-century Glasgow', in A. Slaven and D. H. Aldcroft (eds.), *Business, banking and urban history* (Edinburgh, 1982), pp. 166–92.
5 J. B. Jefferys, *Retail trading in Britain, 1850–1950* (Cambridge, 1954).
6 J. Blackman, 'The food supply of an industrial town', *Business History,* 5–6 (1962–4), pp. 83–97; J. Burnett, *Plenty and want* (London, 1979); D. Alexander, *Retailing in England during the industrial revolution* (London, 1970).
7 G. Shaw and M. T. Wild, 'Retail patterns in the Victorian City', *Transactions Institute British Geogs.,* N.S., 4 (1979), pp. 278–91.
8 Even accounting for variations in the accuracy of directory data the differences are still substantial.
9 Shaw and Wild, 'Retail patterns'.
10 Alexander, *Retailing in England,* discusses the possible effects of settlement type on shop provision during the early nineteenth century; see also M. T. Wild and G. Shaw, 'Population distribution and retail provision: the case of the Halifax–Calder valley area of West Yorkshire during the second half of the nineteenth century', *Journal of Historical Geography,* 1 (1975), pp. 193–210.
11 G. Shaw, 'Changes in consumer demand and food supply in nineteenth-century British cities', *Journal of Historical Geography,* 11 (1985), pp. 280–96.
12 M. T. Wild and G. Shaw, 'Locational behaviour of urban retailing during the nineteenth century: the example of Kingston-upon-Hull', *Transactions Institute British Geogs.,* 61 (1974), pp. 101–18.
13 R. Jones, 'Consumers' co-operation in Victorian Edinburgh: the evolution of a locational pattern', *Transactions Institute British Geogs.,* N.S., 4 (1979), pp. 292–305.
14 P. T. Kivell and G. Shaw, 'The study of retail location', in J. Dawson (ed.), *Retail geography* (London, 1980), pp. 95–155.

15 G. Shaw, *Processes and patterns in the geography of retail change* (Hull, 1978), chap. 1.
16 Upgrading refers to shops changing from a low order trade, such as food retailing, to a higher order non-food function. Downgrading is the reverse of this process.
17 For a discussion of the methods used to identify these shopping centres see G. Shaw, 'The role of retailing in the urban economy', in J. H. Johnson and C. J. Pooley (eds.), *The structure of nineteenth-century cities* (London, 1982), pp. 171–94.
18 P. S. Bagwell, *The transport revolution from 1770* (London, 1974); T. Barker, 'Towards an historical classification of urban transport development since the late eighteenth century', *Journal of Transport History*, 3rd Series, 1 (1980), pp. 75–90.
19 A. Adburgham, *Shops and shopping, 1800–1914* (London, 1964).
20 H. Carter and G. Rowley, 'The morphology of the central business district of Cardiff', *Transactions Institute British Geogs.*, 38 (1966), pp. 119–34.
21 M. J. Bowden, 'Growth of central business districts in large cities', in L. Schnore (ed.), *The new urban history* (New York, 1978).
22 Forsyth, 'Urban economic morphology'; S. G. Checkland, 'The British industrial city as history', *Urban Studies*, 1 (1964), pp. 34–54.
23 J. R. Kellett, *The impact of railways on Victorian Cities* (London, 1969), chap. 10.
24 Bowden, 'Growth of central business districts'.
25 Forsyth, 'Urban economic morphology'.
26 N. Taylor, *Monuments of commerce* (London, 1968).
27 Kellett, *The impact of railways*.
28 C. R. Elrington and P. M. Tillott, 'The growth of the city', in *A History of the County of Warwick* (Victoria County History 7, 1964), pp. 4–26.
29 Blackman, 'Food supply'; K. Grady, 'Commercial, marketing and retail amenities, 1700–1914', in D. Fraser (ed.), *A history of modern Leeds* (Manchester, 1980), pp. 177–99; R. Scola, 'Food markets and shops in Manchester, 1770–1870', *Journal of Historical Geography*, 1 (1975), pp. 153–68.
30 Wakefield Borough Market Bill, *House of Commons Papers*, 24 (1847).
31 F. Sheppard, *London 1808–1870; the infernal wen* (London, 1971), pp. 189–90.
32 Adburgham, *Shops and shopping*.
33 Shaw and Wild, 'Retail patterns'.
34 Adburgham, *Shops and shopping*; H. Pasdermadjian, *The department store* (London, 1954).
35 C. W. Condit, *The rise of the skyscraper* (London, 1952).
36 A. Briggs, *Friends of the people: the centenary history of Lewis's* (London, 1956).
37 *Ibid.*, p. 80.
38 *Ibid.*, pp. 79–94.

17 Morphogenesis, morphological regions and secular human agency in the historic townscape, as exemplified by Ludlow

1 For the conceptual background of this term cf. König's 'global society' (*Global-gesellschaft*) in R. König, *Grundformen der Gesellschaft: die Gemeinde* (Ham-

burg, 1958), p. 26; and Bobek's 'local society' (*Lokalgesellschaft*) in H. Bobek, 'Über den Einbau der sozialgeographischen Betrachtungsweise in die Kulturgeographie', *Deutscher Geographentag Köln 1961* (Wiesbaden, 1962), pp. 148–65; repr. in W. Storkebaum (ed.), *Sozialgeographie* (Darmstadt, 1969), pp. 89–93.

2 Through the distinctiveness of material forms contributed by them to the cultural landscape historico-cultural periods are also morphological periods. As such they are not absolute historical periods like the reigns of monarchs, but relative periods subject to the diffusion of innovations in geographical space from points of origin, with consequent geographical relativity of their definition by date.

3 With regard to the visible townscape in general the term 'historical stratification' is to be taken here in its broader, figurative as well as its literal, archaeological sense.

4 P. Schöller, *Die deutschen Städte*, Erdkundliches Wissen, No. 17 (Wiesbaden, 1967) pp. 30–2.

5 The nature of these processes including the burgage cycle, has been described in some detail in M. R. G. Conzen, 'Alnwick, Northumberland: a study in town-plan analysis', *Institute of British Geographers Publication*, No. 27 (1960, 2nd edn, 1969); M. R. G. Conzen, 'The plan analysis of an English city centre', in K. Norborg (ed.), *Proceedings of the IGU Symposium in urban geography Lund 1960* (Lund, 1962), pp. 383–414, repr. in J. W. R. Whitehand (ed.), 'The urban landscape: historical development and management', *Institute of British Geographers Special Publication*, No. 13 (London, 1981), pp. 25–53. Further references to papers by Conzen reprinted in the volume edited by J. W. Whitehand follow the pagination in that volume.

6 Conzen, 'Alnwick, Northumberland', pp. 108–9, 116–17; Conzen, 'English city centre', pp. 25–53; M. R. G. Conzen, 'Historical townscapes in Britain: a problem in applied geography', in J. W. House (ed.), *Northern geographical essays in honour of G. H. J. Daysh* (Newcastle upon Tyne, 1966), repr. in Whitehand, 'Urban landscape', pp. 55–74 (includes Ludlow); M. R. G. Conzen, 'Geography and townscape conservation', in *Anglo-German symposium in applied geography, Giessen – Würzburg – München, 1973*, Giessener Geographische Schriften (Giessener, 1975), repr. in Whitehand, '*Urban landscape*', pp. 75–86. Its reference to Ludlow is superseded by the present paper.

7 Conzen, 'Historical townscapes', pp. 70–2; Conzen, 'Geography and townscape conservation', pp. 79–83.

8 Figure 17.1 supersedes Figure 4 in Conzen, 'Historical townscapes'. Its sources are as follows. 1A Relief: form lines at 10 foot intervals interpolated from spot levels on the 1:2, 500 O.S. (1926), with adjustments to available contour lines on other O.S. maps, and field observation. 1B Plan Units: interpretation M.R.G.C. of the town plan on the 1:500 O.S. (1885) Sheets Ludlow LXXVIII.7.25/8.11/8.16/8.17/8.21/8.22/12.1 and 1:2, 500 O.S. (1885) Sheets Shropshire LXXVIII.7/8/12. 1C Building Types and 1D Land Utilization: morphological survey M.R.G.C. 1946.

9 Figure 17.2 supersedes Figure 1 in Conzen, 'Geography and townscape conservation', and is based on the morphological Survey M.R.G.C. 1946.

10 On the concept of persistence of forms cf. E. Sabelberg, *Regionale Stadttypen in Italien*, Erdkundliches Wissen No. 66 (Wiesbaden, 1984), pp. 5–9. He traces

the appearance of the concept in the German-language literature beginning with Czajka in 1964.

11 D. Lloyd and M. Moran, *The corner shop, the history of Bodenhams from the middle ages*, Ludlow Research Papers (L.R.P.) No. 2 (Birmingham, n.d., 1978?), pp. 5–7, 23–30; D. Lloyd, *Broad Street, its houses and residents through eight centuries*, L.R.P. No. 3 (Birmingham, 1979), *passim*, and particularly passages, illustrations and sections of the fold-out topograms relevant to the upper (northern) part of Broad Street.

12 Conzen, 'Historical townscapes', p. 60; Conzen, 'Geography and townscape conservation', p. 79.

13 C. Platt, *The English medieval town* (London, 1976), pp. 62–87; M. Laithwaite, 'The buildings of Burford: a Cotswold town in the fourteenth to nineteenth centuries', in A. Everitt (ed.), *Perspectives in English urban history* (London, 1973), pp. 69–85.

14 W. H. St John Hope, 'The castle of Ludlow', *Archaeologia*, 61, part 1 (1908), p. 324. but cf. W. E. Wightman, *The Lacy family in England and Normandy, 1066–1194* (London, 1966), concerning uncertainty of dating.

15 *Rolls Series 36, 44, 51, 57, 58, 82*, and especially *43 (Chronica monasterii de Melsa)*, p. 120, which mentions Ludlow for the period 1135–54 among several *castraetvillae*:'Herforth,Brystowe,Slade,Kary,Ludelowe,OxenforthetMalton'.

16 H. Andersson, *Urbanisierte Ortschaften und lateinische Terminologie: Studien zur Geschichte des nordeuropäischen Städtewesens vor 1350* (Göteborg, 1971), p. 26.

17 Andersson, *Urbanisierte Ortschaften*, pp. 23–4. H. Ludat, *Vorstufen und Entstehung des Städtewesens in Osteuropa,* Osteuropa und der Deutsche Osten, Reihe 3, Buch 4 (Köln-Braunsfeld, 1955), especially pp. 20–3. H. Ludat, 'Frühformen des Städtewesens in Osteuropa', in Theodor Mayer (ed.), *Studien zu den Anfängen des europäischen Städtewesens: Reichenau Vorträge 1955–1956* (Lindau/Konstanz, 1958), pp. 527–53.

18 St John Hope, 'The castle of Ludlow'.

19 A. W. J. Houghton, 'A Roman Road from Ashton, North Herefordshire, to Marschbrook, Salop', *Transactions of the Shropshire Archaeological Society*, (1964), pp. 185–90.

20 1:500 O.S. (1885), as specified in n. 8. I am greatly obliged to Mr David Lloyd for easy access to the information on these sheets.

21 *Pipe Rolls 1168/9–1197/8. Rolls Series 53.*

22 M. de W. Hemmeon, *Burgage tenure in medieval England* (Cambridge, Mass., 1914); J. Tait, *The medieval English borough* (Manchester, 1936), pp. 154–61, and especially 162ff, 176–7.

23 G. M. Trevelyan, *Illustrated history of England* (London, 1956), pp. 178–9.

24 Lloyd, *Broad Street*, p. 10; T. R. Slater, map of Ludlow showing distribution of combined plot head measures (frontages) in perches. Distributed at University of Birmingham Extra-Mural Department and Ludlow Historical Research Group Day Conference (16 Oct. 1982) on 'The Origins of Ludlow'.

25 The morphometric classification, adopted here provisionally, distinguishes *shallow burgages* with E = 4 or less, *medium burgages* with E = > 4–7, and *deep*

burgages with E = > 7. The subject of morphometric burgage types according to historical origin and regional incidence awaits comparative research on a regional and European scale. Slater's recent work in the West Midlands and Devon is important here: T. R. Slater and C. Wilson, *Archaeology and development in Stratford-upon-Avon* (Birmingham, 1977), pp. 9–10; T. R. Slater, *The analysis of burgages in medieval towns*, Working Paper 4, Dept of Geog., Univ. of Birmingham (Birmingham, 1980); T. R. Slater, 'The analysis of burgage patterns in medieval towns', *Area*, 13 (1981), pp. 211–16.

26 The origin of Broad Street has been discussed by Lloyd, *Broad Street*, chap. 2, pp. 8–11, but his interpretation of this admittedly complicated case and its morphological as well as historical context presents too many difficulties to be acceptable.

27 *Palmers' Guild Rental c.1270*, Salop Record Office 1996/16/1.

28 M. Beresford, *New towns of the Middle Ages. Town plantation in England, Wales and Gascony* (London, 1967), p. 151, Table V.1.

29 Beresford, *New towns of the Middle Ages*, p. 599, with a rather indifferently drawn plan on p. 146, Fig. 30.

30 *Ibid.*, pp. 597–8, with an indifferently drawn plan on p. 144, Fig. 28; accurate plan by A. E. Brinckmann in *Deutsche Bauzeitung* (Jan.–Feb. 1910), repr. Royal Institute of British Architects, *Transactions of the Town Planning Conference, London 1910* (London, 1911), p. 174, Fig. 8. None of these illustrations shows the *placeae* or burgages.

31 T. F. Tout, *Medieval town planning* (Manchester, 1934), p. 20. Beresford, *New towns of the Middle Ages*, p. 598 (Monségur). The French *pied* exceeded the English foot by 1 inch.

32 Beresford, *New towns of the Middle Ages*, p. 584; Tout, *Medieval town planning*, Fig. III.

33 E. M. Carus-Wilson, 'The late twelfth and thirteenth centuries', in M. D. Lobel and E. M. Carus-Wilson, *Bristol, Historic Towns Atlas* (London, 1975), p. 6; M. K. James, *Studies in the medieval wine trade* (London, 1971); E. M. Carus-Wilson, *Medieval merchant venturers* (2nd edn, London, 1967), pp. 265ff.

34 Carus-Wilson, 'The late twelfth and thirteenth centuries', p. 6.

35 Lloyd, *Broad Street*, p. 10.

36 *Calendar of Patent Rolls 1232–37*, p. 35; Lloyd, *Broad Street*, p. 11.

37 R. A. Donkin, 'Changes in the early middle ages', in H. C. Darby (ed.), *A new historical geography of England* (Cambridge, 1973), p. 113 Fig. 28, p. 122 Fig. 30.

38 D. Lloyd and P. Klein, *Ludlow, a historic town in words and pictures* (Chichester, 1984), p. 19, with Rolls Series references.

39 Lloyd, *Broad Street*, p. 10.

40 *Calendar of Patent Rolls 1232–37*, p. 35.

41 H. T. Weyman, 'A grant by Walter de Lacy to Ludlow church', *Transactions of the Shropshire Archaeological Society*, 4th ser., 9 (1923), pp. 244–57; E. L. Morley, 'A thirteenth century mystery', *The Shropshire Magazine* (Dec. 1964); Lloyd and Klein, *Ludlow*, p. 121 fn. 3.

42 *Palmers' Guild Rental c. 1270*.

43 Slater's map (see n. 24) illustrates the resulting difficulties of reconstructing original burgage frontages.

44 Lloyd, *Broad Street*, p. 11 fn. 12, mistakes these secondary plots, recorded in the Palmers' Guild Rental of 1270, for primary burgages.

45 Lloyd and Moran, *The corner shop*, describes the gradualness and complexity in the development of one such encroachment at the corner of King Street and Broad Street from the thirteenth to the fifteenth century.

46 At least four examples of such residences are identified in Lloyd and Klein, *Ludlow*: (1) the large house once occupying five former burgages at the bottom of Broad Street (now Nos. 35–7) and built by the successful Council lawyer Edmund Walter in the 1560s to 1570s (pp. 38 and 64); (2) Kingston's Place in King Street (now Nos. 9 and 10) built in 1576 by the Steward of the Council Thomas Hankey (p. 41); (3) Council Secretary Charles Fox's large courtyard house on two former burgages (now Castle Street, Nos. 2–6), its courtyard plan surviving in the present Quality Square (pp. 42–3); (4) Thomas Sackford's (Porter and Keeper of the Prisons in the Marches of Wales) stone house, the present Castle Lodge, built in the 1580s on three former burgages (pp. 42–3).

47 In chronological order: (1) 18 Broad Street: five-bay Georgian town house built 1738, partly adapted with separate entrance for the Old Bank *c*.1816. (2) 15 Broad Street: five-bay Georgian town house, replaced or refronted later to accommodate the Worcester City and County Bank. (3) 16 Broad Street: five-bay Georgian town house, replaced 1879 by the purpose-built imitation Tudor brick and stone structure of Lloyds Bank, the first clear indication of outside architects far removed from the region. (4) 9–10 Bull Ring: first, unsuccessful, attempt to blend with the traditional local style in the imitation 'half timber' building of the Midland Bank 1905, in the Cheshire rather than the Shropshire style, let alone the distinctive timber frame pattern of the Ludlow carpenters. (5) 15 Bull Ring: imitation 'half timber' structure of the National Provincial Bank 1924, in Shropshire, if not exactly Ludlow, style.

48 P. J. Aspinall and J. W. R. Whitehand, 'Building plans: a major source for urban studies', *Area*, 12, 3 (1980), pp. 199–203; J. W. R. Whitehand, 'Land-use structure, built-form and agents of change', in R. L. Davies and A. G. Champion (eds.), 'The future for the city centre', *Institute of British Geographers Special Publication*, No. 14 (London, 1983), pp. 41–59; J. W. R. Whitehand, 'Renewing the local CBD: more hands at work than you thought?', *Area*, 15, 4 (1983), pp. 323–6; J. W. R. Whitehand and S. M. Whitehand, 'The study of physical change in town centres: research procedures and types of change', *Transactions of the Institute of British Geographers*, N.S., 8, 4 (1983), pp. 483–507; J. W. R. Whitehand, 'Commercial townscapes in the making', *Journal of Historical Geography*, 10, 2 (1984), pp. 174–200; J. W. R. Whitehand, 'The architecture of commercial redevelopment in post-war Britain', *Journal of Cultural Geography*, 4, 2 (1984), pp. 41–55; J. W. R. Whitehand and S. M. Whitehand, 'The physical fabric of town centres: the agents of change, *Transactions of the Institute of British Geographers*, N.S., 9, 2 (1984), pp. 231–47.

18 The metrological analysis of early modern planned towns

1 H. Stoob, *Forschungen zum Städtewesen in Europa*, vol. 1: *Räume, Formen und*

Schichten der mitteleuropaischen Städte. Eine Aufsatzfolge (Köln/Wien, 1970).

2 D. Hannerberg, 'Die ältesten skandinavischen Ackermasse. Ein Versuch zu einer zusammenfassenden Theorie', *Lund Studies in Geography*, B 12 (Lund, 1955).

3 H. Delius, *Die Entstehung und Entwicklung des Stadtgrundrisses von Lippstadt i.W.* (Dortmund, 1926). F. Lenz, *Die räumliche Entwicklung der Stadt Lübeck bis zum Stralsunder Frieden 1370* (Hannover, 1936). A. Schiller, 'Gründungsstädte im badischen Rheintal', thesis Karlsruhe 2 vols. (Karlsruhe, 1958). D. Pernice, 'Gründungsstädte in der rechtsrheinischen Pfalz', thesis Karlsruhe 2 vols. (Karlsruhe, 1959).

4 J. Pudelko, 'Rynki w planach miast slaskia' (Market places in the plans of Silesian towns), *Kwartalnik Architektury i Urbanistyki*, 4 (1959), pp. 235–63. J. Pudelko, 'Proba pomiarowej metody badânia planow niektorych miast sredniowiecznych w oparciu o zagadnieniw dzialki', (Plot surveys as a method of investigating the plans of some medieval towns), *Kwartalnik Architektury i Urbanistyki*, 9 (1964), pp. 3–27. J. Pudelko, 'Dzialka lokacyjna w strukturze przestrzennej sredniowiecznych miast slaskich XIII wieku' (Location plot in the spatial structure of medieval towns in 13th century Silesia), *Kwartalnik Architektury i Urbanistyki*, 9 (1964), pp. 115–37. T. Zagrodzki, *Regularny plan miasta sredniowiecznego a limitacja miernicza* (A regular plan of a medieval town and cadastral limitations) (Wroclaw, 1962).

5 J. Lafrenz, 'Friedrichstadt', in H. Stoob (ed.), *Deutscher Städteatlas III/3* (Dortmund, 1979). J. Lafrenz, 'Analisi metrologica di piante cittàdine', in *Enciclopedia Italiana di Cultura* (Rome, 1984). J. Lafrenz, 'Die metrologische Analyse als Instrumentarium zur morphogenetischen Interpretation frühneuzeitlicher Stadtgrundrisse', *Trierer Geographische Studien*, 4/5 (Trier, 1986).

6 See the important publication by E. Taverne, *In't land van belofte: in de nieue stadt. Ideaal en werkelijkheid van de stadsuitleg in de Republick 1580–1680* (Maarssen, 1978).

7 R. Reymers, 'List of the first interested settlers of Friedrichstadt, 1622 May 26'; R. Reymers, 'Justification of surveying and mapping of Friedrichstadt, 1623 June 29': examined in Archiv Remonstrantengemeinde Friedrichstadt.

8 Lafrenz, 'Die metrologische Analyse'.

9 H. Carter, *The study of urban geography*, 3rd edn (London, 1974), p. 138.

10 W. L. Garrison, 'Discussion on urban morphology', in K. Norborg (ed.), *Proceedings of the IGU Symposium in Urban Geography Lund 1960* (Lund, 1962), pp. 463–4.

19 Recent developments in urban morphology

1 M. P. Conzen, 'Analytical approaches to the urban landscape', in K. W. Butzer (ed.), *Dimensions in human geography: essays on some familiar and neglected themes* (Chicago, 1978), p. 135.

2 For example, J. W. R. Whitehand, 'The study of variations in the building fabric of town centres: procedural problems and preliminary findings in southern Scotland', *Transactions of the Institute of British Geographers*, N.S., 4 (1979), pp. 559–75; J. M. Luffrum, 'Variations in the building fabric of small towns',

Transactions of the Institute of British Geographers, N.S., 5 (1980), pp. 170–3; T. R. Slater, 'The analysis of burgage patterns in medieval towns', *Area*, 13 (1981), pp. 211–16; J. M. Luffrum, 'The building fabric of the central areas of small towns in rural England: interurban variations and relationships', *Urban Geography*, 2 (1981), pp. 161–77; J. W. R. Whitehand, 'Fluctuations in the land-use composition of urban development during the industrial era', *Erd-kunde*, 35 (1981), pp. 129–40; H. Carter, 'The internal structure of Welsh towns in the nineteenth century: changing townscapes', *Landscape History*, 4 (1982), pp. 47–60; J. W. R. Whitehand, 'Land-use structure, built-form and agents of change', in R. L. Davies and A. G. Champion (eds.), 'The future for the city centre', *Institute of British Geographers Special Publication*, No. 14 (London, 1983), pp. 41–59.

3 For example, B. Rubin, 'Aesthetic ideology and urban design', *Annals of the Association of American Geographers*, 69 (1979), pp. 339–61; J. A. Jakle, 'Motel by the roadside: America's room for the night', *Journal of Cultural Geography*, 1 (1980), pp. 34–49; M. P. Conzen, 'The morphology of nineteenth-century cities in the United States', in W. Borah, J. Hardoy and G. Stelter (eds.), *Urbanization in the Americas: the background in comparative perspective* (Ottawa, 1980), pp. 119–41; R. Stump, 'The Dutch colonial house and the colonial revival', *Journal of Cultural Geography*, 1 (1981), pp. 44–55; C. Winters, 'Urban morphogenesis in Francophone Black Africa', *Geographical Review*, 72 (1982), pp. 139–54.

4 See, for example, I Möller, *Die Entwicklung eines Hamburger Gebietes von der Agrar- zur Groszstadtlandschaft. Mit einem Beitrag zur Methode der Städt-ischen Aufrissanalyse*, Hamburger Geographische Studien, No. 10 (Hamburg, 1959); R. Stewig, 'Der Grundriss von Istanbul. Vom orientalisch-osmanischen zum europäisch-kosmopolitischen Grundriss', in G. Sandner (ed.), *Kulturraum-probleme aus Ostmitteleuropa und Asien*, Schriften des Geographischen Instituts der Universität Kiel, No. 23 (Kiel, 1964), pp. 195–225; H. Bobek and E. Lichten-berger, *Wien. Bauliche Gestalt und Entwicklung seit der Mitte des 19. Jahrhun-derts* (Graz, 1966); D. Richter, *Geographische Strukturwandlungen in der Weltstadt Berlin. Untersucht am Profilband Potsdamer Platz–Innsbrucker Platz*, Abhandlungen des 1. Geographischen Instituts der Freien Universität Berlin, vol. 14 (Berlin, 1969); A. Scheuerbrandt, *Südwestdeutsche Stadttypen und Städte-gruppen bis zum frühen 19. Jahrhundert*, Heidelberger Geographische Arbeiten, No. 32 (Heidelberg, 1972); J. Lafrenz, *Die Stellung der Innenstadt im Flächen-nutzungsgefüge des Agglomerationsraumes Lübeck. Grundlagenforschung zur erhaltenden Stadterneuerung*, Hamburger Geographische Studien, No. 33 (Ham-burg, 1977); E. Lichtenberger, *Die Wiener Altstadt von der mittelalterlichen Bürgerstadt zur City* (Vienna, 1977).

5 For example, R. W. Bastian, 'The prairie style house: spatial diffusion of a minor design', *Journal of Cultural Geography*, 1 (1980), pp. 50–65; J. R. Curtis, 'Art Deco architecture in Miami Beach', *Journal of Cultural Geography*, 3 (1982), pp. 51–63; R. Mattson, 'Store front remodeling on Main Street', *Journal of Cultural Geography*, 3 (1983), pp. 41–55; R. Fusch and L. R. Ford, 'Architec-ture and the geography of the American city', *Geographical Review*, 73 (1983), pp. 324–40; J. A. Jakle, 'Twentieth century revival architecture and the gentry',

Journal of Cultural Geography, 4 (1983), pp. 28–43.

6 J. E. Rickert, 'House facades of the Northeastern United States; a tool of geographic analysis', *Annals of the Association of American Geographers*, 57 (1967), pp. 211–38; R. W. Bastian, 'Urban house types as a research focus in historical geography', *Environmental Review*, 4 (1980), p. 27.

7 J. B. Leighly, 'The towns of Mälardalen in Sweden: a study in urban morphology', *University of California Publications in Geography*, 3 (1928), pp. 1–134; J. E. Spencer, 'The houses of the Chinese', *Geographical Review*, 37 (1947), pp. 254–73.

8 For example, J. Fritz, 'Deutsche Stadtanlangen', *Beilage zum Programm 520 des Lyzeums Strassburg* (Strassburg, 1894); O. Schlüter, 'Über den Grundriss der Städte', *Zeitschrift der Gesellschaft für Erdkunde zu Berlin*, 34 (1899), pp. 446–62; O. Schlüter, *Die Siedlungen im nordöstlichen Thüringen: ein Beispiel für die Behandlung siedlungsgeographischer Fragen* (Berlin, 1903).

9 For example, T. R. Slater, 'Urban genesis and medieval town plans in Warwickshire and Worcestershire', in T. R. Slater and P. J. Jarvis (eds.), *Field and forest: an historical geography of Warwickshire and Worcestershire* (Norwich, 1982), pp. 173–202.

10 For example, J. W. R. Whitehand, 'Commercial townscapes in the making', *Journal of Historical Geography*, 10 (1984), pp. 174–200.

11 Especially, O. Schlüter, 'Bemerkungen zur Siedlungsgeographie', *Geographische Zeitschrift*, 5 (1899), pp. 65–84.

12 W. Geisler, *Danzig: ein siedlungsgeographischer Versuch* (Danzig, 1918); W. Geisler, *Die deutsche Stadt: ein Beitrag zur Morphologie der Kulturlandschaft* (Stuttgart, 1924).

13 For example, H. Hassinger, *Wiener Heimatschutz und Verkehrsfragen* (Vienna, 1912); H. Hassinger, *Kunsthistorischer Atlas von Wien*, Österreichische Kunsttopographie, No. 15 (Vienna, 1916).

14 G. Schaefer, *Kunstgeographische Siedlungslandschaften und Städtebilder: Studien im Gebiet zwischen Strassburg–Bern–Dijon–Freiburg i. Br.* (Basel, 1928).

15 For a discussion of disciplinary influences on the development of urban morphology in central Europe before the Second World War see J. W. R. Whitehand, 'Background to the urban morphogenetic tradition', in J. W. R.. Whitehand (ed.), 'The urban landscape: historical development and management', *Institute of British Geographers Special Publication*, No. 13 (London, 1981), pp. 2–7.

16 Bobek and Lichtenberger, *Wien*.

17 M. R. G. Conzen, 'The growth and character of Whitby', in G. H. J. Daysh (ed.), *A survey of Whitby and the surrounding area* (Elton, 1958), pp. 49–89; M. R. G. Conzen, 'Alnwick, Northumberland: a study in town-plan analysis', *Institute of British Geographers Publication*, No. 27 (London, 1960); M. R. G. Conzen, 'The plan analysis of an English city centre', in K. Norborg (ed.), *Proceedings of the IGU Symposium in urban geography Lund 1960* (Lund, 1962), pp. 383–414.

18 M. R. G. Conzen, 'Historical townscapes in Britain: a problem in applied geography', in J. W. House (ed.), *Northern geographical essays in honour of*

G. H. J. Daysh (Newcastle upon Tyne, 1966), pp. 56–78; M. R. G. Conzen, 'Geography and townscape conservation', *Giessener Geographische Schriften*, Anglo-German Symposium in Applied Geography, Giessen–Würzburg–München, 1973 (1975), pp. 95–102.

19 H. J. Dyos, *Victorian suburb: a study of the growth of Camberwell* (Leicester, 1961).

20 M. Beresford, 'The making of a townscape: Richard Paley in the east end of Leeds, 1771–1803', in C. W. Chalklin and M. Havinden (eds.), *Rural change and urban growth* (London, 1974), pp. 281–320.

21 For example, F. H. W. Sheppard (ed.), *Survey of London*, vol. 40 (London, 1980), 'The Grosvenor Estate and Mayfair', part 2.

22 See, for example, W. K. D. Davies, 'The morphology of central places: a case study', *Annals of the Association of American Geographers*, 58 (1968), pp. 91–110; R. J. Johnston, 'Towards an analytical study of the townscape: the residential building fabric', *Geografiska Annaler*, Series B, 51 (1969), pp. 20–32.

23 See, for example, J. W. R. Whitehand, 'Building cycles and the spatial pattern of urban growth', *Transactions of the Institute of British Geographers*, 56 (1972), pp. 39–55.

24 For example, D. Harvey, *Social justice and the city* (London, 1973), pp. 153–94.

25 R. Barras, *The returns from office development and investment,* Centre for Environmental Studies Research Series, No. 35 (London, 1979).

26 For example, L. Esher, *A broken wave: the rebuilding of England 1940–1980* (London, 1981); C. A. Jencks, *The language of post-modern architecture*, 3rd edn (London, 1981).

27 J. Springett, 'Landowners and urban development: the Ramsden estate and nineteenth-century Huddersfield', *Journal of Historical Geography*, 8 (1982), p. 129.

28 For example, H. Hobhouse, *Thomas Cubitt: master builder* (London, 1971); S. Buggey, 'Building in mid-nineteenth century Halifax: the case of George Lang', *Urban History Review*, 9 (1980), pp. 5–20.

29 S. B. Warner, *Streetcar suburbs: the process of growth in Boston 1870–1900* (Cambridge, Mass., 1962), pp. 126–32, 184.

30 P. J. Aspinall, *Building applications and the building industry in nineteenth century towns: the scope for statistical analysis*, University of Birmingham Centre for Urban and Regional Studies Research Memorandum, No. 68 (Birmingham, 1978); P. J. Aspinall and J. W. R. Whitehand, 'Building plans: a major source for urban studies', *Area*, 12 (1980), pp. 199–203.

31 Conzen, 'Alnwick, Northumberland', pp. 33–34.

32 J. W. R. Whitehand, 'The architecture of commercial redevelopment in post-war Britain', *Journal of Cultural Geography*, 4 (1984).

33 Whitehand, 'Commercial townscapes', pp. 179–87.

34 Conzen, 'Alnwick, Northumberland', pp. 7–9.

35 Whitehand, 'Commercial townscapes', pp. 180, 182.

36 M. Bowley, *The British building industry: four studies in response and resistance to change* (Cambridge, 1966), p. 390.

37 Whitehand, 'Commercial townscapes', pp. 181–2.

38 *Ibid.*, pp. 174–200.

39 Whitehand, 'Land-use structure', pp. 44–7; R. Barras, *The development cycle in the City of London*, Centre for Environmental Studies Research Series, No. 36 (London, 1979), p. 55, App. 2; Hillier Parker Research, *British shopping developments* (London, 1979), p. 33; O. Marriott, *The property boom* (London, 1967), pp. 27–9.

40 J. W. R. Whitehand and S. M. Whitehand, 'The physical fabric of town centres: the agents of change', *Transactions of the Institute of British Geographers*, N.S., 9 (1984).

41 J. W. R. Whitehand, 'Renewing the local CBD: more hands at work than you thought?', *Area*, 15 (1983), pp. 323–6; J. W. R. Whitehand and S. M. White-hand, 'The study of physical change in town centres: research procedures and types of change', *Transactions of the Institute of British Geographers*, N.S., 8 (1983), esp. pp. 495–6.

42 Conzen, 'Historical townscapes', p. 59.

43 Conzen, 'Whitby', p. 78.

44 Jencks, *Language*, esp. pp. 5–8.

20 Historical geography and conservation planning in British towns

1 N. Pevsner, 'Scrape and antiscrape', in J. Fawcett (ed.), *The future of the past* (London, 1976).

2 A. Barker, *The local amenity movement* (London, 1976).

3 A. Dobby, *Conservation and planning* (London, 1978).

4 A. Dale, *Historic preservation in foreign countries*, vol. I (France, Great Britain, Ireland, Netherlands, Denmark) (I.C.O.M.O.S., 1982).

5 N. Boulting, 'The law's delays: conservation legislation in the British Isles', in Fawcett, *The future of the past*; Cambridgeshire County Council, *A guide to historic building law*, 5th edn (Cambridge, 1984).

6 See particularly *Architectural Review, The Planner, Town Planning Review*.

7 An exception is A. A. Faulkner, 'A philosophy for the preservation of our heritage: three lectures', *Royal Society of Arts Journal*, 126 (1978), pp. 452–80.

8 R. M. Newcomb, 'A business and a charity: conservation in transition', *Reading geographical papers*, 83 (1983).

9 R. J. P. Kain, 'Urban conservation in France', *Town and Country Planning*, 43 (1975), pp. 428–32.

10 D. Lowenthal, 'Conserving the heritage: Anglo-American comparisons', in J. Patten (ed.), *The expanding city: essays in honour of Professor Jean Gottman* (London, 1983), pp. 225–76.

11 D. Burtenshaw, M. Bateman and G. J. Ashworth, *The city in West Europe* (Chichester, 1981).

12 G. Gordon, 'Management and conservation of the historic city', in G. Gordon (ed.), *Perspectives of the Scottish city* (Aberdeen, 1985), pp. 236–79.

13 G. E. Cherry, 'The conservation movement', *The Planner*, 61 (1975), pp. 3–5.

14 G. J. Ashworth and F. Schuurmans, 'Colmar: form and function in a conserved city', *Papers of Geographical Institute, University of Groningen* (1981); see also Burtenshaw *et al.*, *The city in West Europe*.

15 G. J. Ashworth, 'Urban conservation and urban renewal', paper presented to

'Crisis in the City and the Take-Off of Suburbia', International Symposium, Munich/Vienna (1984).

16 D. Eversley, 'Conservation for the minority', *Built Environment*, 3 (1974), pp. 14–15.

17 C. R. Hamnett, 'Improvement grants as an indicator of gentrification in Inner London', *Area*, 5 (1973), pp. 252–61; C. R. Hamnett and P. R. Williams, *Gentrification in London, 1961–71*, Research Memorandum 71, Centre for Urban and Regional Studies, Birmingham (1979).

18 J. E. Tunbridge, 'Whose heritage to conserve? Cross cultural reflections on political dominance and urban heritage conservation', *Canadian Geographer*, 228 (1984), pp. 171–80.

19 P. D. Lowe, 'Amenity and equity: a review of local environmental pressure groups in Britain', *Environment and Planning A*, 9 (1977), pp. 35–58.

20 S. Jenkins, 'The conservationist as politician', *Royal Society of Arts Journal*, 132 (1984), pp. 722–31.

21 P. F. McNamara, 'The control of office development in central Edinburgh 1959–1978', unpublished Ph.D. thesis, University of Edinburgh (1985).

22 Newcomb, 'A business and a charity'.

23 P. J. Larkham, 'Conservation, planning and morphology in West Midland conservation areas, 1968–84', unpublished Ph.D. thesis, University of Birmingham (1986).

24 M. R. G. Conzen, 'Historical townscapes in Britain: a problem in applied geography' in J. W. R. Whitehand (ed.), 'The urban landscape: historical development and management', *Institute of British Geographers Special Publication*, No. 13 (London, 1981), pp. 55–75.

25 M. R. G. Conzen, 'The growth and character of Whitby', in G. H. J. Daysh (ed.), *A survey of Whitby and the surrounding area* (Elton, 1958), pp. 49–89.

26 M. R. G. Conzen, 'Geography and townscape conservation', in Whitehand, *The urban landscape*.

27 J. W. R. Whitehand, 'Commercial townscapes in the making', *Journal of Historical Geography*, 10 (1984), pp. 174–200; *idem*, 'The architecture of commercial redevelopment in post-war Britain', *Journal of Cultural Geography*, 4 (1984), pp. 41–55.

28 Larkham, 'Conservation, planning and morphology'.

29 R. J. Buswell, *Changing approaches to urban conservation: a case study of Newcastle upon Tyne*, Occasional Series in Geography, 8, Newcastle upon Tyne Polytechnic (n.d.).

30 K. Lynch, *The image of the city* (Cambridge, Mass., 1960).

31 K. Lynch, *What time is this place* (Cambridge, Mass., 1972).

32 C. Morris, 'Townscape images: a study in meaning and classification', unpublished Ph.D. thesis, University of Exeter (1978); *idem*, 'Townscape images: a study in meaning', in R. Kain (ed.), *Planning for conservation* (London, 1981).

33 E. Johns, *British townscapes* (London, 1965).

34 G. Cullen, *Townscape* (London, 1961).

35 T. Sharp, *Town and townscape* (London, 1968).

36 D. Lowenthal, *The past is a foreign country* (Cambridge, 1985), pp. 35–69.

37 *Ibid.*

38 H. Louis, 'Die geographische Gliederung von Gross-Berlin', *Länderkundliche Forschung*, Krebs Festschrift (Stuttgart, 1936).
39 E. Cieslak and C. Biernat, *Dzieje Gdanska* (Gdansk, 1975).
40 Kingston-upon-Hull City Planning Department, *Kingston-upon-Hull: the Old Town conservation area* (Hull, 1975).
41 T. Sharp, *Exeter Phoenix* (London, 1945), and see later in this chapter.
42 F. W. B. Charles, 'Timber-framed houses in Spon Street, Coventry', *Transactions Birmingham and Warwickshire Archaeological Society*, 89 (1978–9), pp. 91–122; D. Lloyd, 'Coventry, city of the century', *Built Environment Quarterly*, 2 (1976), pp. 140–50.
43 T. R. Slater and C. Wilson, *Archaeology and development in Stratford-upon-Avon* (Birmingham, 1977).
44 P. Styles, 'The borough of Stratford-upon-Avon', *Victoria Country History, Warwickshire*, 3 (1945), pp. 247–51.
45 L. Fox, *The borough town of Stratford upon Avon* (Stratford-upon-Avon, 1953), pp. 151–9.
46 *Ibid.*
47 P. and L. Abercrombie, *Stratford-upon-Avon: report on future development* (London, 1923).
48 *Ibid.*
49 T. R. Slater, 'Preservation, conservation and planning in historic towns', *Geographical Journal*, 150 (1984), pp. 322–4.
50 A copy of the lists is available in the Shakespeare Birthplace Trust Library.
51 Slater and Wilson, *Archaeology and development*.
52 Fox, *The borough town*, pp. 151–9.
53 R. M. W. Norris, *Stratford-upon-Avon conservation area report* (Stratford-upon-Avon, 1967).
54 R. M. W. Norris, *Stratford-upon-Avon draft town centre map and report* (Stratford-upon-Avon, 1968).
55. *Ibid.*
56 Whitehand, 'The architecture of commercial redevelopment'.
57 Norris, *Stratford-upon-Avon draft town centre map and report*.
58 H.M.S.O. *Report on the Census of Distribution and other services 1971, Pt. 9* (London, 1975).
59 Companies redeveloping include a local department store and F. W. Woolworth, Boots and W. H. Smith.
60 The former streetscape of Bridge Street and elsewhere can be appreciated in L. Fox, *Stratford past and present* (Oxford, 1975).
61 Notably Sir Frederick Gibberd's group of shops which replaced the Victorian Market Hall on the corner of High Street and Sheep Street.
62 Restoration in Ely Street has been primarily by the local authority, for example. A notable private restoration is the mid-Victorian Gothic bank, on the corner of Ely Street and Chapel Street, for Midland Bank plc.
63 W. G. Hoskins, *Industry, trade and people in Exeter, 1688–1800* (Manchester, 1975).
64 Exeter City Council, *Central conservation study Exeter* (Exeter, 1977).
65 W. G. Hoskins, *Two thousand years in Exeter* (London, 1969), chap. 10.

66 Exeter City Council, *Central conservation study*, and Exeter City Council, *Exeter draft plan report* (Exeter, 1981), chap. 7.

67 R. M. Newcombe, *Planning the past* (Folkestone, 1979).

68 R. M. Newcombe, 'The Arhus, Denmark Village Project: applied geography in the service of the municipality', *Geographical Review*, 67, 1 (1977), pp. 86–92.

69 G. Shaw and R. Cullingford, 'Constructing a data base mapping system for central area planning in an historic town', *Proceedings of the Urban Data Management Symposia* (The Hague, 1985), pp. 1–8.

70 D. Denecke, *Historische Geographie und räumliche Planung* (Hamburg, 1985), chap. 7.

21 Future developments in Anglo-German studies of urban historical geography

1 H. Bobek, 'Innsbruck. Eine Gebirgsstadt, ihr Lebensraum und ihre Erscheinung', *Forschungen zur deutschen Landes- u. Volkskunde*, 25, 3 (1928). H. Dörries, *Die Städte im oberen Leinetal, Göttingen, Northeim und Einbeck* (Göttingen, 1925). For developments of this work see H. Bobek and E. Lichtenberger, *Wien. Bauliche Gestalt und Entwicklung seit der Mitte des 19. Jahrhunderts* (Graz, 1966).

2 E. Lichtenberger, 'The German-speaking countries', in R. J. Johnston and P. Claval (eds.), *Geography since the Second World War* (London, 1984), chap. 8, pp. 156–84.

3 R. Geipel, 'The Landscape Indicators School in German geography', in D. Ley and M. S. Samuels (eds.), *Humanistic geography: prospects and problems* (London, 1978), chap. 10, pp. 155–72.

4 M. P. Conzen, 'Analytical approaches to the urban landscape', in K. W. Butzer (ed.), *Dimensions in human geography: essays on some familiar and neglected themes* (Chicago, 1978), pp. 128–65.

5 A. R. H. Baker, R. A. Butlin, A. D. M. Phillips and H. C. Prince, 'The future of the past', *Area*, 4 (1969), pp. 46–51.

6 R. A. Butlin, 'Developments in historical geography in Britain in the 1970s', in A. R. H. Baker and M. Billinge (eds.), *Period and place: research methods in historical geography* (Cambridge, 1982), pp. 10–16.

7 D. Gregory, 'New towns for old: historical geography at the IBG', *Historical Geography Newsletter*, 4 (1974). See also D. Gregory, 'Re-thinking historical geography', *Area*, 8 (1976), pp. 295–9.

8 M. Billinge, 'In search of negativism, phenomenology and historical geography', *Journal of Historical Geography*, 3 (1977), pp. 55–67.

9 A. R. H. Baker, 'Historical geography in Britain', and H. Jäger, 'Historical geography in Germany, Austria and Switzerland', in A. R. H. Baker (ed.), *Progress in historical geography* (Newton Abbot, 1972), chap. 5, pp. 90–110, and chap. 3, pp. 45–62.

10 Jäger, Historical geography', pp. 46–7.

11 Baker, 'Historical geography', p. 108.

12 E. Lichtenberger, 'The impact of institutional forces on the state of University geography in the Federal Republic of Germany in comparison with Britain',

in R. J. Bennett (ed.), *European progress in spatial analysis* (London, 1981), pp. 112–30.

13 A. Buttimer (ed.), *The practice of geography* (London, 1983), chap. 1, pp. 1–19.

14 M. Phillips and T. Unwin, 'British historical geography: places and people', *Area*, 17 (1985), pp. 155–63.

15 J. H. Johnson and C. G. Pooley, 'The internal structure of the nineteenth-century British city – an overview', in J. H. Johnson and C. G. Pooley (eds.), *The structure of nineteenth-century cities* (London, 1982), chap. 1, pp. 3–35.

16 Baker, 'Historical geography'; see also L. W. Hepple, 'Epistemology, model-building and historical geography', *Geographical Articles*, 10 (1967), pp. 42–8.

17 Baker *et al.*, 'The future of the past'.

18 D. Gregory, 'Human agency and human geography', *Transactions of the Institute of British Geographers*, 9 (1981), pp. 1–18. P. Jackson, 'Social geography: convergence and compromise', *Progress in Human Geography*, 7, 1 (1983), pp. 116–21. J. P. Thompson, 'The theory of structuration: an assessment of the contribution of Anthony Giddens', in J. P. Thompson, *Studies in the theory of ideology* (Cambridge, 1984), chap. 4.

19 J. Hadju, 'Towards a definition of postwar German social geography', *Annals of the Association of American Geographers*, 58 (1968), pp. 397–410.

20 Some of these problems of terminology have been discussed in contemporary urban geography in T. Wild, *Urban and rural change in West Germany* (London, 1983), Preface and Glossary of German words and phrases. See also as a further example of the complex problems of urban terminology the discussion of the term 'Stadtkern' by D. Denecke, 'Stadtkern und Stadtkernforschung. Ein Beitrag zur Terminologie und Fragestellung', in H. Jäger (ed.), 'Stadtkernforschung', *Städteforschung*, A 27 (Köln, 1988), pp. 11–21.

21 See, for example, P. J. Aspinall, 'The use of nineteenth century fire insurance plans for the urban historian', *Local Historian*, 11 (1975), pp. 343–9; G. Rowley, *British fire insurance plans* (Hatfield, 1984). G. Shaw, 'British directories as sources in historical geography', *Historical Geography Research Series*, 8 (Norwich, 1982).

22 See the different contributions made by urban historians and geographers to H. Heineberg (ed.), *Innerstädtische Differenzierung und Prozesse im 19. und 20. Jahrhundert. Geographische und historische Aspekte*, *Städteforschung*, A 25 (Köln, 1987), pp. 133–57.

Index